# Limitations and Possibilities of Dialogue among Researchers, Policy Makers, and Practitioners

Studies in Education/Politics
Mark B. Ginsburg, *Series Editor*

THE POLITICS OF EDUCATORS'
   WORK AND LIVES
edited by Mark B. Ginsburg

POLITICS, RACE, AND SCHOOLS
*Racial Integration, 1954–1994*
by Joseph Watras

POLITICS AND EDUCATION IN ISRAEL
*Comparisons with the United States*
by Shlomo Swirski

STAFF, PARENTS AND POLITICS IN
   HEADSTART
*A Case Study in Unequal Power, Knowledge
   and Material Resources*
by Peggy A. Sissel

WHOSE EDUCATION FOR ALL?
*Recolonization of the African Mind*
by Birgit Brock-Utne

A CLASS ACT
*Changing Teachers' Work the State, and
   Globalization*
by Susan L. Robertson

RETHINKING ACADEMIC POLITICS IN
   (RE)UNIFIED GERMANY AND THE
   UNITED STATES
by John A. Weaver

DEMOCRATIZING EDUCATION AND
   EDUCATING DEMOCRATIC CITIZENS
*International and Historical Perspectives*
edited by Leslie J. Limage

LIMITATIONS AND POSSIBILITIES OF
   DIALOGUE AMONG RESEARCHERS,
   POLICY MAKERS, AND PRACTITIONERS
*International Perspectives on the Field of
   Education*
edited by Mark B. Ginsburg and
   Jorge M. Gorostiaga

# Limitations and Possibilities of Dialogue among Researchers, Policy Makers, and Practitioners
*International Perspectives on the Field of Education*

Edited by **Mark B. Ginsburg** and **Jorge M. Gorostiaga**

ROUTLEDGEFALMER

Published in 2003 by
RoutledgeFalmer
29 West 35th Street
New York, New York 10001

Published in Great Britain by
RoutledgeFalmer
11 New Fetter Lane
London EC4P 4EE

RoutledgeFalmer is an imprint of the Taylor & Francis Group.

Copyright © 2003 by RoutledgeFalmer

Printed in the United States of America on acid-free paper.

All rights reserved. No part of this book may be reprinted or reproduced or utilized in any form or by any electronic, mechanical, or other means, now known or hereafter invented, including photocopying and recording, or in any information storage or retrieval system, without permission in writing from the publishers.

Cataloging-in-Publication Data is available from the Library of Congress.

ISBN 0-415-945453

CONTENTS

Acknowledgments and Dedication — vii

Series Editor's Introduction: Dialogue Isn't Necessarily More Efficient, but It's More Democratic and, Therefore, More Effective — ix
MARK B. GINSBURG

Chapter Summaries — xiii

About the Authors — xix

Chapter 1
**Dialogue about Educational Research, Policy, and Practice: To What Extent Is it Possible and Who Should be Involved?** — 1
MARK B. GINSBURG AND JORGE M. GOROSTIAGA

Chapter 2
**Dancing in the Dark: The Relationship between Policy Research and Policy Making in Dutch Higher Education** — 37
ANNE KLEMPERER, HENNO THEISENS, AND FRANS KAISER

Chapter 3
**Linking Research, Policy, and Strategic Planning to Education Development in the Lao People's Democratic Republic** — 61
DON ADAMS, GEOK HWA KEE, AND LIN LIN

Chapter 4
**Teacher Peripheralization in Comparative Education: Causes, Consequences, and Some Responses** — 83
PAUL R. FOSSUM AND PATRICIA K. KUBOW

## Chapter 5
**Researching Women's Literacy in Mali: A Case Study of Dialogue among Researchers, Practitioners, and Policy Makers**      95
LAUREL PUCHNER

## Chapter 6
**"Other" Perceptions: Intersubjectivity in the Research Dialogue Process**      109
SANDRA L. STACKI

## Chapter 7
**Reinventing Research for Educational Reform: Advocacy Research and the Promotion of Participation**      125
CRAIG G. WISHART AND JOSEPH DESTEFANO

## Chapter 8
**Ideology in Educational Research and Policy Making in the United States: The Possibility and Importance of Transcendence**      143
MICHELE S. MOSES AND MARINA GAIR

## Chapter 9
**Dialogue between "Academic" and "Community" Researchers: The Possibilities and Challenges of Participatory Research**      161
KEVIN J. GORMLEY

## Chapter 10
**Enhancing Dialogue among Researchers, Policy Makers, and Community Members in Uganda: Complexities, Possibilities, and Persistent Questions**      183
JOSEPH CARASCO, NANCY CLAIR, AND LAWRENCE KANYIKE

## Chapter 11
**Policy Making, Critical Analysis, or Both—What Role for Educational Research?: The Example of "Lifelong Learning"**      207
HOLGER DAUN

## Chapter 12
**"Designed" Dialogues: The *Real* Politics of Evidence-Based Practice and Education Policy Research in England**      219
SUSAN L. ROBERTSON AND ROGER DALE

Index      237

# Acknowledgments and Dedication

Like all books, this volume has benefited from the contributions of many people. As editors of a collective work, we especially want to thank those who authored chapters. Their willingness to cooperate with us on this project has only been surpassed by their capacity to help us understand more fully and deeply the issues that we have sought to address herein. We also wish to express our sincere appreciation to Nelly Stromquist, who not only invited us to edit a special issue of the *Comparative Education Review,* on which this book is based, but also helped develop our thinking with constructive feedback on the work as we proceeded. Similar expressions of gratitude are due to those colleagues/friends who reviewed drafts of chapters or participated in conference sessions or university seminars devoted to discussions of one or more of the chapters.

During our lives, both of us have been strongly influenced by people whose main identities were as researchers, policy makers, and/or practitioners. Their sage advice, probing questions, and inspiring examples have not always been heeded fully, responded to adequately, or modeled successfully. Nevertheless, we believe that whatever is valuable about this book can be attributed to our opportunities to interact—and, sometimes, engage in dialogue—with them. As individuals who identify ourselves—and are identified by others—as researchers, we have engaged in our own personal struggles to comprehend and appreciate the thoughts and actions of educational policy makers and practitioners. This is not to suggest, somehow, that dialogue with other researchers is easy, but only to highlight that we have personally experienced—and probably helped to construct—the cultural and structural barriers that often limit joint reflection and action among researchers, policy makers, and practitioners.

This volume is also dedicated to people closer to home, literally. For Jorge, they include his wife Cecilia and his children Luján and Andrés, who are a constant source of meaning and joy in his life. For Mark, they include his wife Barbara; his children Jolie, Kevin, and Stefanie; his parents Norman and Blanche; and, particularly, one of his grandparents, Fred, whose encouragement and inquiries have animated his life.

# Series Editor's Introduction
*Dialogue Isn't Necessarily More Efficient, but It's More Democratic and, Therefore, More Effective*

MARK B. GINSBURG

"Take education out of politics!" "Education should not be a political football!" "Keep politics out of the schools!" "Educators should not be political!" These and similar warnings have been sounded at various times in a variety of societies. Such warnings, however, miss (or misconstrue) the point that education *is* political. Not only is education constituted by and constitutive of struggles over the distribution of symbolic and material resources, but education also implies and confers structural and ideological power used to control the means of producing, reproducing, consuming, and accumulating symbolic and material resources (see Ginsburg 1995; Ginsburg and Lindsay 1995).

Political struggles about and through education occur in classrooms and nonformal education settings; school and university campuses; education systems; and local, national, and global communities. Different groups of students, educators, parents, business owners, organized labor leaders, government and international organization officials, and other worker-consumer-citizens participate (actively or passively) in such political activity. These struggles not only shape educational policy, educational practice, and educational research; they also are dialectically related to more general relations of power among social classes, racial/ethnic groups, gender groups, nations, and regional/multinational blocs. Thus, the politics of education and the political work accomplished through education are ways in which existing social relations are reproduced, legitimated, challenged, or transformed.

The Studies in Education/Politics series is designed to include books that examine how in different historical periods and in various local, national, and global contexts education *is* political. The focus is on what groups are involved in political struggles in, through, and about education; what material and symbolic resources are of concern; how ideological and structural power are implicated; and what consequences occur for the people directly involved and for social relations more generally.

The purpose of this series, however, is not only to help educators and other people understand the nexus of education and politics. It is also concerned with facilitating their active involvement in the politics of and through education. Thus, the issue is not whether education should be taken out of politics, nor whether politics should be kept out of schools, nor whether educators should be apolitical. Rather, the concerns are toward what ends, by what means, and in whose interests educators and other worker-consumer-citizens should engage in political work in and about education.

This volume edited by Jorge Gorostiaga and me, the ninth book to appear in the Studies in Education/Politics series, focuses on the work and lives of educational researchers and their relationships with a variety of individuals/groups involved in conceiving and executing educational policy and practice. The editors (in their introductory chapter) and the authors of the eleven other chapters not only illuminate how educational research itself can be seen as a political activity; they also analyze how the distribution of power as well as material and symbolic resources shapes and is shaped by the nature of relations that are socially constructed by researchers, policy makers, practitioners, and other community members. Moreover, the cases presented in this volume are located in a variety of countries, including Brazil, England, Lao People's Democratic Republic, Mali, the Netherlands, South Africa, Uganda, and the United States, thus providing an international vista of such dynamics.

Gorostiaga and I frame the volume with reference to Paulo Freire's (1970) conception of *dialogue,* joint reflection, and action. Additionally, we—with the help of the contributions of the other authors—describe how the following six approaches to linking research, policy, and practice measure up to this standard: (1) translation/mediation, (2) education, (3) role expansion, (4) decision-oriented research, (5) collaborative action research, (6) collective research and praxis. While identifying a number of challenges faced in employing any of these approaches, we call for efforts—viz., the latter approaches—that offer more opportunities for dialogue between and among researchers, policy makers, practitioners, and other members of local, national, and global communities.

We favor collaborative action research and collective research and praxis because of our commitment to more "public" democratic (versus "privatized" democratic or professionalized/expert) forms of politics (see Sehr 1997). Our preference is also based on the belief that in the long run dialogue and participation by a wide range of stakeholders produce better and more relevant educational research, policy, and practice. As Coulter and Wiens (2002, pp. 17–18) argue, in discussing Hannah Arendt's political philosophy: "Good judgment is ... a result of intersubjectivity ... 'look[ing] upon the same world from [others'] standpoint[s]' ... (Arendt, 1968, p. 51) ... [and r]especting diverse standpoints requires dialogue with other people." Certainly, it may be easier—and, in that sense, more efficient—for researchers, policy makers, and practitioners in education to engage in action (or even in praxis) in isolation of members of the other groups. However, the decisions that are made and the actions that are pursued are likely to be less effective. This is the case not only because the quality of judgments may be lower but also because the activities of one group may detract from or cancel out those of other groups.

## References

Arendt, Hannah. 1968. *Between Past and Future: Eight Exercises in Political Thought.* New York: Penguin Books.
Coulter, David, and Wiens, John. 2002. "Educational Judgment: Linking the Actor and Spectator." *Educational Researcher* 31 (4): 15–25.
Freire, Paulo. 1970. *Pedagogy of the Oppressed.* New York: Seabury Press.
Ginsburg, M. ed. 1995. *The Politics of Educators' Work and Lives.* New York: Garland.
Ginsburg, M., and Lindsay, B., eds. 1995. *The Political Dimension in Teacher Education: Comparative Perspectives on Policy Formation, Socialization and Society.* New York: Falmer.
Sehr, David. 1997. *Education for Public Democracy.* Albany: State University of New York Press.

# Chapter Summaries

### Chapter 1   Dialogue about Educational Research, Policy, and Practice: To What Extent Is it Possible and Who Should be Involved?
*Mark B. Ginsburg and Jorge M. Gorostiaga*

Chapter One introduces the themes of the book and indicates how these are developed in the other chapters. We first discuss different models of knowledge utilization (instrumental, conceptual, and strategic) to identify the variety of ways in which educational theory/research may influence educational policy/practice. Next we present and raise questions about the two cultures thesis for explaining the limited communication between these theorist/researcher and policy maker/practitioner groups: (a) whether more than one dominant cultural portrait exists for each group; (b) whether each group is heterogeneous with respect to activities and power, as well as beliefs and values; and (c) whether there is significant overlap in membership between the two groups. We also call attention to the absent presence of another group in this discourse: the other members of the local, national, and global communities in which educational praxis occurs. Then we discuss six approaches for enhancing the connections among theorists, researchers, policy makers, practitioners, and community members: (1) translation/mediation, (2) education, (3) role expansion, (4) decision-oriented research, (5) collaborative action research, (6) collective research and praxis. Finally, we consider the possibility of dialogue—joint reflection and action—among the variety of individuals and groups who are involved in education at institutional, local, national, and international levels.

### Chapter 2   Dancing in the Dark: The Relationship between Policy Research and Policy Making in Dutch Higher Education
*Anne Klemperer, Henno Theisens, and Frans Kaiser*

The relationship between research and policy making is analyzed by examining three cases of international comparative research commissioned by various Dutch government organizations. Based on the work of Weiss and Hoogerwerf, a simple, heuristic model is drawn up and used as a first step toward being able to classify different uses of research. This model is then examined in the light of discussions about the complex nature of the policy process. Some additions to the simple model used are proposed.

## Chapter 3   Linking Research, Policy, and Strategic Planning to Education Development in the Lao People's Democratic Republic
*Don Adams, Geok Hwa Kee, and Lin Lin*

After providing a brief overview of the changing social and economic context within which Lao education functions, Chapter Three describes the use and nonuse of research in national efforts in education policy making and planning and examines both the processes and the products of decision making involved in a Lao Government/Asian Development Bank–sponsored education sector assessment. The chapter also suggests ways to improve the effectiveness of Lao policy and planning through building a tradition of use of research and outlines a modified role of international donors in contributing to the development of research capabilities.

## Chapter 4   Teacher Peripheralization in Comparative Education: Causes, Consequences, and Some Responses
*Paul R. Fossum and Patricia K. Kubow*

Comparative education scholars often examine patterns of insularization and exclusion within societies and the ways these patterns affect and are reflected in educational institutions and practices. Yet the field itself functions as a society. And like other societies, comparative education has its own privileged and excluded groups. Specifically, schoolteachers, who hold crucial roles as street-level (non)implementers of policy, tend to have little meaningful conversation with scholars or policy makers, and as a result occupy the peripheral terrains of comparative education. The voices of teachers in the field's discourses is absent—let alone teachers' engagement in genuine dialogue. These circumstances are explicable in part because comparative education's pursuit of recognition as a scholarly field mirrored that of social sciences' quest for academic legitimacy—a quest that has been characterized by the establishment of methods and discipline geared toward the production of knowledge that, while technical, is not genuinely practical. The policy milieu reinforces a preference for technical knowledge, with the term "policy" itself construed in ways that preclude teacher involvement and that make the theory-to-practice divide even more intractable.

## Chapter 5   Researching Women's Literacy in Mali: A Case Study of Dialogue among Researchers, Practitioners, and Policy Makers
*Laurel Puchner*

Chapter Five examines the limited dialogue that occurred between a researcher and practitioners/policy makers during a study that was carried out to assess the impact of literacy program participation on women in rural Mali. Going beyond the popular notion that such dialogue problems exist because of cultural differences between researchers and practitioners/policy makers, the case is used to illustrate (a) the overlapping roles among those involved in the project and (b) the difficulty of untangling cultural differences associated with researcher and practitioner/policy maker perspectives from cultural differences associated with Western and non-Western country perspectives.

## Chapter 6   "Other" Perceptions: Intersubjectivity in the Research Dialogue Process
*Sandra L. Stacki*

The kind and amount of communication that occurs between researchers and practitioners depend upon the characteristics of the researcher, the relationships he or she establishes before and during the research, and the methodological approach adopted in the field. My interpretive, naturalistic study in Uttar Pradesh, India, using a critical, feminist lens, illustrates how being a "friend of UNICEF" and an "American woman in an Indian patriarchal field" constrained and enabled my efforts to develop dialogic and friendship relationships with educational practitioners and other respondents. Such efforts were facilitated by my actions and experiences while I was immersed in the daily lives of some respondents; new shared spaces were created as these respondents and I came to understand that our "advocacies" and values were similar. This precipitated essential trusting relationships to grow and propelled a movement from public-level, researcher-researched relationships to private-level friendships.

## Chapter 7   Reinventing Research for Educational Reform: Advocacy Research and the Promotion of Participation
*Craig G. Wishart and Joseph DeStefano*

This chapter argues for the reinvention of social science research for educational reform. From a postmodern stance, we discuss the purpose and function of research as a means of advocacy, rather than an objective means of data gathering and information sharing. Committed to including all stakeholders, especially the least advantaged in terms of power and material resources, we offer a practical framework for examining the nature and context of stakeholder participation in educational reform. Ideally, such a participatory approach not only is more democratic but also contributes to better policy and practice. Three cases—situated in Brazil, South Africa, and the United States—are presented to illustrate the possibilities and limitations of advocacy research.

## Chapter 8  Ideology in Educational Research and Policy Making in the United States: The Possibility and Importance of Transcendence
*Michele S. Moses and Marina Gair*

Can ideological perspectives be transcended within educational policy research? If so, how should we proceed? In Chapter Eight we examine the seemingly intractable problem of the influence of political ideology on research questions, results, and use. We briefly discuss the struggles over bilingual education in Arizona and California and the debate about school voucher effects in Florida to illustrate how ideology is an undeniable element within educational policy research and policy making. We then draw on Freire's notion of critical cultural workers and Guttman's and Thompson's concept of deliberative democracy to sketch a strategy for transcending, not eliminating, ideology in the policy arena. Next we note the challenge of pursuing a critical deliberative strategy, given existing inequalities in power as well as in economic, social, and cultural capital. Nevertheless, we argue that this strategy can be helpful in transcending ideology in the use of research in relation to controversial policy issues and we discuss the debate over remedial education in colleges and universities to demonstrate how this strategy can contribute.

## Chapter 9  Dialogue between "Academic" and "Community" Researchers: The Possibilities and Challenges of Participatory Research
*Kevin J. Gormley*

Participatory research (PR) is a unique form of scientific investigation that is conducted with coresearchers who work and live in disadvantaged conditions. This chapter reports on research undertaken in Brazil to assess the degree to which a PR project lived up to its theoretical assertions, which include bringing together "academic" and "community" researchers, creating knowledge, and expediting societal transformation. The effectiveness of PR is examined by reviewing the stories of the researchers themselves, specifically by considering what they said about this union between academic and community interests and by appraising whether their efforts created sustainable change.

## Chapter 10  Enhancing Dialogue among Researchers, Policy Makers, and Community Members in Uganda: Complexities, Possibilities, and Persistent Questions
*Joseph Carasco (deceased), Nancy Clair, and Lawrence Kanyike*

Participatory action research (PAR) is one possible solution to the lack of dialogue between researchers, policy makers, and practitioners. PAR involves communication, investigation, and action and includes local people in the research process. Findings from an interpretive study of PAR in the context of the Improving Educational Quality project in Uganda are discussed in terms of three interrelated themes: power, dependence, and resource distribution. While there are enormous dilemmas of using participatory approaches and enhancing dialogue among education stakeholders, there is evidence that some stakeholders were able to collaborate in new ways to improve the quality of their local primary schools.

## Chapter 11   Policy Making, Critical Analysis, or Both—What Role for Educational Research?: The Example of "Lifelong Learning"
*Holger Daun*

During the past two decades, new trends have emerged in the relationships between the realm of educational research, on the one hand, and decision makers and economic interests, on the other. Educational researchers have become involved in studying concepts defined by policy makers. This chapter discusses how the concept of "lifelong learning," originally developed in the context of socialization research, has been distorted to focus only on workforce preparation. In this context, educational researchers are being asked to work in relation to this narrower notion of lifelong learning rather than in relation to a broader set of concerns about human development.

## Chapter 12   "Designed" Dialogues: The *Real* Politics of Evidence-Based Practice and Education Policy Research in England
*Susan L. Robertson and Roger Dale*

Chapter Twelve examines the relationships among researchers, practitioners, and policy makers in the context of the politics of a "designed dialogue" engineered by the state (in part through the actions of a subgroup of policy makers) within the education sector in England. The government in England has recently promoted a notion of "evidenced-based practice" as a basis for improving the communication between researchers and schoolteachers. This initiative can be seen as seeking to control the research topics and the research methods employed by university-based scholars concerned with schooling, while also striving to limit practitioners' and policy makers' conceptions of the goals and strategies of teaching and learning. The rationales and consequences of state efforts to control academic researchers are analyzed in relation to the state's moves since 1980 to exercise more control over teachers and teacher educators and to connect their activities more closely to the "needs" of the economy.

# About the Authors

**Don Adams** is an Emeritus Professor of Education at the University of Pittsburgh. His current international research interests include strategic educational planning and implementation.

**Joseph Carasco,** who died in an airplane crash on January 30, 2000, was a professor in the Department of Biochemistry, Makerere University, and served as the principal researcher for Uganda's Improving Education Quality (IEQ) project. He was a nationally recognized and respected champion of better standards in primary education in Uganda.

**Nancy Clair** is an independent researcher. Her areas of interest are qualitative and participatory research methods, teacher development, and the equitable inclusion of multilingual learners in school reform. From 1997 to 1999 she served as senior research advisor, Education Development Center (EDC) Inc., with Uganda's Improving Education Quality (IEQ) project.

**Roger Dale** is Professor of Education at Auckland University, New Zealand. He has written widely on globalization, the state, and education policy and has a major interest in the global governance of education.

**Holger Daun** is Professor in International and Comparative Education at the Institute of International Education, Stockholm University, Sweden. Research areas are sociology of education, knowledge production and distribution, globalization and education, educational restructuring, and cultural issues and education.

**Joseph DeStefano** is a senior partner of the Busara Group, as well as the Vice President for networking of Learning Communities Network, Inc.. His research and consulting efforts have focused on international education policy, planning, administration, governance, evaluation, and reform.

**Paul R. Fossum** is Assistant Professor of Education at the University of Michigan-Dearborn. His current research and teaching emphases include the professionalization of teaching, social and philosophical aspects of education technology, and interinstitutional organizations and cooperation in higher education.

**Marina Gair** is a doctoral candidate in the Division of Educational Leadership and Policy Studies at Arizona State University. Her academic interests include sociology of education, educational anthropology, and visual ethnography. Her current research focuses on the socialization of preservice teachers, specifically investigating the ways in which elements of hidden curricula function in teacher training practice.

**Mark B. Ginsburg** is Professor of Administrative and Policy Studies (Education) and Sociology (Arts and Sciences) as well as Codirector of the Institute for International Studies in Education at the University of Pittsburgh. His research and teaching interests include the politics of teachers' work, teacher education, and educational research.

**Kevin J. Gormley** is a researcher and institutional grants administrator for the National Security Education Program (NSEP), a U.S. federal program that provides funding for undergraduate scholarships, graduate fellowships, and institutional grants that focus on less commonly studied regions, languages, and cultures around the world. His research interests include underrepresentation in overseas education, international development education, and participatory democracy.

**Jorge M. Gorostiaga** has recently completed his doctoral program in Social and Comparative Analysis in Education program at the University of Pittsburgh. His research focuses on educational reform, especially decentralization, in Latin America and globally.

**Geok Hwa Kee** is a doctoral student in anthropology of education in the Social and Comparative Analysis in Education program at the University of Pittsburgh. Her research interests include school level management in Southeast Asia.

**Frans Kaiser** graduated in public administration at the University of Twente in 1986. He began work at CHEPS in 1988 and became coordinator of the Center for Higher Education Policy Studies (CHEPS) Higher Education Monitor in 1994. His current research interests include systems approaches to the analysis of complex problems and the use of indicators in higher education research and policy.

**Lawrence Kanyike** is currently a researcher with the Enhancement of Universal Primary Education in Kampala (EUPEK) project. He served as research leader for Uganda's Improving Education Quality (IEQ) project.

**Anne Klemperer** graduated with an M.A. in higher education from the Ontario Institute for Studies in Education, University of Toronto, Canada, in

November 1995. She has been working as a researcher at CHEPS since 1997. Her main research interests are research policy and research funding systems, as well as comparative analysis of policy developments in (western) European higher education.

**Patricia K. Kubow** is an Assistant Professor in the School of Leadership and Policy Studies at Bowling Green State University in Bowling Green, Ohio. Her research and teaching interests include comparative and international education, democratic citizenship education and pedagogy, teacher education, and educational policy.

**Lin Lin** received her Ph.D. in Social and Comparative Analysis in Education at the University of Pittsburgh in 1999. Having worked as a consultant on international development projects, she is currently a visiting scholar at Pitt's Institute in International Studies in Education. Her research interests include higher education and policy analysis.

**Michele S. Moses** is an Assistant Professor in the Division of Educational Leadership and Policy Studies at Arizona State University. Her research centers on issues of educational equality and social justice, particularly focusing on education policies related to multiculturalism and poverty, and issues of educational research and policy, especially as related to ideology and ethics.

**Laurel Puchner** is a Lecturer at Southern Illinois University–Edwardsville. She is currently carrying out research examining learning that takes place in learning centers in elementary school classrooms in the United States. She is also interested in the relationship between different types of education/schooling and cognitive and socioeconomic outcomes in low-print environments in developing countries.

**Susan L. Robertson** is a Reader in the Sociology of Education at the Graduate School of Education, University of Bristol. Susan has held academic appointments in Australia, Canada, New Zealand, and England. Her teaching and research interests are in state formation, the policy process, labor studies, and globalization.

**Sandra L. Stacki** received her Ph.D. in Educational Policy Studies/Comparative and International Education and Curriculum and Instruction from Indiana University, Bloomington. She currently teaches at Hofstra University in Long Island, New York. Her research interests include gender and cross-cultural studies, qualitative and feminist inquiry, policy analysis, and teacher education and empowerment.

**Henno Theisens** graduated in 1998 from the faculty of Public Administration of the University of Twente. His master's thesis focused on the impact of the different distributions of power and the institutional contexts on the implementation of a policy in a former polytechnic and a chartered university in the United Kingdom. He joined CHEPS in 1999 as a research trainee (Ph.D.). His research interests are centered on policy studies and the application of institutional theory in this field.

**Craig G. Wishart,** Ph.D. is a cofounder of Learning Leadership Partners, Inc., as well as the director of Learning Communities Institute. His research and consulting efforts have focused on sustainable community development, education reform, organizational change management, and transformational leadership.

CHAPTER 1

# Dialogue about Educational Research, Policy, and Practice
## *To What Extent Is it Possible and Who Should be Involved?*[1]

MARK B. GINSBURG
JORGE M. GOROSTIAGA

### Introduction

There is a long history of concern with the impact of research on policy and practice, "roughly ... [dating from] the emergence of empirical policy research, including censuses and social surveys, in nineteenth-century Europe and North America."[2] In education as in other fields, concerns have been expressed about the limited extent and effectiveness of communication between theorists and researchers, on one side, and policy makers and practitioners, on the other.[3] Many educators, whatever the primary nature of their activity, agree that policy makers and practitioners "should dramatically increase utilization of research [knowledge] in education."[4] Support for greater and more effective one-way communication from theorists/researchers to policy makers/practitioners is based on the belief that vital decisions within educational systems "are taken without sufficient knowledge and information."[5] For example, Noah[6] suggests that "reliable description ... directs us to search out and try to understand forces and factors at work that ... can feed directly into policy making and decision taking." At the same time many people[7] concur that more extensive and effective communication from policy makers/practitioners to theorists/researchers is also critical if we want to improve the policy/practice relevance of the theory and research that is developed in education and other fields.[8]

### Models of Knowledge Utilization

In discussing communication as transmission and use of knowledge, however, we should follow Weiss's advice to avoid relying on a single, simple model of knowledge utilization.[9] As Biddle and Anderson[10] observe, disappointment about the level of communication between theorists/researchers and policy makers/practitioners is "based, in part, on misunderstandings about ... the ways in which its knowledge can affect institutions such as education." Similarly, Watkins calls attention to the "conceptual confusions resulting from problems in the practice of research dissemination [and utilization] that ha[s] previously been examined solely from an instrumental perspective."[11]

Here we discuss three general categories of knowledge utilization: instrumental, conceptual, and strategic. The **instrumental** model of knowledge utilization has two versions that represent the process in terms of people using knowledge directly in making specific decisions:

- *knowledge-driven* (basic research → applied research → development → application)
- *problem-solving* (policy/practice problem arises → preexisting research is identified or research is commissioned to fill knowledge gap → problem solution is determined)[12]

The **conceptual** model of knowledge utilization[13] also includes two versions, both of which draw attention to a more complex, indirect, and diffuse process:

- *interactive* (research findings are used along with experience, political insight, and opinions from a variety of actors in a nonlinear process of decision making)
- *enlightenment* (concepts, theoretical perspectives, and research findings diffuse in society and shape decision makers' general thinking about issues, which subsequently become relevant to specific policy and practice decisions)[14]

The **strategic** model of knowledge utilization,[15] often characterized pejoratively as the *mis*use of knowledge,[16] has three versions in which the process is portrayed as people drawing on or referring to research findings or the research process to support a predetermined position related to a policy or practice decision:

- *political* (research findings are used selectively to provide support for a previously adopted position in relation to a policy or practice decision)
- *tactical* (the fact that research is being undertaken or has been commissioned is used to enhance the credibility of policy makers or practitioners and whatever (non)decisions or (in)action they pursue)[17]
- *promotional* (research or evaluation activity serves to disseminate and promote the implementation of policy and practice decisions to individuals who may not have been involved in the decision-making process)[18]

In their contribution to this volume (Chapter Two), Anne Klemperer, Henno Theisens, and Frans Kaiser employ a similar conceptualization. They distinguish among enlightening, political, and problem-solving uses of research, which correspond to varying degrees with what we have termed conceptual, strategic, and instrumental models of the utilization of knowledge. In addition, Klemperer and colleagues present a simple heuristic model, which postulates that the three types of uses of research will be dominant at three different stages of the policy process. In their initial model they propose that the use of research for enlightenment purposes will dominate at the "designing" stage of the policy process, the political use will be most evident at the "deciding" stage, and research will be used primarily for problem solving during the "implementing" stage. Klemperer and colleagues then analyze three policy-driven, comparative studies (market mechanisms in higher education, university research funding, and student selection procedures) conducted under contract for the Dutch government by the University of Twente's Center for Higher Education Policy Studies to examine the utility of this heuristic model. They conclude that the model serves them fairly well in their analysis of these case studies, although they identify a number of limitations of the model, including that research was used for more than one purpose at a given stage of the policy process.[19]

Furthermore, the distinction between "evidence-based" and "evidence-informed" practice, which Susan Robertson and Roger Dale (Chapter Twelve) make in their critique of how state agents in England have sought to regulate researchers and teachers, is similar to the contrast we made earlier between instrumental and conceptual uses of knowledge. And Craig Wishart and Joseph DeStefano's promotion of what they call "advocacy research" is a call for a version of what we labeled earlier as the strategic use of knowledge (see Chapter Seven).

### The Two Cultures Thesis[20]

Despite the aforementioned valuing of unidirectional communication (i.e., the transmission and use of knowledge), such interaction between theorists/researchers and policy makers/practitioners occurs relatively infrequently.[21] Why is this the case? Of the variety of explanations that have been posited,[22] the most "widely employed" is the "two communities theory," which draws "attention to the cultural basis of the differences between social scientists and policy makers."[23] As Levin observes, more specifically, educational policy makers/practitioners and educational theorists/researchers "represent two different cultures."[24] In Chapter Twelve of this volume Robertson and Dale discuss how this two cultures thesis was promoted by state agents in England in justifying their efforts to redirect the educational research enterprise and redefine the nature and content of interaction (a "designed dialogue") between researchers and practitioners.

Theorists and researchers in education and related fields are said to "believe that [their] singular duty is to the rigorous employment of the methodological canons of social science"[25] and to subscribe to a view of knowledge as "objective, factual, dispassionate truth."[26] The image is that theorists and researchers "constantly ... reexamine and challenge their own assumptions ... [and] pepper the analysis they offer ... with appropriate cautions about the very limited circumstances in which they can claim to make valid generalizations."[27] Theorists and researchers are said to engage in scholarship in isolation from policy makers and practitioners, who have the "obligation ... to understand the importance of, and to apply correctly, the findings [researchers] have so meticulously generated."[28] The assumption seems to be that "good science"[29] will "trickle down to the level of practice and inform practitioners [and policy makers] on what to do and what not to do."[30] A cultural portrait of researchers and theorists also highlights how they select topics based on long-term concerns among scholarly colleagues,[31] undertake projects that take a relatively long time to complete, use specialized terminology, and attend less often to issues of concern to policy makers and practitioners.[32] For example, Psacharopoulos argues that comparative educators are too concerned about theoretical paradigm labeling, what he calls "classificatory mystification," and as a result "few comparative lessons can be drawn [from comparative education literature] to assist decision makers in educational planning."[33] And Heyneman claims that comparative education is "dead ... [because] attention is devoted to academic issues with no obvious product."[34] However, in Chapter Four of this volume, Paul Fossum and Patricia Kubow challenge Pscharopoulos's and Heyneman's conclusions, arguing that higher level policy makers are active participants in the discourse in the field of comparative education, both contributing to and gaining insights from the theory-, research-, and policy-oriented literature. However, Fossum and Kubow note that teachers are "peripheralized" from this discourse.[35] Although many teachers perceive theorists/researchers as experts producing and possessing knowledge, they often reject such knowledge as "opaque, overly esoteric, or otherwise less than useful." Moreover, the field's privileging of policy over practice concerns, and the way policy is conceived within the field, excludes practitioners from the conversation.

Policy makers and practitioners, in contrast, are portrayed as "not [being] interested in the minor details that may be intellectually interesting to researchers or relevant to a few individuals."[36] Their culture is characterized as valuing research that addresses particular questions on their agenda; generates conclusions that are compatible with their beliefs, ideologies, and preferred practices; is written in an understandable way for nonexperts; is provided in a timely fashion; and takes political and economic constraints into consideration.[37] In these senses, it is claimed that within policy maker/practitioner culture, knowledge is "partial, biased, incomplete, self-serving, and politically compromised."[38] Evidence of this, at least from the perspective of theorists and researchers,[39] is that policy makers and practitioners obtain information from nonresearcher groups (e.g., administrators, practitioners, politicians, planners, journalists, clients, interest groups, aides, friends) and make use of sources of knowledge other than research (e.g., experience, political insights, political pressures).[40] Thus, the influence of theory and research on policy and practice decisions is limited, so the argument goes, because policy maker/practitioner culture is "often refractory to ideas from the research domain."[41] In his contribution to this volume, Kevin Gormley (Chapter Nine) indicates that teachers, school directors, and other community members, who formed the team for a participatory research project undertaken in a *favela,* or shantytown, in Brazil, were more concerned with achieving practical "results" and obtaining needed "resources" than with issues of theory and research methodology. Also germane to this cultural portrait of policy makers and practitioners is the observation by Don Adams, Geok Hwa Kee, and Lin Lin (Chapter Three) that research utilization in the policy process was limited because of the "politicization" and dominance of ideological concerns in policy making in the Lao People's Democratic Republic (PDR).

## Limitations of the Two Cultures Thesis

While the issues raised in the two cultures thesis are instructive,[42] we need to be mindful that, like any other explanatory model, it may oversimplify or exaggerate in order to illuminate certain important features of human experience. Here we focus on three ways in which this thesis is built on stereotypic portrayals of the two cultures: (1) it presents only one dominant portrait of each culture; (2) it ignores the heterogeneity of membership in each cultural group; and (3) it overstates the extent to which individuals are members of only one of the two cultural groups.

*Alternative Cultural Portraits*

The dominant representation of each culture can be contrasted with an alternative, less pervasive image. Importantly, the alternative portrait of the theorist/researcher culture is similar to the dominant depiction of policy maker/practitioner culture, while the alternative image of the policy maker/practitioner culture is similar to the dominant view of theorist/researcher culture—facts that encourage us to consider the similarities in as well as differences between the cultures of the two groups.

The *alternative narrative of theorist/researcher culture* emphasizes the assumption that "no knowledge is objective; ... all knowledge is a cultural and historical artifact; and ... all knowledge serves the interests of certain individuals and groups and is counter to the interests of others and consequently knowledge is inevitably political."[43] In this alternative portrayal, research is political in decisions about "the directions and topics," the design and methods, and the interpretation of "the results of research."[44] For instance, in contrast to the dominant model of theorist/researcher culture, but similar to the prevailing view of policy maker/practitioner culture, in this alternative model "different interpretations [of research findings are perceived to] grow from deeply held ideological and value differences" among scholars.[45] As Erwin Epstein[46] observes, no matter how much "we may have improved our application of technological and quantitative tools to the analysis of educational problems, we have progressed nary a step in becoming disinterested, ideologically unbiased observers of school-society relations."

In this volume, Michele Moses and Marina Gair (Chapter Eight) describe how ideology influences the research-based debates about bilingual education and school vouchers in the United States, while proposing a strategy (critical deliberation) for transcending, not eliminating, the influence of ideology on various phases of the processes of research and policy making. In promoting the concept of "advocacy" research, Wishart and DeStefano (Chapter Seven) take a related, but somewhat different, tack, arguing that the researcher's role should be explicitly political, self-consciously oriented to serving the interests of less economically privileged groups. Also, in Chapter Six of this volume, Sandra Stacki describes her struggle with these issues during her dissertation study of the Teacher Empowerment Program in India. From her feminist interpretive perspective she believes that research is a subjective (rather than objective) process—and is shaped by ideology and politics. At the same time she hesitated to make public her own ideological perspective and political commitments because of concerns that doing so would discourage some potential informants from participating in the study or bias what they said during interviews.[47] In reflecting upon her experiences as a researcher, an American woman, and "friend of UNICEF," however, she also notes that at times when she revealed her "advocacies," she was able to establish stronger and deeper (even "friendship") relationships with some practitioners in this setting, thus enabling her to collect richer data.[48]

This alternative model of theorist/researcher culture also draws attention to the political role played by those who do (or do not) provide the needed or desired resources for scholarly activity: local, provincial, and national governments; bilateral and multilateral organizations; and local, national, and global philanthropic organizations.[49] To illustrate, "it is common to find the research problems and the research approach being specified by the sponsor"[50] and the "results of outsourced research projects for government instrumentalities are likely to be filtered [and, thus, "sanitized"] through a tight screen of the political agendas, priorities, and urgencies of the organization that commissions the research."[51]

In Chapter Two of this volume, Klemperer and colleagues illustrate how researchers may be viewed as objective or apolitical, while at the same time they serve the interests of political actors, in part by allowing government officials or other groups financing their research to define the questions to be addressed.[52] Robertson and Dale (Chapter Twelve), in their critical case study of "designed dialogue" and "research-based practice" in England, also draw our attention to how state agents seek to prescribe what is relevant research. At the same time they document how these agents strive to regulate the form of communication between researchers and practitioners and the conception of the goals and processes of education adopted by these groups. And Holger Daun (Chapter Eleven) criticizes the way researchers have tended to uncritically accept—and take on roles as monitoring and assessing adults in relation to—the narrower, workforce development conception of lifelong learning that has been promoted by international organizations that fund (or set the terms for other organizations that fund) much of the research in adult education.

An *alternative narrative about policy maker/practitioner culture* presents the work of policy makers and practitioners as being an objective and a technical process. Psacharopoulos, for example, identifies the activity of planners as "the examination of many feasible alternatives and choice among them according to an objective."[53] And, in his critique, Schon[54] describes this image of practitioners' activity as being "instrumental, consisting of adjusting technical means to ends that are clear, fixed, and internally consistent." In contrast to the dominant representation of policy maker/practitioner culture, but similar to that prevailing view of theorist/researcher culture, in this alternative model policy makers and practitioners operate in a systematic, technically rational, and objective manner.

The comparison between the two cultures becomes even more challenging if we consider that the members of each cultural group are not homogeneous. Here we will briefly discuss heterogeneity in activities, beliefs/values, and power, first, between and among theorists and researchers and, second, between and among policy makers and practitioners.

*Heterogeneity between/among Theorists/Researchers*
Subgroups of researchers and theorists engage in different activities. First, a mental versus manual distinction is often made between theorists (the thinkers) and researchers (the doers).[55] Second, following Kuhn,[56] one can contrast those who do "normal science," pursuing knowledge within the current dominant paradigm, and those whose work unleashes a "scientific revolution," resulting in a new paradigm being enthroned. Among theorists there are distinctions between those who produce "grand" theories and those who contribute to "middle range" theories.[57] In comparative education, furthermore, theorists/researchers work in a variety of organizational settings, each with somewhat different responsibilities and opportunities: local, provincial, and national government units; bilateral and multilateral agencies; nongovernmental organizations, including think tanks, consulting firms, and foundations; and universities.[58] We wish to highlight from a world-system perspective[59] the material differences in the research experience between those based in institutions in the center and those situated in the periphery. As Vulliamy and colleagues[60] observe, "while some issue of research design, execution and analysis may be generalizable, ... different circumstances lead to different constraints and possibilities concerning the process of research."

The theorist/researcher group also is heterogeneous with respect to beliefs and values. For instance, in the field of education, as in the social sciences and related fields, theorists can be grouped into various subcultures (e.g., functionalists, conflict theorists, interpretivists).[61] Additionally, researchers subscribe to different epistemologies (positivism, interpretivism, or critical science) and perform different rituals to collect data (e.g., experiments or quantitative survey research, participant observation or ethnographic interviewing).[62] And one should mention the divergence and lack of cooperation among social science disciplines (inside and outside the field of education) which is accentuated by institutional arrangements at universities and by disciplinary specialization in leading journals.[63] Moreover, as Campbell and Greenberg discuss, "gender and ethnic or racial background are important components of who [researchers] are and affect [their] work and [their] findings."[64] We also call attention to differences in the beliefs and values between theorist/researcher groups in center versus those in periphery locations within the world system, including center-periphery relations both within and between countries.[65] This point is illustrated by Diambomba's warning of the danger if international development research activity is reduced to "a mere exercise in the re-creation of 'Western research environments' in the Third World"[66]—a phenomenon that Husén refers to as "methodological neocolonialism."[67]

In terms of status and power differentials, we need to consider differences in faculty ranks (professor, associate professor, assistant professor, lecturer), the possession or not of tenure, and formal organizational positions (faculty member, chair, dean, etc.) in universities.[68] Moreover, through their gatekeeper roles as editors (of journals, books, and book series), professional organization conference program chairs, and reviewers (of conference presentation proposals, journal articles, book prospectuses, and grant applications), some theorists and researchers clearly exercise more power than others in shaping the knowledge and ways of knowing in a given field during a particular period.[69] And let us not forget that there is an international as well as intranational division of labor or power structure in this regard; thus, researchers in the center, compared to their colleagues in the periphery, account for a disproportionate share of the published and cited work.[70] Robertson and Dale (Chapter Twelve) indicate that the state can play a key role in differentiating the status and power hierarchies among theorists/researchers, in that some scholars' ideas may be promoted by the state in efforts to regulate the ideas and actions of researchers (as well as practitioners).

*Heterogeneity between/among Policy Makers/Practitioners*

With respect to differences in activity, we note that the notion of implementation of policy into practice signals a division of labor between policy makers and practitioners,[71] between those who conceptualize the plans and those who are responsible for executing them.[72] And certainly it is important to point out that policy makers and practitioners often specialize in subsectors of education (preschool, primary, middle, secondary, and higher education levels as well as nonformal and adult provision); that policy makers and administrative practitioners may focus on curriculum, personnel, finance, transportation, infrastructure, and other issues; and that teachers and supervisors are divided with respect to subject matter (e.g., music and art, literacy, mathematics, science, social studies).[73]

In terms of differences in beliefs and values between policy makers and practitioners, we note that:

> Policy makers, planners and administrators want generalizations and rules which can apply to a wide variety of institutions with children of rather diverse backgrounds. ... Classroom practitioners are, however, at a loss with generalizations which only can apply "on the whole" or "by and large", because they are concerned with the local and timely, the particular child here and now.[74]

Based on this distinction in orientations and perceived knowledge needs, Husén argues that comparative education research—at least that undertaken within the positivist tradition—tends to be perceived as more useful by policy makers and higher level administrators than by lower level administrators and teachers.[75]

This theme is at the heart of the contribution to this volume by Fossum and Kubow (Chapter Four). They trace how teachers have been "peripheralized" in relation to the "core" discourses of comparative education, as scholars in the field in their quest for scientific legitimacy, mirroring dynamics in the social sciences more generally, came to emphasize knowledge grounded in "technical" (versus "practical") interests associated with a positivist paradigm. As a result policy makers and administrators are more fully, but not completely, incorporated into comparative education discourses than teachers.

Saha and colleagues[76] however, indicate that the issue of intragroup diversity is more complicated; they report differences among lower level administrators (i.e., principals) in Australia and the United States: Those who had "a strong sense of professional commitment" and had undertaken "postgraduate training" tended to "view research as integral to their responsibilities" and have "a high regard for educational research knowledge." The reference to higher and lower level administrators, of course, reminds us that differences in status and power also characterize the community of policy makers and practitioners. We also call attention to potential differences in power of policy makers operating at the institutional, local, provincial, national, and international levels and to hierarchies among educational practitioners employed at all of these levels (e.g., director versus deputy director, administrator versus teacher, subject or grade level teacher leader versus regular classroom teacher). Differences also exist between the power and resources of national level policy makers in large and small states[77] as well as between more and less privileged/powerful countries. In Chapter Twelve, Robertson and Dale illuminate the differences in ideological and fiscal resources between national level policy makers and school practitioners, documenting how these state agents sought to regulate teachers' (and researchers') conceptions of what counts as relevant research knowledge as well as their understandings of what are the important problems to be addressed through evidence-based practice.

## Overlapping Membership

As with most cultural analyses,[78] the cultural difference thesis is based on an assumption of the separateness of the membership of cultural groups. However, we know that frequently the groups have overlapping memberships. To illustrate, Altbach[79] provides international evidence that during the course of their careers some professors (i.e., university-based theorists/researchers) move in and out of policy-making or practitioner roles in government as well as in for-profit and nonprofit organizations, while Wilson[80] examines the "dual roles played by ... [international education] agency personnel who continue to undertake 'academic' research and publication, even though not based in academia." Furthermore, Wagner[81] provides evidence contradicting "the presumption that researchers and [administrators] are different kinds of people doing different kinds of things." And speaking of teachers, Ludden and Woods[82] explain that "practitioners often are also researchers in particular settings." Finally, we draw attention to the concept of praxis (the conjunction of theory and practice)—signaled in Benson's[83] statement that at least implicitly "[t]heoretical arguments have practical, built-in concerns, and practical interventions usually have theoretical presupposition"—which suggests that theorists and practitioners are not two completely separate groups engaged in totally distinct activities.

Five of the chapters in this volume illustrate the blurred line between the theorist/researcher group and the policy maker/practitioner group. In Chapter Five, Laurel Puchner reflects on her dissertation experience when studying literacy programs for women in Mali, noting that (a) as a researcher, she also became involved in the policy/practice aspects of the program she was studying, and (b) the administrators and practitioners of the program also assisted her in collecting data for her research. In Chapter Six, Stacki notes that during the course of her research in India two of her teacher informants also accompanied her during data collection trips and conferred with her as she analyzed her data. In Chapter Seven, Wishart and DeStefano illustrate how within an "advocacy research" tradition, those who collect and analyze data are also involved in shaping the framework for and outcomes of policy dialogue. In Chapter Nine, Gormley reports on a participatory research project in a *favela* in Brazil in which educators and other community members also became active in the process of research. And in Chapter Ten, Joseph Carasco, Nancy Clair, and Lawrence Kanyike discuss how in the context of participatory action research activities, undertaken within the Improving Educational Quality project, those primarily identified as researchers also participated to varying degrees in activities normally associated with educational policy makers and practitioners, while those primarily identified as policy makers and practitioners (viz., district officials, school administrators, and teachers) served as members of the core research team.

In contrast, in this volume Klemperer and colleagues' analysis of policy research in the Netherlands (Chapter Two) and Adams and colleagues' examination of a sector study in the Lao PDR (Chapter Three) portray situations where there was a clear and strong separation between theorist/researcher and policy maker/practitioner roles.

**Community Members, Democracy, and Professionalism**

In the previous discussion of the two cultures thesis, one can note an absent presence of members of local, national, and global community members who do not happen to be theorists, researchers, policy makers, or practitioners. While they are not an explicit focus of attention and, thus, are absent from the analysis of either of the two cultures, they are nonetheless present, implicitly, in the sense that it is difficult to imagine constructing educational theory/research or developing educational policy/practice unless there were students, parents, and other community members who are implicated in educational systems to be studied and organized. Therefore, unless we submit to "the idea that the world has grown too complex to be ... [governed by] democratic processes ... and must be guided [only] by research-wielding technocrats,"[84] we need to consider the roles to be played by other community members in educational theory, research, policy, and practice.

The degree to which community members' involvement in these activities is promoted depends, in part, on whether one subscribes to a *public* or a *privatized* conception of democracy.[85] In the "public" notion of democracy, the common people are "the only ones who [can] guarantee that the government would not be corrupted" because they do not have privileged positions to preserve, and thus their active involvement in governing is essential.[86] In contrast, the "privatized" notion of democracy, which implies a less active role for citizens in general, is grounded on the belief that

> people come together in political society for protection against constant exposure "to the invasion of others." In this way, people effect the "mutual preservation of their lives, liberties, and estates." ... [T]hese ideas... encourage "antipathy toward direct democracy"... [in part because of] fears about the people's ability to govern itself, without threatening established property relations.[87]

Community members' direct involvement in discussing, let alone determining, educational policy, for instance, would likely be less encouraged under a privatized versus a public conception of democracy.[88]

The preferred level of community member participation in educational theory, research, policy, and practice also depends on how much emphasis one gives to the distinction between "professional" and "nonprofessional." While some have sought to treat professionalism as a scientific term, it is more compelling to conceive of professionalism as an ideology, "not only an image which consciously inspires collective or individual efforts, but a mystification which unconsciously ... obscures real societal structures."[89] Importantly, in relation to our discussion here, although some versions of the ideology of professionalism

Table 1.1 Six Approaches for Facilitating Communication and Promoting Dialogue between/among Theorists/Researchers, Policy Makers/Practitioners, and Other Community Members

| APPROACH | POLICY MAKERS/ PRACTITIONERS | THEORISTS/ RESEARCHERS | OTHER COMMUNITY MEMBERS | COMMUNICATION AND DIALOGUE (JOINT REFLECTION AND ACTION) |
|---|---|---|---|---|
| 1. **Translation/Mediation** between the groups, through individuals who facilitate communication of knowledge | Maintain traditional roles without changes | Maintain traditional roles without changes | Maintain traditional roles without changes | One- or two-way communication may improve, but dialogue is not promoted since groups remain separated |
| 2. **Education** of individuals for better communication with members of another group | Perhaps develop their commitment and capacity to seek out, interpret, and use research and theory | Perhaps use more accessible language and outlets for communicating research results or develop their policy-making/practice understandings | Perhaps develop their research/theory capacities as well as their policy-making/practice understandings | One-way communication is stressed, perhaps enabling joint reflection but not joint action (essential to dialogue) |
| 3. **Role Expansion:** weakening the boundaries between the activities of members of the groups | Perhaps take on theory/research activities as part of their responsibilities | Perhaps devote a proportion of time to perform roles of practitioners and policy makers | Perhaps become more involved in policy-making, practice, theory, or research activities | Does not necessarily increase communication since groups may remain separated |

| | | | |
|---|---|---|---|
| 4. **Decision-Oriented Research:** orienting and research toward policy and practice concerns | Perhaps collaborate in part of the research process (identification of problem and interpretation of findings) | Seek practitioners', policy makers', or community members' input for specific stages of research process | Perhaps collaborate in part of the research process (identification of problem and interpretation of findings) | Enhances two-way communication and facilitates a limited form of dialogue about aspects of research activities |
| 5. **Collaborative Action Research:** active role of practitioners/policy makers in research process | Perhaps participate actively in all stages of the research process | Assume the role of collaborators with policy makers, practitioners, or other community members in research activities | Perhaps participate actively in all stages of the research process | Promotes communication and dialogue, but focused only on research activity |
| 6. **Collective Research and Praxis:** joint construction of theory and research as well as policy and practice | Participate actively and jointly with other groups in all aspects of the theory, research, policy-making, and practice activities | Acknowledge and act on their political commitment by engaging in praxis with both professionals and nonprofessionals | Participate actively and jointly with other groups in all aspects of the theory, research, policy-making, and practice activities | Promotes communication and dialogue in relation to theory, research, policy, and practice activities |

represent professionals' interests as in harmony with those of clients and the general public, in practice this is not necessarily the case.[90] For instance, Esland[91] notes:

> A major characteristic of the professional mandate is that it is dependent on a somewhat negative view of the lay public.... Another crucial aspect of the mandate is that professions have the power to speak for the society on matters which they claim to be expert.... Most professions have developed strategies and techniques... for keeping clients [and other lay community members] "in their place" and for minimizing their intrusion into professional definitions and routines of work.

Community members' participation in educational research, policy, and practice, therefore, could be restricted because of the claims by researchers, policy makers, and educators that they (the "professionals") have a monopoly on relevant expertise.

The chapters in this volume present a range of levels of community member participation, perhaps signaling that different conceptions of democracy or professionalism are operating in the various contexts. For example, Klemperer and colleagues (Chapter Two) and Adams and colleagues (Chapter Three) paint a picture in which only researchers, policy makers, or administrators/practitioners—and not other community members—participate in such activities. In contrast, Wishart and DeStefano (Chapter Seven) report on the involvement of community members in research-, policy-, or practice-related activities in three societal contexts: Brazil, South Africa, and the United States; Gormley (Chapter Nine) portrays the roles played by parents and community organizers as well as teachers and school directors on a team with which he collaborated in conducting a participatory research project in Brazil; and Carasco and colleagues (Chapter Ten) describe how in Uganda students, parents, and other members of rural communities participated in the collection and analysis of data as well as the decisions about school policy and classroom practice.

### Facilitating Communication and Promoting Dialogue[92]

In this section we discuss six approaches toward enhancing the connections among theorists, researchers, policy makers, practitioners, and other community members: (1) translation/mediation, (2) education, (3) role expansion, (4) decision-oriented research, (5) collaborative action research, (6) collective research and praxis.[93] (See Table 1.1 for summary descriptions of the six approaches.) Singly or in combination these approaches could be used to enhance communication. From the earlier discussion, however, it should be evident that our concerns about linkages and communication pertain not only to relations between theorist/researcher groups and policy maker/practitioner groups. We are also interested in interaction among the members of each of these overlapping and somewhat heterogeneous groups as well as between people identified with these groups and other community members.

As we explore strategies for facilitating communication between and within these groups, moreover, we want to consider possibilities of going beyond the one-way or even two-way transmission and utilization of knowledge (theory/research findings or policy/practice issues) to a form of interaction referred to as *dialogue*. Drawing on Freire,[94] we distinguish (a) one-way communication, "the act of one person [or group] 'depositing' ideas in another;" (b) two-way transmission of ideas, "a simple exchange of ideas to be 'consumed' by the discussants;" and (c) dialogue, a process of "united reflection and action." This emphasis on joint *reflection and action* means that we are interested in relationships between/among theorists, researchers, policy makers, practitioners, and other community members that are more extensive and more intensive than (a) theory/research being communicated and influencing the ideas of policy makers, practitioners, and other community members; (b) knowledge about policy/practice issues being communicated and influencing the ideas of theorists, researchers, and other community members; or even (c) two-way communication of ideas (without joint reflection and action) between/among theorists, researchers, policy makers, practitioners, and other community members. As Glass[95] observes, for Freire, dialogue is "characterized by participatory, open communication focused around critical inquiry and analysis, linked to intentional action seeking to reconstruct the situation."

The first approach focuses on *mediation* or *translation* as a means of enhancing communication between and among these groups. Variously referred to as "knowledge brokers,"[96] "intermediaries,"[97] "linkers,"[98] "research brokers,"[99] and "translators,"[100] these "bilingual" or "bicultural" individuals have the responsibility for facilitating at least the one-way transmission of knowledge from theorists and researchers to policy makers and practitioners.[101] Hallinan,[102] for instance, calls for the "creation of a formal position... [occupied by] a person who can act as a bridge between researchers and practitioners... [a]n informed entrepreneur who both understands and appreciates research findings and can package them in a form that educators can use to improve their schools." Expanding their audience to include community members in general, Cabatoff[103] urges program evaluators to "act as policy entrepreneurs... [to shape] public opinion" and Willinsky[104] argues for "an expanded model in which... translation is supported by a website portal strategy for public... engagement with the relevant research in the context of policy and practice." In Chapter Three of this volume, Adams and colleagues describe how mediation or translation was part of the role to be played by the team conducting the Asian Development Bank–funded sector assessment in Lao PDR. The team's charge included identifying, synthesizing, and disseminating to policy makers relevant research that had been previously conducted and published by others. However, we should note that while one- or even two-way communication may be improved through the mediation or translation approach, it is unlikely that joint reflection and action will occur. Indeed, the translator's role depends on the groups remaining in their separate spheres.

The second approach involves the *education* of individuals so that they can better communicate with members of the other cultural group. One variant of the "education" approach entails developing the capacity and commitment of theorists/researchers so that they can communicate more effectively and credibly the results of the research in language[105] and through outlets that are more accessible to different groups of policy makers, practitioners, and other community members. Such outlets include publications, presentations, training sessions, or seminars (targeted to audiences other than theorists/researchers) as well as via mass media.[106] Fossum and Kubow (Chapter Four) offer a clarion call for comparative educators to become more effective in communicating research-based knowledge with teachers; they propose teacher education programs, international educational exchanges, conferences, and publications as channels to develop for this purpose. Puchner (Chapter Five) also stresses the importance of researchers being committed to and effective in communicating their research findings to other people, but describes some of the cultural and structural barriers to achieving this goal, especially in the context of dissertation study undertaken by an American researcher in a country like Mali.

A second variant of the "education" approach consists of developing the commitment and capacity of policy makers and practitioners[107] as well as other community members. The goal here is to encourage them to seek out and make use of theory/research[108] as well as develop their ability to interpret scholarly knowledge produced within a variety of theoretical and methodological paradigms. Adams and colleagues (Chapter Three) identify the potential benefits of national government and international organization policy makers participating in such educational experiences. While those promoting this approach have stressed education as a means of improving communication of knowledge from theorists/researchers to policy makers/practitioners, similar arguments could be made for increasing capacity and commitment of the latter group to communicate knowledge about policy/practice issues to the former group. Additionally, school- and community-based citizen education programs seek to develop community members' capacity and commitment to communicate more effectively with policy makers and practitioners.[109] Even if such communication between and among the various groups is achieved, however, there is no guarantee that joint reflection and action will follow. The division of labor between and within the groups and perhaps their beliefs and values remain unchanged; the intended change is for more effective communication—without the need for a translator.

The third approach, which we call *role expansion,* encourages a weakening of the boundaries between the work activities of the groups. One variant of this approach calls for at least teachers and administrators to take on theory/research activities as part of their responsibilities. For example, Anderson and Herr[110] have promoted the idea of "practitioner research"—"a broad-based movement among school professionals to legitimate knowledge produced out of their own lived realities as professionals."[111] Examples of practitioner research include the ideas of "administrators as researchers"[112] and "teacher research."[113] Moreover, there is no logical reason to exclude the idea of "policy maker research" or "community member research." A second variant of this approach is signaled in calls for university-based theorists/researchers, especially those in professional fields like education, to devote a proportion of their time every week or to arrange extended periods of time during periodic sabbaticals performing the roles of policy makers, administrators, counselors, teachers, and so forth.[114] Note, however, that this approach does not necessarily augment communication between and among theorists/researchers, policy makers/practitioners, and other community members.[115] For example, Puchner (Chapter Five) describes how despite the facts that she (as a researcher) assisted in policy and instructional materials development in relation to the literacy program for women in Mali and that some of the program's practitioners were conducting research as part of a diploma course, there was only limited communication between her and her Malian contacts. And it is possible that as theorists/researchers and policy makers/practitioners expand their respective roles, they may devote less time and energy to communicating with other community members.

The fourth approach partially challenges the traditional division of labor between theorists/researchers and policy makers/practitioners, while also enhancing two-way communication and facilitating a limited form of dialogue. Variously called "applied research,"[116] "case study,"[117] "clinical partnerships,"[118] "evaluation research,"[119] "interest-driven research,"[120] "solution-driven research,"[121] "policy-relevant research,"[122] "policy research,"[123] "practice-oriented research,"[124] and "practice-driven research,"[125] this approach seeks to improve the relevance of research and theory by orienting theorists/researchers toward policy and practice concerns.[126] Here we employ the term *decision-oriented research*, drawing on the writings of Cooley and Bickel.[127] A key element in this approach from the researcher's standpoint is a "client orientation," operationalized through an "on-going educational dialogue"[128] in which researchers "work hard at trying to understand the information needs of the client and to meet those needs."[129] Following this approach, theorists/researchers interact with clients (usually defined as policy makers or administrators, although logically they could be teachers, students, parents, and other community members) to get clients' input in determining the focus of the research as well as to discuss how the research findings might be interpreted. Thus, while theorists/researchers are not involved directly in making policies or in engaging in practice, policy makers, practitioners, and/or other community members collaborate with theorists/researchers in the problem-identification and the findings-interpretation stages of the research process. Thus, a limited extent of dialogue (i.e., joint reflection and action) does occur in this approach with respect to some—but not all—phases of the research activity. In this volume the comparative policy research in the Netherlands examined by Klemperer and colleagues (Chapter Two) and the Lao PRD education sector study discussed by Adams and colleagues (Chapter Theree) represent examples of this approach to improving the relationship between theorists/researchers and policy makers/practitioners. In some ways this approach is the one being promoted by state agents to foster research-related communication between researchers and teachers in England; however, as Robertson and Dale (Chapter Twelve) observe, the form and content of the "dialogue" are not being negotiated between the two groups directly involved but instead are being "designed" by a third group, national level policy makers.

The fifth approach further blurs the division of labor and promotes a somewhat more extensive dialogue between (and perhaps among) theorists/researchers, policy makers/practitioners, and other community members. We label this approach *collaborative action research,* a term popularized in the field of education by Lawrence Stenhouse.[130] This approach entails not only communication about, but also joint reflection and action in relation to, research by "researchers" and "practitioners" (usually defined as teachers), although logically educational administrators, policy makers, and community members could be involved. This model builds on the notion that all people normally engage in inquiry and that such activity can be enhanced if they devote more time and energy to a more systematically planned and implemented process of research.[131] Nonetheless, a division of labor still exists. Even though "practitioners" (and perhaps "policy makers" and other community members) assume rights and responsibilities in the research process,[132] "researchers" are involved primarily as a collaborator in research design, data collection, and data analysis, remaining somewhat detached from the "professional" and "political" activity of educational policy making and practice.[133] Thus, this approach primarily implicates role changes for policy makers, practitioners, and community members, and the dialogue that occurs remains focused only on research activity. For instance, in describing the use of "participatory evaluation" in nonformal educational projects aimed at "empowering" indigenous Mexican communities, Brunner and Guzman[134] note that

> [p]rofessional evaluators...play the role of methodological consultants in the evaluation process, not of decision makers. The social groups, together with their [program] facilitators, decide when an evaluation should take place, what should be evaluated, how the evaluation should be carried out, and what should be done with the results.

In Chapter Nine, Gormley describes in similar terms his experiences as an "academic" researcher working with "community" researchers examining the educational needs of people living in a *favela* in Brazil. Although the ten teachers, three school directors, three community organizers, and 4 other parents/community members on the research team did engage in actions—to purchase land for a school and to challenge government officials regarding the limited educational provision in their neighborhood—Gormley's dialogue with the "community" researchers was focused primarily on planning, conducting, and interpreting the findings from the "participatory research" project.

The sixth approach, which we label *collective research and praxis,* implicates theorists, researchers, policy makers, practitioners, and other community members in expanding their traditionally distinct roles. This approach, which is at least partly rooted in Freire's efforts to develop "liberation pedagogy within... adult education,"[135] also offers the possibility of the most extensive form of dialogue, focused on the activities of constructing theory and research as well as of developing policy and practice. Related approaches include (a) "fourth generation evaluation," described as a "sociopolitical process" in which the evaluator not only "solicits and honors stakeholder inputs... with respect to the *methodology* of the evaluation itself" but also "divests him- or herself of the role of passive observer and recognizes and embraces the role of change agent,"[136] and (b) "empowerment evaluation," in which evaluators, practitioners, policy makers, and other community members collaboratively "shape the direction of the evaluation, suggest ideal solutions to their problems, and then take an active role in making social change happen."[137]

The collective research and praxis approach is also similar to what Wagner[138] calls "co-learning agreements," in which the "division of labor... [is] more ambiguous, as both researchers and practitioners are regarded as agents of inquiry and as objects of inquiry... [and] both are engaged in action and reflection," and to what Reimers and McGinn[139] call "informed policymaking," which entails active participation in policy research and policy making by researchers, policy makers, practitioners, and other stakeholders. It should be noted that Wagner as well as Reimers and McGinn draw on the work on "organizational learning" by Peter Senge,[140] who focuses on business enterprises and who gives more attention to promoting efficiency and effectiveness than to achieving equity, meeting human needs, and preserving the environment.

The latter goals are more likely to be prioritized by those subscribing to a critical theory perspective and those employing the term *praxis*[141] or stressing activism or participation[142] in relation to their approach to linking theorists/researchers, policy makers/practitioners, and community members. For example, Lather[143] describes the "research as praxis" approach as one "that goes well beyond the action research concept.... The vast majority of this work operates from an ahistorical, apolitical value system." Similarly, McTaggert[144] characterizes "participatory action research" as a "process of using critical intelligence to inform action, and developing it so that social action becomes praxis through which people may consistently live their social values."[145] Moreover, researchers operating within at least the critical tradition of the collective research and praxis approach start "from social and political intentionality which is explicit and articulated in solidarity with the dominated and poor... groups of the society."[146] Solidarity with oppressed and impoverished groups is at the heart of "advocacy research," as discussed by Wishart and DeStefano (Chapter Seven), and "participatory research," as discussed by Gormley (Chapter Nine), although this element was realized to varying degrees in the projects they describe.

Core assumptions of the "collective research and praxis" approach are that (a) researchers acknowledge and act upon their political commitments, and (b) they do so in the context of engaging in theorizing and practice (i.e., praxis) with both professionals and nonprofessionals, such as students and other community members.[147] In this way, the boundary between research and politics is broken down and the distinction between theorist/researcher, policy maker/practitioner, and other community member groups becomes blurred; those who identify (or are typified) primarily as playing one (or none) of these roles, in fact, play more than one. Policy makers, administrators, teachers, students, and other community members participate in research, and "researchers" become active participants in various settings, working with others to understand *and* change schools and society. Members of these various groups engage in dialogue—joint reflection and action—with reference to theory and research as well as policy and practice.

In this volume the sixth approach is exemplified in Carasco and colleagues (Chapter Ten) participatory action research activities in the context of the Improving Educational Quality project in Uganda. Although the power and resource relations between the authors (as non-community-based researchers) and the local teacher, parent, and student researchers remained unequal and the changes brought about through this project certainly could not be described as socially transformative, there is ample evidence that all groups involved participated in research activities as well as deliberations about policy and practice. Moreover, the "advocacy research" model, presented by Wishart and DeStefano (Chapter Seven), overlaps substantially with the "collective research and praxis" approach. In their model, policy-relevant knowledge is not limited to "objective" facts obtained by expert "researchers" and shared only with high-level policy makers. All stakeholders, especially those who are disadvantaged in terms of power and resources, should be involved in—or at least have access to the findings from—policy studies. This is because the model promotes a broad-based participatory style of decision making regarding public sector policy and practice issues.

Putting this model in practice, of course, is not a simple matter, as the three cases presented by Wishart and DeStefano (Chapter Seven) attest. In Brazil the Programma de Pesquisa e Operacionização de Politica Educational (PPO) was supported by international agency representatives and orchestrated by government officials and professionals/experts, who partnered with practitioners, parents, pupils, and other community members to gather and interpret data. While the policy and practice recommendations were crafted during relatively elite deliberations and then disseminated to educators and the public at large, these recommendations were believed to emerge from and reflect the experiences and opinions of all stakeholders. For the South African case an Assessing Policies for Education Excellence (APEX) team was created and used "Policy Options Workshops" to collect and share data as well as stimulate a policy dialogue involving a range of stakeholder groups, including the least advantaged. While the research was guided and managed by specialists, these researchers did not view themselves as neutral disseminators of facts but as change agents working in partnership with other stakeholders. The case in the United States focuses on the dynamics of the organization called District Community Voices Organized and Informed for Change in Education (DC VOICE), "a broad-based collaborative of parents, teachers, and community representatives." DC VOICE conducted an action research project, which gathered input from an even broader segment of the population and then convened "community dialogues" during which a wide range of stakeholders discussed the findings and possible educational policy/practice implications. The research activity as well as the policy/practice deliberations involved researchers, policy makers, practitioners, and other community members, thus blurring the lines between the roles of these various groups and making the processes more democratic. Important questions to address in follow-up studies of the three cases discussed by Wishart and DeStefano are whether such participatory processes continue over the longer term and what educational and economic benefits accrue to the least advantaged and other stakeholders as a result of such "advocacy research" activities.

**Conclusion**

We have focused our attention on the limited extent and effectiveness of communication between theorists and researchers, on the one hand, and policy makers and practitioners, on the other. And while not wishing to ignore some general cultural differences between these two groups, we have discounted the two cultures thesis for explaining the communication gap, arguing that neither group is homogeneous culturally and that there is overlap in the membership of the two groups. We also called attention to the need to consider these groups' interaction with other community members. We then discussed six approaches toward closing the communication gap (translation/mediation, education, role expansion, decision-oriented research, collaborative action research, collective research and praxis), analyzing the likelihood that they would promote dialogue (joint reflection and action) between and among theorists/researchers, policy makers/practitioners, and other community members. Although the first two approaches retain a traditional separation of roles, the other four promote varying degrees of movement toward more involvement of policy makers, practitioners, and other community members in theory/research activities and, in some cases, more involvement of theorists, researchers, and other community members in policy/practice decisions and actions. As we have noted, the fourth and fifth approaches imply some form of dialogue, but only the sixth approach, *collective research and praxis*, facilitates dialogue—that is, communication, reflection, and action—concerning both theory/research and policy/practice. We recognize that these latter approaches threaten or undermine what some would see as an "efficient" division of labor, substituting arrangements that require more time and resources to sustain and perhaps undermining the legitimacy of researchers' contributions (see Chapter Two by Klemperer et al.). However, we see value in the potential for such an approach to promote democratric structures and to yield richer theory/research and policy/practice (see Chapter Six by Stacki and Chapter Seven by Wishart and DeStefano).

However, we are not naively suggesting that this or any division of labor ensures dialogue. Remember that, following Freire, dialogue involves joint reflection and action among individuals or groups who do not engage in "banking" relations, in which one party "deposits" ideas into the heads of another:

> Because dialogue is an encounter among [people] who name [and thus begin to transform] the world, it cannot be reduced to a situation where some [person] names on behalf of others. It ... must not serve as a crafty instrument for the domination of one [person] by another.... Unfortunately, however, ... [change agents] often fall for the banking line of planning program content from the top down.[148]

Thus, we need to scrutinize the motives and actions of those involved in dialogic efforts. While Freire was clearly aware and concerned that people might claim they are pursuing "dialogue" when, in fact, they were employing communication as "a technique for manipulation,"[149] this has not prevented critics of Freire's dialogic method from claiming that it is merely a subterfuge for indoctrination.[150] Relevant here is the point that Moses and Gair (Chapter Eight) make in this volume, that individuals and groups who possess greater amounts of economic, social, and cultural capital are likely to be more influential both in shaping and interpreting research and in framing and making decisions about controversial educational policy issues. Thus, they propose combining Freire's notion that researchers should serve as critical cultural workers (acting as progressive agents in concrete political struggles in the public domain) with a conception of "deliberative democracy" in formulating their proposed ideal strategy (critical deliberation) for undertaking dialogue about research, policy, and practice.

In the field of comparative and international education this issue surfaces in the context of communication between powerful/privileged actors (e.g., those representing bilateral or multilateral agencies, universities in center locations) to impose over actors of periphery their own views about research questions, design, and findings interpretation.[151] In Chapter Six, Stacki discusses how she tried to get practitioners and policy makers in India to reflect on and discuss gender issues without trying to impose her own views on them. Like Stacki, Puchner (Chapter Five) identifies this as a personal concern that she dealt with as a researcher from a "Western" country while studying and interacting with policy makers and practitioners in the "non-Western" or "developing" country of Mali in West Africa. Puchner suggests that part of the reason that she may have not shared her interpretation of her findings was that she worried about imposing her "Western," feminist perspective on the Malians with whom she interacted.[152] It should be noted that Freire would not encourage the strategy followed by Puchner (and likely other researchers, not to mention some consultants[153] who are engaged in technical assistance and training projects in less privileged/powerful countries). In response to Shor's questions, Freire emphasizes that educators (and researchers) should evince humility and demonstrate (versus assert) their competence, but notes that this "does *not* mean that [they] deny that [they] know! It would be a lie, an hypocrisy."[154] One might also question whether Puchner's decision not to share her views avoided the problem of imposing ideas on her counterparts in Mali. The other, more technical interpretations of her findings that she shared with her associates in Mali may also have swayed their thinking, if only by reinforcing their previously held ideas, which could now be "supported" by the scientific/empirical research of a doctoral student "scholar" from the United States.

Furthermore, it is important to remember that relationships are constructed by the various individuals and groups in interaction (not just the researchers). It may be that, no matter how hard theorists and researchers from more "privileged/powerful" countries strive to achieve co-agency or power-with relations[155] with policy makers, practitioners, and other community members from less "privileged/powerful" countries, the latter groups may continue to devalue the contribution of their own perspectives, knowledge, and skills, and thus not participate fully and equally in the joint activities of theorizing, researching, policy making, and/or educating. In effect, they help create and sustain a "banking" relationship with researchers from privileged/power locations, despite a commitment by such researchers toward a more dialogic form.

We believe that the problem of *overblown deference* to "developed" country ideas, methods, and people by "developing" country policy makers, practitioners, and other community members poses a significant problem for actualizing a dialogic relationship, no matter which approach is employed to facilitate communication in international development education projects.[156] In this volume Adams and colleagues (Chapter Three), Puchner (Chapter Five), Gormley (Chapter Nine), and Carasco and colleagues (Chapter Ten) provide glimpses of how this may be occurring. We should note that (a) the problem of overblown deference also exists in the relationship between and among theorists/researchers, policy makers/practitioners, and other community members who are all from the same country; (b) not all policy makers, practitioners, and other community members suffer from this condition of overblown deference; and (c) some policy makers, practitioners, and other community members may feign such a condition if this is perceived as a necessary part of a strategy for receiving financial or other resources for themselves or the educational systems with which they are associated.

Moreover, there are situations where the theorists and researchers may defer—at least publicly—to the ideas of educational policy makers, practitioners, and perhaps other community members, thus limiting the possibility for true dialogue.[157] In Chapter Two, Klemperer and colleagues describe examples of how the Center for Higher Education Policy Studies (CHEPS) researchers operated in response to Dutch government officials, restricting their input to issues that were framed by the policy makers. And Adams and colleagues illustrate in Chapter Three how researchers from both more and less privileged/powerful countries may defer to policy makers/practitioners in multilateral agencies, who not only are potentially part of the dialogue but also provide much of the funding for the research activity and policy planning and implementation. A similar form of deference may have occurred in the situation described by Carasco and colleagues (Chapter Ten), with U.S. and Ugandan researchers being reluctant to enter fully into open discussion and action in relation to the United States Agency for International Development, which supported financially the research and policy/practice initiatives. Finally, in Chapter Eleven, Daun discusses how researchers have for the most part refocused their energies on a narrower concept of lifelong learning, eschewing a broader, humanistic notion concerned with adult development in favor of a notion of workforce development. He argues that researchers have generally come to devote themselves to monitoring and assessing individuals across a range of life situations, but with a focus on this narrower, economistic notion of adult learners who are "naturally" embedded within commodified, capitalist, productive and social relations. He also posits that this shift in focus in researcher activity as well as in researcher–policy maker relations has occurred not only because international organization policy makers fund much of the research, but also because of ideological and structural dynamics associated with economic globalization and the restructuring of the state. Nevertheless, Daun points to spaces in which researchers might pursue a strategy of critical analysis and resistance, rather than one of uncritical acceptance of these dynamics and the notions of lifelong learning associated with them.

These examples remind us that while people construct their social relations, they do so within structural and ideological contexts that predate their own thoughts and actions.[158] Thus, we need to consider more than just the beliefs, attitudes, and actions of individual theorists, researchers, policy makers, practitioners, and community members; we should examine how broader structures and ideologies constrain and enable actors' involvement in dialogue.[159] Misgeld,[160] for example, identifies "psychologically operative repressions" as a constraint on dialogue, but sees such individual features as depending at least in part on "(1) conditions of economic scarcity [and] (2) conditions of social and political inequality." In this volume, both Gormley (Chapter Nine) and Carasco and colleagues (Chapter Ten) indicate that teachers' and community members' involvement in participatory projects may be difficult to sustain without financial or other material resources being secured to "facilitate" or compensate people for their efforts. And, in Chapter Three, Adams and colleagues suggest how powerful actors, such as the Asian Development Bank, may need to alter the way they operate if dialogue about theory/research and well as policy/practice is to become a reality.

In a way we are restating Habermas's[161] contention that the conditions of the "ideal speech situation" are isomorphic to the conditions of "an ideal form of life:"

> [T]he conditions of the ideal speech situation must insure not only unlimited discussion but also discussion which is free from all constraints of domination, whether their source be conscious strategic behavior or communication barriers secured in ideology.... Thus, the conditions for ideal discourse are connected with conditions for an ideal form of life; they include linguistic conceptualizations of the traditional ideas of freedom and justice.[162]

This means that our individual and collective efforts to achieve dialogue between and among theorists/researchers, policy makers/practitioners, and other community members are not likely to be easy. Nevertheless, like the goal of a world characterized by peace, freedom, and justice, the goal of enhancing the conditions, commitments, and capacities for dialogue between and among different groups of people is one for which we should struggle.

Thus, as we engage in activities as comparative and international educators, we need to be vigilant concerning how our own and others' views and (deliberate or inadvertent) actions may construct relations between and among members of the groups that limit the possibility of dialogue. At the same time we need to attend to and struggle to overcome the cultural/ideological and political economic constraints to dialogue.

## Notes

1. This is a revised and expanded version of our editor's introduction [Mark Ginsburg and Jorge Gorostiaga, "Relationship between Theorists/Researchers and Policy Makers/Practitioners: Rethinking the Two Cultures Thesis and the Possibility of Dialogue"] to a special issue of the *Comparative Education Review* [45 (2) (May 2001): 173–96] focused on the theme signaled by the title. Besides the ideas stimulated by authors of the other chapters in this book, we would like to acknowledge with gratitude the following people for their feedback on earlier drafts of this manuscript and/or their contributions to discussions on the topic during a special topics seminar organized at the University of Pittsburgh during May and June 2000: Hamood Al-Harthi, Santi Ambarrukmi, Mohamed Azab, Annie Budzik, Chiharu Kondo, Nagwa Megahed, Marilyn Patete, Simona Popa, Noriko Tsurui, Erry Utomo, Vanessa Villalobos, Mika Yamashita, and Minho Yeom.
2. William Dunn, "Studying Knowledge Use: A Profile of Procedures and Issues," in *Knowledge Generation, Exchange and Utilization*, ed. George Beal, Wimal Dissanayake, and Sumiye Konoshima (Boulder, CO: Westview Press, 1986), p. 369. Dietrich Rueschemeyer and Theda Skocpol ["Conclusion," in *States, Social Knowledge, and the Origins of Modern Social Policies*, ed. Dietrich Rueschemeyer and Theda Skocpol (Princeton, NJ: Princeton University Press,

1996), pp. 297 and 310] make the interesting observations that in the context of the contradiction of political democratization and economic inequalities and divisions (resulting from capitalist industralization) in Europe and North America, "it was [the state's] knowledge needs that instigated the early development of social sciences.... After as well as before the emergence of the modern social sciences, social knowledge and its bearers primarily helped to identify and characterize 'social problems' on which states could act, and helped to rule in or out conceivable sorts of policy options."
3. Maureen Hallinan, "Bridging the Gap between Research and Practice," *Sociology of Education* 69 (extra) (1996): 131–34; Bruce Biddle and Don Anderson, "Social Research and Educational Change," in *Knowledge for Policy: Improving Education through Research*, ed. Don Anderson and Bruce Biddle (London: Falmer, 1991); S. Heyneman, "Quantity, Quality, and Source," *Comparative Education Review* 37 (November 1993): 6–15; George Psacharopoulos, "Comparative Education: From Theory to Practice, or Are You A:/neo.* or B:/*.ist?," *Comparative Education Review* 34 (3) (1990): 369–80.
4. Fernando Reimers and Noel McGinn, *Informed Dialogue: Using Research to Shape Education Policy around the World* (Westport, CT: Praeger, 1997), p. 5.
5. Wanda Rokicka, "Introduction," in *Educational Documentation, Research and Decision-Making: National Case Studies*, ed. Wanda Rokicka (Paris: International Bureau of Education, 1999), p. 7; see also Reimers and McGinn, p. 5; Carol Weiss, "The Many Meanings of Research Utilization," in *Knowledge for Policy: Improving Education through Research*, ed. Don Anderson and Bruce Biddle (London: Falmer, 1991), p. 179. In contrast, some view the utilization of research by policy makers and practitioners as having negative consequences, for example: "supporting the status quo[, which presumably exhibits negative features,] or facilitating actions that are questionable" (Biddle and Anderson, p. 17).
6. Harold Noah, "The Uses and Abuses of Comparative Education," *Comparative Education Review* 28 (4) (1984): 552.
7. We suspect that this group would be comprised of most policy makers and practitioners, but relatively fewer theorists and researchers in the field of education.
8. Dunn, "Studying Knowledge Use," p. 370; Weiss, "The Many Meanings," p. 181; John Meyer and David Baker, "Forming American Educational Policy with International Data: Lessons from the Sociology of Education," *Sociology of Education* 69 (extra) (1996): 123; Andrew Pettigrew, "Contextualist Research: A Natural Way to Link Theory and Practice," in *Doing Research That Is Useful for Theory and Practice*, ed. Edward Lawler, Allan Mohrman, Susan Mohrman, Gerald Leoford, and Thomas Cummings (Washington, DC: Jossey-Bass, 1985), pp. 225–26; Psacharopoulos, p. 380. Those who balk at the notion worry that scholars would be co-opted and lose their "objectivity" [J. Bradley Cousins and Kenneth Leithwood, "Current Empirical Research on Evaluation Utilization," *Review of Evaluation Research* 56 (3) (1986): 331–64] become "cheap consultants" [ Robert Burgess, "Contractors and Customers: A Research Relationship?" in *Educational Research and Evaluation: For Policy and Practice?*, ed. Robert Burgess (Washington, DC: Falmer, 1993), p. 25] rather than independent researchers "examining basic theoretical, conceptual, and methodological issues" [Dunn, "Studying Knowledge Use," p. 394]; eschew feminist and other critical perspectives [Catherine Marshall, "Researching the Margins: Feminist Critical Policy Analysis," *Educational Policy* 13 (1) (1999): 60]; and tend to serve the interests of dominant groups [Michael F. D. Young, "Introduction," in *Knowledge and Control: New Directions for the Sociology of Education*, ed. Michael F. D. Young (New York: Collier-Macmillan, 1970)].
9. Weiss, "The Many Meanings."
10. Biddle and Anderson, p. 6. Although Biddle and Anderson, among others [e.g., Thomas Barone, "Introduction," *International Journal of Educational Research* (Special Issue on "The Uses of Educational Research") 23 (2) (1995): 107–12; Cousins and Leithwood]), focus on the communication of knowledge from theorists/researchers to policy makers/practitioners, we suggest that similar issues arise when we consider how theorists/researchers utilize the knowledge of policy/practice concerns that may be transmitted to them by policy makers/practitioners. Perhaps, given that most of the literature we reviewed was based on the writings by members of the theorist/researcher community, it is not surprising that very little attention is devoted to the other direction of communication.
11. John Watkins, "A Postmodern Critical Theory of Research Use," *Knowledge and Policy: The International Journal of Knowledge Transfer and Utilization* 7 (4) (Winter 1994): 74. Watkins

observes that "a critical realist theory of research use is fundamentally at odds with the traditional, modernist [positivist] views of knowledge and its use, including the view of its objectivity and universality, the linear perspective of dissemination and use, and the absence of a process for the critique of its own ideology (p. 62). Although the emphasis on ideology critique distinguishes a critical realist from an interpretivist approach, both approaches differ from positivism in viewing knowledge as "cognitively and socially constructed" and, thus "not disseminable *per se*, needing "to be reconstructed in any use setting" (p. 72).

12. Weiss, "The Many Meanings."
13. William N. Dunn ["Conceptualizing Knowledge Use," in *Knowledge Generation, Exchange and Utilization,* ed. George M. Beal, Wimal Dissanayake, and Sumiye Konoshima (Boulder; CO: Westview Press, 1986), p. 336] notes that many authors have distinguished conceptual and instrumental uses of knowledge, but argues that "instrumental use is a particular type of conceptual use." Carol Weiss ["Perspectives on Knowledge Use in National Policy Making," in *Knowledge Generation, Exchange and Utilization,* ed. George Beal, Wimal Dissanayake, and Sumiye Konoshima (Boulder, CO: Westview Press, 1986), p. 420] states that utilization is best seen as a continuum between instrumental and conceptual use (as decision makers do not recall specific studies but report use of research in their decisions). Ray Rist and M. Kathleen Joyce ["Qualitative Research and Implementation Evaluation: A Path to Organizational Learning," *International Journal of Educational Research* (Special Issue on "The Uses of Educational Research") 23 (2) (1995): 127–36] combine the instrumental and conceptual use models into what they term "double-loop" learning and which they view as the best way for evaluation and research findings to contribute to "good organizational decisionmaking."
14. Weiss, "The Many Meanings." In his discussion of externally funded, policy-oriented research in "developing" countries, Kenneth King ["Dilemmas of Research Aid to Education in Developing Countries," *Prospects* 11 (3) (1981): 350], notes: "Whatever the record on implementation of the results of such research, it is at least arguable that work of a more theoretical nature may equally be implementable (cf. the work of Freire, which... has reached and affected many people with responsibility for literacy policy)."
15. We label this model "strategic" rather than "political" both because one of its forms (identified by Weiss, "The Many Meanings") is called "political" and because of the generally negative connotation of the term, "political" [see Mark Ginsburg, *The Politics of Educators' Work and Lives* (New York: Garland, 1995)].
16. Guy Benveniste, *The Politics of Expertise* (San Francisco: Boyd and Fraser, 1977); Laura Leviton and Edward Hughes, "Research on the Utilization of Evaluations: A Review and Synthesis," *Evaluation Review* 5 (4) (1981): 525–48; T. Lovelace, "The Use and Misuse of Research in Educational Reform," in *Brookings Papers on Educational Policy,* ed. Diane Ravitch (Washington, DC: Brookings Institute, 1998).
17. For a discussion of "political" and "tactical" uses of knowledge, see Weiss, "The Many Meanings."
18. For illustrations of the "promotional" form of research knowledge utilization, see Don Adams, Mark Ginsburg, Thomas Clayton, Martha Mantilla, Judy Sylvester, and Yidan Wang, "Linking Research to Policy and Practice to Improve Educational Quality," in *New Approaches to Studying Educational Policy Formation and Appropriation,* ed. Bradley Levinson and Margaret Sutton (New York: Ablex, 2000).
19. Klemperer et al. (Chapter Two) also found the linear, stage model of the policy process to be overly simplistic, especially when one takes into consideration the broader context within which any particular policy process occurs. They thus came to agree with Weiss ["Perspectives on Knowledge Use," pp. 410–11], who argues for dynamic, nonlinear models, in which the "process is not one of linear order from research to decision but a disorderly set of interconnections and back-and-forthness that defies neat diagrams." On different models for analyzing policy-making processes, see also Rita Kelly and Dennis Palumbo, "Theories of Policy-Making," in *Encyclopedia of Government and Politics,* ed. Mary Hawkesworth and Maurice Kogan (New York: Routledge, 1992).
20. Our focus here has some affinities with, but is not identical to, Charles Percy Snow's [*The Two Cultures and the Scientific Revolution* (Cambridge, England: Cambridge University Press, 1959)] two cultures thesis, articulating his concern about the lack of communication and understanding between those trained in the natural sciences and those schooled in the humanities.

21. See, for example, Rita Brause and John Mayher (eds.), *Search and Re-Search: What the Inquiring Teacher Needs to Know* (London: Falmer Press, 1991); Maureen Hallinan, "Bridging the Gap between Research and Practice," *Sociology of Education* 69 (extra) (1996): 131; Mary Kennedy, "The Connection between Research and Practice," *Educational Researcher* 26 (7) (October 1997); Cheol Oh, *Linking Social Science Information in Policy-making* (Greenwich, CT: JAI Press, 1996), pp. 56–70; Psacharopoulous.
22. In addition to the two cultures (mis)communication model (to be discussed later in the chapter), Dunn ["Conceptualizing Knowledge," p. 328] also identifies what he terms "quasi-physical process" metaphors of knowledge utilization (e.g., carried from source to receiver like a bucket carries water, travels like a bullet shot at a target, spreads like an infectious disease). Each of these models focuses attention on the transmission process rather than the cultural characteristics of the transmitting or receiving entities.
23. Dunn, "Conceptualizing Knowledge Use," pp. 329–30. Similarly, Bridget Somekh ["Inhabiting Each Other's Castles: Towards Knowledge and Mutual Growth through Collaboration," *Educational Action Research* 2 (3) (1994): 367] notes that "the castle of the academy and the castle of the school have different tests for truth when evaluating the product of research and are, therefore, inclined to approach methodological issues from different points of view." Thus, Neville Jennings ["Building Bridges in School-Focused Research: The Australian Experience," in *The Politics & Machinations of Educational Research: International Case Studies*, ed. Susan McGinty (New York: Peter Lang, 2001), pp. 87–97] discusses the need for "building bridges" when undertaking collaborative "school-focused" research.
24. Henry Levin, "Why Isn't Educational Research More Useful?" in *Knowledge for Policy: Improving Education through Research*, ed. Don Anderson and Bruce Biddle (London: Falmer, 1991), pp. 72 and 77.
25. Barone, p. 109.
26. Weiss, "Perspectives on Knowledge Use," p. 415.
27. Sally Brown, "Research in Education: What Influence on Policy and Practice?" *Knowledge and Policy: The International Journal of Knowledge Transfer and Utilization*, 7 (4) (Winter 1994): 97.
28. Barone, p. 109.
29. William Foote Whyte, "Introduction," in *Participatory Action Research*, ed. William F. Whyte (Newbury Park, CA: Sage, 1991), p. 8.
30. A. Gitlin, K. Bringurst, M. Burns, V. Cooley, B. Meyers, K. Price, R. Russell, and P. Tiess, *Teachers' Voices for School Change: An Introduction to Educative Research* (New York: Teachers College Press, 1992), p. 25.
31. This focus on academic colleagues helps to define policy makers and practitioners as "others" (see related discussion by Stacki in Chapter Six).
32. Levin; Weiss, "Perspectives on Knowledge Use." Nadia Auriat ["Social Policy and Social Enquiry: Reopening Debate," *International Social Science Journal* 50 (2) (1998): 278] notes that two of the four reasons that researchers become involved in the policy arena are tied to scholar community values ("to become a reputable and respected social scientist" and "to advance the cause of analytically based decision-making"), while the other two ("to make a difference" and "to advocate a particular political position") may be seen as more in line with policy-maker/practitioner norms.
33. Psacharopoulos, p. 369.
34. Heyneman, p. 386.
35. Similarly, Joyce Epstein ["New Connections for Sociology and Education: Contributing to School Reform," *Sociology of Education* 69 (extra) (1996): 13] observes that sociologists of education and other educational researchers "are even less prepared to connect with educators than with policy makers and have little experience of success in seeing their work influence daily practice."
36. Joyce Epstein, p. 10. See also Katherine Marshall; Steven Miller and Marcel Fredericks, "Social Science Findings and Educational Policy Dilemmas: Some Additional Distinctions," *Education Policy Analysis Archives* 8 (3) (2000): 4–5, http:/epaa.asu.edu.epaa/v8n3.
37. Biddle and Anderson; Robert Donmoyer, "Empirical Research as Solution and Problem: Two Narratives of Knowledge Use," *International Journal of Educational Research* 23 (2) (1995): 152; Joyce Epstein; Torsten Husén, "Educational Research at the Crossroads? An Exercise in Self-Criticism," *Prospects* 19 (3) (1989): 351–60; Kennedy; Levin; Louis; Marshall; Miller and Frederick; William Reese, "What History Teaches about the Impact of Educational Research

on Practice," *Review of Research in Education* 24 (1999): 8; Reimers and McGinn; Rokicka, p. 17.
38. Weiss, Perspectives on Knowledge Use," p. 415. Richard Allington and Haley Woodside-Jiron ["The Politics of Literacy Teaching: How 'Research' Shaped Educational Policy," *Educational Researcher* 28 (8) (1999): 11] conclude that "the use of 'research' as a policy advocacy tool seems less dependent on the reliability of synthesis of research than on the ability to place 'research' summaries that support particular policy agendas into the hands of advocates and policymakers."
39. An important limitation of this discussion is that it is based on literature produced by theorists/researchers. Thus, the two cultures are being viewed from the (admittedly multiple) perspectives of members of only one of the communities.
40. Weiss, "Perspectives on Knowledge Use," pp. 410–11; see also Rokicka. Dunn ["Studying Knowledge Use," p. 390] also distinguishes social science research knowledge from "common sense," "casual empiricism," and "thoughtful speculation and analysis," but argues categorical distinctions, such as "'science-based' and 'ordinary' knowledge [as well as] 'professional social inquiry' and 'casual empiricism' [are] a product of the meanings and subjective judgments of researchers, and not of those whom such categories are applied."
41. Biddle and Anderson, p. 16.
42. Moreover, Gene Hall ["The Local Educational Change Process and Policy Implementation," in *International Perspectives on Educational Reform and Policy Implementation*, ed. David Carter and Marnie O'Neille (Washington, DC: Falmer Press, 1995), p. 101] makes the interesting observation that not only is there a "perennial ... gap in perspectives, semantics, and scope" between policy makers and practitioners, but a similar gap exists between "researchers of policy and [researchers of] practice."
43. Donmoyer, p. 157; see also Reese, p. 13.
44. D. Pan, "Ivory Tower and Red Tape: Reply to Adler," *Telos* 86 (1990): 12; see also Peter Cookson, Joseph Conaty, and Harold Himmelfarb, "Introduction," *Sociology of Education* 10 (1996): 1–4; Mark Ginsburg, Don Adams, Thomas Clayton, Martha Mantilla, Judy Sylvester, and Yidan Wang, "The Politics of Linking Educational Research, Policy and Practice: The Case of Improving Educational Quality in Ghana, Guatemala, Mali," *International Journal of Comparative Sociology* 41 (2000): 27-47; Thomas Popkewitz, *A Political Sociology of Educational Reform: Power/Knowledge in Teaching, Teacher Education and Research* (New York: Teachers College Press, 1991).
45. E. Vance Randall, Bruce Cooper, and Steven Hite, "Understanding the Politics of Research in Education," *Educational Policy* 13 (1) (1999): 8; see also Miller and Fredericks.
46. Erwin Epstein, "Currents Left and Right: Ideology in Comparative Education," *Comparative Education Review* 27 (1) (1983): 5.
47. As noted earlier, Marshall ("Researching the Margins") expresses the concern that researchers' efforts to communicate more regularly with policy makers/practitioners might lead researchers to eschew feminist and other critical perspectives.
48. Stacki (Chapter Six) also reports that she was also able to develop solid, trusting relationships with some male informants and others who did not share her feminist perspective and commitments. She was able to do this by finding other matters on which she and they held common views—for example, about the quality of certain educational institutions. This is reminiscent of what Fred Erickson ["Gatekeeping and the Melting Pot: Interaction in Counseling Encounters," *Harvard Educational Review* 45 (1975): 44–70] labels as "co-memberships," which were relied on by counselors to facilitate their cross-racial/ethnic group interaction with some, but not all, students in a community college in the United States.
49. Biddle and Anderson; Urszula Clark, "The Researcher and National Government-Sponsored Curriculum Research: Dilemmas, Contradictions, and the 'Squaring Circles,'" in Susan McGinty (ed.), *The Politics & Machinations of Educational Research: International Case Studies* (New York: Peter Lang, 2001), pp. 23–40. Note that although sometimes the research sponsor/funder can be viewed as a third party, at other times research and evaluation studies are financially supported by policy-maker and practitioner organizations (e.g., local, provincial, and national governments; international agencies; and teacher or administrator organizations).
50. Robert Burgess, "Biting the Hand That Feeds You? Educational Research for Policy and Practice," in *Educational Research and Evaluation: For Policy and Practice?*, ed. R. Burgess (London: Falmer, 1993), p. 1. See also Ginsburg et al., "The Politics of Linking."

51. Denis Ladbrook, "Pitfalls in Doing Research for Government Bureaucracies," in *The Politics & Machinations of Educational Research: International Case Studies*, ed. Susan McGinty (New York: Peter Lang, 2001), pp. 75–76.
52. Note how all three of the studies that Kemperer et al. discuss could be considered to be focused on the economic functions of higher education as conceived within a functionalist or neoliberal framework: market mechanisms, competitive research funding, and limiting student enrollment in higher education.
53. Psacharopoulos, p. 370. Don Adams ["Analysis without Theory Is Incomplete," *Comparative Education Review* 34 (3) (1990): 381–85] reminds Psacharopoulous that he (Adams) does not view the technocratic rationality perspective on educational planning as most adequate. See also Don Adams, "Extending the Educational Planning Discourse," *Comparative Education Review* 32 (November 1988): 400–15.
54. Donald Schon, "The New Scholarship Requires a New Epistemology," *Change: The Magazine of Higher Learning* 27 (6) (1995): 29; quoted in Gary Anderson and Kathryn Herr, "The New Paradigm Wars: Is There Room for Rigorous Practitioner Knowledge in Schools and Universities?" *Educational Researcher* 28 (5) (1999): 13. As he continues, however, Schon [Anderson and Herr, p. 29] indicates that knowledge from theorists/researchers is needed to take practice to a higher, professional level, stating that "the instrumental practice becomes professional when it is based on the science or systematic knowledge produced by the schools of higher learning."
55. On the importance of the distinction between mental and manual labor in the ideology of professionalism, see Mark Ginsburg, "Professionalism or Politics as a Model for Educators' Work and Lives," *Educational Research Journal* 11 (2)(1996: 133–46.
56. Thomas Kuhn, *The Structure of Scientific Revolutions* (Chicago: University of Chicago Press, 1962).
57. Robert Merton, "On Sociological Theories of the Middle Range," in *Social Theory and Social Structure* (New York: The Free Press, 1968).
58. For example, Margaret Sutton ["Policy Research as Ethnographic Refusal: The Calculus of Women's Literacy in Nepal," in *New Approaches to Studying Educational Policy Formation and Appropriation*, ed. Bradley Levinson and Margaret Sutton (New York: Ablex, 2000)] discusses the differences in "norms of practice" between researchers based primarily in universities, on the one hand, and those consulting for or serving as a regular employee in international education development assistance agencies, on the other. Edmund King ["Observations from Outside and Decisions Inside," *Comparative Education Review* 34 (3) (1990): 392–93] notes, however, that "[e]ven practically oriented scholars as those observing educational decision making from the World Bank, the Organizational for Economic Cooperation and Development (OECD), or other international organizations may be just as remote from reality and just as arrogant as those looking down from the 'dreaming spires' of academe. Moreover, they are the slaves of fashion."
59. Terence Hopkins and Immanuel Wallerstein, *World Systems Analysis: Theory and Methodology* (Beverly Hills, CA: Sage, 1982).
60. Graham Vulliamy, Keith Lewin, and David Stephens, *Doing Educational Research in Developing Countries* (London: Falmer Press, 1990), p. 4.
61. See Rolland Paulston, "Social and Educational Change: Conceptual Frameworks," *Comparative Education Review* 21 (June and October 1977); Gail Kelly, "Debates and Trends in Comparative Education," in *Emergent Issues in Education: Comparative Perspectives*, ed. Robert Arnove, Philip Altbach, and Gail Kelly (Albany: State University of New York Press, 1992); Erwin Epstein, "Currents Left and Right"; Raymond Morrow and Carlos Alberto Torres, *Social Theory and Education: A Critique of Theories of Social and Cultural Reproduction* (Albany: State University of New York Press).
62. See Thomas Popkewitz, "Paradigms in Educational Science: Different Meanings and Purposes to Theory," in *Paradigm and Ideology in Educational Research: The Social Functions of the Intellectual* (New York: Falmer Press, 1984); Vandra Masemann, "Critical Ethnography in the Study of Comparative Education," in *New Approaches in Comparative Education*, ed. Philip Altbach and Gail Kelly (Chicago: University of Chicago Press, 1986). Biddle and Anderson [p. 12] argue that "[v]arious forms of research are associated with the production of different types of knowledge elements," which have meaning because they are embedded within systems of thought and investigation (paradigms), and thus research produces different types of knowledge which may (or may not) be useful to diverse educators.

Dialogue about Educational Research, Policy, and Practice • **31**

63. Auriat identifies the disciplinary divide as one of the obstacles for conducting policy relevant research.
64. Patricia Campbell and Selma Greenberg, "Gender in Research, Achievement, and Technology," in *Gender and Education,* ed. Sari Biklen and Diane Pollard (Chicago: National Society for the Study of Education, 1993), p. 67.
65. Vulliamy et al., p. 212.
66. Miala Diambomba, "Research and External Aid: A View from the Recipient Side," *Prospects* 11 (3) (1981): 355.
67. Torsten Husén, "Policy Impact of IEA Research," *Comparative Education Review* 31 (1) (1987): 42.
68. See Burton Clark, *The Higher Education System: Academic Organization in Cross-National Perspective* (Berkeley: University of California Press, 1983).
69. With this power structure in mind, Randall et al. [p. 8] claim that as "the cloak of neutrality in both research and education is being discarded.... [G]oing 'political' could challenge the hegemony of those in charge of the research enterprise, the distribution of research monies, the publication of results, and the awarding of tenure."
70. See Philip Altbach, *The Knowledge Context: Comparative Perspectives on the Distribution of Knowledge* (Albany: State University of New York Press, 1987); Birgit Brock-Utne, *Whose Education for All: The Recolonization of the African Mind* (New York: Falmer Press, 2000); John Weaver, *Rethinking Academic Politics* (New York: RoutledgeFalmer Press, 2000).
71. For example, see Peter Cowden and David K. Cohen, *Divergent Worlds of Practice: The Federal Reform of Local Schools in the Experimental Schools Program* (Cambridge, MA: Huron Institute, 1979); Michael Fullan with Suzanne Stiegelbauer, *The New Meaning of Educational Change,* 2nd ed. (New York: Teachers College Press, 1991); Hall. However, following Bradley Levinson and Margaret Sutton ["Policy as Practice: A Sociocultural Approach to the Study of Educational Policy," in *New Approaches to Studying Educational Policy Formation and Appropriation,* ed. Bradley Levinson and Margaret Sutton (New York: Ablex, 2000)], it seems useful not to overstate the division between policy and practice. They reconceptualize "the notion of policy itself as a complex social practice, an ongoing process of normative cultural production constituted by diverse actors across diverse social and institutional contexts" (p. 1). Similarly, Donmoyer [p. 152] comments that "classrooms are important policy making arenas and ... teachers are significant policy-makers;" Joyce Epstein [p. 12] suggests that "educational policies are expressed by teachers and administrators in their daily activities with children, families, and other educators"; and Reimers and McGinn [p. 118] consider that policy making actors include "parents and students[,] ... teachers and principals[,] and the larger communities where schools are located, etc."
72. On the topic of the separation of conception and execution as a part of the proletarianization process, see Harry Braverman, *Labor and Monopoly Capital: The Degradation of Work in the Twentieth Century* (New York: Monthly Review Press, 1974); Magali Larson, "Proletarianization of Educated Labor," *Theory and Society* 9 (11)(1980): 131–75.
73. See Stephen Ball and Colin Lacey, "Subject Disciplines as the Opportunity for Group Action: A Measured Critique of Subject Sub-Cultures," in *Teacher Strategies: Explorations in the Sociology of the School,* ed. Peter Woods (London: Croom Helm, 1980).
74. Husén, "Educational Research at the Crossroads," p. 359.
75. Husén, "Educational Research at the Crossroads." Note how Husén's conclusion contradicts the arguments of Psacharopoulos and Heyneman (discussed earlier). In another place, Husén ["Policy Impact of IEA Research," p. 29] argues that the research interests/needs of policy makers and practitioners "cannot, however, be regarded as clearly distinct from each other. What is policy-relevant research is often closely dependent on a given time and place. The same applies to practice-relevant research."
76. Lawrence Saha, Bruce Biddle, and Don Anderson, "Attitudes Towards Education Research Knowledge and Policymaking among American and Australian School Principals," *International Journal of Educational Research* 23 (2) (1995): 123–24.
77. Mark Bray and Steve Packer, *Education in Small States: Concepts, Challenges and Strategies* (New York: Pergamon Press, 1993).
78. John Hawkins and Thomas La Belle (eds.), *Education and Intergroup Relations: An International Perspective* (New York, Praeger, 1985).
79. Philip Altbach, "Professors and Politics: An International Perspective," in *The Politics of Educators' Work and Lives,* ed. Mark Ginsburg (New York: Garland, 1995); see also Jeanne

Guillemin and Irving Louis Horowitz, "Social Research and Political Advocacy," in *Ethics, the Social Sciences, and Policy Analysis,* ed. Daniel Callahan and Bruce Jennings (New York: Plenum Press. 1983), pp. 187–211.
80. David Wilson, "Comparative and International Education: Fraternal or Siamese Twins," *Comparative Education Review* 38 (4) (1994): 453.
81. Jon Wagner, "Administrators as Ethnographers: School as Context for Inquiry and Action," *Anthropology and Education Quarterly* 21 (3) (1990): 211–12.
82. LaVerne Ludden and George Wood, "Practice Driven Research: A Model for Bridging the Gap between Research and Practice," *Lifelong Learning* 10 (5) (1987): 25.
83. J. Kenneth Benson, "The Underdevelopment of Theory and the Problem of Practice," *Comparative Education Review,* 34 (3) (1990): 385–92. Similarly, Paul Goodman ["Critical Issues in Doing Research That Contributes to Theory and Practice," in *Doing Research that is Useful for Theory and Practice,* ed. Edward Lawler, Allan Mohrman, Susan Mohrman, Gerald Leoford, and Thomas Cummings (Washington, DC: Jossey-Bass, 1985)] notes that different definitions of research (as a process and/or as forms of knowledge) and of practice (as behavior and/or as cognitive processes) lead to different conclusions concerning how research and practice can/should be linked.
84. John Willinsky, "The Strategic Education Research Program and the Public Value of Research," *Educational Researcher* 30 (1) (2001): 9.
85. BryanTurner, "Contemporary Problems in the Theory of Citizenship," in *Citizenship and Social Theory,* ed. B. Turner (London: Sage Publications, 1993), p. 9.
86. David Sehr, *Education for Public Democracy* (Albany: State University of New York Press, 1997), p. 34; see also D. Heater,*Citizenship: The Civic Ideal in World History, Politics and Education* (New York: Longman, 1990), p. 217.
87. Sehr, p. 32. Similarly, Heater distinguishes between "participatory/democratic" and "conservative/élitist" models of citizenship, explaining that the élitist model, based on the assumption that the masses are "slothful and ignorant," views the government [as] a device to keep them apathetic lest their propensities to selfishness and violence undermine communal life.... The conservative élitist would rather emphasize the right of the individual to exercise his [or her] freedom *not* to participate. His [or her] ideal is the private, not the public citizen" (pp. 215–16).
88. For a discussion of different conceptions of democracy as they relate to education and teacher education, see Mark Ginsburg, "Democracy, Worker-Consumer-Citizens, and Teacher Education," in *Democratizing Education and Educating Democratic Citizens,* ed. Leslie Limage (New York: RoutledgeFalmer, 2001), pp. 169–91.
89. Magali Larson, *The Rise of Professionalism* (Berkeley: University of California Press, 1977), p. viii.
90. For a discussion of various aspects of the ideology of professionalism in relation to education and teachers' work, see Mark Ginsburg, Robert Meyenn, and Henry Miller "Teachers, Professionalism, and Trades Unionism: An Ideological Analysis, in *Teacher Strategies,* ed. Peter Woods (London: Croom Helm, 1978), pp. 179–212.
91. Geoff Esland, "Professions and Professionalism," in *The Politics of Work and Occupations,* ed. G. Esland and G. Salaman (Milton Keynes, England: Open University Press, 1980), p. 246.
92. This section draws upon and elaborates discussions presented in Adams et al., "Linking Research to Policy and Practice to Improve Educational Quality"; Ginsburg et al., "The Politics of Linking"; Mark Ginsburg and Leopold Klopfer (with Thomas Clayton, Michel Rakotomanana, Judy Sylvester, and Katherine Yasin), "Choices in Conceptualizing Classroom-Anchored Research and Linking It to Policy/Practice to Improve Educational Quality in 'Developing' Countries," *Research Papers in Education* 11 (3) (1996): 239–54.
93. Some of the proposed approaches involve changing individuals and/or group cultures [see Reimers and McGinn, p. 23], while others have targeted changing the working relationships of members of the two groups [see L. Neville Postlethwaite, "Research and Policy Making in Education: Some Possible Links," in *Knowledge for Policy: Improving Education through Research,* ed. Don Anderson and Bruce Biddle (London: Falmer, 1991)]. The former activities (what might be called capacity development) are likely to be a necessary part of the latter. However, changing individuals' knowledge, skills, and attitudes is unlikely to be sufficient for bringing about the structural changes implied in the latter set of approaches.
94. Paulo Freire, *Pedagogy of the Oppressed* (New York: Seabury Press, 1970), p. 77. Some might question the use of Freire's concept of dialogue, which he developed in the context of analyzing pedagogical relations between teachers and students, as appropriate for framing a discussion

of the relationship between theorists/researchers and policy makers/practitioners. However, on should remember that Freire (a) focused much of his attention on adult education, (b) gave importance to research activity as a means of collaborative naming/changing the world, and (c) devoted some attention to the activities of research specialists in the context of what we term "collective research and praxis" (see discussion later in this chapter). On the latter point, Freire [*The Politics of Education: Culture, Power and Liberation* (New York: Bergin & Garvey, 1985), p. 156] comments: "Precisely because consciousness is not transformed except in praxis, the theoretical context [which offer reasons, for example, of peasants' condition of oppression and exploitation] cannot be reduced to an *uninvolved* research center" (emphasis added).

95. Ronald Glass, "On Paulo Freire's Philosophy of Praxis and the Foundations of Liberation Education," *Educational Researcher* 30 (2) (March 2001): 19.
96. Biddle and Anderson, p. 12.
97. Michael Huberman, "Research Utilization: The State of the Art,"*Knowledge and Policy: The International Journal of Knowledge Transfer and Utilization,* 7 (4) (Winter 1994): 13–33.
98. Ronald G. Havelock, *Planning for Innovation though Dissemination and Utilization of Knowledge* (Ann Arbor: Center for Research on Utilization and Scientific Knowledge, Institute for Social Research, University of Michigan, 1969).
99. J. Sunquist, "Research Brokerage: The Weak Link," in *Knowledge and Policy: The Uncertain Connection,* ed. Lawrence Lynn (Washington, DC: National Academy of Sciences, 1978).
100. Paul F. Lazarsfeld and Jeffrey G. Reitz, *An Introduction to Applied Sociology* (New York: Elsevier, 1975).
101. Dunn, "Conceptualizing Knowledge Use," p. 328.
102. Hallinan, pp. 133–34.
103. Kenneth Cabatoff, "Translating Evaluation Findings into 'Policy Language,'" *New Directions for Evaluation* 86 (2000): 52.
104. Willinsky, p. 7. Willinsky's proposal is to use the Internet not only as a mechanism for disseminating research findings but also to "enable users to post comments, questions, and proposals on the big and small questions provoked by this research and its various agendas" (p. 12). The democratizing potential of the Internet, of course, is limited by the "digital divide" that exists in the United States and, even more so, globally.
105. Joyce Epstein, p. 6.
106. Biddle and Anderson.
107. Brown, p. 104; Joyce Epstein, p. 6.
108. Saha et al.
109. For example, see Sheldon Berman and Phyllis La Farge (eds.), *Promising Practices in Teaching Social Responsibility* (Albany: State University of New York Press); Katherine Isaac, *Civics for Democracy: A Journey for Teachers and Students* (Washington, DC: Essential Books, 1992); Leslie Limage (ed.), *Democratizing Education and Educating Democratic Citizens: International and Historical Perspectives* (New York: RoutledgeFalmer, 2001); David Sehr, *Education for Public Democracy* (Albany: State University of New York Press, 1997).
110. Anderson and Herr [p. 16] explain that "practitioner research" has its own forms of validity (outcome, process, democratic or local, catalytic, dialogic).
111. Ibid., p. 20.
112. Carolyn Riehl, Colleen L. Larson, Paula M. Short, and Ulrich Reitzug, "Reconceptualizing Research and Scholarship in Educational Administration: Learning to Know, Knowing to Do, Doing to Learn," *Educational Administration Quarterly,* 36 (3) (2000): 391–427; Wagner, "Administrators as Ethnographers."
113. M. Cochran-Smith and S. Lytle, *Inside/Outside: Teacher Research and Knowledge* (New York: Teachers College Press, 1993); Dixie Goswami and Peter Stillman, *Reclaiming the Classroom: Teacher Research as an Agency for Change* (Upper Montclair, NJ: Boynton/Cooke, 1987). Michael Huberman and Miriam Ben-Peretz ["Disseminating and Using Research Knowledge," *Knowledge and Policy: The International Journal of Knowledge Transfer and Utilization,* 7 (4) (Winter 1994): 5–6], acknowledge the contributions of "teacher research," but note that the "danger ... is that these local practices will gradually exclude the desire or the capacity to engage with more classically scientific work."
114. See Joyce Epstein, p. 19.
115. Nevertheless, Joyce Epstein suggests that the involvement of practitioners (and, by implication, policy makers and other community members) in research activities may provide more opportunities and make it easier for them to communicate with theorists and researchers.

116. Dunn, "Studying Knowledge Use," p. 370.
117. Michael Crossley and Robin Burns ["Case Study in Comparative and International Education: An Approach to Bridging the Theory-Practice Gap," in *Comparative and International Studies and the Theory and Practice of Education*, ed. Barry Sheehan (Proceedings of the Eleventh Annual Conference of the Australian Comparative and International Education Society, Hamilton, New Zealand, 1983) pp. 1 and 13] describe case study in comparative and international education as a way to address "an apparent polarization between theorists and practitioners," since it provides "a way to interrelate the theory and 'reality' of education.... [Focusing on] the actual day-to-day activities of educational practitioners and their clients ... can lead to ... greater cross-fertilization ... between theory and practice."
118. Jon Wagner, "The Unavoidable Intervention of Educational Research: A Framework for Reconsidering Researcher-Practitioner Cooperation," *Educational Researcher* 26 (7) (1997): 16. Wagner observes that "all educational research in schools involves [communication and] cooperation of one form or another between researchers and practitioners" [p. 13], but notes that such communication generally gets formalized as "data-extraction agreements" (negotiated so that researchers can do the research they have designed) [p. 15].
119. Cousins and Leithwood; Jennifer Greene, "Stakeholder Participation in Evaluation Design: Is It Worth the Effort?" *Evaluation and Program Planning* 10 (1987): 379–93; Michael Patton, *Utilization-Focused Evaluation*, 3rd ed. (Thousand Oaks, CA: Sage, 1997).
120. Auriat, p. 275.
121. Don Adams and Gary Theisen, "Comparative Education Research: What Are the Methods and Uses of Comparative Education Research?" in *International and Comparative Education: Practices, Issues and Prospects*, ed. R. Murray Thomas (Oxford: Pergamon, 1990), p. 286.
122. Peter Coleman and Linda LaRoque, "Linking Educational Research and Educational Policy via Policy-Relevant Research," *The Alberta Journal of Educational Research* 29 (3) (1983): 243.
123. Reimers and McGinn [p. 23] explain that policy research "is designed to anticipate the consequences of action ... as opposed to research designed to explain why the world is the way it is without describing how it could be made different."
124. Evelyn Jacobs, "The Council on Anthropology and Education as a Crossroads Community: Reflections on Theory-Oriented and Practice-Oriented Research," *Anthropology and Education Quarterly*, 32 (3) (September, 2001): 266–75. Jacobs states that "it is useful to think of the 'roads' intersecting ... as two continua. One axis involves low to high theory orientation; the other involves low to high practice orientation. In this view, orientations to theory and practice are not oppositional, but are complementary dimensions" (p. 267).
125. Ludden and Wood, pp. 21–25.
126. Weiss ["The Many Meanings" p. 181] concludes that "it is time for social scientists to pay attention to the imperatives of policy-making systems and to consider soberly what they can do, not necessarily to increase the use of research, but to improve the contribution that research makes to the wisdom of social policy." See also Meyer and Baker; Pettigrew, pp. 225–26; Psacharopoulos, p. 380.
127. William Cooley and William Bickel, *Decision-Oriented Educational Research* (Boston: Kluwer-Nijhoff, 1986).
128. Ibid, p. 27. Note that "conversation" would be the more appropriate term here, given the way we have defined dialogue in this chapter.
129. Ibid, p. 36.
130. Lawrence Stenhouse, *Introduction to Curriculum Research and Development* (London: Heinemann, 1975). Although Stenhouse and his colleagues at the University of East Anglia in England popularized and legitimized collaborative action research in education, Stephen Corey [*Action Research to Improve School Practices* (New York: Teachers College Press, 1953)]—drawing on ideas of Kurt Lewin ["Action Research and Minority Problems," *Journal of Social Issues* 2 (1) (1946): 34–46], who coined the term action research—may have been the first to promote this approach in education.
131. See Brause and Mayher (eds.); Joe Kincheloe, *Teachers as Researchers: Qualitative Inquiry as a Path to Empowerment* (Bristol, England: Falmer Press, 1991); H. Preskill, "Evaluation's Role in Enhancing Organizational Learning," *Evaluation and Program Planning* 17 (3) (1994): 291–97.
132. Cousins and Leithwood, p. 361; Goodman; Reimers and McGinn, p. 25. Karen Seashore Louis ["Making Meaning of the Relationship between Research and Policy: An Epilogue," *Educational Policy* 13 (1) (1999): 211] provides the important insight that unless one assumes

Dialogue about Educational Research, Policy, and Practice • 35

that research generates generalizable conclusions (as is the case in the positivist paradigm), "[i]nvolving the users in research will not necessarily make the research more useable—except at that particular site."
133. Whyte.
134. Ilse Brunner and Alba Guzman, "Participatory Evaluation: A Tool to Assess Projects and Empower People," *New Directions in Program Evaluation* 42 (1989): 10–11.
135. Carlos Alberto Torres, "Participatory Action Research and Popular Education in Latin America," *Qualitative Studies in Education* 5 (1) (1992): 53. Torres notes that "Pablo Latapí ["Participatory Research: A New Paradigm?" *Alberta Journal of Educational Research* 34 (1) (1988): 310–19] argues that "participatory methodologies have developed [from, among other sources:] ... *thematic research* (Freire's original approach) ... [and] *militant research*, which emphasized the political component of action-research methodologies (well represented in the work of Miguel and Rosiska Darcy de Oliveira, members of the [Institute for Cultural Action], an institute founded by Freire and a group of Brazilian exiles in Geneva)" (pp. 53–54).
136. Egon Guba and Yvonna Lincoln, *Fourth Generation Evaluation* (New York: Sage, 1989), pp. 253, 260, and 261.
137. David Fetterman, "Empowerment Evaluation: An Introduction to Theory and Practice," in David Fetterman, Shakeh Kaftarian, and Abraham Wandersman (eds.), *Empowerment Evaluation: Knowledge and Tools for Self-Assessment and Accountability* (Thousand Oaks, CA: Sage, 1996), p. 13.
138. Wagner, "The Unavoidable Intervention," p. 16. It is also synonymous with what Joyce Epstein [p. 16] identifies as the "highest level of involvement" that educational theorists/researchers (viz., sociologists of education) can have in educational reform efforts.
139. Reimers and McGinn, p. 38.
140. Peter Senge, *The Fifth Discipline: The Art and Practice of the Learning Organization* (New York: Doubleday, 1990).
141. Y. Bodemann, "The Problem of Sociological Praxis," *Theory and Society* 5 (1978): 387–420; G. Vio Brossi and R. de Wit (eds.), *Investigación Participativa y Praxis Rural* (Lima, Peru: Mosca Azul, 1981); Orlando Fals Borda, "Por la Praxis: El Problema de Cómo Investigar la Realidad para Transformarla," in *Crítica y Política en Ciencias Sociales: El Debate sobre Teoría y Práctica,* Tomo I (Bogotá, Colombia: Simposio Mundial de Cartagena/Punta de Lanza, 1978); Patti Lather, "Research as Praxis," in *Getting Smart: Feminist Research and Pedagogy with/in the Postmodern* (New York: Routledge, 1991); Heinz Moser, "La Investigación-Acción como Nuevo Paradigma en las Ciencias Sociales," in *Crítica y Política en Ciencias Sociales: El Debate sobre Teoría y Práctica,* Tomo I (Bogotá, Colombia: Simposio Mundial de Cartagena/Punta de Lanza, 1978).
142. Wilfred Carr and Stephen Kemmis, *Becoming Critical: Education, Knowledge and Action Research* (London: Falmer Press, 1986); Michelle Fine, "The Politics of Research and Activism," *Gender and Society* 3 (4) (1989): 549–558; Gitlin et al.; James Ludwig and Jennifer Gore, "Extending Power and Specifying Method within the Discourse of Activist Research," in *Power and Method: Political Activism and Educational Research,* ed. Andrew Gitlin (New York: Routledge, 1994): 227–38; Robin McTaggart, "Principles for Participatory Action Research," *Adult Education Quarterly* 41 (3) (1991).
143. Lather, p. 56.
144. McTaggart, p. 176.
145. Reimers and McGinn [p. 110] make an important point that a "major difficulty with participatory approaches in education policy dialogue is that many organizational and political cultures are not supportive of participation and democracy. Public administration in some countries is highly hierarchical and participatory approaches represent a major cultural change."
146. Torres, "Participatory Action Research," p. 56.
147. See also Shulamit Reinharz, "Dimensions of Experiential Method," in *On Becoming a Social Scientist* (New Brunswick, NJ: Transaction Books, 1984), pp. 308–68.
148. Freire, *Pedagogy of the Oppressed,* pp. 77–83.
149. Paulo Freire's words in Ira Shor and Paulo Freire, *A Pedagogy for Liberation: Dialogues on Transforming Education* (South Hadley, MA: Bergen & Garvey Publishers, 1987), p. 98.
150. See Peter Berger, "'Consciousness Raising' and the Vicissitudes of Policy," in *Pyramids of Sacrifice: Political Ethics and Social Change* (New York: Basic Books, 1974); Jim Walker, "The

End of Dialogue: Paulo Freire on Politics and Education," in *Literacy and Revolution: The Pedagogy of Paulo Freire*, ed. Robert Mackie (London: Pluto Press, 1980).
151. Joel Samoff, "Institutionalizing International Influence," in *Comparative Education: The Dialectic of the Global and the Local*, ed. Robert Arnove and Carlos Alberto Torres (Oxford: Rowman & Littlefield, 1999).
152. See also Marshall, "Researching the Margins."
153. For a related discussion about the challenges for and the possibility of "authentic communication" between international educational consultants and "indigenous" groups, see Christine Fox, "Listening to the Other: Mapping Intercultural Communication in Postcolonial Educational Consultancies," in *Social Cartography: Mapping Ways of Seeing Social and Educational Change*, ed. Rolland Paulston (New York: Garland, 1996).
154. Shor and Freire, p. 101.
155. Seth Kreisberg, *Transforming Power: Domination, Empowerment, and Education* (Albany: State University of New York Press, 1992).
156. See also Kathryn Anderson-Levitt and Ntal-I'Mbirwa Alimasi, "Are Pedagogical Ideals Embraced or Imposed? The Case of Reading Instruction in the Republic of Guinea," in *New Approaches to Studying Educational Policy Formation and Appropriation*, ed. Bradley Levinson and Margaret Sutton (New York: Ablex, 2000).
157. Relevant here is the claim by Martin Carnoy and Joel Samoff [*Education and Social Transition in the Third World* (Princeton, NJ: Princeton University Press, 1992)] that often research judged to be relevant to educational policy making treats existing political and economic structures as a given rather than problematizing them.
158. On the related issue of "duality of structure," see Anthony Giddens, *Central Problems of Social Theory: Action, Structure and Contradictions in Social Theory* (Berkeley: University of California Press, 1979).
159. This provides insights regarding the conclusion by Kennedy [pp. 9–10] that "the connection between research and practice is not one in which research influences practice ... nor one in which practice influences research ... but rather one in which both research and practice are influenced by, and perhaps are even victims of, the same shifting social and political context." This conception is partly related to the model for linking research and policy that Weiss ["The Many Meanings," pp. 174–80] labels as "Research as Part of the Intellectual Enterprise of Society," where research and policy are both influenced by "the larger fashions of social thought."
160. Dieter Misgeld, "Emancipation, Enlightenment, and Liberation: An Approach toward Foundational Inquiry into Education," *Interchange* 6 (1975): 35. We first came across this quote in Raymond Morrow and Carlos Alberto Torres, *Social Theory and Education: A Critique of Theories of Social and Cultural Reproduction* (Albany: State University of New York Press, 1995), p. 241.
161. Jürgen Habermas, *Communication and the Evolution of Society*, trans. Thomas McCarthy (Boston: Beacon Press, 1979); Jürgen Habermas, *The Theory of Communicative Action*, volume 1, trans. Thomas McCarthy (Boston: Beacon Press, 1984); Jürgen Habermas, *The Theory of Communicative Action*, volume 2, trans. Thomas McCarthy (Cambridge, MA: Polity Press, 1987).
162. Thomas McCarthy, "Translator's Introduction," in Jürgen Habermas, *Legitimation Crisis* (London: Heinneman, 1976), p. xvii. Morrow and Torres explain that the notion of participatory action research as well as Freire's vision of liberatory pedagogy have been influenced by Habermas's writings; for instance, Habermas's concern about constraints on the "ideal speech situation" informs understandings of the value of and the challenges to dialogue in both participatory action research and liberatory pedagogy.

CHAPTER 2

# Dancing in the Dark
## *The Relationship between Policy Research and Policy Making in Dutch Higher Education*[1]

ANNE KLEMPERER
HENNO THEISENS
FRANS KAISER

**Introduction**

The idea that research is directly useful in the policy process has been widely disputed,[2] and much has been written about the differences between the contexts or "cultures" in which research is produced and in which policy is made.[3] A number of authors, however, have pointed out indirect ways in which policy makers may make use of research findings or have tried to find more complex ways of understanding and describing the relationships between researchers and policy makers.[4] It has been proposed, for example, that the categories of researcher and policy maker are not always mutually exclusive and that interactions between all actors involved in this process could be better described as two-way, rather than only as one-way, interactions.[5]

In our experience, the relationship between policy making and policy research resembles "dancing in the dark," where the dancers do not completely see each other, the movements are complex, and the environment influences the flow of the dance. In this chapter we want to reflect upon the complexities involved in this dance.

Different approaches to understanding the relationship between policy and research are addressed herein. While keeping in mind the discussions of the complexity of the relationship between research and policy, we want to see if we can identify and classify the uses made of a few particular cases of comparative research. By examining a few specific cases of research commissioned to the Center for Higher Education Policy Studies (CHEPS),[6] we hope to explore in more detail the (direct and indirect) ways in which this research had an influence on the policy process.[7] In doing so, we have assumed a static, rational perspective, and we limit our discussion to an examination of only one direction of influence—the influence of research on the policy process. We do not think that this is the only or the best way to understand the relationship, but we hope that this serves as a starting point for a discussion about the usefulness and limitations of such frameworks. We use our framework as a heuristic device that helps us to make sense of the intricate relationship between policy and policy research. The framework is not a full explanatory model. In our conclusions we return to the ideas about the more complex nature of the relationship between policy and policy research.

The main questions that will be addressed in this study are: (a) Is it possible to classify how and at what stages in the policy process research results are used? (b) Can an examination of the strengths and weaknesses of such a classification help to contribute to the ongoing discussions of the complex relationship between research and policy?

## Theoretical Issues

### Perspectives on the Policy Process

There are a wide variety of theories on policy processes. According to Hoogerwerf, in a goal-rational sense, policy can be bluntly defined as the striving for certain goals, with certain means.[8] These goals are to solve certain problems that an actor or a group of actors perceives.[9] Within this same goal-rational framework, problems may be defined as the discrepancy between an ideal situation an actor wishes and the real situation an actor perceives. Policy, or the implementing of means, is used to change a situation from the real to the ideal. From this goal-rational point of view, the policy process may be seen as consisting of three stages that are linearly connected: designing, deciding, and implementing.

The first stage of the policy process is the *designing* stage. At this stage, the problem is analyzed and policy makers attempt to come to a shared definition of the problem and to see what elements of the system are directly tied to the problem and what factors might influence the problem. In addition, policy makers look for solutions in terms of policy instruments to help them overcome the problem and try to define which approaches may be taken. A variety of actors may be involved at this stage of the policy process. Actors include policy makers, researchers, various intermediate government bodies, advice organs, and interest groups.

The second stage of the policy process is the *deciding* stage. During this stage policy makers, politicians, and often stakeholders in the policy field decide how the problem is going to be solved and what approach will be used. The instrument(s) that are going to be applied are chosen from a range of potential instruments, theoretically on the basis of their rank ordering using objective criteria.

The third or *implementing* stage of the policy process involves implementation and also follow-up. During this stage the steps that should be taken to make the policy instruments work include choosing or creating an organization that can operate the instruments, creating legal frameworks, providing funds, and opening communication channels. At this stage a variety of actors may again be involved: civil servants at the operational levels, evaluation bodies, various stakeholders.

Although we defined these stages more or less in terms of rational "steps," we do not wish to imply that these stages are, in reality, linear in time. When a decision cannot be made, the problem might have to be reanalyzed or different solutions may have to be developed. In addition, the stages may be parallel in time: deciding and designing are sometimes interwoven, as when policy designers decide to develop certain solutions/instruments and not others. Despite the fact that we know that these complications exist in reality, we have chosen to create a simple model, which views these parts of the process as linear steps. This aspect of our model is reexamined in the conclusions.

These are, of course, not the only phases identified in the literature, and these phases may be classified differently. For example, Coleman and LaRocque discuss aggregation and allocation phases, which correspond loosely to the deciding phase described earlier.[10] Many people have emphasized the importance of research in the evaluation of policy (sometimes called the "oversight phase").[11] In addition, there may be phases of reengineering policies based on experience or the outcomes of implementation. In this study, however, we limit ourselves to the three phases mentioned earlier, since we will use our framework as a heuristic device and need a simple model instead of a complete description of the policy process.

### The Use of Policy Research in the Policy Process

The stages distinguished here might help us to answer *where* in the policy process policy research was used. We are also interested in exploring *how* policy research is used. Policy research is often done with at least the intention that it will contribute to policy making. Whether and in what ways this is actually the case are matters for debate. Before discussing the more complex facets of the relationship, we want to see if it is possible to make a simple classification of ways in which this research was used. Based on the work of Weiss,[12] we distinguish three different types of use: problem-solving, political, and enlightening uses of policy research.

Research used for *problem solving* is research that is used to solve a particular problem, for example, to find the right policy instrument. A preferred way of solving the problem is not given. There is agreement between the researchers and policy makers concerning the goals of the research. It is expected that the research will clarify the situation and have a direct influence on the policy decisions to be made.

*Political* uses of research, on the other hand, refer to a situation in which research is used to back up (political) opinions that have already been formed. In this use of research, the (preferred) "solution" to the problem can be found

|  | Designing | Deciding | Implementing |
|---|---|---|---|
| Enlightening | ■■■■■■ |  |  |
| Political |  | ■■■■■■ |  |
| Problem solving |  |  | ■■■■■■ |

**Figure 2.1.** Stages in the policy process and the use of policy research.

in the way in which the problem is spelled out. In this use of research, findings that do not conform to or support the political point that is being made are generally neglected.

Research used for *enlightening* purposes refers to the ways in which research may be used to provide generalized notions or may help in the process of shaping ideas or conceptualizations of the problem. This type of research provides background information or helps to define problems rather than providing solutions to problems. This kind of use of knowledge is much less direct than problem-solving or political uses, and it is rarely possible to identify direct uses of this research. In order to analyze this type of use, one must therefore look for ways in which ideas or concepts have been used in policy making that has some connection with research.

*Toward a Heuristic Model*

Combining our ideas about *stages* in the policy process and the *uses* of policy research we can draw a 3 × 3 matrix. What we expect (see Figure 2.1) is that in the designing stage policy research will have predominantly an enlightening function. We expect this to be the case because at the initial stages of the policy process the concept of the problem is still being developed. Therefore, research that helps to shape the definition of the problem or research that provides general ideas or concepts is expected to be the most useful. During the deciding stage, as problem definitions and solutions are chosen and political interests are at stake, we expect more political uses of policy research. At this stage the questions and problems have been worked out and defined, and what remains is for a political choice to be made. Here we expect that research findings conflicting with the decision that is being made will be ignored, and that only research that supports the decision will be used. Finally, when political struggles have been fought and the analytical problems are reduced within the boundaries of a chosen problem definition and potential solutions, we expect policy research to be used mostly for problem solving.

*Criticism of the Goal-Rational Approach*

As mentioned in the introduction, the goal-rational perspective implied by the "steps" outlined here has been under severe criticism. According to Hoogerwerf,[13] the policy process—the dynamic flow of action and interaction with regard to a certain policy—is often not a unitary governed, linear process of designing, deciding, and implementing. On the contrary, other authors, such as

Lindblom and Cohen,[14] have characterized the formulation of policy as a process of "muddling through." Similarly, Cohen, March, and Olsen have described the formulation of policy within higher education institutions as functioning as a "garbage can" process, and Kingdon has taken this idea and applied it to the policy process as a whole.[15]

Lindblom and Cohen point out that, in practice, policy making is not the rational process described here. In complex situations rational policy making requires simply too much intellectual capacity and more sources of information that humans can handle. Moreover, there are no clear values on which everybody agrees and on which decisions can be based. Where Lindblom and Cohen focus on the decision making by the individual actors in the policy process, Kingdon looks at a more aggregated level. He sees policy formation as the result of the joining three streams, namely, problems, politics, and policies. According to Kingdon, each of these streams arises and flows largely independently of one another. The key to understanding policy change is the coupling of these streams. The separate streams come together at critical times. At particular moments a problem is recognized, a solution is available, and the political climate is favorable: In short, a policy window opens and things start happening. These two approaches suggest that both on an individual and an aggregate level, unpredictability and potential irrationality characterize the policy process. We can thus conclude that our model has some obvious shortcomings:

- The model lacks dynamics and ignores power struggles.
- The model presupposes too much goal rationality.
- The stages are not related on a one-to-one basis to uses of policy research.

The framework we have presented is rather static. The stages seem to be fixed in the linear order of designing, deciding, and implementation. This is not realistic. In the first place, Pressman and Wildavsky[16] have shown that policy is in fact a continuous iteration of designing, deciding, and implementing, from very abstract values down to the actual use of policy instruments. Moreover, policy can bounce back and forth between the stages; if an impasse arises in the deciding stage, for example, it might be necessary to return to the designing stage to come up with viable policy alternatives. External changes might also lead to a shift from one stage to another in the policy process. These policy dynamics are partly the result of the fact that policy is rarely only made by one central actor. Most of the time several stakeholders strive for their own interests in the different stages of the policy process. The policy process is not purely an intellectual enterprise, but is also a power struggle. The policy process has been rightly characterised by Hoogerwerf as a combination of a game of chess and a boxing match in which the allowed moves on the chessboard depend on the course of the boxing match.[17]

The second shortcoming of our framework is its focus on goal rationality. Obviously, there are many other factors governing the policy process than the goal. We already mentioned the existence of power struggles: the existence of different actors with different goals means that the power relations among these actors, as well as their access to policy arenas, have an impact on the policy process and its outcomes.[18]

A third element that we neglected is the fact that the different uses of policy research are not straightforwardly related to the stages of the policy process. In the first place, the enlightening research might be used as a political means to influence decision making. Often it is very important to be able to influence the terms in which the policy discussions are framed. For example, it makes a big difference whether discussions about the funding of higher education are made from the perspective of economic growth or social mobility. Thus, actors might try to use enlightening research to introduce a certain perspective in the deciding stage of the policy process. By the same token, the political use of research is also possible in the designing and deciding stages. Obviously, if one can influence the available policy alternatives during the decision stage one may have a big impact on the outcomes of the policy process. Also, in the implementation stage, actors can try to hold up or influence implementation by requesting more detailed research. Finally, problem-solving research is also used in the designing and deciding stages of the policy process. If a policy design is only built on enlightening research, without the backing of more applied research, it is likely to contain many gaps and uncertainties that make it not viable in the deciding stage of the policy process. Problem-solving research may also be used in the decision-making stage, as a political tool. The use of expertise and contra-expertise to show whether or not policy proposals are effective or efficient is a clear example of this.

The question now is, how shall we deal with these amendments to our framework without loosing its simplicity? We have chosen to operationalize our framework as if we could ignore the preceding reflections. We have done so because, at this point, we feel it is better and more realistic to use a simple model flexibly and for heuristic purposes than to develop a more complicated model. A simple model can act as a first step toward a better understanding of complex phenomena. We come back to these reflections in the conclusions and discuss the ways in which the complex reality can or cannot be captured by our model and what consequences that has for our framework.

## Operationalization

On the basis of the definitions (from the previous section) of the *stages of the policy process* and the *types of research use* found in the literature, we have chosen a number of variables to help us in examining our three cases. A short summary of these points can be found in Table 2.1. According to Weiss,[19] research is used for enlightenment purposes in rather indirect ways: Generalizations

**Table 2.1** Evidence of Different Types of Use of Research/Stages of the Policy Process: Expected Outcomes

| | SET-UP | | | OUTPUT/USE OF THE RESEARCH | | | |
|---|---|---|---|---|---|---|---|
| | SCOPE OF THE RESEARCH: NARROW OR BROAD | TYPES OF RESEARCH QUESTIONS: OPEN AND EXPLORATORY OR SPECIFIC | REASONS FOR COMMISSIONING THE RESEARCH | HOW QUICKLY WAS THE RESEARCH USED? (IN THE SHORT OR LONG TERM?) | HOW IMPORTANT WAS IT TO MEET THE DEADLINES? | WAS THE RESEARCH USED WHOLLY, PARTIALLY, OR NOT AT ALL? | WAS THE RESEARCH USED DIRECTLY OR INDIRECTLY? |
| **Enlightening/ Designing** | Broad | Open, exploratory | To provide background information/to help define the problem | Longer term, not right away | Less important | Partially | Indirectly; difficult to point to exact examples |
| **Political/ Deciding** | Narrow | Specific; expected or desired outcome is implied in the question | To provide evidence that the predefined choice is the "right" one | Very short term | Important | Wholly or not at all | Directly |
| **Problem-solving/ Implementing** | Narrow | Specific; no predefined outcome implied | To solve a particular problem | Relatively short term | Relatively important | Partially | Directly |

are drawn from the research, and research is used to help define problems (rather than solve particular problems). Therefore, we assume that during the designing stage, the use of research will be indirect, the scope of the research will be broad, and the questions will be rather open-ended and exploratory. Furthermore, we expect research to be commissioned in order to provide background or general knowledge. Along the same lines, we also expect that the use of research is likely to be partial or fragmented rather than holistic because certain ideas will (eventually) be picked out of the results while others will be left behind. Weiss also explains how enlightenment uses of research may not occur right away; that is why we expect the use to be over the long term and for there to be less emphasis placed on meeting the deadlines of the project.

In Weiss's description, the political use of knowledge is defined by the emphasis on using research to support opinions that have already been made. When research is commissioned for political purposes, we expect it to have a rather narrow focus (specifically on the issue at hand). We also expect that the desired outcome will be evident in the questions that are asked and/or the way the research is set up. Furthermore, we expect that the research will be commissioned in order to support the opinions of the organization sponsoring the research, and that research outcomes that conform to these expectations will be directly and wholly used, and that research outcomes that contradict these expectations will be ignored. Because we expect this type of research to be commissioned close to moments of political decisions, we also expect that use will be made of research in the short term and that meeting deadlines will be considered very important.

Problem-solving research, according to Weiss, addresses a particular problem in a specific context, but a preferred solution to the problem is not given. We therefore expect this type of research to be narrow in scope, to focus on particular problems, and to aim at solving these problems. Because of this rather practical view of the relationship between research and the policy process, we also expect the results to be used directly and in the short term, and we expect that reaching deadlines will be relatively important. This type of research is likely to provide policy makers with a range of potential solutions to the problem. We therefore assume that we will see partial use of the results: Some options will be chosen and implemented while others will be left aside.

In Table 2.1 we provide an overview of the types of concrete evidence we expect to be able to find for the different stages/types of uses of research. The following section will describe several cases of actual policy research. On the basis of these cases we will see to what an extent we find conformity with the expected pattern presented in this table.

## Cases

Here we discuss the uses made of three research projects commissioned to CHEPS from various government agencies. These three cases have been chosen because they were thought to more or less cover the three different uses of research (enlightening, political, and problem-solving) and because they are examples of international comparative research. The titles of the three projects chosen are (1) market orientation in higher education, (2) university research funding, and (3) selection procedures in higher education. In terms of the international comparative content, these cases are quite typical of contract research undertaken by CHEPS.[20] The second case (university research funding) was somewhat unusual in that the agency contracting the research made clear statements at the start of the research contract negotiations about its point of view (described later in the chapter). Most contracts that CHEPS undertakes are more open ended or less explicit in their aims. In this sense, the first and third cases are more typical of contract research at CHEPS.

Table 2.2 presents a summary of how the evidence from the actual cases fits into the model presented in Table 2.1. Shaded text in Table 2.2 indicates places where the evidence from the cases deviates from the model of expected results (presented in Table 2.1). The aim is to try to discuss the feasibility and validity of using a static, goal-rational model for understanding the relationship between research and policy.

Sources of information included documents related to the commissioning of the research (research set-up, preliminary ideas, development of the research questions); all documents associated with the research process, follow-up, and discussions of the issues; policy documents; and interviews with researchers and policy makers.

It is necessary to say a few words about the specific context in which the research in these cases was carried out. All three of the cases studied involve contract research carried out by CHEPS for various Dutch government bodies, and in this sense there is only a limited variation in the cases. It is probable that the national context played a strong role in shaping the types of use that occurred and in setting a particular tone for the conversations between researchers and contractors. For example, in comparison with many other countries, we would argue that the Dutch government is fairly receptive to the idea of using research in general (and international comparative research in particular[21]) in formulating policy. Compared with many European countries, the Dutch Ministry of Education, Science and Culture spends a considerable amount of money on contract research. In addition, we would argue that there exists a fairly traditional image of the "proper" distance between researchers and policy makers. In the Netherlands research is generally valued in the policy-making process for its "unbiased," fairly detached, and independent point of view.[22] It would generally not be considered acceptable, for example, for researchers to be too closely involved in the politics of the policy-making process.[23]

The fact that all three cases that are examined here are examples of contract research is obviously also an important contextual fact. We would argue that all types of contract research could be considered to have some kind of political

**Table 2.2** Evidence of the Different Types of Uses of Research/Stages of the Policy Process: Examples from the Three Case Studies (Market Mechanisms, University Research Finance, and Selection Procedures)

| | SET-UP | | | OUTPUT/USE OF THE RESEARCH | | | |
|---|---|---|---|---|---|---|---|
| | SCOPE OF THE RESEARCH: NARROW OR BROAD | TYPES OF RESEARCH QUESTIONS: OPEN AND EXPLORATORY OR SPECIFIC | REASONS FOR COMMISSIONING THE RESEARCH | HOW QUICKLY WAS THE RESEARCH USED? (IN THE SHORT OR LONG TERM?) | HOW IMPORTANT WAS IT TO MEET THE DEADLINES? | WAS THE RESEARCH USED WHOLLY, PARTIALLY, OR NOT AT ALL? | WAS THE RESEARCH USED DIRECTLY OR INDIRECTLY? |
| Market Mechanisms (Enlightening/ Designing) | Very broad | Open and exploratory; later more specific questions | For background information/to help define the problem; some aspects related exactly to Dutch situation | Longer term, not right away | Not very important | Partially | Indirectly |
| University Research Finance (Political/ Deciding) | Narrow | Particular problems, with an expected or desired outcome | To provide support for the opinion that was already formed | Medium term | Somewhat important | Wholly | Directly (expected) |
| Selection Procedures (Problem Solving/ Implementing) | Narrow | Focus on particular problems, but no predefined outcome specified | To solve a particular problem | Short term | Quite important | Partially | Directly |

Shaded areas indicate differences with expected outcomes (as defined in Table 2.1).

orientation, as the contractors have reasons for commissioning the work and ideas about what they want to get out of it. There may be large variations between cases in terms of how hidden or obvious the views of the contractors are, but we would argue that the political element exists in most cases of contract research to some degree. Furthermore, Weiss[24] has pointed out different ways in which research that is not actively sought out and paid for also can play an important role in the policy process. These uses of research will not be studied here. All of these contextual factors are important in the policy-research relationship and influence the type and tone of interactions, as well as the type of research use. Given this, we urge caution concerning the extent to which the conclusions reached and model presented can be transferred to other contexts.

*Case 1: Market Mechanisms in Higher Education*

Over the past several years, the Dutch government has been introducing market elements into many different public sectors (health care system, higher education, etc.). The expectation is that market mechanisms will, in the long run, improve the efficiency and the quality of the public sector. In 1999, international comparative research on market mechanisms in higher education was commissioned by the Dutch Ministry of Education, Culture and Science. A report was produced in 1999.[25] This research was commissioned to contribute to the writing of an important policy discussion document (the Higher Education and Research Plan, or HOOP) produced every two years by the Ministry.[26]

The study focused on comparing three particular markets within higher education: the market for contract research as well as the markets for initial and postinitial education. Five (national) settings were analyzed: France, Germany, Michigan (United States), the Netherlands, and the United Kingdom. These five higher education systems were studied in terms of how many barriers (such as legal, financial, due to system or institutional characteristics, etc.) to competition (or the introduction of competition) exist in the functioning of the three markets described earlier. The existence of (or lack of) a "level playing field" for all higher education institutions was examined in each setting. In other words, the degree to which there are differences among the institutions within a system concerning the basic operating conditions (for example, access to public funding, the ability to select students, etc.) was examined. The different systems were then compared to each other and each was roughly "ranked" according to the extent to which competition exists in the system. Insofar as information was available, positive and negative consequences of the competition were mentioned.

The research was very broad in scope. The research questions covered many aspects of market mechanisms. Questions posed by the Ministry in the first round of negotiations concerning the research included, "What is the definition of 'external' or 'third-party' funding in other national contexts (does it include some forms of public sector funding)? Where is the border between public and private?" Other questions included, "What types of rules set the framework for market mechanisms in higher education?" The original questions posed by the Ministry did not specify which market mechanisms or particular functions of the higher education system (research vs. teaching functions, initial degree or postinitial degree programs) should be addressed.

The broad scope of the questions asked indicates that the information provided was not intended to solve a particular problem, but instead to give general background information and to help define the problems associated with market mechanisms. At one stage in the research process, representatives of the Ministry asked the researchers to provide comments concerning the connections between different elements of market orientation (the possible conflicts between the freedom of individual institutions to initiate degree courses, on one hand, and the transparency of qualification and accreditation, on the other hand). This clearly indicates that the information was being used more in terms of defining the problem than for direct problem solving.

There were, however, some aspects of the research that could be characterized as more political than enlightening. For example, in the process of negotiating the operationalization of the questions and the research set-up, the commissioners of the research posed a few additional, more specific questions and asked for information concerning one particular part of the higher education sector (postinitial degree programs). In addition, the Ministry also posed some very specific questions concerning the legal conditions for market mechanisms. In the process of negotiating the framework for the research, the Ministry decided to commission a separate study (from a consultancy agency) to answer these questions. The fact that more specific questions were also asked could indicate that the use of the research was likely to be a combination of enlightening as well as problem-solving or political aspects.

The commissioners of the research could not answer questions concerning exactly where, when, and how the research would be used (other than how it would contribute ideas that could be used in the discussion document described earlier). They mentioned that the information would be useful as background knowledge. This research can therefore clearly be seen as contributing indirectly to an ongoing discussion by providing general information. The results were meant to be used in the long rather than in the short term. This is also reflected in the fact that the deadlines did not seem to be terribly important. For instance, it did not seem to cause many problems when the date for the final report was extended.

The results of the research did not enable the researchers to judge the effectiveness of market mechanisms. It is problematic to relate market orientation with performance. The fact that one must consider the larger context—differences in traditions, cultures, higher education structures, and environments—makes it very difficult to offer any clear statements about effectiveness. As was mentioned earlier, the value of this research was more related to understanding relationships between market mechanisms and different elements in the system and in gaining insight into what is being done in other countries.

Considering this, it is not surprising that there are few signs of direct use of this research. The discussion policy document (HOOP 2000) does not specifically mention the report. However, one can point to quite a few examples of indirect use of the research. The topic of market mechanisms was featured prominently in the HOOP 2000 document. "An orientation toward the market is not an aim in itself, but is an instrument for innovation in teaching and research.... 'public entrepreneurialism' can provide added value.... Contract activities can be fruitful and stimulate innovation when they are in agreement with the primary mission of the higher education institutions."[27]

Again, despite the fact that no direct reference was made to the research, issues that were touched upon in the research report also appear in the document. For example, a discussion of the potential conflict between institutional accountability and quality, on the one hand, and the freedom of institutions to create new programs, carry out contract research, and respond flexibly to the market, on the other, was presented by the Ministry in the HOOP 2000 document:

> Universities should have greater possibilities for creating their own distinct profiles.... Due to rapid changes in all areas of knowledge it is no longer necessary for all universities to be active in all subject areas.... The development of individual profiles [however] must never lead to the loss of high quality.[28]

Despite the fact that one can describe the use of research in this case as a mixture of different types, we feel that it fits best into the classification of enlightening. If one fills in the boxes given in Table 2.1 with information from this particular study (see Table 2.2), then it is possible on this basis to conclude that this research was used more in enlightening than political or problem-solving ways.

*Case 2: University Research Funding*

This research was commissioned by the Dutch Organisation for Scientific Research (NWO).[29] The aim of the research was to compare the funding arrangements for research in Dutch universities with those in five other countries (Belgium, Finland, Germany, Switzerland, and the United Kingdom).[30] The NWO has been claiming for many years that the portion of public research funding for universities awarded in competitive ways (research council funding) is much too low in comparison with basic research funding the universities receive as part of their operating budgets directly from the government. A report was submitted to the NWO early in 2000.[31]

Statistical information was gathered from national sources concerning the sources of university research funding. Funding categories that are commonly used in the Netherlands were used, and the researchers tried to rework the statistics from other countries to make them more directly comparable with those used in the Netherlands. Three basic categories of funding from the Dutch system were used: basic public (noncompetitive) funding, public competitive (research council) funding, and all other sorts of (third-party or external) funding. Interviews were conducted with people involved with producing statistical information (or working with this information) in all of the countries in order to gain insight into how university-sector financial statistics are collected and categorized. In order to see if there had been changes in funding patterns over time, a nine-year period, 1990–1999, was examined.

The approach to classifying research funding in universities mirrored that employed in a 1990 study on the subject by Irvine, Martin, and Isard,[32] which is quoted widely by different stakeholders in the Dutch policy debates (and in many other countries as well). The research commissioned by the NWO in 1999 was partially an attempt to update the findings of this previous study, as the statistics reported in the 1990 study were viewed to be too old to be useful in current policy debates.

As was mentioned earlier, the research was commissioned to substantiate the claim that the NWO's portion of university research funds is low in comparison with funding from similar organizations in a number of other western European countries. The scope of the research questions was quite narrow. The researchers were asked to stick to collecting the "hard facts" (i.e., statistical information) and not to spend too much time looking into the effects of different funding methods or other related topics. Part of the reason for this focus on collecting information rather than on interpreting had to do with the limited budget of the project and the difficulty of attaining reliable and comparable statistical information. It was thought that the collection of good data would be time-consuming; therefore, the NWO wanted to limit the scope of the study.

This study is a good example of a political use of research because the (desired) outcome of the research was quite clear from the initial discussions concerning the research project. Furthermore, when asked how they anticipated using the results of the study, the representatives of the NWO said that this would depend very much on the outcomes of the research. This could indicate that whether or not (and in what capacity) the results would be used depended upon whether or not the results were considered "favorable" from the NWO's point of view.

At the time this study was undertaken, no other research was commissioned by the NWO to other groups. Other databases of statistics are, however, regularly used in political discussions on research finance in the Netherlands. The most commonly used databases are those of Eurostat and the OECD. For the specific purposes of the NWO, however, these do not contain specific enough information. When commissioning this study, the NWO was interested in the breakdown of public funding into competitive and noncompetitive sources, which are not distinguished by these databases.

The research was commissioned shortly after a heated debate in the parliament about the way in which university research is supported. In 1999 the parliament came close to passing a new initiative that would have taken a substantial amount of universities' direct basic budgets and given this money to the NWO to distribute on a competitive basis. The research was clearly commissioned to support the NWO's side of this debate. At the time of the parliamentary debate, the NWO asked some researchers to produce quickly an overview of the types of research funding in various western European countries, relying on information that was readily available from the researchers themselves. This brief study was used at the time of the debates, and it appeared that the information was interesting enough to warrant the commissioning of a longer study, which is the one discussed here. Because the parliamentary debate happened essentially while the research project was being formulated, the pressure for short-term results decreased. This could perhaps explain why the original deadlines set for the final report were extended several times. The commissioners of the research made it clear, however, that they were actively interested in the results and that too many delays would not be acceptable.

The general conclusions of the research were that there is a trend in the six European countries studied toward a decline in government basic (noncompetitive) funding, a stagnation in government competitive (research council) funding, and an expansion in external funding. The commissioners of the research at NWO have indicated that they are pleased with the results and they are in the process of publishing the entire report. Although to date the report has not been used publicly used in political discussions, based on the fact that representatives of the NWO feel that the results support their point of view, it is likely that the results will be used in budget discussions with the government.

*Case 3: Numerus Fixus in Higher Education*
One of the principles of Dutch higher education is that it be accessible to all qualified applicants. However, some programs have a limited number of places (for financial and/or labor market reasons). Most of the programs with limited access are in the health sector (medicine, veterinary sciences, physiotherapy), but some business administration programs are also included.

Prior to 1999, selection to these courses was determined by a "weighted lottery" system. The main criterion for admissions was average grades at graduation from upper secondary school (weighted in such a way that people with higher grades had better chances of gaining admission). In 1995 a lively public debate concerning these selection procedures began. This discussion stemmed from a well-publicized case in which a secondary school graduate with very high grades was denied admission to a medical program.

As a result of the public debate that was sparked in 1995, the government, under pressure to make changes to the system, decided to form a committee (known as the Drenth Committee) to make recommendations. This committee commissioned researchers at CHEPS to undertake a comparative study of selection mechanisms in eight countries (Belgium, Denmark, Finland, France, Germany, Norway, Sweden, and the United Kingdom).[33] The committee wanted to see if any of the admissions procedures used in these countries would be appropriate in the Dutch context. A report was produced at the end of 1996.[34]

The questions posed by the committee were quite specific, and the scope of the research was relatively narrow. The general research questions were, "How can the selection procedures used in other countries be described?" and "What experiences have people had with using these procedures?" The first general question encompassed specific issues: What are the rules and regulations? Who are the actors involved, and what are their responsibilities? What criteria are used? How is assessment carried out? What costs are involved? Can rejected applicants appeal? The second general question related to the acceptability of the system in the wider societal context and focused on issues of effectiveness, transparency, feasibility, and the ability to guard against misuse or fraudulence. It was the second question that was at the core of the research because the controversy that flared up as a result of the well-publicized case was the reason why the Drenth Committee was created to study the problem.

Information was collected on admissions procedures in the eight countries (on the basis of documents and interviews). The systems were compared and "scored" in terms of a number of (potential) benefits and problem areas (such as transparency, efficiency or objectivity, and the potential for fraudulent use of the system). The advantages and disadvantages of various admission procedures were discussed.

The research was commissioned at a time when the government was under pressure to change the existing system, before a decision had been reached concerning what alternative methods could be (or would be) used. It can therefore be concluded that this research was being used to help solve a particular problem at the "deciding" phase of the policy process. However, the focus on the acceptability of the selection procedures by various actors, in combination with the lively political discussion regarding the acceptability of the Dutch procedures, might give us some reason to classify the use of the study as political. Characterizing the use of the study as enlightening does not seem very plausible, as the characteristics do not conform to our operationalization of enlightening use of research (broad questions that help to define the problem, etc.; see Table 2.1).

Because the research was intended to provide direct input for the work of the committee, formed by the government that was under pressure to consider alternative selection procedures, time was of the essence and meeting deadlines was emphasized. The research was carried out in September–November 1996, and the advice was given to the government in January 1997.

The CHEPS research produced was one of three studies commissioned by the Drenth Committee in the process of producing advice for the government.

The first of the other two studies gave a description of the discussions going on at that time in a historical (national) context, and the second was an empirical study of the effectiveness of the Dutch procedure being used at that time in the medical disciplines. The first of these can be classified as being used in a somewhat more enlightening way because this report was intended to give background information concerning the subject and was not intended to be used for problem solving. The second report can be described as more problem solving, as it focused on the question of whether or not the (then) existing system could be described as successful and therefore viable. The second report can also be considered political, as it was clear at the time that the political climate favored a change in the system.

The Drenth Committee's final report made considerable, direct use of the CHEPS study, including lengthy discussions of the advantages and disadvantages of various selection procedures used in other countries:

> [The CHEPS researchers] noted that the use of selection criteria other than "qualifying diplomas" can result in less transparency.[35]
>
> Questions about the motives for selection have played an important role in this discussion. The comparative study of the literature showed that there is a large variety in the aims for selecting students in higher education systems. It is necessary to differentiate between motives for limiting the number of students due to limited capacity, and other reasons for selecting students.[36]

Moreover, although no explicit references were made to the CHEPS study in the policy debates at the parliamentary level, the Dutch Minister of Education referred to issues that were covered by the study. For instance, in both his reaction to the committee's report[37] and his response to questions from the parliament on the issue,[38] the minister referred to the following issues addressed in the study: decentralizing selection, including working experience as a (potential) criteria, using quotas, and implementing waiting lists.

In 1997 a follow-up study was commissioned on one particular selection criteria (previous work experience) by an organization set up to advise the government on educational issues (the Onderwijsraad[39]). The use of work experience as a selection criteria was mentioned by the minister in a policy document in 1995[40] as one possible criterion that could solve some of the problems of the acceptance of the Dutch weighted lottery system. The fact that there was a discussion about this particular criterion over a longer period of time indicates that the use of this research was partially political (i.e., was partially used to support a preexisting policy idea).

In the time since the Drenth Committee came out with its advice there have been changes in the rules governing the selection of students. A new law on access to higher education was implemented in April 1999.[41] This law gives higher education institutions the right to admit a certain percentage of applicants (in certain fields) according to criteria that they determine themselves. The law suggests some criteria that the institutions may wish to use. For example, among other types of selection criteria, the document mentions previous work experience.

If one compares the details of this case study to the expected pattern given in Table 2.1, it is possible to conclude that it fits best into the category of "problem-solving" use of research. As with the other two cases presented, this case does not fit perfectly into the framework we have developed (see Table 2.2). Even though this case also represents some kind of mixture of uses, it is possible to conclude that it fits best with the characterization of problem-solving use of research.

**Discussion and Conclusions**

The model presented in Table 2.1 shows our attempt at finding a way to classify actual cases of research according to the uses of research and the phases of the policy process. Table 2.2 provides a summary of the information taken from the three cases presented in the previous section, indicating in what ways it does or does not fit into the model. By comparing Table 2.1 with Table 2.2, one can see that the three cases fit fairly well into the framework; it was possible to roughly classify the cases in terms of research uses and phases of the policy process as specified in the model. However, as was mentioned earlier, there are a number of complexities that cannot be captured in this simple heuristic model. A number of factors should be incorporated into a revised model:

1. Using the model, it should be possible to classify actual cases of research as being mixtures of different uses of research.
2. Dynamics and changes that occur over the course of the whole policy process should be taken into consideration.
3. Interactions between different stakeholders and the larger context of policy making should be considered.

Although it may be useful to classify research use as being predominantly oriented toward one type, our model should define uses of research less rigidly and should allow one to see the ways in which different uses are made of the same piece of research. As we have seen in the descriptions, all three cases examined here can be considered mixtures of different types of research. One example of this involves the Case 3 (selection procedures). The mismatches between the model (Table 2.1) and the evidence from the description of the research (Case 3, see shaded areas Table 2.2) may be explained in terms of the use of this research being a kind of hybrid of problem solving and political aspects. While the set-up of the research suggests a problem-solving orientation, some of the output elements indicate political use. The facts that the research deadlines were emphasized and the research was used in the short term, for example, indicate a political orientation.

The second complicating factor in the policy process is its dynamic nature and the changes that take place over the course of the policy process. The three cases we presented display some elements of policy dynamics and change over time. For example, the case involving the market mechanisms research (Case 1) shows some movement during the research process. At the initial stages of the research, the policy stage/research use category of designing/enlightening seems most apt. As the research progressed, however, the commissioners of the research wanted attention paid to particular issues and thus posed more specific questions. This type of question and the narrower orientation of the research conform more to the pattern described by an implementing/problem-solving category.

Similarly, some differences between the university research finance case (Case 2) and the model may be explained by the fact that events in reality happened in a different order (or at different times in the research process) than we predict from the simple model. On the basis of our model, we expect that research commissioned for political use will be completed before the moment when the political decision is taken formally. In the case concerning university research finance, however, the political decision was actually reached while the research was still being formulated. This could explain why the deadlines were not so important and why the research was used in the medium term, rather than in the very short term (as was expected on the basis of the model). The crucial moment of decision making passed, and the pressure to produce research results therefore eased. One might expect (from our model) that interest in the research results might be dropped altogether once a political decision was made. This did not occur in this case. This can perhaps be explained by the fact that the political process is very complex and decisions are rarely made only once at one particular moment by one actor. In most cases, discussions concerning important issues go on over a period of time, and different (even contradictory) decisions may be taken at different times by different actors. In the case of the university finance research, the findings are clearly still of interest and can be used in the next round of budgetary discussions and in future discussions concerning the role of the NWO.

The third complexity is formed by the interactions between different stakeholders in the policy process. To understand the role of research in the policy process, it is necessary to see the research as forming one part of a much larger context. Within this context there are many interest groups that play a role. In the three cases examined here, we described how there were sometimes other groups commissioned to undertake research. We did not, however, analyze the nature of interaction, if any, between the CHEPS researchers and these other groups; whether the different research findings supported or contradicted each other; or how the various findings were interpreted *and* used by various groups, including the contractor of the research. Although it is difficult to examine the role played by various groups in the policy process, it is important to examine the broader context in which various stakeholder groups (students, collective associations of universities, industry, etc.) make use of research as they participate in the policy-making process. We need to consider the possibility that different groups use the same study in different ways or for different purposes even at the same point in time.

Based on the comments made here, we would like to suggest ways in which the model could be altered to better take into account some of the more complex aspects of the relationship between research and policy making. In the first place, the model should allow for a classification of mixtures of different types of uses. Research could then be classified as, for example, highly political/slightly problem solving. Second, the model needs to include factors that have to do with the research process in addition to the set-up and output. One could examine, for example, whether or not substantial revisions were made to the original research concept and which actors influenced these changes. One might also try to measure the extent to which the researchers themselves were able to determine the topic of the study or the methodology used. It would be interesting to know if these choices were influenced or steered by others. Third, the model needs to locate the research-policy interaction within the larger policy-making context. It should enable and encourage an examination of the role of different groups in relation to each other as well as the impact of more than one study being commissioned or drawn upon in the policy-making process.[42]

This chapter has been an attempt to understand the complex relationship between research and policy making in terms of a simple, heuristic model and using cases of contract research as examples. Much of the literature on the subject of the relationship between research and policy making does not refer specifically to individual cases of actual research, but rather describes the relationship in abstract terms. In this chapter we have tried to see how general descriptions of different uses of research could be applied to real cases of research.

While the simple model we propose is relatively successful in classifying different types of uses of research during different stages of the policy-making process, the limitations of it also point to the fact that the interaction between policy and policy research is (more) complicated. The uses of policy research and the stages in the policy process are often of a hybrid nature. The interactions between policy and research are dynamic, both in the sense that policy shifts back and forth over the stages and in the sense that the use of research changes during the policy process. Research is one factor among many that have an impact on the policy process. It is difficult to find any order in the whirlwind of actors and factors that constitutes the policy process.

In this chapter we made a modest attempt to shed some light on the process of dancing in the dark. Although we feel we have understood some things, much remains obscure. It is clear that the interaction between policy and research is an interesting area for further research.

## Notes

1. This chapter was originally published in the special issue of the *Comparative Education Review* [45 (2) (May 2001): 197–219] focused on "The Relationship between Theorists/Researchers and Policy Makers/Practitioners."
2. H. R. van Gunsteren, *The Quest for Control: A Critique of the Rational-Central-Rule Approach in Public Affairs* (London: John Wiley, 1976).
3. See, for example, Henry M. Levin, "Why Isn't Educational Research More Useful?", in *Knowledge for Policy: Improving Education through Research*, ed. D. S. Anderson and B. J. Biddle (London: Falmer Press, 1991); Robert Birnbaum, "Policy Scholars Are from Venus; Policy Makers Are from Mars," *The Review of Higher Education* 23 (2) (Winter 2000): 119–132; Clifton F. Conrad and Ramona Gunter, "To Be More Useful: Embracing Interdisciplinary Scholarship and Dialogue," *New Directions for Higher Education* 110 (Summer 2000): 49–62.
4. For example, see Janet A. Weiss, "Using Social Science for Social Policy," *Policy Studies Journal* 4 (3) (1976): 234–38.
5. Mark Ginsburg and Jorge Gorostiaga, "Relationships between Theorists/Researchers and Policymakers/Practitioners? Rethinking the Two Cultures Thesis and the Possibility of Dialogue," *Comparative Education Review* 45 (May 2001): 173–96.
6. CHEPS, founded in 1984, is an academic research institute based at the University of Twente in the Netherlands. CHEPS combines basic research with more applied, practically oriented studies funded by a variety of national and international sources.
7. It is an interesting question whether or not comparative studies have a unique relationship with policy making and whether there is a greater potential for comparative studies to be used in particular ways. These questions will not be addressed here because we only examine comparative international research; to draw any conclusions regarding this issue both comparative and single-country studies would have to be examined.
8. A. Hoogerwerf, "Beleid, Processen en Effecten," in *Overheidsbeleid*, ed. A. Hoogerwerf (Alphen aan den Rijn: Samsom Uitgeverij, 1989).
9. The term "problem" is used here not in the limited sense of a particular aspect or feature that should be changed, but in a broader sense that includes undefined ideas (such as market orientation; see description of Case 1) an actor or group of actors would like to introduce. In this particular case (Case 1) a lack of market orientation in the system is the problem that is perceived.
10. Peter Coleman and Linda LaRocque, "Linking Educational Research and Educational Policy via Policy-Relevant Research," *The Alberta Journal of Educational Research*, 29 (3) (September 1983): 242–55.
11. Janet A. Weiss; Coleman and LaRocque.
12. Carol H. Weiss, "The Many Meanings of Research Utilization," in *Knowledge for Policy: Improving Education through Research*, ed. D. S. Anderson and B. J. Biddle (London: Falmer Press, 1991). In addition to these three types, Weiss describes three other types of research use: knowledge-driven, interactive, and tactical, but we feel that they are of a different order. The interactive model focuses not so much on the way in which policy research is used, but much more on the process through which it enters the policy arena, namely, through scientists in interaction with many other actors in a policy field. The category of knowledge-driven research derives its name not from the use of the knowledge by policy makers but from the way in which basic research may develop through different stages toward applicable knowledge. The tactical model is, in our view, a subcategory of the political use of knowledge: It is research used as a political tool to delay policy, deflect criticism, and so on.
13. Hoogerwerf.
14. Charles E. Lindblom and David K. Cohen, *Usable Knowledge: Social Science and Social Problem Solving* (New Haven, CT, and London: Yale University Press, 1979).
15. Michael Cohen, James March, and Johan Olsen, "A Garbage Can Model of Organizational Choice," *Administrative Science Quarterly* (March 17, 1972): 1–25; John W. Kingdon, *Agendas, Alternatives, and Public Policies* (New York: Harper Collins College Publishers, 1995).

16. Jeffrey L. Pressman and Aaron Wildavsky, *Implementation: How Great Expectations in Washington Are Dashed in Oakland—Or Why It Is Amazing That Federal Programmes Work at All* (Berkeley: University of California Press, 1974).
17. Hoogerwerf.
18. See, for example, Graham T. Allison, *Essence of Decision-Making: Explaining the Cuban Missile Crisis* (Boston: Little, Brown, 1971).
19. Carol H. Weiss.
20. The majority of the research carried out at CHEPS can be described as international and comparative.
21. Given the fact that the Netherlands is a small country and due to the increasing importance of the European dimension in higher education, the Dutch government seems quite aware of the (potential) usefulness of looking across borders when seeking solutions to national problems. There tends, however, to be an emphasis on studying other European (and occasionally North American) countries, and in this sense the international focus is somewhat limited.
22. One can, of course, argue that no research is truly "independent." But we would still claim that the idea (perhaps illusion) of this exists more strongly in this context than in many others, and that this has an influence on the way research is used and on the interactions between the different actors involved in the process.
23. This is not to say that researchers never play political roles such as in giving advice to the government. However, in cases of contract research (which is the focus of this study), a greater distance between the researcher and the political decision making would be expected. Obviously in practice there may be at times a considerable amount of overlap in these roles, but we would argue that the idea of a separation between these functions is fairly strong in this national context.
24. Carol H. Weiss.
25. Frans Kaiser, Peter van der Meer, Jasmin Beverwijk, Anne Klemperer, Bernard Steunenberg, and Anne van Wageningen, *Market Type Mechanisms in Higher Education* (Enschede: Center for Higher Education Policy Studies, 1999).
26. Dutch Ministry of Education, Culture and Science, *Hoger Onderwijs en Onderzoek Plan (HOOP) 2000* (Den Haag: Dutch Ministry of Education Culture and Science, 1999). This document outlines the government's position and future plans concerning a range of issues related to higher education. Changes proposed in this document do not automatically become law. The document sets out a framework, provokes discussion, and outlines the government's intentions for the coming two-year period.
27. Dutch Ministry of Education, Culture and Science, *Hoger Onderwijs en Onderzoek Plan (HOOP) 2000*, p. 67. Translation by author.
28. Dutch Ministry of Education, Culture and Science, *Hoger Onderwijs en Onderzoek Plan (HOOP) 2000*, p. 70. Translation by author.
29. The NWO is an organization that funds publicly supported research (such as research councils in other countries or organizations such as the National Science Foundation in the United States).
30. These countries were chosen on the basis that they are all western European countries (and presumably, therefore, somewhat similar to the Netherlands) and because they are all have rather high research outputs.
31. Heide Hackmann and Anne Klemperer, *University Research Funding: An International Comparison—Report for the Dutch Organisation for Scientific Research* (Enschede: University of Twente, 2000).
32. J. Irvine, B. R. Martin, and P. Isard, *Investing in the Future: An International Comparison of Government Funding of Academic and Related Research* (London: Edward Elgar, 1990).
33. The selection of countries was made together by the researchers and members of the Drenth Committee. The researchers were asked to select countries that are located fairly close to the Netherlands; some variety in admissions systems was also desired.
34. Frans Kaiser, Sandra de Lange, and Egbert de Weert, *Vergelijkend Onderzoek Selectie-Procedures voor het Hoger Onderwijs in een Antal West-Europese Landen* (Enschede: CHEPS, 1996).
35. Drenth Committee, *Gewogen Loting Gewogen: Rapport van de Commissie Toelating Numerus Fixusopleidingen* (Den Haag: SDU, 1997), p. 36. Translation by author.
36. Drenth Committee, p. 41. Translation by author.

37. Tweede Kamer, *1996/97, 25000 VIII nr. 99* (official record of Dutch Parliamentary budget discussion), 1997.
38. Tweede Kamer, *1997/98, 25600 VIII, nr. 5* (official record of Dutch Parliamentary budget discussion), 1997.
39. The *Onderwijsraad* gives independent advice to the Minister of Education concerning drafts of new laws.
40. Dutch Ministry of Education, Culture and Science, *Hoger Onderwijs en Onderzoek Plan (HOOP) 1996* (Den Haag: Dutch Ministry of Education, Culture and Science, 1995).
41. Staatsblad, *170* (official publication of Dutch law) (April 1999).
42. For example, in two of the cases examined (Cases 1 and 3—market mechanisms and selection procedures) studies were commissioned to other researchers around the same time as the studies described here were commissioned to CHEPS. To go beyond the model presented here, one could examine the potential interactions between the processes and products of the different studies as well as investigate how different stakeholder groups reacted to and sought to use the different studies.

CHAPTER 3

# Linking Research, Policy, and Strategic Planning to Education Development in the Lao People's Democratic Republic[1]

DON ADAMS
GEOK HWA KEE
LIN LIN

**Introduction**

Although academic researchers frequently decry the infrequent use of research by policy makers, globally, information, analysis, and research are playing an increasingly important role in shaping education decisions. Indeed, policy makers and senior education administrators in some developing countries appear to suffer from "studies fatigue" as a result of the scores of local and donor-sponsored empirical investigations. Unfortunately, such studies, even when significant in number, frequently have not been convincing to policy makers and planners as to their relevance. Wanted may not only be additional research but more useful research. To many policy makers research remains an uncertain investment.[2]

Although narrowed in many circumstances, the long-standing gap tends to persist between education research and policy and planning decisions. Particularly in developing countries relationships between research and policy are often tentative and uncertain. The reasons lie both with the amount and quality of research found and in the political and organizational contexts. The available research has often been too narrow in scope, too slow in evolving, and too costly to become part of policy deliberations. Research has been most successful in identifying "educational problems," such as the general conditions of inequity in the opportunities for schooling, inefficiencies in the progress of students through school, and poor quality of instruction—conditions policy makers and planners claim to know about already. The extant research is less successful in helping to shape decisions in the processes of policy making and planning and, least successful of all, in assisting in the processes of implementing and sustaining educational reforms. Moreover, communication between policy makers and researchers is often flawed. Policy makers may expect research to "solve problems," a view that researchers have not sufficiently discouraged, while research has often primarily indicated the complexity of educational change.[3]

A variety of conditions in developing countries may explain the absence of a well-developed research tradition and capability to generate educational research relevant to the needs of policy and planning. The dominance of ideology in politics may leave little room for the discipline and time required for traditional research, and when bureaucrats and politicians are indistinguishable, research may be stunted. Revolutionary or crises governments tend to exist in an environment where policy symbolism outweighs seeking new insights to cope with complex educational problems. Likewise, if nation building is still taking place within the context of deep ethnic antagonisms and inequalities, little independent research will take place. In the poorest countries few, if any, universities or other institutions exist with research capabilities in education. The state[4] and patterns of governance are still evolving in many developing countries with fairly recent introduction of programs of privatization and localization, and the extent of attention to research capacity is still largely left to the limited resources of the public sector. Under such conditions research information is not a priority in the management of education.

Many models and metaphors have been developed to capture variations in relations between research and policy making.[5] However, generic descriptions of linkages between "research" and "policy" are of little value since the information and knowledge needed to support policy, at minimum, varies by type and purpose of policy and the policy context. Reimers and McGinn[6] suggest three models to illustrate relationships between research and the development and implementation of educational policy. Model 1: Research assists in persuasion as a necessary condition in achieving goals established a priori. Under this model knowledge derives its power from its persuasiveness. Model 2: Research contributes to knowledge under conditions when policy development emphasizes negotiation. Under this model researchers and policy makers continue to play separate roles but knowledge is utilized in a way that explicitly acknowledges the broader political and social conditions in which the policy makers must choose their information options. Model 3: Research is part of a constructivist view of knowledge production and utilization where policy making is seen as participation and organizational learning, that is, policy making is an ongoing dialogue.[7] To a degree, these are seen as reflecting levels of increasing technical sophistication and democratization of educational policy making. That is, to Reimers and McGinn,[8] more research-informed, participatory dialogue contributes to more effective educational systems. In the case study that follows, these models are useful referents in examining current linkages between education research and the policy and planning processes and in considering a possible future model of policy making and strategic planning.

To further clarify description of policies, a distinction will also be made between rhetorical policy, enacted policy, and implemented policy. Rhetorical policy refers to broad statements of educational goals often found in national addresses of senior political leaders. Enacted policies are the "authoritative statements," decrees, or laws that give explicit standards and direction to the education sector. Implemented policies are the enacted policies, modified or unmodified, as they are being translated into actions through systemic, programmatic, and project-level changes.

This chapter is organized around three main sections. The first provides a brief overview of the social and economic environment within which Lao education functions. The second describes the use and nonuse of research in education policy and planning by focusing on both the processes and the products of decision making involved in a Lao government/Asian Development Bank (ADB)–sponsored education sector assessment.[9] The third examines ways to improve the effectiveness of Lao policy and planning through building a tradition of use of research and outlines a modified role of international donors in contributing to the development of research capabilities.

**Social, Economic, and Educational Contexts**

Although several positive changes are underway, economically, socially, and educationally, the Lao People's Democratic Republic (PDR) currently is one of the poorest countries in the world. Lao social and education policies are embedded in a heritage of colonialism, socialist revolution, and, most recently, some movement toward a market economy and privatization.[10] A national reform beginning in 1975 saw the elimination of French colonial control and the emergence of the independent Lao People's Democratic Republic under control of the Communist Party. The early national tasks were to elaborate the party structure and integrate it with the government apparatus. Control over the economy was established through a series of national laws in which centralized fiscal and economic authority were defined.[11]

Dissatisfaction with the performance of the economy led, in the 1980s, to a new economic reform, the New Economic Mechanism (NEM). NEM, as a macro-economic policy, was formally initiated in 1986 to move the country incrementally from a centrally planned economy toward a market-oriented economy and to reduce the government's direct involvement in production and trade. The new reform was characterized by satisfactory improvement in the Lao economy, which from 1986 to the mid-1990s grew at an annual rate of 5–8 percent, fueled largely by small industries using low and intermediate technologies. However, since 1997 economic conditions have deteriorated, reflecting the fiscal crisis and economic slowdown in Asia, particularly as found in neighboring Thailand.[12]

Demographically, Lao PDR has a young, largely rural population; a moderately high population growth rate; and a high youth-dependency ratio. The distribution of population largely to rural areas has adverse financial implications for the cost of delivery of schooling at all levels. Further, since education systems are highly sensitive to the size of the school-age cohort, the young Lao population puts a heavy burden on human and fiscal resources for schooling. Asian countries with lower youth dependency ratios than Lao PDR have been able to invest more per child in education and social services with similar levels of funding.[13]

The Lao population of 4.9 million includes over forty-seven ethnic and linguistic groups. School attendance, literacy, and other indicators of educational attainment vary greatly among these groups. Census data from 1995 reveal that 23 percent of the Lao ethnic group have never attended school, as compared with 34, 56, and 67 percent for the Phutai, Khmu, and Hmong, respectively. Among two of the smallest ethnic groups, 94 percent of the Kor and 96 percent of the Musir have never attended school. Lao, the official and instructional language, is spoken by about 50 percent of the population. Women remain underrepresented at every level of the education system and in the technical and professional ranks of labor. The largest number of employed women is found in agricultural and fishery occupations. Other occupation groups, which include larger percentages of women, are clerical and service workers, where women frequently hold lower level positions.[14]

Although Lao PDR is still classified by international donors as a "least developed country," a category that includes such Asian countries as Afghanistan, Bangladesh, Bhutan, Cambodia, Maldives, Myanmar, and Nepal, the last decade has seen significant social and educational progress.[15] The chances of child survival have improved, many children and youth are acquiring more schooling, adult literacy rates have increased, and the annual population growth rate has been reduced to 2.4 percent. However, on several human development indicators, Lao PDR continues to rank among the lowest countries in Asia. The Lao population is characterized by high mortality, with an average life span of 51 years, and chronic malnutrition of children persists with only 20 percent of children immunized. On three human development indicators, the Human Development Index (HDI), the Human Poverty Index (HPI), and the Gender Development Index (GDI), Lao PDR tends to be placed with the poorest South and Southeast Asian counties.[16]

In terms of percent of population served, and the efficiency and the quality of education delivered, the education system is in an early stage of development. Crude benchmarks, such as indicators of illiteracy, enrollment ratios, and educational expenditure as a percent of GDP, suggest Lao PDR educationally is among the lowest countries in Asia. Moreover, the enrollment projections contrast sharply with the ambitious targets for growth found in the current and forthcoming national five-year plan.[17] Another indicator that Lao education has not matured as a system is its lack of efficiencies within primary, secondary, and tertiary cycles. If, for example, the primary and secondary cycles have meaning and represent distinct programs of education, then selection would be expected to be largely between cycles and not within cycles as in the case of Lao PDR.

At the primary level, for example, out of every one thousand entrants to grade 1 approximately 45 percent drop out before graduation, 35 percent survive with repetition, and only 20 percent survive without repetition. At the school level, for about half of the pupils in grade 1 the language of instruction is not the language the child speaks; thus, the non-Lao-speaking child begins schooling with a significant disadvantage in all subjects. Moreover, the style of classroom instruction in the lower grades is essentially "read-copy" or "copy-copy," where the teacher either reads from a textbook or writes on a board and pupils copy to a notebook. Currently, the system may provide basic literacy to those who graduate from primary school. As Lao PDR further industrializes and utilizes more intermediate and advanced technology in all sectors, including agriculture, the current quality of basic education will be inadequate even for those who complete it.[18]

**Utilization of Educational Research in Lao Policy and Strategic Planning**

This section focuses on the education policy-making and strategic planning processes and a major attempt to develop a comprehensive critique of the education sector. Research-based insights and research-informed dialogue are identified within the context of (1) the development and review of the current national five-year educational plan (1996–2000), (2) preparation for the next five-year plan (2001–2005), and (3) a collaborative sector assessment in education financed through ADB loans and involving a group of international and Lao consultants.

*Decision-Making Structure in Education*

The Lao People's Revolutionary Party (LPRP), the major policy-making body in the country, plays the key role throughout the national policy and planning processes. Generally, other stakeholders at the center, province, and district levels have little direct input into national education policies and participate in very limited ways in policy dialogue. The LPRP holds a national congress every five years to discuss major national issues and pass resolutions that establish the broad economic and social policy framework, sectoral objectives, and, sometimes, specific targets for the next five or more years.[19]

The Leading Party Committee in each sector deliberates and produces guiding documents for the congresses. The Leading Committee for Human Resource Development (LCHRD), whose vice chair is the minister of education, reviews education planning documents in their developmental stage before they are sent to the National Assembly, which promulgates necessary decrees. The Sixth Party Congress in 1996 emphasized the need to expand and modernize the educational system, orienting it toward producing youth and adults with the skills and knowledge required to achieve the government's goals of national development. At every planning stage at each administrative level discussions are led by a party unit. Within the Ministry of Education (MOE), for example, there is a Leading Party Committee (LPC) which consists of the minister and selected department directors, which can suggest priorities to the national LCHRD. Educational bureaucrats, particularly first- and second-echelon personnel, may contribute to policy through drafted memoranda at the requests of the party. Similarly, there is a party committee leading deliberations within the MOE units at each provincial and district level.

The responsibility for translating these broad policy statements of party congresses into national plans rests with the State Planning Committee (SPC), the national body with intersectoral authority, and the line ministries. As shown in Figure 3.1, national planning in education in Lao PDR, like planning in other social sectors, is a complex process involving many technical and administrative bodies at the national and local levels. The SPC, interacting with the line ministries, develops sectoral plans and a national (five-year) "socioeconomic plan" that includes a Public Investment Programme.[20] A plan document exists for the current national education plan (1996–2000), and a draft document exists

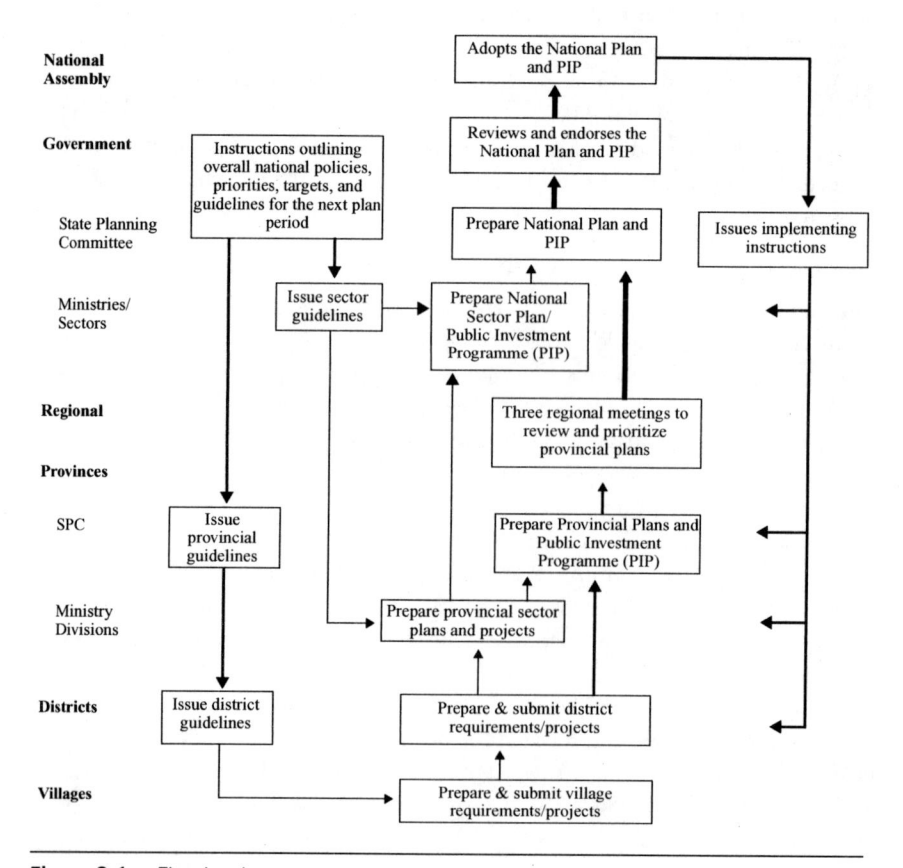

**Figure 3.1.** The planning process.

for the forthcoming plan (2001–2005). A longer-term "perspective plan" 2001–2020 is under development.[21] This process is sometimes viewed as highly centralized, with powerful central agencies exercising control over, and demanding compliance from, provincial and district education authorities. Yet local values, particularly with the support of the provincial governor, may influence the inclusion of specific projects and, thus, help shape the implementation of national plans. The future may see increased educational responsibilities devolving to the province, district, and village.

However, information available within MOE is currently not being sufficiently analyzed and used in planning decisions, partly because of a traditional lack of interdepartmental sharing of information—a condition severely limiting the effectiveness of strategic planning. Thus, within MOE, and in the broader policy-making arena, it is not necessarily the absence of data and data analysis that inhibit a more analytical and data-based approach to policy making and planning. Rather, it is also the absence of supporting demand. Because policies in the form of broad laws and goals are issued from deliberations by party leadership, often advocacy with emphasis on appropriate goals, not research, is the strategy to create new or different policies. The challenge for the department directors in MOE and senior administrators of other institutions associated with education is to present arguments to attain relevant "decrees" (authoritative statements or policies that have not attained the full stature of law) complementary to party goals and supportive of the functions of their departments. Information, if significant, is part of the argument to persuade, not define, policy making. Moreover, once a decree is in place, debate or critique is effectively discouraged.

Neither the decision process within the highest levels of the party nor the planning or negotiation process that results in the development and content of annual and multiyear educational plans is fully transparent. The data, analyses, and discussions leading to the content of official plan documents are difficult to identify. Typically, the national education plans present long lists of goals and targets associated largely with expansion of the existing system at all levels. Neither the analysis upon which future educational growth is based, nor enrollment projections, nor identification of programs to be reduced, nor budgets are found in these documents. Viewed as a development process other limitations are also apparent. First, there is a lack of integration of objectives, priorities, and budget in the early stages of the planning process. Second, planning and administration at all levels tend to focus on projects that respond to donor-driven initiatives and resources. Third, the impacts of such project investments on future recurrent costs are not fully explored. Fourth, there is an absence of involvement in major decisions by stakeholders outside the highest political and bureaucratic circles.[22]

As suggested, the influence of international donors on the priorities and projects of national plans can be substantial. This condition holds for the establishment of broad priorities, for example, basic education, which donors tend to favor, and in the case of specific donor-recommended projects, for example, teacher in-service training. Priorities, programs, and projects emerging from donor involvement can be expected to be informed by research-based information, either commissioned, in-country studies or existing international research. Further, linked to donor loans or grants, research may be seen as support of conditions to be met by the government as it seeks international funding. Other than donor influence within Lao political and bureaucratic process, the limited and rare role of research in policy making and strategic planning is found at the earliest stages of the process and particularly associated with *rhetorical* policy. That is, policy pronouncements, typically associated with tenets or aspirations of the party, may refer to available information or studies in order to add to their stakeholder legitimacy. *Enacted* policies and accompanied national plans would be expected to incorporate selective available data or, possibly, the results of commissioned studies. For example, studies of expected enrollment trends and their cost consequences may be cited by an MOE director of an education subsector as he or she informs the appropriate Leading Committee drafting policies related to the subsector growth and change. The extremely small cadre of researchers within MOE, thus, may be involved in providing data to support positions already decided upon by the higher echelons of government. However, the researchers have little voice in discussion of either research or policy priorities.

Directors in MOE have little ownership of either policy or the process of its development. Moreover, typically they lack organizational resources to carry out enacted policy. At the provincial and district levels during the rhetorical and enactment policy stages little discretion is expected. Yet, in the absence of adequate resources to implement plans and programs, local administrators may become de facto policy makers as they are forced to rely on experiential knowledge and community resources and to cope in innovative ways to keep schools in operation.

At the stage of enacted policy some reality testing takes place as budgets are approved by the Ministry of Finance and program modification becomes necessary. Directors of the subsectors may find some space to defend their programs and projects. Modifications presented by directors may be screened by the MOE cabinet; however, decisions are reserved for the minister's office. Movement from policy enactment to policy implementation requires a high level of specification of the program content and the magnitude of necessary resources and costs. At this stage, project delay, postponement, and radical modification or redesign are not uncommon. The more active provincial governments generate additional revenues to protect and even extend favored projects.

The lack of a significant, consistent role of research in policy-making and planning processes relates to both the supply of and the demand for research capabilities. Neither research-based information nor processed and interpreted data from international research studies are generally available. The short supply of research activities can be traced to the exodus of highly educated Laotians at the time of revolution; the current underdeveloped education system, which has virtually no output of education researchers; and the initial Lao government priorities, which focused on nation building, national defense, and development of national language and symbols. Within the context of these priorities there has been little demand for or resources to build research capabilities or tradition.

*Developing the Education Sector Assessment and Investment Plan*

As a centerpiece in its educational assistance, ADB funded and, in collaboration with the Lao government, managed the development of a sector assessment and investment plan. The aim of this activity was to provide the Lao government, ADB, and other international donors with a comprehensive, current interpretation of education conditions, provide a set of recommendations, identify priorities, and develop an investment plan around suggested programs. Integral to this technical assistance project were (1) encouragement of policy dialogue involving, as participants, Lao officials, "other stakeholders," and the consulting team and (2) demonstration of the use of research and data analysis in establishing education priorities and strategies as part of national planning in Lao PDR. In preparation of its reports, the ADB team of international and Lao consultants was not expected to conduct extensive original research, but rather to review any existing research, interpret it, and validate other relevant available data and information. New or different knowledge and insights were expected, essentially, to emerge from such collaborative analysis and from the expected dialogue and the "constructed" synthesis developed by the consultants and their counterparts in the Lao Ministry of Education. From the viewpoint of ADB, ideally the forthcoming national 2001–2005 Education Plan would reflect the analyses of the ADB consulting team and incorporate the recommendations of its final report.

The Sector Assessment was developed over a five-month period in 1998–1999 with consultant contracts of varying lengths. The activities of the ADB team were coordinated by the Department of Planning and Cooperation (DPC) within MOE,[23] and each international consultant had as a counterpart an official from MOE, typically the deputy director of a department. Involvement of stakeholders in the development of the sector analysis and investment plan was largely limited to MOE officials. However, a national workshop and investigative trips into the provinces (supplemented with mailed surveys) permitted some interaction with personnel from Provincial Education Services (PES) and District Educational Services (DES) as well as direct contact with a few parent school committees.[24]

Discussion here is limited to three major priorities for developing a more effective Lao education system identified in the Sector Assessment.

1. *Providing an adequate recurrent budget for the education sector.* The Lao education investment budget is subsidized heavily by international donors,[25]

and the requirements for recurrent funds to complement investments often have not been carefully planned or the government may not have the resources for such recurrent funds. For example, some projects of school construction have not fully specified complementary recurrent funds to pay teachers, purchase day-to-day teaching supplies, and carry out necessary school maintenance.

The international and Lao consultants working on the ADB project developed a financial model to provide estimates of yearly recurrent costs for the years 2000–2005. The model allowed examination of the future behavior of the core system and the effects of implementing the recommendations of the Sector Assessment. The direct research inputs to development and application of the model included analyses of unit costs of schooling, enrollment progression rates of primary schooling, future educational needs (estimated based on assumptions of growth and development of the economy), and characteristics of Lao PDR's education and economy compared with other poor Asian countries. The investment model was discussed with and had input from a steering committee composed of department directors from MOE. Reviews in its developmental stage also took place with the Ministry of Finance.

*2. Continuing to strengthen basic education.* All Lao children have a constitutional right to education. However, as noted earlier, there are significant geographic, ethnic, gender, and wealth disparities in distribution of education services. Schools are simply not available in many remote areas. Teachers, particularly in rural areas, are inadequately prepared, have few materials of instruction, and are poorly (and often infrequently) paid. In the absence of adequate central support many local areas, often with support from nongovernmental organizations (NGOs) but with little central guidance, are making great sacrifice to maintain and repair school buildings, provide housing for teachers, and assist particularly needy students. In order to address concerns with both access and efficiency, two central recommendations of the ADB team were for expansion of multigrade teaching to extend availability of complete primary schooling and redeployment of teachers to areas of high demand. Other major recommendations especially directed toward quality improvement were to direct more resources to (1) teacher salaries, (2) school and classroom levels for teaching and instructional materials, and (3) regular maintenance of schools.

A priority to further develop basic education was perhaps a foregone conclusion before the Sector Assessment was undertaken. Over the last decade ADB has become strongly committed to giving priority to adequate basic education in less developed member countries. This commitment has grown out of international calls for "education for all"[26] and from international research showing the effects of basic education on the life chances of individuals, the quality of family life, and the economic and social development of societies.[27] Given the low net primary enrollment ratio, exceedingly high dropout rates, the wide disparities of opportunities for schooling across and within provinces, and, generally, the low quality of instruction, ADB readily and consistently identified improved basic education as the highest priority. The Lao government has agreed with this priority.

The Sector Assessment team, in collaboration with researchers from MOE, engaged in a number of small-scale studies that at least indirectly may have influenced the development of enacted policy and subsequently may impact on policy implementation. These included validation of such standard indicators as dropout, repetition, and progression rates; mapping distribution of primary school students by gender, age, and ethnicity across provinces; and cost analyses for policies related to different scenarios for expanding the system at all levels. Explicit research carried out by the project team led to adjustments in certain indicators being used by MOE and to modification of existing and forecasted dropout and repetition rates. Mapping variations in access and efficiency at the provincial and district levels led to MOE discussions of localized distribution of allocated resources. The results of theses studies were discussed with the Steering Committee but not directly with the Leading Committee of the education sector. During its development the Sector Assessment was reviewed and to a degree redefined through meetings with the steering committee, national workshops that included education officials at all levels, and a full-day presentation to a broad spectrum of ministry officials and the donor community.

The timing of the team's research was crucial to its effects. For example, in the studies related to the distribution of schooling the findings of the project team were reinforced by an important investigation carried out by an international team prior to the Sector Assessment. Research undertaken by Mingat and colleagues[28] described the mismatch between teacher supply and demand by quantifying the oversupply and undersupply of teachers across provinces and districts. These researchers also quantified the cost savings of equitable teacher redeployment. Because rural areas of Lao PDR have many incomplete (two to four years) primary schools, a suggestion for redeployment of teachers was coupled with the policy recommendation of utilizing multigrade schools and multigrade teachers as needed. Before the Sector Assessment was completed the explicit recommendation to increase access to basic education by use of multigrade teaching and teacher redeployment received verbal support from the minister of education and, thus, at minimum, became an component of rhetorical policy.

3. *Maintaining balance in the development of the education system.* The basic legal, administrative, and curricula requirements for a functioning, articulated Lao educational system are in place. A major task of policy makers and planners is to help plan and shape a system that allows and encourages complete cycles of learning at each system level. Additionally, as enrollments expand, new pathways need to be developed for education and training and for transferability across programs. A major task of administrators and teachers is to

improve the efficiencies of existing programs and to participate in adapting their operationalization to reflect evolving priorities. However, the Lao system in a number of ways is not "balanced." As one example, the rapid expansion of new entrants to secondary school is occurring outside of any formal planning effort. An early consequence of such uncontrolled expansion can be that an increased proportion of the limited education budget will be diverted to a rapidly expanding secondary education, resulting in greater difficulty in achieving the highest priority, that is, universalizing adequate primary education.

Joint efforts of the project team and MOE researchers were able to verify existing enrollment data, demonstrate the cost implications of recent enrollment trends, consider multiple future enrollment scenarios, and discuss the effects of different enrollment patterns on agreed-upon priorities. The team was able to demonstrate that continuation of recent growth rates in secondary education would not be sustainable if the goals of basic education were to be met. Projections of enrollment growth rates for primary and secondary education from 1996 to 2005 show a significant change in the relative size of the subsectors. Given the higher unit cost of secondary education, financing such system growth would probably not be possible. For a balanced system in terms of agreed-upon priorities expansion of each level of the system needs to take place within a planning framework. This analysis and conclusion were discussed at length with MOE directors. The information was seen as important but not necessarily compelling. Some directors remained committed to giving high priority to both primary and secondary education.

## Building a Research Tradition to Improve the Effectiveness of Educational Governance, Policy, and Planning

Building a tradition and larger body of relevant education research and increasing the utilization of research in the policy and planning processes of Lao PDR, at minimum, require two major sets of actions: (1) modifying the Lao pattern of educational governance, planning, and management and (2) developing a more effective role for donors. Neither set of actions by itself necessarily guarantees rapid increases in research-based policy dialogue. Both of these changes are fundamental to the production, analysis, and use of research-based information. However, both sets of actions are complex, require long-term commitment, and can be aborted at any time.

### Improving Educational Governance, Planning, and Management

In Lao PDR, as in many countries, detailed planning mechanisms may help give policy an illusion of objectivity and detachment. However, in Lao PDR policy development is a nontransparent process centered on deliberations of the party. Moreover, a number of international and Lao observers have commented on the shortcomings in management in the Lao public sector.[29] Reviews of administrative behavior emphasize such characteristics as (a) cautious behavior of bureaucrats; (b) lack of technical, including evaluation, skills; (c) insufficient commitment to strategic planning; (d) absence of functioning information systems; (e) little horizontal communication across ministries and departments within ministries; and (f) reduced organizational memory because of frequent transfers of personnel.[30]

Effective educational governance, planning, and management may require a different model, one characterized by the reduction in politicization of policy, extension of participation in education decisions, promotion of policy-related institutional and individual research, and recognition of an educational role for the private sector.[31] The newer model implies that certain responsibilities should be assumed at the national, while others need to be fulfilled at the local, level.[32] At the national level such responsibilities include developing and sustaining equity in attaining basic education, developing and implementing R & D programs, developing demonstration and experimental programs, and evaluating and disseminating information on the behavior of the educational system. At the provincial and local levels such responsibilities include facilitating communication and exchange networks, better utilization of supervisors and supervision, and analysis and feedback to schools of data forwarded from the school level. Given the old responsibilities carried forward and the newly acquired authorities, major long-term training and capacity-building efforts will be crucial.

How quickly can adoption and implementation of such roles be expected in Lao PDR? The political significance of the education sector in the country's future is recognized increasingly by the Lao government. Moreover, the education bureaucracy that extends from the center to the village level contributes both to central control and legitimacy. Under these conditions political decentralization in Lao PDR during the next few years appears unlikely. Giving up political power, including control of patronage, and reforming bureaucracies that are nested in the centralized system could thus weaken both party and government and probably will not happen without significant pressure internally from stakeholders and externally from major international donors. However, administrative decentralization already underway may be expected to expand.[33] The relatively slow speed with which these changes take place may be of concern to those recommending a swifter expansion in responsibilities and participation of local communities, teachers, and school managers. At the same time we should remember that a swift transfer of financial, planning, and personnel problems to the community level without preparation could be a managerial disaster.[34]

Data and information regularly collected and analyzed by the MOE largely serve routine administrative reporting requirements rather than planning and management purposes. However, several recent developments are promising to extend policy and planning discussions: New MOE units allocating resources to girls' education and private education have been created, and a major attempt at lateral coordination—including a cross-department strategic planning committee—is underway. Another promising development is the information systems being developed within several departments of the MOE. At present, these systems are not completely operational, failing to collect and process all necessary data and not effectively linked together to serve system-level planning. The challenge to using more fully existing information capabilities is both a technical and a management issue.

As the various forms of localization unfold, policy and planning decisions may be shared more widely.[35] Faced with such day-to-day crises as teacher absenteeism and collapse of facilities, however, administrators may give low priority to research information. And it is not likely that national policies and decrees will be sufficient to motivate increased involvement and use of data analysis by administrators at the province, district, and school levels. Planners need to consider what incentives, economic or professional, are necessary to stimulate local initiatives, organizations, or networks to develop and take root.

*Refining the Roles of Donors*

According to documents of the World Bank (WB) and the ADB, two of the largest international donors in education in Asia, the donor-country relationship should emphasize collaboration and partnership in activities in education when donor financing is involved. ADB-sponsored sector assessments and subsequent program and project technical assistance, thus, are expected to be defined and refined through extensive and continuing dialogue involving ADB personnel with government officials and "other" stakeholders. In the Lao case these expectations were not fully met.

During the Sector Assessment there were frequent exchanges between team members and MOE counterparts. Typically, however, these did not constitute a process in which information needs were collaboratively defined and interpretations were intensely examined over time, allowing maximum mutual learning to take place. Working relationships were cordial and, particularly in the early stages of the project, some support within MOE could be found for the importance of developing dialogue between team members and MOE officials. Informal evidence, however, suggests that there were not many senior officials who shared the team's enthusiasm for these open discussion and transparent decision-making processes such an approach tends to foster. Thus, interactions between international consultants and counterparts often focused on identification of specific information needs rather than collaborative inquiry or analysis. Extensive transferring of personnel during the project, with many officials, including the director of DPC, changing positions within MOE, required the establishment of new relationships. Moreover, the changes in personnel took place over a period of several weeks during which time the focus of attention of officials tended to be on their indefinite future.

Despite a number of discussions involving team members and MOE counterparts to clarify the working relationships, some differences in role perceptions persisted. Time constraints affected the behavior of both MOE officials and ADB consultants. Officials received no released time for project assistance. Consultants, for their part, were required to produce a series of reports by specific dates and they sometimes viewed "dialogue" as persuading officials of their interpretations. Moreover, both international and Lao consultants had limited experience in participating in prolonged dialogue. The MOE counterparts and other involved MOE officials tended to see themselves essentially as informants whose function was to add knowledge and correct misconceptions of consultants. Working closely in a collaborative manner with donors was not an experience with which they were comfortable or highly familiar. Further, in attempting to reach closure in discussions and agreement on interpretations of issues or interventions, satisfying internal politics took precedent over meeting the expectations of external clients, for example, international donors.

For the next several years international donors are expected to continue to make major, perhaps crucial, contributions to Lao education development. What can be done to make the involvement of donors more effective in collaboration with Lao policy makers in development and utilization of relevant research based information?

*1. The concept of donor-country partnership should be better operationalized.* ADB, WB, and other donors widely use the term "partnership" when characterizing their relationship with recipient countries. The concept of partnership would seem to suggest that both donor and country benefit from this relationship and that this benefit is best arrived at when a task (agreement) is conducted in an egalitarian manner. The brief description earlier of relationships of an ADB project team and MOE officials suggests a few of the operational difficulties in "partnerships." The dimensions of ownership within a "partnership" or other collaborative efforts must be made clear and subsequently demonstrated by trust, opportunities to take risks, and tolerance of mistakes as policies, plans, and projects evolve and change. Developing a more mutually beneficial relationship between donor and Lao government may be difficult and probably frustrating. However, even incremental progress in this area may help achieve mutual goals.

*2. Mutual learning should characterize training programs.* Both ADB and WB have emphasized that a major role in recipient countries in the coming decade will be capacity building and developmental processes related to policy making and management that extend from the center to the management of schools. However, the need for capacity building can apply to both the Lao government and donors. Thus, actions initially might include a joint program of capacity building focused on the Lao government as well as ADB. This joint program should be based upon understandings of how these two bureaucracies set priorities, formulate plans, and evaluate their results and should offer better advance preparation for actors in the recipient country and the international consultants for participation in information-based dialogue. Such training would assist in developing in both organizations research-friendly leadership that appreciates, seeks, and uses information. Training should concentrate on the interactions of research, policy, and planning as the interactions attempt to clarify the complexities of educational change. Understanding the potential benefits and serious constraints of informed dialogue is a precondition of planned change. But research, to be utilized, must appeal to politicians-bureaucrats in terms of their professional challenges and political constraints. Senior bureaucrats, whether in the Lao government or ADB, need to interpret the congruence of proposed changes with their organizations' principles. They need to judge which key stakeholders win or lose, what the costs are, and who pays. In the real world of planned change partnerships are bounded, and when the boundaries are clear, the likelihood of implementation is increased.

*3. Longer-term donor commitment should be negotiated.* Problems of policy and program planning, implementation, and long-term sustainability are a concern of the Lao government and donors. A new mechanism, Adaptable Program Loans (APLs), has been proposed by the World Bank and is designed to provide phased and sustained support through a series of loans, for the implementation of long-term development programs. In general, each phase of a seven- to ten-year supported program would last three to five years. APLs are expected to allow for greater flexibility in adapting project design and financing over time to meet development objectives as borrower conditions and partnerships evolve. This particular mechanism may not become WB or ADB policy, and at least some Lao officials believe that APLs would restrict flexibility in rethinking priorities. Nevertheless, some extended commitment is necessary for improved long-term technical assistance simply because the complexity of educational issues often will not yield to quick solutions but requires continuous management. Thus, the need for data analysis and insightful information persists. Even well-developed research-informed policy planning over time will not eliminate the complexities of education; such planning may help in understanding how to cope with the ongoing problems and perhaps how to chip away at the many mysteries of educational change.

*4. Research capacity and research tradition should be developed.* For the next several years prospective Lao educational researchers will need to receive their advanced training outside of Lao PDR. Good, short-term specialist training programs are available in neighboring Asian countries, often sponsored by regional organizations. Long-term training typically translates into multi-year graduate programs in highly industrialized countries. The latter programs, in particular, suggest an investment of such magnitude as to warrant careful monitoring. Unfortunately, graduate degrees abroad do not automatically produce effective researchers.

A range of both quantitative and qualitative research models and methods can be relevant to support policy making and planning in Lao PDR. The roles played and skills needed by researchers vary across policy development, implementation, monitoring, and evaluation phases and according to the decision-making process. Statistical analysis has been the stock-in-trade of researchers in formulation of policy and developing strategic plans, and remains a core technology. As policy making and planning become more participatory, users become key stakeholders, and dialogue merges with inquiry, qualitative research approaches also become crucially important. For example, when considering program and project monitoring and evaluation, researchers may need to cope with involvement of multiple local actors and capture tacit knowledge in deciding how programs should be investigated and results utilized.

In addition to the usual role of producer of knowledge, talented researchers can play many other respected roles in contributing to educational reforms. One common and important role is to make regional and international information part of ongoing policy dialogue. Influences from research, plans, and practices from other countries may bring benefits, extending and deepening meaningful policy dialogue and discussion about successful innovations and reforms. However, the researcher must become a critic, for some of the educational concerns and capabilities of Lao PDR may be different from those of neighbors and, most assuredly, are different from many of those of the highly industrialized countries. In some countries the linkage between research and policy comes through appointment of researchers as major decision makers, for example, director-generals or ministers of education. Occasionally those who are familiar with both research and practice become knowledge brokers who communicate research findings to political and policy actors and clarify for researchers information needs of policy makers. Given the current status and relative youthfulness of researchers, such is unlikely to take place in Lao PDR in the near future.

**Conclusion**

Policy development in Lao PDR is politicized, with control highly centralized in the Lao People's Democratic Party and structured to reach from the center to the village level. The process of making or avoiding major educational choices includes only a narrow range of stakeholders and lacks transparency. The processes of policy making and national planning have tended to avoid uncertainties and complexities and as a consequence have ignored the potentially central place of data gathering and analysis in educational decision making.

An optimistic scenario of policy making and planning in Lao PDR in the year 2010 would describe a local capability to assess education needs and collect and analyze data, an expanded research unit in MOE and the beginnings of nongovernmental research capabilities in education, middle level management in MOE with formal training in the technology of modern planning and program evaluation, and top leadership in government (and international donor agencies) who understand and advocate the use of research-based information in negotiating, constructing, and implementing policy.

In considering future potential for policy dialogue in education informed by research in Lao PDR it is important to understand that actions to extend the use of research in improving policy, planning, and management must go beyond acquisition of a few new specific skills by education officials. In addition to technical requisites, such planned systemic change in education requires experienced planning and policy bodies and leadership that are part of a structure of national decision making. Such a structure would (1) generate a shared strategic vision that systems, and not their parts, are the overarching concern of policy makers and strategic planners; (2) create a willingness of involved institutions to share information; (3) demonstrate political will for implementing stringent measures; and (4) negotiate effective partnerships with donors. The further development of such capabilities, at minimum, requires significant fiscal resources, long-term capacity building of institutions of planning, evaluation, and administration. Given adequate funding and collaboration between donors and the Lao government, the necessary technical skills may be acquired over a few years; how quickly the Lao society and government can commit to utilization of technical knowledge and fully adapt to open decision processes and participatory planning is more difficult to predict.[36]

These observations do not ignore the many examples of positive changes identified earlier and are currently are underway in Lao PDR. However, these and other specific changes grow and flourish best when they accompany or follow fundamental changes in the organizational and policy environment.

## Notes

1. This chapter was originally published in the special issue of the *Comparative Education Review* [45 (2) (May 2001): 220–41] focused on "The Relationship between Theorists/Researchers and Policy Makers/Practitioners."
2. Fernando Reimers and Noel McGinn, *Informed Dialogue: Using Research to Shape Education Policy around the World* (Westport, CT: Praeger, 1997), pp. 21–28.
3. M. Lockheed and A. Verspoor, *Improving Primary Education in Developing Countries* (Washington, DC: The World Bank, 1991), B. Fuller and P. Clarke, "Raising School Effects While Ignoring Culture? Local Conditions and the Influence of Classroom Tools, Rules and Pedagogy," *Review of Educational Research* 64 (1) (1994); A. Hargreaves, A. Liberman, M. Fullan, and D. Hopkins (eds.), *International Yearbook of Educational Change* (Dordrecht: Kluwer, 1998), Parts 1 and 2.
4. World Bank, *World Development Report: The State in a Changing World* (New York: Oxford, 1997); Yidan Wang, Public-Private Partnerships in the Social Sector: Issues and Country Experiences in Asia and the Pacific (Tokyo: Asian Development Bank Institute, March 2000).
5. Merilee S. Grindle and John Thomas, *Public Choices and Policy Change: The Political Economy of Reform in Developing Countries* (Baltimore: Johns Hopkins University Press, 1991); T. Hussein, "Education, Research and Policy Making," in *International Encyclopedia of Education*, 2nd ed. (Oxford: Pergamon Press), pp. 1857–64; Henry Mintzberg, *The Rise and Fall of Strategic Planning* (Toronto: The Free Press, 1994); Henry Mintzberg, Bruce Ahlstrand, and Joseph Lampell, *Strategic Safari* (New York: The Free Press, 1998).
6. Reimers and McGinn, Chapters 4, 5, 6.
7. C. E. Lindblom, *Inquiry and Change* (New Haven, CT: Yale University Press, 1990); J. Friedmann, *Planning in the Public Domain: From Knowledge to Action* (Princeton, NJ: Princeton University Press, 1987); D. Adams, "Extending the Educational Planning Discourse: Conceptual and Paradigmatic Explorations," *Comparative Education Review* 32 (1988): 400–15.

8. Reimers and McGinn, Chapter 6.
9. One set of outputs of the Sector Assessment includes a comprehensive education sector analysis identifying trends, problems, and priority interventions for each subsector within education. The second general output, presented separately but substantively integrated with the first, is an investment plan suggesting overall education investment and priority projects for the period 2000–2005. Neither the contractor (Hickling Corporation, Ottawa, Canada), ADB, the Lao government, nor other involved consultants necessarily agree with the views expressed here.
10. ADB, *Social Sector Profiles Study: LAO PDR* (Manila: ADB, 1998).
11. IMF, *Lao Peoples Democratic Republic: Recent Economic Developments. IMF Staff Country Report No. 98/77* (Vientiane: IMF, 1998); Lao PDR, National Statistics Centre, *Lao Expenditure and Consumption Survey (LECS)* (Vientiane: National Statistics Centre, 1997). Lao PDR, National Statistics Centre, *Basic Statistics about the Socioeconomic Development in Lao PDR* (Vientiane: National Statistics Centre, 1996).
12. Lao PDR remains overwhelmingly an agricultural country, with over 80 percent of the workforce engaged in subsistence agriculture. The largest grouping of employment is in the informal or self-employed sector and unpaid family workers. The smallest grouping is found in the formal sector of the economy, the civil service, and those working as employees in state enterprises, joint government/private ventures, and the private sector. This latter group, formal sector employment outside the civil service, is expected to grow as further economic growth takes place. It is also the core group usually thought of as the target for education programs especially designed to provide the knowledge and skills for economic development.
13. ADB, *Lao PDR, Country Profile* (Manila: ADB, 1995).
14. ADB, *Lao PDR Women's Education Project* (Manila: Final Report, March 1997); ADB, *Social Sector Profiles Study: Lao PDR* (Manila: ADB, 1998). UNICEF, *UNICEF and Lao Women's Union and Development for Women and Families 1998–2002* (Vientiane: UNICEF, 1998). J. Chagnon, *Women in Development: Lao People's Democratic Republic* (Manilla: Asian Development Bank, 1996).
15. D. Adams (ed.), *Education and National Development in Asia: Trends, Issues, Policies, and Strategies* (Manila: ADB, 1998). This study examined regional trends among the forty member countries of ADB. Five booklets related to the study are being published jointly by the Asian Development Bank and the Comparative Education Research Centre, The University of Hong Kong.
16. The data source for these indicators is UNDP (*Human Development Report*, [Paris: UNDP, 1997], p. 123). The HDI (Human Development Index) is a simple average of the life expectancy index, educational attainment index, and adjusted real GDP per capita (PPP$) index. HPI (Human Poverty Index) measures deprivation using the same dimensions as the HDI. "The variables used are the percentage of people expected to die before age 40, the percentage of adults who are illiterate, and overall economic provisioning in terms of the percentage of people without access to health services and safe water and the percentage of underweight children under five" (Ibid., p. 14). The GDI (Gender-related Development Index) also uses the same variables as the HDI—life expectancy index, educational attainment index, and adjusted real GDP per capita (PPP$) index. "The difference is that the GDI adjusts the average achievement of each country in life expectancy, educational attainment, and income in accordance with the disparity in achievement between women and men" (Ibid., p. 123).
17. MOE, *Education Development Programs, 2001–2005* (Vientiane: MOE, 1998).
18. ADB, *Future Strategic Directions: Lao PDR Human Development* (Manila: ADB, 1996).
19. ADB, *Lao PDR Country Profile* (Manila: ADB, 1995); UNDP, *Organisation of the Government of the Lao PDR* (Vientiane: The Prime Minister's Office, 1996); B. Boase, *Public Administration Reform in the Lao PDR: An Assessment and Future UNDP Public Administration Project* (Vientiane: UNDP, 1996).
20. State Planning Committee, *Planning and Reporting Reference Manual for Provincial Authorities, Vol. 1., Guidelines for Planning, Project Documentation and Reporting: Lao People's Democratic Republic* (Vientiane: SPC, February 1998).
21. MOE, *Education Sector Development Plan, 1996–2000* (Vientiane: MOE, 1995); MOE, *Mid-Term Education Plan 1997–2000* (Vientiane: MOE, 1998); Ministry of Education, *The National Education Strategy 2001–2020 (Draft)* (Vientiane: MOE, 1998).

22. Operational responsibility for implementing primary and secondary education rests with local arms of MOE, i.e., the Provincial Education Service (PES) and District Education Bureau (DEB). PES reports to the governor or, in the case of municipality, to the mayor. The governor, technically equivalent to a minister in rank, has considerable power in establishing intersectoral priorities and appointments of PES personnel. Moreover, provincial governors have discretionary funds that they may allocate to the education sector. The DEB, the lowest branch of the national educational administration, assists schools and communities in their planning of primary and preprimary education and prepares district plans for each academic year and each school term.

23. Within MOE, the relatively new Department of Planning and Cooperation (DPC) is designated as the unit that coordinates education relationships with international organizations. DPC has assumed the responsibilities for all short- and long-term education sector planning and in this role must coordinate the plans of all MOE departments and manage internationally funded projects. The departments in MOE, all of which are involved in subsector planning, lack supporting technical skills and experience in coordinating efforts to engage in strategic, sector-level planning [MOE, *Decree No. 4361. ED. Regulations of Educational Staff* (Vientiane: MOE, 1994)].

24. To facilitate collaboration and develop a policy and planning dialogue involving MOE personnel and the consulting team, frequent formal and informal meetings were held between the team members and their counterparts. The director of DPC supported the idea of continuing interaction between team and MOE members and during his time in office met at least once a week with the team leader. The structure of interaction between team members and counterparts typically consisted of (1) one-on-one meetings initiated by the international members of the consulting team with their counterparts and (2) group meetings that included a broad range of MOE senior staff. Participation in meetings or workshops, when concern focused on major issues or draft interim reports of the team, included other international donors and other Lao ministries. The workshop in which the final report was presented included MOE personnel, donor groups, and representation from relevant other ministries.

25. On the two indicators devoted to public expenditures spent for education, the percent of GDP and percent of total public expenditures, Lao PDR ranks below the economically faster growing countries of Asia. However, the largest contrast with other Asian countries lies in the division between recurrent and development expenditures. The ADB team could find comparable data from no other Asian country in which recurrent expenditures was as low a percentage of GNP as in Lao PDR.

26. For details regarding the World Conference on Education for All, held in Bangkok, Thailand, March 5-9, 1990, see UNESCO, *World Conference on Education For All: Catalogue of Documents* (Paris: UNESCO, 1990); UNESCO, *Aftermath of the World Conference on Education for All* (Bangkok, Thailand: UNESCO Principal Regional Office for Asia and the Pacific, 1992).

27. Asian Development Bank, *Women in Development: Issues, Challenges and Strategies in Asia and the Pacific* (Manila: ADB, 1994); M. Lockheed & A. Verspoor, *Improving Primary Education in Developing Countries* (Washington, DC: The World Bank, 1991); M. E. Young, *Investing in Young Children* (Washington, DC: The International Bank for Reconstruction and Development/The World Bank, 1995).

28. A. Mingat et al., *Elements on the Cost and Financing of Education in Lao PDR* (Dijon, France: University of Dijon, 1996); A. Mingat, *Assessment of Some Basic Education Policy Issues in Lao PDR from a Cost and Financing Analysis* (Dijon, France: University of Dijon, 1998).

29. For example, see ADB, *Institutional Strengthening of the Social Sciences* (Manila: ADB, 1996).

30. B. Boase, *Public Service Reform in the Lao PDR: An Assessment of the Future* (Vientiane: UNDP, 1996); World Bank, *Lao PDR: Financing and Management of Education, Strategic Considerations for Strengthening the Education Sector* (Vientiane: World Bank, 1997).

31. See also ADB, *Medium-Term Strategic Framework 1995–1998* (Manila: The President's Office, March 1995); Vieira da Cunha and Maria Valeria Junho Pena, *The Limits and Merits of Participation* (Washington, DC: World Bank, 1997).

32. The preferred model is based on certain assumptions, for example, that (1) lasting improvements in educational quality require knowledge and insights of those professionals and stakeholders from different levels of the system, including those closest to the processes of teaching and learning (e.g., teachers, principals, supervisors); (2) planning is a generative process and opens new communication channels to help dialogue at all levels and initiate

actions; (3) local-level personnel and institutions, by themselves, often lack fiscal and technical resources to affect continuing change; (4) parental and community involvement are necessary in both the planning and implementation of successful educational change; (5) research and evaluation to be utilized must focus on problems relevant to particular phases of policy and planning cycles and to particular sets of stakeholders; and (6) new, simple, user-friendly techniques for assessment of educational quality and efficiency are needed to support increased participation of teachers and school-level administrators in decision making.

33. Within the current context of nation building, and under strong centrist control, there are, nevertheless, certain local initiatives in education decision making. Even under severe fiscal constraints well-managed, productive schools can be found throughout Lao PDR. Communities realizing that limited fiscal or technical support will be forthcoming from the center have begun to assume certain management responsibilities for their own schools.

34. The difficulty and complexity of planning and management are not diminished through increased participation and localization of functions. Indeed, many persisting issues and problems of the center will be revisited at local levels and many of the technical skills needed in the center will also be needed in the provinces and districts. Further, under deconcentration, new problems may emerge related to resource generation, resource allocation, and staff development. Both administrative and political reforms in Lao PDR need to consider the possible negative consequences of reinforcing or extending the education gaps between the comparatively advantaged and the disadvantaged areas. Efficiency gains through better management and in the delivery of locally relevant schooling may be traded for increased burdens for the poor communities and regions both in the provision of schooling and in the quality of instruction within schools. Should decentralization include additional costs to parents, only central authorities may be able to ensure that poor communities and poor parents are provided necessary financial support.

35. D. Adams, *Education and National Development in Asia*.

36. As new approaches to policy making and planning inch their way into Lao PDR, important questions persist: To what extent can the single political party accept open policy dialogue? Can the political leadership achieve its goals through a more decentralized and participatory decision making process in education? Or, what are the political costs of a new model of policy making, planning, and management built on transparency, research-generated information, and commitment to continued inquiry? Under what conditions does participation create better school or system performance? What categories of education policy should be subjected to dialogue? What range of options will local communities demand? How much variation in education programs across communities is tolerable in the center? Without political commitment, what are the limitations of administrative reforms in reducing corruption in the utilization of resources? Must Lao PDR first have ownership of the process of knowledge production before significant capacity building can take place and before research can influence policy? Under what conditions does reform follow capacity building? In sum, how long will it take in Lao PDR to transform policy making and routine planning into powerful processes of inquiry and reform? Explicit answers to these questions need not necessarily precede reform but need to be integral to policy dialogue.

CHAPTER 4

# Teacher Peripheralization in Comparative Education
## Causes, Consequences, and Some Responses[1]

PAUL R. FOSSUM
PATRICIA K. KUBOW

**Introduction**

Not all concepts originate with self-proclaimed scholars, that is, with specialists in the manipulation of ideas and large bodies of data. Many, indeed perhaps most, concepts originate among participants in the "real world." And scholars are sometimes among the last, rather than the first, to perceive the utility of these concepts.[2]

This volume grapples with a concern often voiced in the field of comparative education as elsewhere throughout the social sciences—namely, that of effectively addressing gaps between theory and practice. The dominant analyses of this theory/practice divide have productively questioned interactions between two different cultures engaged in educational work—particularly within the policy arena at large. But as Ginsburg and Gorostiaga have suggested in Chapter one, viewing the theory-to-practice divide strictly as a mismatch of cultures—in simple terms between a culture of knowledge users and a culture of knowledge producers—is limited. The cultural difference model tends to rely on stereotypical conceptions of both the theorist/researcher and the policy maker/practitioner cultures; it often ignores or underestimates the heterogeneity of the members of each culture, and it can neglect the fact that the boundary separating the two groups is less permeable than assumed.

We aim in this chapter to draw attention to a further limitation of the cultural difference outlook. Specifically, the model's explanation of the theory-to-practice problem presumes that policy makers' main cultural affiliations lie with the practitioner. Because of the ways in which knowledge is valued and produced, policy makers are in important respects more clearly aligned with theorists and researchers than with practitioners. While cultural and structural divisions between scholars and policy makers certainly constrain communication and dialogue between them in ways that other contributors to this volume have demonstrated, researchers and policy makers in other ways constitute an elite that occupies, we argue, the field's core terrain. From this vantage, then, it is the educational practitioner—the classroom teacher—who inhabits a separate (and peripheral) cultural realm.

Practitioners' detachment and exclusion from the discourses of comparative education mirror patterns of marginalization similar to those that theory within the field itself has critiqued, we argue. The history of comparative education's emergence and development as a field reflects how the ways knowledge is valued have affected teacher peripheralization. We argue also that the operative conception of "policy" within the policy circles of the academy, of ministries, and of transnational organizations is narrowed in a way that discards the practitioner's roles as lying outside the realm of policy, *per se,* and outside the arena of focus.[3] That situation further excludes practitioners from genuine participation in comparative education's discourses. The problematic definition of "policy" is best understood in terms of epistemological dissonance. The "melioristic" impetus of the research and policy network may facilitate interaction between researchers and policy makers,[4] but it tends to place teacher practitioners at the receiving end of a one-way flow of information and prescriptive suggestions. A more comprehensive definition of "policy" would arguably include practitioners and stress their vital roles as major implementers of policy.

Our discussion also provides examples of ways in which the epistemology of practical knowledge might be more suitably accommodated. Here, we emphasize ways in which practitioner participation in comparative education discourses can benefit teacher practitioners, but promises also to benefit theorists, researchers, and policy makers—those whose roles in shaping comparative education discourses and outputs have heretofore occupied the field's more central terrain.

As a society of scholars, we in comparative education appear to resemble other societies in that we have our own included and excluded strata. Despite the apparent cosmopolitanism of the field's questions, venues, disciplinary specialties, methodological identities, and personal associations, comparative education remains provincial and exclusive in important respects. By engaging teacher practitioners more generally, comparative education's discussions stand to become far more inclusive. This will warrant, among other steps, recognition of the ways in which knowledge has come to be produced and in which it continues to be valued.

## Practitioner Peripheralization and Exclusionary Discourse

In the field of comparative education, world systems theory frequently has been employed to analyze unequal political, economic, and educational relations among societies. We adopt world systems theory as a model for critiquing the community of comparative education, focusing on social relations of knowledge production and use. Systems theory asserts the existence of a global social structure or system, suggesting how some parties within this system exercise central or "core" positions and exploit the system's less powerful or "peripheral" parties.[5] The theory further suggests the existence of coalitions that bridge national boundaries, allying privileged sectors of core and peripheral members at the expense of less privileged sectors in different societies.[6] The same situation exists within comparative education. Like world societies, the field has its own patterns of unequal social relations. As such, the field functions as a society or system that has its own "core" and "peripheral" strata.

The systems perspective in our analysis, then, is transposed from its traditional role as an analytical tool employed *within* the field to a model used to critique the nature of the discourses *of* the field. The roles and interests of teachers are pressed toward the periphery in at least three ways. First, positivistic empirical forms of knowledge remain the norm, standard, or core for policy makers, administrators, and researchers. In fundamental respects, knowledge generated from positivistic investigations is not "practical" and is by its nature of limited suitability for teaching practice. Second, even researchers who pursue a non-positivistic tradition—in despite the fact that they often work more closely with teachers—tend to eschew generalization, leaving at the periphery the business of applying or extending the knowledge they produce. Third, the term "policy" itself is constructed in ways that tend to push teachers toward peripheral roles while drawing others, such as policy makers, researchers, and administrators, toward the center or core of policy activity. These circumstances contribute to the theory/practice problem in significant ways and have a substantial negative impact on comparative education discourses aimed at educational improvement. If genuine dialogue requires a sense of parity as well as reciprocity—as Freire[7] maintains—the ways in which knowledge is identified, accumulated, and propagated may limit or even preempt such dialogue between researchers and practitioners.

*Positivistic Knowledge at the "Core"*
Jürgen Habermas's epistemological critique offers an explanation for the limited success of the proposed classroom practices and policies emerging from social scientific processes.[8] Habermas associates the processes most readily deemed "scientific" with the pursuit of knowledge based on technical interest. "Science," from the technical perspective that Habermas critiques, tends necessarily to exclude practitioners precisely because of the specialized expertise and the controlled setting upon which the production of technical knowledge depends. Neither of these circumstances applies to the world of teachers. Teachers, instead, are likely to have a practical orientation toward discovering and valuing knowledge—a motive based upon "practical interest." If the social sciences were geared more toward the production of "practical knowledge," practitioners such

as teachers would occupy roles as capable analysts and producers of knowledge in their own right. But practitioner expertise receives short shrift in a world dominated by the pursuit and application of technical knowledge.

In line with the social sciences' movement to privilege the production and utilization of technical knowledge, comparative education has elevated knowledge associated with a technical interest as the desirable or "core" aim of scholarship on human phenomena. This corresponded with the effort by comparative educationists to move from the periphery to the firmer ground of a higher status within the academic core. Academic and administrative circles[9] join policy makers[10] in distinguishing themselves as members of a professional elite through their access to and expertise in this core form of knowledge, relegating knowledge associated with a practical interest—and practitioners such as teachers—to a more "peripheral" status.

Popkewitz has used the term "instrumentalized" to describe the net result of the favored position that technical knowledge asserts over teacher behavior—a circumstance under which teachers are essentially beholden to knowledge they have no meaningful role in creating. Moreover, Popkewitz has argued compellingly that, particularly in the United States, specialization in research helped administrators displace teachers as the country's recognized professional educators—not least because forging societal acceptance for administrative specialization created career paths from which women could be excluded.[11] Prescriptions for practice arising from the academy effectively distance the teacher practitioner from autonomy and meaningful decision making, a hallmark of the professional by many analyses.[12] Because the academic and administrative experts have assumed favored roles within social institutions like schools, context-sensitive conceptions of teaching have become discredited. Hence, research conducted by those outside the immediate environment, with less investment in the research findings, have been favored over research conducted by those closest to the issues or topics studied. The knowledge produced—and the proposed practices derived from such knowledge—through technical research are difficult to reconcile and integrate with classroom environments that are less controlled. Moreover, with pressure nonetheless to use this knowledge and adopt these practices as part of a policy directive, the practitioner's decision-making domain is further narrowed.

In some respects, the relationship between the school practitioner and the academic researcher is paradoxical and characterized by ambiguity. On the one hand, teachers continue to perceive academics as possessing exceptional expertise in the production and understanding of knowledge; on the other hand, the knowledge produced by academics is often rejected by teachers as opaque, overly esoteric, or otherwise less than useful.[13] What tends to be less ambiguous about this relationship, however, is that researchers continue to have considerable social—if not actual—distance from practitioners. Noting the degree to which university-based researchers and school-based teachers occupy separate worlds, for instance, Anderson and Herr observed that LeCompte, Millroy, and Preissle's *Handbook of Qualitative Research in Education*[14] "makes no reference to practitioner research in its 881 pages."[15]

*Limited Application of Nonpositivistic Research*

Positivistic empirical inquiry, then, adopts technical interest in seeking to objectify and manage nature; it is fundamentally rooted in this same imperative of lending predictability to natural environments. This, to be clear, is what is meant by positivistic empiricism's commitment to "prediction and control." Positivistic empiricism pursues control because of its aim in producing information that is "technically utilizable."[16] Despite its utility in many natural contexts, however, technical interest is limited in social situations, which, like teaching, emphasize human interaction in circumstances that are more unpredictable. Not all problems, in short, are subject to solution through technical interest's control orientation. Thus, paradoxically perhaps, while the notion of technical utility may ring of practicality, efforts undertaken in the name of technical interest are often ill suited in the social world, producing results that are "negative for people."[17] Genuine "practicality" is best supported by a way of valuing knowledge based upon practical interest.

Yet, despite heated "paradigm wars"—and notwithstanding growing acceptance of nonpositivist methodologies informed by interpretive and critical science—knowledge stemming from such approaches continues to be termed "alternative" even by those working within these approaches.[18] In addition, researchers who employ nonpositivist methodologies do so partly within the framework of legitimizing their own expertise as researchers. Because of the traditional structures and practices regarding rewards and advancement within the academy, researchers of all methodological stripes have a continuing interest in nurturing their reputations as scholarly authorities. Many academics embracing both nonpositivistic and positivistic epistemologies, therefore, share the goal of building and maintaining distance and difference from practitioners.

Comparative education's trait as a home of multidisciplinarity, of differing methodological persuasions, and of diversity of research orientations spanning basic and applied realms has not in general engendered the kind of inclusive discourse it might have. Positivistic research continues to satisfy the appetite of governments and international agencies for data thought to be more precise and indicative. Nonpositivist researchers, meanwhile, have not emphasized the value of their findings in practical terms, generally failing to capitalize on the human tendency to pursue the general from the specific.[19] The policy-enriching potential of certain perspectives and ways of knowing is elevated while the potential of others is diminished. In addition, however, nonpositivistic methods are often used for the positivistic aim of assessing the implementation of prescriptive policy.[20] Nonpositivistic researchers—themselves sometimes peripheralized as "less scientific"—are not strong advocates of the practical merits of their work.

This reinforces an even more excluded status for practitioners, who are often the focus of interpretive research work.

*The Peripheralizing Construction of "Policy"*

Egon Guba[21] distinguished three general definitions of "policy":

- "Policy-as-intention," focusing on statements about policy—on policy as a written product
- "Policy-in-implementation," describing the process of acting on policy
- "Policy-in-experience," which, unlike the other definitions, attends chiefly to policy from the viewpoint of those a policy most directly targets

Policy production in the field of comparative education and elsewhere has tended to emphasize policy-as-intention, although increasingly policy-in-implementation has become a focus of comparative educators engaging in research, evaluation, and technical assistance. In these instances, however, both policy-as-intention and policy-in-implementation tend to embrace technical approaches aimed at control and replication. While review of implementation issues suggests that policy-in-implementation is a more context-sensitive conception than policy-as-intention,[22] implementation study tends often to focus on the successes and failures concerning prescribed practices rather than on the generation of policy.

The field of comparative education has not accorded much attention to what is highlighted in the conception of "policy-in-experience," thus devaluing the pursuit of knowledge associated with a practical interest, with which teachers may be more likely to be identified.[23] The conceptions regarding which sort of knowledge is valued in the policy process and, thus, decisions as to who should be involved in the policy process have implications for the kind of interaction that occurs or does not occur in a field like comparative education. The kind of knowledge that practitioners hold about enacted educational policy should be central to the evaluation and modification of that policy. Yet the tendency to equate education policy with work outside the world of the practitioner further privileges technical knowledge over practical knowledge, excluding teachers from policy debates and other discourses within comparative education. Those associated with policy conception, adaptation, and adoption, regardless of their national identities as representatives of developed or developing societies, comprise a core constituency, while the implementers of these policies—often teachers—assume a peripheral role.[24]

The work of teachers and other front-line policy implementers "in the trenches" is often relegated to a lesser status, as knowledge gained within the field often is targeted to high policy circles, such as government bureaucracies and international organizations. Moreover, when action research is conducted by teacher practitioners on issues that are of great concern to them, the findings are discounted by academics and high-level policy makers as being distorted, biased, or subjective, on the grounds that teachers are "too close" to the topic under study. This line of thinking, then, marginalizes teachers' concerns, silences their voices on issues that are highly salient to education, stymies their initiatives to conduct their own research, and dismisses the knowledge of those whose responsibility is to implement educational policy at the most basic levels.

## Historical Roots of Teacher Peripheralization in Comparative Education

Arguably, then, the roots of teacher-practitioners' lack of engagement in the discourses of educational research and educational policy in general are epistemological in nature—and not solely a matter of cultural differences between teachers and researchers or policy makers. Further, the epistemological tensions, exemplified by the practical interests of teachers versus the technical interests of most comparative education researchers and policy makers, are linked with historical precedents concerning the development of the field of comparative education. Since comparative education uses the social sciences for disciplinary identity and for methodological mooring,[25] we will begin with a brief sketch of the history of the social sciences.

During their formation in the late nineteenth and early twentieth century, the social sciences embraced the production of technical knowledge, modeling themselves largely after the natural sciences. Among the several historical factors that coalesced to help precipitate this development, Darwin's successes were particularly important in compelling academics of the 1880s to believe "that 'real' science . . . built its theories closely on empirical observation."[26] While Darwin's interest was not altogether in controlling the natural circumstances he studied, his theories sought nonetheless to lend coherence and predictability to patterns that had seemed random, uncontrolled, and inexplicable prior to his inquiry. The end in view of scientific inquiry was therefore consciously dedicated to an epistemology of technical interest. In the wake of Darwin, scholars recast their work in evolutionary—and often biological—terms. Spencer's evolution-based theories, for instance, reinforced sociologists' impressions of their own scientific identity[27]—their sense that there was a discrete "sociology" distinguishable from the realm of economics with which it had been traditionally associated as a subfield.

In addition to the compelling nature of the grand theory of evolution, the throes of the Industrial Revolution further pressed the social sciences toward an epistemology supporting the production of technical knowledge. The so-called hard sciences enabled people to ameliorate limitations imposed by their physical environment, bringing sweeping change in transportation, architecture, and communication.[28] The discoveries that spurred industrialization—the invention of the engine, the creation of mechanized fabrication, and so forth—also spawned a number of pressing social challenges such as demographic displacement from rural to urban settings.[29] The societal expectation that emerged in tandem with this social upheaval was that the scientific model of technical discovery, if rigorously applied in human and social contexts, could be as powerful as it had been in material realms.[30]

The professional ideal of specialization is another factor central to the social sciences' movement toward an epistemology focused primarily on technical interest. In the United States,[31] the influences of the German *Universität* strengthened this principle[32]: Germany and the United States faced similar challenges in which "increasingly complex technology and social organization gave rise to an enlarged demand for educated specialists."[33] According to Ross, American academics studying in Germany were "impressed by the scientific success and the relatively high status"[34] of the professorate in that country, and thus sought to adopt the formal professional trappings, including graduate seminars, the Ph.D. degree, and journals and associations, of German institutional practices. Yet significantly, American academics embraced knowledge production through positivistic means but without a spirit of circumspection that had tended to remind their German counterparts of the limits of these forms of knowledge.[35]

Like the social sciences more generally, comparative education has also struggled to establish its own legitimacy as an academic pursuit and has followed a path that privileges the production of technical knowledge. Decades after Spencer, scholars in comparative education also adopted the language of biology in describing the world they sought to explore—King, describing schools as "social organisms," for instance.[36] Further, specialization within the field—in interpretive and naturalistic methods as well as in particular regions, in specific issue realms, and so forth—is quite evident, mirroring the specialization that has proliferated across the social sciences at large. The boundaries that have developed among various sectors within comparative education allow disparate perspectives to "agree to disagree" regarding divergent explanations for phenomena of broad general interest. Further, the sense of quasi-disciplinary boundedness that accompanies specialization in a particular content orientation or methodological perspective facilitates some sense of direction and unity within that interest area. On the other hand, communication across these interest specialties is more limited. And it is important to recognize that specialization appears to have given rise to intrafield disciplinary and methodological hierarchies. For instance, region-specialized naturalistic case research has offered legitimacy and stature within the field, but questions as to how the experiences of one region might inform the experiences of another are not routinely explored. Such generalization remains a province of the positivistic core in the field while the nonpositivist specialists continue to reside substantially in the periphery of the policy realm. The discourse that nonpositivistic research engenders is therefore insularized, occurring chiefly within subgroups of comparativists and not across the comparative education community as a whole.

## Conclusion

George Bereday stated that "it is self-knowledge born of the awareness of others that is the finest lesson comparative education can afford."[37] The intent of this chapter has not been to indict the field of comparative education as much as to suggest that the field might better open its arms to educator practitioners and might in this way make the work of comparative educators more useful in important ways. Not only might knowledge about education internationally be more fully grounded in practice, but such knowledge would also be drawn upon more often by practitioners.

Although one can readily find acknowledgment of the need to extend the conversation in the field to include teachers, the discourses within comparative education remain disconnected from and unresponsive to practitioner-oriented audiences. To remedy this problem, comparative educators should seek to open channels of communication between teachers and themselves as well as between teachers and policy makers. Such efforts might include expanding comparative education's use as a tool in pre-service and in-service teacher education, multiplying opportunities for teachers to participate in international education study tours and exchanges, and involving teachers more thoroughly as partners in international collaborative research and evaluation activities.

To foster communication (and perhaps joint reflection and action) by scholars, policy makers, and practitioners concerning critical issues in education around the world, comparative educators also need to reserve more space within conferences and publications for teachers and their viewpoints. For instance, at the U.S.-based Comparative and International Education Society's (CIES) recent annual meetings, sessions devoted to development agencies and aid organizations were plentiful. While these sessions are helpful in their way, no doubt, we need to consider how such sessions might promote the separation of a "policy circle" and might reify narrow and exclusive conceptions of policy. CIES has sought over the past few years to include school site visits and observations in local classrooms for comparative scholars at the conference's chosen venue, but more efforts toward involving practitioners and practitioners' voices in conference sessions are needed. Similar initiatives should be made to increase the participation of teachers in writing and reviewing journal articles, book chapters, and books in comparative education.

This core/periphery analysis of the field of comparative education suggests how the voices of practicing educators have been made peripheral by the field's preference for positivist forms of technical knowledge and by the way "policy" is conceived and policy making is structured by those in the field. Because the realms of practical knowledge tend to be devalued, the work of teaching and the voices of teachers tend to be relegated to the periphery of discourses in the field. Unless the field of comparative education wishes to endorse with its practices a view that administrators, but not teachers, are the schools' true professionals or that "high" policy makers rather than practitioners are the school's true policy shapers, teacher practitioners should be more involved in the field's discourses. If a primary purpose of comparative education is to improve educational policy and practice, educator practitioners must become and can become meaningful participants in the conversation (as well as joint reflection and action) in the field.

## Notes

1. This chapter is based in part on ideas developed in Patricia K. Kubow and Paul R. Fossum, in a book tentatively entitled *Comparative Education: Exploring Issues in International Context*. (Upper Saddle River, NJ: Prentice Hall/Merrill Education, in press).
2. Immanuel Wallerstein, *The Capitalist World Economy* (New York: Cambridge University Press, 1979), pp. x–xi.
3. For more on the recontextualization and translation of educational policy, see Stephen J. Ball "Big Policies/Small World: An Introduction to International Perspectives in Education Policy," *Comparative Education* 34 (2) (1998):119–30.
4. Joseph P. Farrell, "A Retrospective on Educational Planning in Comparative Education," *Educational Researcher* 41 (3) (1997):277–313, p. 278.
5. Wallerstein; also Immanuel Wallerstein, *The Modern World System* (New York: Academic Press, 1974).
6. Johan Galtung, *The True Worlds* (New York: Free Press, 1980).
7. Paulo Freire, *Pedagogy of the Oppressed* (New York: Seabury Press, 1970).
8. Jürgen Habermas, *Knowledge and Human Interests*, trans. J. Shapiro (Boston: Beacon Press, 1971). Habermas argues that "technical interest," which encourages the production of technical knowledge, is grounded in the human activity of work, interacting with the physical environment in order to "appropriate nature" (p. 28) to satisfy material needs—especially shelter and food. Habermas' "practical interest," which animates the production of practical knowledge, is a way of conceiving and valuing knowledge that has its grounding in the experience of human interaction. In supporting that claim, Habermas draws on Marx's contention that the production of goods through labor leads to social problems (e.g., how to distribute the surpluses accruing from their physical labor) that are beyond those of the technical imperatives of manipulating and appropriating nature. These kinds of social problems require human interaction geared toward the goal of practical human understanding—a goal that is much different from the aims of prediction and control associated with technical knowledge. Moreover, for Habermas, when practical action is separated from interaction in deference to the verifiable world of instrumental action characteristic of technical interest, communicative experience—a clear and authentic hallmark of the human social enterprise—is "eliminated in favor of repeatable experience" (p. 191).
9. Popkewitz Thomas S. Popkewitz, "Professionalization in Teaching and Teacher Education," *Teaching and Teacher Education* 10 (1) (1995): 1–14, p. 4, noted that in education, professionalism has "served as a slogan for those 'at the top,' including administrators and university professors, denoting specialization"—but, significantly, excluding practicing teachers.
10. Ball.
11. Notably, Donald Schön, unlike Popkewitz, has described the world of practice as subject to adjustments in technical means in order to suit aims that are stable and well understood [see Donald Schön, "The New Scholarship Requires a New Epistemology," *Change: The Magazine of Higher Education* 27 (6) (1995): 27–34]. Hence, Schön and Popkewitz reach opposite conclusions about the effects of the circumstances they describe on teacher professionalism. Schön's claim is that knowledge gained from theory and research and produced in the academy promises to elevate teaching professionally—presumably because the knowledge they deploy will be the product of the higher quality that specialization in research affords the academic. Schön's argument would be convincing if the results of prescriptive education improvement efforts were routinely successful. Yet efforts to bring the results of technical science to fruition within the unpredictable world of social practice have often been incomplete, disappointing, or frustrating. The social context that defines life in schools seems, by definition, to exist outside the realm of predictability and control. Thus, Popkewitz's critique of the overinstrumentalization of teacher behavior is compelling.

12. Myron Lieberman, *Education as a Profession* (Englewood Cliffs, NJ: Prentice Hall, 1956); R. Soder, *Professionalism and the Profession: Notes on the Future of Teaching,* Center for Education Renewal occasional paper no. 4 (Seattle: University of Washington, 1986).
13. David Hopkins, *A Teacher's Guide to Classroom Research* (Philadelphia: Open University Press, 1993); C. Argryris and Donald A. Schön, *Theory in Practice: Increasing Professional Effectiveness* (San Francisco: Jossey-Bass, 1975).
14. Margaret D. LeCompte, Wendy L. Millroy, and Judith Preissle (eds.), *The Handbook of Qualitative Research in Education* (San Diego: Academic Press, 1992).
15. Gary L. Anderson and Kathryn Herr, "The New Paradigm Wars: Is There Room for Rigorous Practitioner Knowledge in Schools and Universities?" *Educational Researcher* 28 (5) (1999): 12–22, p. 13.
16. Habermas, p. 76.
17. Cited in D. L. Coomer and F. H. Hultgren, "Considering Alternatives: An Invitation to Dialogue and Question," in *Alternative Modes of Inquiry in Home Economics Research,* ed. D. L. Coomer and F. H. Hultgren (Washington, DC: American Home Economics Association, 1989). Habermas's critique clearly challenges the hegemony of positivistic research. However, it is worth emphasizing that Habermas did not seek to reject "technical interest" and empiricism in general, but instead to remind us of the epistemological commitments of technical interest—and of the methods that must spring from such—and to reveal the limitations of technical knowledge in situations which, like teaching, emphasize human interaction in inherently unpredictable circumstances. Not all problems are subject to solution through technical interest's control orientation. People cannot, for instance, "fix" misunderstandings with other people through such simple remedies.
18. Coomer and Hultgren.
19. See Robert E. Stake, "The Case Study Method in Social Inquiry," *Educational Researcher* 6 (7) (1978): 5–8, for more on the human tendency to interpret particular and specific circumstances in terms that generalize to familiar realms.
20. Thus, nonpositivist researchers occupy a position similar to the *lumpen proletariat;* they benefit through their association with a privileged group—gaining access to an augmented pool of research funding and realizing increased institutional and disciplinary status, for instance—and ultimately through the continued existence of a peripheral class.
21. See Egon Guba, "The Effect of Definitions of 'Policy' on the Nature and Outcomes of Policy Analysis," *Educational Leadership* 42 (2) (1984): 63–70. Guba argues that one's conception of policy "determines the kinds of policy questions that are asked, the kinds of policy relevant data that are collected, the sources of the data that are tapped, the methodology that is used, and, finally, the policy products that emerge" (p. 63).
22. John E. Craig, *Implementing Educational Policies in Sub-Saharan Africa: A Review of the Literature* (Washington, DC: World Bank, Research Division, Education and Training Department, 1986).
23. Margaret Sutton and Bradley A. U. Levinson (eds.), *Policy as Practice: Toward a Comparative Sociocultural Analysis of Educational Policy* (Stamford, CT: Ablex Publishing, 2001).
24. This scenario, of course, parallels observations that global exclusionary dynamics are interclass more than international; core/peripheral relationships can sometimes rely on a sort of collusion between privileged classes within the centers of both core and peripheral societies [see Andre Gunder Frank, *Lumpenbourrgeoisie and Lumpendevelopment* (New York: Monthly Review Press, 1972); Galtung].
25. See Anthony R. Welch, "Knowledge and Legitimation in Comparative Education," *Comparative Education Review* 35 (3) (1991): 508–31. While the social sciences have only come to dominate as the conceptual/methodological foundation of comparative education since the middle of the twentieth century, this identity is entwined with the efforts of comparative educators to pursue disciplinary definition for the field.
26. Dorothy Ross, "The Development of the Social Sciences," in *The Organization of Knowledge in Modern America* (Baltimore: Johns Hopkins University Press, 1979), p. 114.
27. Ross, p. 112.
28. Francis Fukuyama, *The Great Disruption: Human Nature and the Reconstitution of Social Order* (New York: The Free Press, 1999); Popkewitz.
29. Popkewitz. For a number of reasons, this rural to urban migration engendered societal upheaval, including the fact that as the agrarian village culture declined, religious and ethnic identity dimmed, and, in the vernacular of F. Tönnies [see *Community and Association*

(London: Routledge and Kegan, Paul, 1955)], the social norms of village *Gemeinschaft* culture gave way to a social environment characterized by *Gesellschaft*'s norms: "Society" replaced "community."

30. Popkewitz.
31. The chapter's focus is largely, although not solely, on the United States. This is necessary primarily because, as Altbach has noted, universities in the United States and a few other industrialized nations "are the major producers of scholarly knowledge, as well as the major distributors" of this knowledge [Phillip G. Altbach, *The Knowledge Context: Comparative Perspectives on the Distribution of Knowledge* (Albany: The State University of New York Press, 1987), p. 62]. Although there are presently other sources of knowledge outside the United States and the industrialized west, and although there have been other knowledge-producing centers in different eras, the West's universities—those in the United States in particular—function as major centers of knowledge production. Because this circumstance is in most important respects the focus of our commentary, the narrative uses the United States quite persistently as its source of examples and as the object of its critique. While our means in the chapter are Western-centric at face value, then, our aims are not.
32. Although German postsecondary institutions and practices enjoyed considerable influence throughout the nineteenth century, a surge of migration overlapped with the growth in industrialization in the United States (Ross, p. 119).
33. Fritz K. Ringer, "The German Academic Community," in *The Organization of Knowledge in Modern America* (Baltimore: Johns Hopkins University Press, 1979), p. 409.
34. Ross, p. 199.
35. The American and German academic responses to social pressures accompanying the Industrial Revolution were different, according to Ringer. While American academics imported certain elements of the German higher education scene, American academics did not adopt the so-called mandarin tradition [Ringer, p. 411; see also Hans-Joachim Hans, *Education and Society in Germany* (Oxford: Berg, 1998)]—a tradition that favored education for its own sake and eschewed applied education and that made "German intellectuals particularly resistant to the fallacies of a doctrinaire positivism" (Ringer, p. 412).
36. Edmund King, *Comparative Studies and Educational Decisions* (Indianapolis: Bobbs-Merrill, 1968), p. 59.
37. G. Z. F. Bereday, *Comparative Method in Education* (New York: Holt, Rinehart, and Winston, 1964), p. 6.

CHAPTER 5

# Researching Women's Literacy in Mali
*A Case Study of Dialogue among Researchers, Practitioners, and Policy Makers*[1]

LAUREL PUCHNER

## Introduction

Ideally, results of research are used to improve policy and practice. For this to happen, communication must occur between those who carry out research and those who might use the results for some practical or policy-related purpose.[2] This chapter presents a case study about dialogue that occurred between myself and others as I planned, carried out, analyzed, and wrote about a research study on women's literacy in rural Mali. I did engage in dialogue with some individuals who might have utilized the information in policy or practice, but the dialogue was insufficient to bring about change. In this chapter I describe the dialogue that occurred and analyze why it was insufficient. I argue that the common conception that researchers have different agendas and different cultural understandings than practitioners and policy makers can be used to a certain extent to understand the communication problems.[3] At the same time, however, the case study supports the suggestion of others that the different cultures thesis is too simplistic.[4] It is too simplistic, first of all, because some of the people involved in the study, myself included, played somewhat overlapping roles as researchers, practitioners, and/or policy makers.[5] It is also too simplistic because although there were definitely cultural differences between myself and many of the practitioners and policy makers with whom I collaborated, it is difficult to untangle cultural differences attributable to researcher versus practitioner/policy maker from differences attributable to Western versus non-Western country perspectives.

## The Gap between Research, Policy, and Practice

As was just alluded to, most writings about problems linking research to policy and practice focus on the differing agendas or even different cultures of researchers, policy makers, and practitioners.[6] It is argued that researchers focus on narrow issues that interest them and that are consistent with the latest research, while policy makers and practitioners want immediate solutions that they can apply to specific situations within existing constraints.[7] Researchers are hesitant about making global recommendations and strive to please other researchers in their field rather than policy makers or practitioners. Some educators have even gone so far as to describe different political agendas of researchers, policy makers, and practitioners. For example, in a case study of history education in the United States, Barton and coauthors relate how researchers in that field are interested in transforming the status quo, policy makers are interested in maintaining it, and practitioners are interested in whatever it takes to get good standardized assessment results.[8]

In the literature there are three basic types of solutions provided for the different agenda problem. The first type involves changing the research that is done to fit policy maker and practitioner needs.[9] It is suggested, for instance, that researchers perceive themselves as "producers" who must cater to their "clients," the policy makers,[10] and that local level administrators and policy makers be involved in identifying problems and seeking solutions.[11] The second type of solutions consists of changing how research information is disseminated so that it is more palatable and accessible to policy makers and practitioners.[12] Creating documents that summarize research findings and translate them into a briefer and more user-friendly format for policy maker and practitioner audiences is seen as one way to bridge the gap. The third type of solutions is based on the assumption that it is unrealistic that research can directly inform policy and practice given the political nature of decision making. Instead, researchers should aim to change the ways that policy makers and practitioners think about problems, thus indirectly influencing their future actions.[13]

Some authors have challenged the idea that the communication gap between researchers, on the one hand, and policy makers and practitioners, on the other, is best explained by cultural differences between the groups.[14] Ginsburg and Gorostiaga argue that this thesis is too simplistic, since the differences between researcher and policy maker/practitioner may not be as large as is imagined, many people perform more than one of the roles simultaneously, and there are large within-group differences in cultures among researchers and among practitioner/policy makers.[15]

In the terms of the last issue, cultural differences between individuals from non-Western and those from Western nations need to be considered when examining the supposed cultural differences between researchers and practitioners/policy makers.[16] Educators have written about researchers applying developed or Western country paradigms to non-Western or developing country situations where they do not readily apply,[17] but individual researchers may also be particularly hesitant about applying solutions to cultural contexts that differ substantially from their own.

## Mali Research Project: A Case Study

In 1994–1995 I spent nine months in rural Mali undertaking a qualitative and quasi-experimental study examining the impact of adult literacy programs for women in four villages. I collected data through household observations, literacy class observations, interviews with female learners and teachers, and surveys and tests. I found that few women became literate through the literacy program and that being able to read and write had very little impact on the lives of women who were literate. I concluded that local level ideological forces—in particular, those pertaining to the role of women in village life—strongly influenced how that literacy program was implemented and how literacy skills could be used by women; thus, any "effects" of literacy on women that may have been envisioned by policy makers could not occur. For literacy programs to have positive socioeconomic benefits for women, I argued, one would have to do more than simply insert literacy classes into villages. One would have to change the entire sociopolitical structure of the villages, which would not only be difficult but may not even be desirable. I questioned whether women's literacy programs are always the best option for improving the lives of women, although I also made specific recommendations for improving the existing program in case one were to decide to take that route.[18]

Planning for the study began about a year before I actually left the United States for Mali. I wanted to do my dissertation fieldwork on women's literacy in francophone Africa. I was employed by a literacy research office at my university, and this research office had a collaborative relationship with an international aid organization that I refer to in this chapter as Aid Africa.[19] Aid Africa had a functional literacy program in one area of southern Mali, so they agreed to work with me as part of the larger collaboration between their organization and my university. Most of my financial support came from a dissertation fellowship, but I still needed access to a literacy program and to literacy participants. Hence, I negotiated with Aid Africa to provide me with access and logistical support for my research, and in return I would provide technical support for their local development program in areas where they thought I could be of assistance.[20]

This agreement between myself and Aid Africa's education office set the stage for a theme of mutual assistance that characterized my relationship with Aid Africa throughout the data collection process in Mali. First of all, Aid Africa provided me with much logistical support. For example, they transported my family and me to and from the airport in Bamako (the capitol of Mali) and between Bamako and Biaka, the town in southern Mali where the literacy program is based. Aid Africa personnel in Bamako housed us whenever we were in the capitol, helped us obtain visas, and authorized logistical help for us at the local level in Biaka, among other things.

While the Aid Africa office in Bamako provided me with important logistical support, I worked most closely with the Biaka-based education office. My reaction to the first meeting I had with them illustrates the generally positive view I held of our relationship, a perspective that continued throughout the data collection process:

> Yesterday afternoon I had a meeting with Solo and the rest of the education group. He had said he wanted to meet me and give me an overview and history of the education sector. He did that and then I asked some questions, and then I presented my study. It was all much better than I expected. They seemed to think [my study] was fine as written, and feasible. They were very positive about the whole thing, and seemed genuinely looking forward to working with me. The other issue that surprised me a little was the extent to which all that they said [fit] exactly with what [the field director in the Aid Africa office in Bamako had] said, in terms of issues they wanted help with. Also, they were extremely *au courant* with my objectives and reasons for being here, and very well prepared mentally to deal with me. Much more than I had expected. (Fieldnotes, October 18, 1994)

In Biaka I worked particularly closely with Solo Diarra, the head of the education sector. He provided much advice and logistical help in carrying out my data collection. He began by listening to what I wanted to accomplish, and then advised me to work in four particular villages, mainly on the basis of proximity, since transportation was a major constraint. He and other members of his staff also traveled with me to villages during the first few visits to introduce me to village leaders, literacy teachers (all of whom were villagers), and participants and to explain to villagers what my goals were. I needed Aid Africa's help at this stage in order to gain trust and cooperation from people in the villages and because I did not speak the local language, Bambara, very well. Bambara is one of the national languages of Mali and is also the language in which literacy was taught to adults in the region and in which development activities were conducted in the villages. French is the official language of Mali, and also the language I used to communicate with Aid Africa personnel; however, very few people in the villages spoke French. Later on in the research process Solo also found me a research assistant to help me administer a questionnaire and test to sixty women and to facilitate other parts of the data collection process.

In addition to facilitating my work in the villages, Solo and some of his colleagues were important study informants, answering many questions that I had about the basic structure of literacy programs and the development projects[21] as well as about Malian village life. Solo was a particularly good informant. He had been a scholar of community life and community issues, which meant that he recognized what was interesting to outsiders, and he explained issues clearly. Possibly because the topics were interesting to him as well, he appeared to enjoy answering my questions about village social structures, the local economy, and gender roles, for example.

Although Solo was well educated and employed by an international nongovernmental organization, he was also an insider, and he was quite traditional in many ways himself. Thus, while he understood the perspective of outsiders, his own views on many practices matched more closely with the views of an insider. For example, at one point, even though I had seen much child labor in the villages in Mali and felt that I understood it, I asked him about a case I thought might have been excessive. The question pertained to a child of six or seven who had been "loaned" to or adopted temporarily by one of my study participants in a village. I had observed the child unwillingly make five or six trips in a row to get water at the request of the woman, which had seemed inappropriate. Solo's response, as recorded in my fieldnotes (January 22, 1995) was, "If I am the mother of that child, and I come and I see my child in the household doing nothing, I will be angry and take my child away. The child has to learn to work properly." He added, however, that if the loads are too big, or the woman makes an adopted child work more than her own children, then it is bad. Usually, however, the community will look down on it and put pressure on the person to stop.

Although my spouse and I provided some assistance to Aid Africa personnel based in Bamako,[22] I provided the most technical assistance to those working in the education sector in Biaka. During our first meeting the education personnel identified the areas in which they wanted my help: developing literacy program curricula, creating postliteracy materials, and designing action research projects on which two of them were working in relation to a higher education diploma program. I complied with the requests, working on most of these projects throughout my nine months in Mali. Specifically, I helped with the development of a second-year curriculum for the adult literacy program, provided recommendations for improving the first-year curriculum, helped develop a "Baby Book" for women (a postliteracy document modeled after Western baby books), and made a list of general suggestions pertaining to postliteracy efforts. I also helped Solo and other members of the staff develop their action research proposals, which focused on the impact of development on the rural environment (Solo's project) and the impact of adult literacy education on women and children in a village with a women's literacy center.

I enjoyed the contributions I made and considered them an integral part of my research as they helped me to understand the development process at Aid Africa in Biaka. Aid Africa treated me in many respects like a member of its staff, expecting me to attend weekly Monday morning meetings, where, like other personnel based in Biaka, I gave an outline of what I had accomplished the previous week and what I intended to do the current week. I also attended and participated in the larger and longer monthly meetings attended by the entire Aid Africa personnel in Mali, as well as many meetings involving only those working in the education sector. My reports at the weekly and monthly meetings, like those of most of the Aid Africa personnel members, were focused on how I spent my time (presented in list form) and not on reflection or discussion of issues such as research findings. Some questions and issues were raised at these meetings, but it would not have occurred to me to promote discussion about my research, mainly because I believed that the staff would have thought it irrelevant to the development work they were carrying out.

Meetings with members of the education sector were usually limited either to discussion pertaining to technical assistance or to my asking for clarification or information to fill in gaps in my data collection process. Most of these meetings involved discussions about such items as the curriculum, for example, or about why many of my study participants appeared to believe that consuming too much oil causes malaria. The most in-depth communication of my study findings occurred at a meeting, which I convened in April 1995 (seven months into my fieldwork) and which was attended by one member of the education sector as well as members of a newly formed women/child/impact team. During this meeting I outlined preliminary findings: (a) that women did not appear to gain much from the literacy program in the villages involved in my study and (b) that the few women who were literate did not appear to use their skills very much. Although only one member of the education sector was there, I had also communicated these findings informally over time to Solo, generally during the meetings described earlier that I had initiated to ask him questions that I had about village life or about puzzling aspects of my data. We did not discuss my findings in detail, however, partly because at the time I generally considered myself to be in the process of collecting rather than interpreting or drawing conclusions from data, and partly because no one asked. In general, he responded to my findings concerning low levels of literacy ability and use of literacy by saying that, unfortunately, I had studied villages in which literacy classes—and women's literacy—were poorly implemented. If it had not been for transportation constraints, he continued, I could have conducted the study in other villages that had much more successful literacy programs.

Some other conclusions based on my research were communicated more indirectly, as I utilized them when giving technical advice to the education sector. The development of curricula for the Aid Africa adult literacy program, for example, provides an illustration of how my research results guided some of the technical assistance that I provided. My observations of literacy classes in the villages indicated that Aid Africa's first-year literacy curriculum was poorly linked to possible everyday uses of literacy. Those working in the education sector felt that functionality was important. However, they tended to define "functional" narrowly in terms of how skills might contribute to the specific development programs they had in place for improving health and agriculture, rather than more broadly in terms of what people in the villages considered useful. My interviews with women as well as my survey data indicated that women who were motivated to become literate tended to be motivated for one major reason—to increase their earnings from their own small-scale commercial activities (petit commerce). Hence, in a document that I prepared for the education sector entitled (in translation) "Suggestions for the Preparation of Lesson Plans for the First-Year Adult Literacy Program" one of my recommendations was that numeracy skills be tied to each woman's individual "petit commerce" projects. Although I had talked to Solo about the possibility that literacy skills in the program could be linked to more than just Aid Africa–initiated development activities, in retrospect I should have made clearer the data source for my advice and tried harder to engage in dialogue about this issue, especially since the topic is relatively noncontroversial.

The technical advice that I gave also often had a feminist agenda, once again stemming both from my personal background and from my research data. In a document[23] prepared in January 1995, I provide suggestions for improving the Baby Book as drafted by personnel working in the education sector. Excerpts from my document include the following.

- I suggest replacing this text with a text that is less negative and in which a woman instead of a man is the central character.
- I suggest replacing this text with a text that talks about the joy of having a child without giving the message that a woman is not valuable until she has a child.
- In my opinion, one should allow the women to form their own opinion about the book instead of talking for them [referring to a section of the Baby Book entitled "I like this book"]. Thus I suggested removing this text.

Another way in which my research findings influenced the technical assistance I provided is that I gave advice that was not solicited, but that my research had indicated might be useful. For example, although the education personnel requested help with the development of a second-year adult literacy curriculum, my observations indicated that improving the current first-year curriculum might help women gain more literacy skills from the program; thus, I also provided suggestions to that effect. Further, in addition to providing technical assistance with the development of the Baby Book, I prepared a document offering further suggestions for enhancing the print environment in general.

Although I communicated some of my study findings to Aid Africa personnel during the fieldwork, there were issues stemming from my research findings that I did not raise. For example, although some of my advice might have been described as feminist, as mentioned earlier, it was fairly low-key, and I did not bring up more complex and problematic issues. For example, I never addressed the fact that women's literacy classes were held at night in many villages (from 8:30 P.M. to 10 P.M. in three of the four villages I studied). Aid Africa personnel and village literacy teachers had proudly explained to me that holding classes late was done to accommodate women, who were too busy to attend class during the day. My data indicated that the classes simply added another burden for women, taking away what would have otherwise been an important time for women to relax and socialize. My conclusion was reinforced by the fact that women tended to go to class out of pressure from others, another issue that I hesitated to discuss because it appeared to be considered normal by Aid Africa education personnel and was in fact reinforced by the way they encouraged and talked about women's literacy in the villages. For example, during the literacy "mobilization" sessions that Aid Africa personnel held in the villages they promoted women's literacy as a way to make women better mothers for their children and better cooks for their husbands, among other things. Their attempts to get women to go to class by making it palatable to men in the villages was perhaps the only strategy that might have worked without attempting to make broad sociocultural changes, which I can understand Aid Africa not wanting to do and which I did not want to suggest.

Another issue I did not bring up was what I perceived to be the somewhat circular nature of literacy development in the area. Adult literacy was taught in the local language, Bambara, which, according to my research, had little use or prestige outside the realm of development projects. The following is an excerpt from my fieldnotes illustrating one of the very first questions I asked myself in the field.

> The question is whether [Aid Africa], or it could be any NGO, has basically created a self-perpetuating, yet completely circular literacy market. People learn literacy in Bambara from Aid Africa, and then they are able to participate in activities generated by Aid Africa which need Bambara literacy, a main one of which is teaching Bambara. (Fieldnotes, October 16, 1994 )

Another of my major conclusions that I did not raise with practitioners or policy makers in Mali was the notion that for women's literacy to have a positive impact, the entire sociopolitical structure of the communities would need to change. Most of these issues are developed in my dissertation, but since I had no communication with Aid Africa in Mali after I left the country, they have no knowledge of these conclusions.[24]

Although I did not communicate with Aid Africa in Mali after my return to the United States, I did discuss and communicate my study findings in several venues in the states. The first was via a paper presentation at the annual conference of the Comparative and International Education Society as part of an adult literacy panel in March 1996 in Williamsburg, Virginia. I also did a presentation a few days later at an International Literacy Institute conference in Philadelphia, Pennsylvania. Although I do remember that Malians attended these presentations, I do not recall discussing my findings with anyone at these events. A year later (in 1997) I made a roundtable presentation at the annual meeting of the American Educational Research Association, but this was attended only by two friends/colleagues from my own university. In all of these presentations I emphasized my conclusions that social, economic, and political forces greatly restricted the acquisition of literacy skills by women and the use of literacy skills once acquired.

In addition to the conference presentations, I gave a presentation about my findings at a university-based workshop for midlevel literacy professionals from developing countries, held during the summer of 1997. A representative from Aid Africa's U.S. headquarters attended my talk, and during the workshop we talked about the possibility of scheduling a time for me to come and discuss and/or present my findings at Aid Africa's U.S. office. Unfortunately, such a talk was never scheduled. Another interesting aspect of the presentation at the workshop was that there was some dissent from workshop participants about my conclusions, as some participants (mis)perceived my message to be that it is not a good idea to teach literacy skills to women. This reaction necessitated a clarification from me that my message was not that women's literacy should be abandoned as a goal. Rather, I was arguing that certain conditions may need to be met in order for literacy skills to be acquired and used, and that these conditions were not met in the case of the villages involved in my study.

The final post-Mali piece that I did, besides discussions with my dissertation committee, was initiated by Aid Africa in 1998. Aid Africa had hired a consultant to prepare a book of case studies to help in the training of trainers. Aid Africa suggested that the consultant ask me to provide a written description of the Biaka functional literacy program, which I did. My account was deliberately descriptive, mainly involving a discussion of how the program was organized and run. However, as directed, I included a section on problems, in which I outlined factors that contributed to ineffective implementation of the program: (1) low compensation of teachers, (2) limited skills among those doing the teaching, (3) poor conditions in which classes were held, and (4) lack of motivation for women to attend classes. I did not raise any of the more controversial issues because I did not want to appear critical of the program or of Aid Africa and because it was clear from the format they provided for the case study that interest lay not in my research but in my knowledge of the mechanics of the implementation of the program.

The only additional conversations that I had about the study upon my return were with members of my dissertation committee. Two of the three committee members welcomed and encouraged the critical approach to literacy development that my research provides. Although one of the two is not in the field of education, the other is an important researcher and policy maker in the field of literacy who considered my work to be an important contribution and who is interested in disseminating my findings via scholarly publications. The third committee member is a scholar and policy maker in the field of literacy development who had hoped that my study would provide clear evidence that adult literacy programs work. Based on his comments to me and to others about the project, I believe he was somewhat disappointed that my study did not provide clear support for the effectiveness of adult literacy for women. Members of my dissertation committee neither encouraged nor discouraged me from sharing my findings with members of Aid Africa in the United States or in Mali.

**Reasons for a Lack of Effective Dialogue**

During my fieldwork in Mali I engaged in some discussion about my study's findings with literacy practitioners and policy makers. And although I had no communication with any Aid Africa personnel in Mali after my return, I was in communication with a number of relevant individuals in the literacy field through presentations at conferences in the United States, a report I prepared for an Aid Africa consultant, and interactions with my dissertation committee. However, my findings were not used to effectively change the approach to women's literacy development in Mali or elsewhere. This section addresses possible reasons why the dialogue was insufficient. It is important to note that I consider myself responsible for the limited dialogue and believe that dialogue would have been improved if had I made better decisions. The goal of the analysis is to examine some of the situational variables that influenced the decisions I made in the hopes of improving dialogue in the future.

As was stated earlier, the poor communication can be explained to a certain extent by the differing agendas and even different cultures between researcher and practitioners and policy makers. For example, one problem in the Malian study was that the topic was generated by myself, the researcher, based on my own interests and on what I felt would be interesting to other researchers. No practitioner or policy maker within Mali or within Aid Africa asked me to carry out the study or had input into the topic. Thus, I was the one who selected the topic, and the practitioners and policy makers with whom I worked in Mali, although they agreed to having the study conducted, never came to identify with the topic or view it as something that would inform their decisions and practices. Applying some of the problem-solving strategies identified under the different cultures thesis might have helped, such as taking a more consumer-oriented approach and involving local level administrators and policy makers in specifying the research problem.

The different cultures thesis also helps to explain why I had very perfunctory communication with officials from the Malian Ministry of Education. During my first week in Mali, before I departed for Biaka, I did make formal contacts with the relevant Malian education officials. I considered these contacts necessary because of protocol and because the agency that funded me required them. Some of these meetings were very brief and formal. However, I did have meetings with individuals from the official Malian adult literacy organization, which were more meaningful, and during which officials displayed an interest in my work. I did not pursue collaboration with this group, however, because I was most concerned with collecting data for my study as written, and such collaboration would have been time-consuming and expensive. For example, officials in charge of the women's literacy unit said they would be very pleased to show me their successful literacy programs. They needed me to provide a vehicle and chauffeur, however, which I simply did not have the means to do. In short, more and better attempts to link what I was doing with government literacy projects and interests would have been a good idea, but my goals, albeit narrow, were to carry out the work I had committed to do in my dissertation research proposal.

While in Mali my preoccupation was with collecting my data, and when I returned my primary goal was to write up my dissertation. I did not question the dissertation format, which, like other writing that researchers are encouraged to do, yields a document that is generally not much use to practitioners and policy makers. As Duke and Beck assert, "the dissertation in [its current] format is ill-suited to the task of training doctoral students in the communicative aspects of educational research, and is largely ineffectual as a means of contributing knowledge to the field."[25] One can rework and rewrite the dissertation afterward to create articles for publication and other purposes, but the process of writing the dissertation itself is so long that the task of creating more useful works from it becomes delayed for years.[26] Krathwohl and others have argued, and convincingly so, that alternative formats to the traditional dissertation, such as a series of ready-to-publish articles, would be more useful.[27] I could have and should have attempted to use an alternative format for my dissertation, perhaps comprised of a series of papers including reports in French and English aimed at practitioners and policy makers associated with Malian as well as other national and international institutions.

While the differing cultures thesis can provide a partial explanation, it is clear that the premise that researchers have different agendas, or are different culturally from practitioners and policy makers, cannot fully explain the communication difficulties that occurred. One of the problems, as mentioned earlier, is that practitioners, policy makers, and researchers held somewhat overlapping roles during the study.[28] My primary role was that of researcher, but I also acted as a practitioner in many respects. I contributed to curriculum development and materials development, helped to organize symposia, monitored literacy development activities, and participated in regular meetings of the Aid Africa personnel. Unlike outside experts and many educational researchers, I brought my whole family to the study region, rented a house, traveled to villages, ate village food on a regular basis, and stayed for an extended period of time (relatively speaking). Other overlapping roles occurred with many of the practitioners in Biaka who were developing proposals for research projects that they planned to carry out, and dissertation committee members who were researchers and policy makers to differing degrees at the same time.

Since I participated in development work, I was able to understand somewhat the practitioner perspective. Rather than aiding my ability to communicate, however, I believe it hindered it. I understood how difficult practitioner work was, and that many of my conclusions and recommendations were impractical or controversial. For example, I felt strongly that instead of holding classes for women at night it would be much better to hold them during the day, while distributing work tasks more equally among men and women and giving women and men equal freedom in deciding how to spend their time. However, this was not something practitioners could implement as it would involve changing the culture and political structure of the communities. Furthermore, making such a suggestion to policy makers at any level would have been controversial, and I did not want to raise controversy.

In fact, the differing cultures thesis clearly does not account adequately for the fact that one of the reasons for my failure to communicate and discuss findings was a simple distaste for creating political turmoil and for overtly questioning the status quo. Many of the controversial issues were not necessarily research issues, and I can think of several practitioner and policy maker roles in which I would have generated the same questions. I had met with some resistance from Aid Africa personnel when I questioned relatively uncontroversial but accepted practices, such as the necessity of making all literacy activities for villagers be directly related to Aid Africa development activities. Raising more controversial issues might have jeopardized not only the positions of some of the practitioners and policy makers with whom I worked in Aid Africa but also my own position and those of foreign researchers in Mali in the future.

I also hesitated to raise controversial issues because of my position as a cultural outsider. I worried, for example, that the differences in perspectives between my Malian contacts and me had less to do with the differences in our positions (researcher versus practitioner/policy maker) and more to do with our location in the world system (Western versus non-Western countries).

For example, during an interview with Mariam, a member of the Aid Africa women's promotion sector, I was surprised to discover that one of her hobbies was excision of girls.[29] Excision, she explained, was necessary in a polygamous culture (where husbands do not have a lot of time for each wife) to prevent women from seeking extramarital affairs and hence risking a divorce. Mariam was careful to point out in the interview that while she felt excision was necessary in her own culture, it may not be in other cultures. One subtle implication was that I should not consider myself in a position to criticize excision for Malians, just as she does not criticize the fact that people in the United States do not practice it. I knew that many Malians would have questioned my ability to make appropriate interpretations of village life and that I did not in fact have an adequate cultural understanding to avoid misinterpretations and inappropriate conclusions.

It is difficult to bring up issues of sexism in many contexts, especially when one knows there will be resistance from both men and women. However, when I dispense advice on the issue in the United States, even if I know some people resent me and do not believe me, I am at least reasonably confident that my interpretations of events and consequences are accurate. When examining such issues in Mali, however, I am not nearly as confident, which makes articulating conclusions about sensitive issues much more problematic. It is much safer to put controversial conclusions in a dissertation or academic journal, which is far away and which few will read, than it is to have face-to-face dialogue with the individuals who might actually be affected.

The limitations of the different cultures thesis can be seen in that the strategies proposed in the literature to solve the problem are unlikely to be sufficient. For example, one proposed solution is to disseminate results in a form that is user-friendly to practitioners and policy makers. Although such dissemination in the Malian study would doubtless have been better than not disseminating results at all, it would not have made it likely that controversial issues would be addressed by practitioners or policy makers nor would it alter the perceptions of Malian practitioners and policy makers that I am a cultural outsider.

As stated earlier, involving policy makers and practitioners in the process of planning the study probably would have improved dialogue and the chances of results being utilized effectively. Indeed, the practice of Western researchers generating a question in isolation in the United States and then going into a non-Western or developing country to try to answer it should be called into question. At the same time, however, involvement of practitioners and policy makers may have reduced the scope of possible topics, since the mainly male practitioners and policy makers may have avoided and discouraged certain important issues, especially those related to women. In organizing my study around my own research questions I believe I came up with findings about women's literacy that could be of interest to scholars in the field. On the other hand, if these findings do not contribute to practice or policy, there may be little use to them. In order to resolve the problem, it is likely that a profound change in the relationship between researcher, practitioner, and policy maker would need to occur. As Ginsburg and Gorostiaga describe, practitioners, policy makers, and researchers probably ought to undergo "substantial role changes," simultaneously asking questions about themselves and each other, and truly acting as researchers, practitioners, and policy makers at the same time.[30]

## Notes

1. This chapter was originally published in the special issue of the *Comparative Education Review* [45 (2) (May 2001): 242–56] focused on "The Relationship between Theorists/Researchers and Policy Makers/Practitioners."
2. P. A. Haensly, A. E. Lupkowski, and J. F. McNamara, "The Chart Essay: A Strategy for Communicating Research Findings to Policymakers and Practitioners," *Educational Evaluation and Policy Analysis* 9 (1987): 63–75; R. E. Slavin, "On Making a Difference," *Educational Researcher* 19 (April 1990): 30–34.
3. K. C. Barton, M. T. Downey, T. L. Epstein, L. S. Levstik, P. Seixas, S. J. Thornton, and B. A. VanSledright, "Research, Instruction, and Public Policy in the History Curriculum: A Symposium," *Theory and Research in Social Education* 24 (Fall 1996): 391–415; M. T. Hallinan, "Bridging the Gap between Research and Practice," *Sociology of Education* (extra issue) (1996): 131–134; S. P. Heyneman, "Universal Adult Literacy: Policy Myths and Realities," in *World Literacy in the Year 2000*, ed. D. A. Wagner and L. D. Puchner, vol. 520, *The Annals of the American Academy of Political and Social Science* (Newbury Park, CA: Sage Publications, 1992), pp. 27–31; J. Ryan, "Literacy Research, Policy and Practice: The Elusive Triangle," In *World Literacy in the Year 2000*, ed. D. A. Wagner and L. D. Puchner, vol. 520, *The Annals*

of the *American Academy of Political and Social Science* (Newbury Park, CA: Sage Publications, 1992), pp. 36–41; R. J. Shavelson, "Contributions of Educational Research to Policy and Practice: Constructing, Challenging, Changing Cognition," *Educational Researcher* 17 (October 1988): 4–11; Slavin.

4. Mark B. Ginsburg and Jorge Gorostiaga, "Relationships between Theorists/Researchers and Policymakers/Practitioners? Rethinking the Two Cultures Thesis and the Possibility of Dialogue." *Comparative Education Review* 45 (May 2001): 173–96.
5. Ibid.
6. Barton et al.; Hallinan; Heyneman; Ryan; Shavelson; Slavin.
7. Heyneman, pp. 31–32; Ryan, pp. 37–40; Shavelson, pp. 4–11.
8. Barton et al., pp. 393–97.
9. E. R. Hines, "Policy Research in Higher Education: Data, Decisions, Dilemmas, and Disconnect," *Mid-Western Educational Researcher* 12 (1999): 2–6; Heyneman, pp. 31–32.
10. Heyneman, p. 31.
11. K. Mwiria, "Major Issues in Educational Research," *Kenya Journal of Education* 4 (1989): 177–93; Ryan.
12. Haensly, Lupkowski, and McNamara; Hallinan, pp. 131–34.
13. Shavelson, p. 4.
14. Ginsburg and Gorostiaga; Mwiria, pp. 184–85; R. Husen, "Research Paradigms in Education," *Interchange* 19 (1988): 2–13.
15. Ginsburg and Gorostiaga.
16. Ibid.
17. Husen; Mwiria; Ryan, p. 38.
18. L. D. Puchner, "The Socio-Economic Impact of Literacy Program Participation on Women in Rural Mali," University of Pennsylvania doctoral dissertation, 1998.
19. Names of organizations, individuals, and most places have been changed to protect anonymity.
20. Although most of the initial arrangements were worked out in negotiations involving my boss, members of the U.S.-based Aid Africa education office, and me, I did have one meeting with the Aid Africa field director for Mali, Paul Simmons (not his real name), before beginning the research. Paul was an American based in Mali, but our meeting was held in New York while he happened to be visiting the United States. At that meeting, which took place in February 1994, Paul and I discussed some of the areas in which he thought I could help them out. We also discussed the feasibility of my study.
21. Aid Africa had development programs in the Biaka district in the following domains: child survival, natural resources management (agriculture and environment), small business/credit/savings, promotion of women, and education (support to the formal school system, a village school program, and adult functional literacy). Although there were a few other organizations who carried out projects in the district (including a Swiss organization that dug wells), Aid Africa was the most visibly active organization in the area.
22. Bamako-initiated projects that my spouse and I worked on included development of an evaluation of the Aid Africa Village School project (in collaboration with the Malian national pedagogical institute) and development of a system of statistical indicators for determining the impact of Aid Africa programs in Biaka.
23. Remarks about the texts that accompany the Baby Book, submitted by Laurel Puchner to Solo Diarra, January 1995; translated from the French.
24. Recently, in September 2000, I did try to contact Solo Diarra in the Aid Africa office in Biaka in an effort to restart some dialogue by asking for an update on the literacy program. I obtained confirmation that he had received the email that I sent via a third party, but as of this writing I have not received a reply.
25. N. K. Duke and S. W. Beck, "Education Should Consider Alternative Formats for the Dissertation," *Educational Researcher* 28 (April 1999): 31–36.
26. Ibid, p. 32.
27. Krathwohl, in Duke and Beck, p. 34; Duke and Beck, p. 34.
28. See Ginsburg and Gorostiaga.
29. Excision is the total or partial removal of women's external genitals.
30. Ginsburg and Gorostiaga.

CHAPTER 6

# "Other" Perceptions
## Intersubjectivity in the Research Dialogue Process

SANDRA L. STACKI

## Introduction

Five years ago, in conjunction with my Ph.D. dissertation, I conducted field research in India. My study,[1] which subsequently won the Comparative and International Education Society's "Gail Kelly Award" for the best dissertation in 1999, took a critical feminist and phenomenological approach to understanding the partnerships, processes, and perspectives of stakeholders involved in this Teacher Empowerment Program (TEP).[2] In this study I strove to answer several overlapping questions, including whether the environment, processes, and partners in the TEP facilitated participating women teachers to become empowered professionals and social change agents. A primary goal was to understand the lived realities and perspectives of women teachers involved in an empowerment program in a non-Western, strongly patriarchal country.

Initiated by UNICEF officers, the TEP in India, although not designed specifically for women teachers, provided what I believed was a perfect opportunity to conduct a critical feminist, qualitative study that integrated issues of teacher development and gender. However, as my excitement regarding a meaningful research opportunity grew, so did my anxiety. I wanted this field experience to be both professionally and personally fulfilling, yet a pragmatic question subdued my eagerness: Would I be prepared to conduct an intersubjective study as an outsider and as a woman in a strongly patriarchal culture? I knew that my presence, my subjectivities, and the respondents' perceptions of me would influence the quality and direction of the research dialogue process. While indigenous people might become familiar with the principles, objectives, and approaches that a donor agency such as UNICEF advocates, they might find my principles, values, and intentions, at least initially, to be less transparent and perhaps mysterious or even threatening. My culture, ideology, feminist views, and ethics might be unwelcome or challenged. Therefore, whether to reveal my subjectivities or advocacies became a question on which I reflected.

A preferred level of interaction between the researcher and others is dialogue, a process of joint reflection and action that ensures indigenous voices are heard equally and as often as external voices.[3] This process parallels the transactional and constructivist approaches to curriculum and pedagogy that educators use to encourage teacher and student interaction.[4] Similar to guiding students to discover their own directions, problems, and solutions, a process of joint reflection and action can encourage intersubjective negotiations in our research efforts and mutual adaptation and consensus for decision making in policy dialogue. Yet to reach this level of dialogue, relationships must be formed, trust must be built, and intersubjective negotiation must occur among stakeholders who often perceive one another as "others."

In this chapter, I link issues of methodology and my particular research, actions, and experiences to the possibilities for dialogue. I provide context and key findings of my research and fieldwork in late 1995 and early 1996; however, I focus on varied examples of engagement with respondents who were "others." These allow me to explore the roles of myself as the researcher—my perceptions and theirs—and to illustrate relationship building that improved dialogue with various respondents, especially the women, in this cross-cultural context. My experiences, reflections, and reflexive responses during the initial fieldwork—colored also by my recent trip during summer 2001 to confer again with several key respondents—led me not only to reach certain conclusions about the possibilities of contributing to dialogue through an interpretive research process but also to raise questions about the implications that sharing advocacies may have for policy and practice.

## Methodology for Dialogue

The methodology and methods a researcher chooses have everything to do with the kind and amount of interaction—or lack of it—that occurs with and among the various respondents in a study. In my research, policy makers, donor officers, trainers, and teachers were among those respondents whose views all contributed to a case study with multiple perspectives and layers. Thus, for me, any discussion of approaches to enhance the relationships and dialogue among researcher and respondents overlaps with the purposes of naturalistic, interpretive, or qualitative methodology. These approaches to research explore multiple perspectives and focus on "culture, meanings and processes... rather than variables, outcomes and products."[5] By interacting with people in their natural environments and through intersubjective experiences,[6] interpretive researchers can more clearly understand subjective perspectives or standpoints[7] and their respondents' social constructions of reality. Recognition of individual, subjective experience in the construction of knowledge is a part of emphasizing a flexible flow between public/private systems for all individuals.[8] Thus, knowledge creation is a dialogic and dialectic interaction among individuals and various groups and between individuals and the policies, structures, and institutions that constitute the context within which they live.

Dialectics focuses on internal contradiction as the driving force of change.[9] Individuals and institutions are perceived not as resisting each other from extreme positions or focusing on dichotomies, but rather as interacting intersubjectively to create dialogue and social change that could benefit both individuals and institutions. Initial standpoints may lead people to perceive one another as "others," yet dialogue can create new, shared space that benefits those involved. This epistemological position, in line with what Ginsburg and Gorostiaga (in their introduction to this volume) discuss as an alternative, less dominant portrait of theorist/researcher culture, emphasizes that no knowledge is objective—all knowledge is socially constructed (i.e., it is a cultural and historical artifact) and political (i.e., it serves the interests of certain individuals and groups). Different interpretations of research findings are perceived to grow from deeply held differences in ideologies and value among scholars. In other words, our subjectivities[10] affect our findings and interpretations, and thus we need to abandon the idea of absolute truth in favor of varied subjective perspectives on truth.

As do many researchers, I believe that the days of nonparticipant observer research are gone. Yet relationships with respondents can range on a continuum from stranger to friend.[11] In a feminist interpretive approach,[12] the researcher establishes close relationships with respondents. People who begin to know each other well share more honestly and openly their beliefs and feelings about the intimacies of their lives. The respondent who does not know the researcher is more likely to offer less honest information because little trust has been established.

My strong interpretive orientations, including my feminist and phenomenological prioritizing, influence my definition of dialogue as I strive primarily to document lived realities and respondents' understandings of the daily activity in their natural contexts.[13] Face-to-face interaction between myself and respondents through interview conversations and my immersion in their daily lives enhanced intersubjectivity. As a lone researcher, I interacted with different stakeholders at different times. When more than one respondent was present, more opportunities—and challenges—for joint reflection among us all existed.

In efforts to increase understanding and dialogue, I believe researchers should help respondents to be reflective and reflexive about their roles and action and vice versa. Encouraging respondents to think more deeply about a political issue—such as patriarchy—does not have to mean persuading them to adopt the researchers' views. Yet researchers must think reflectively about their own roles and action. Researchers can learn important essences about themselves when they wrestle with issues of subjectivity and conscience—when they are reflective and reflexive in their roles as inquirers. Researchers must recognize "the multiple, overlapping and contradictory oppressive and privileging aspects of their own identities."[14]

As a cross-cultural researcher, these aspects of my identity, advocacies, and ethnocentrisms had to be the subject of careful reflection. As an American feminist from white European ancestry with a critical approach and commitments to social justice and social action, I needed to understand that gender roles and constructs in India would be different than my norm and that this would affect my relationships. I had to be sensitive to and understand India's cultural traditions and not impose my ideas about feminism or other values in an insensitive, judgmental way. As a Western feminist, I wanted to build bridges and yet not reject feminist and critical theory, even though I recognized that I had to be open to "question, modify and adapt the theory" to make sense of specific (other) discourses.[15] As a qualitative researcher, I was committed to understanding and accurately representing the "other" as well as to presenting reflexively and critiquing myself by challenging my values in relation to the respondents' values. That is, I strove to experience *verstehen*, "a sympathetic entrance into the cultural worlds of others."[16] I believed that the more I came to understand myself and how my ethics and subjectivities affect the research process, the stronger would be the possibilities that dialogue (i.e., joint reflection and action) could occur.

## Context of the Research[17]

In general, Indian policy documents prior to the 1980s viewed teachers as passive agents at the bottom of an extremely hierarchical system. In a deteriorating, centralized formal primary education system, teachers received most of the blame for students' lack of success. However, some teachers blamed the victims—especially the students from the poorest and lowest caste families. The environment was one of distrust: Teachers believed government officials were corrupt and did not care about the status or welfare of teachers or the children; officials expressed that many teachers were lazy, absent, and uncommitted.

The 1986 and the (revised) 1992 National Policy on Education promotes teacher professionalism and expresses a view that highly values teachers, quality teacher education, and female education.[18] Furthermore, decentralization reform in 1992 increased the promise for more teachers to be involved in in-service education programs. Yet practical improvements at the local level were slow in coming.

In response to and within the guidelines of the National Policy on Education, TEP evolved to become a partnership[19] among UNICEF, the government of India, four state governments,[20] and one of the state's union of government primary schoolteachers.[21] The TEP began to function in the state of Uttar Pradesh[22] in October 1994, with teachers from six districts. The design of the TEP evolved to facilitate universal primary education and to begin to meet the professional needs of teachers that these policy documents identified: improved status, teaching skills, and materials; more participation and decision making in governance and program development; training in pedagogy that is more joyful for both the students and the teachers; and more in-service training. General goals included increased attendance, higher completion rates through class five (especially for girls), and higher achievement levels through empowerment of the teachers.[23]

The lateral "teacher-teach-teacher" training approach has stressed equality, reduced power issues, and giving teachers more respect and confidence. Even though government officials and teachers often viewed each other as "others" and lacked trust, increasing dialogue among the involved stakeholders, including UNICEF trainers, teachers, and often government officials, was an essential goal of the participatory process. This aided the hearing of multiple perspectives, concerns, and needs for the program to be successful. Thus, the program had a built-in, dialogue-promoting process among groups that were composed mostly of Indians but were still sometimes "others." Moreover, the program sought to facilitate some critical and feminist approaches, especially in Uttar Pradesh, through an explicit discussion of patriarchy and gender equity.[24]

**Relationships with Others**

Researchers encounter situations in the field and make decisions that affect their relationships with respondents—and not only those who are directly involved in such interactions. Since establishing and maintaining relationships with a variety of respondents are prerequisites to obtaining multiple perspectives on the focus of inquiry, what researchers do in such situations and whether and how they communicate their advocacies and subjectivities have implications for the quality of data obtained. For example, the topic a researcher selects and how she or he frames questions for the study give respondents some knowledge of the researcher's interests and advocacies. Thus, can researchers avoid having respondents interpret their views, and, if not, should researchers seek to communicate these more directly? Does sharing such information with one group of respondents enhance or reduce trust and openness in the relationship between a researcher and that group? And what implications do such actions have for a researcher's relationships with other groups of respondents?

I address these questions by examining some of my experiences in the field. I describe situations and relationships that developed, identify lessons learned, and raise questions for further consideration. Ultimately, I am interested in facilitating more extensive and intensive relationships with all the groups and in becoming engaged in joint reflection and action (i.e., dialogue) with them.

*Friend of UNICEF*

My relationships with various groups of respondents were framed in part in terms of my being a "friend of UNICEF." There is no question in my mind that my connections with UNICEF made my research in India possible. Had I not begun to establish a relationship with the people in UNICEF's New York office, who wrote letters of introduction and asked for field assistance on my behalf, access to respondents in India would have been much more difficult and time-consuming. Having these connections helped me to be less anxious about the trip and more comfortable once I arrived. I took advantage of the access help that UNICEF offered because I had never been to India and my time constraints required that I plan ahead.

I explained to people that I did not work for UNICEF. Yet the reality that the agency was facilitating my access did not go unheeded by them. Respondents knew of UNICEF's work and at least one of the agency's representatives; therefore, the formal connections facilitated my entree into their world. Their knowledge of UNICEF's relationship in India[25] helped my respondents to be more comfortable with my presence in their world.[26] As I strove to understand the TEP and stakeholders' needs and feelings, all the people I asked for help or information treated me with respect, from government officials to the teachers and the relatives and friends of the teachers.[27] My friend-of-UNICEF status not only facilitated communication with participants in the program, but also enhanced feelings of trust with UNICEF staff responsible for developing the program.[28]

My role as "friend of UNICEF," however, also created some challenges for me. First, although I was committed to establishing egalitarian relationships that feminist research attempts to realize, upon reflection I recognize that even though friendships grew with several people, I had entered their world as someone who at least appeared to have higher status and power. Second, even though the agency did not fund my research, shape directly my research questions or my research approach, or have control over the dissemination of my findings, my research may have been construed as serving the agency's interests. Thus, my "friend-of-UNICEF" status may have shaped how people in the field responded to my questions, limiting the depth, breadth, and validity of the data I collected.

For example, while my association with UNICEF allowed me to become closer to many respondents much more quickly, with some respondents—typically government officials—my interactions were limited to one formal interview. Some of those whom I interviewed only once, I believe, made time for me in respect for UNICEF, but had no desire to build a longer-term, deeper relationship. My role as "friend of UNICEF" may also have biased my interview data. For instance, would policy makers say unfavorable things about a donor with whom India has had a relationship for years? Would teachers complain about aspects of the program when many had no other in-service training for years and were thus grateful? Were some of them simply tolerating my presence because of this UNICEF connection, even though they mistrusted outside researchers in general or feared I was reporting to the government? Might some people have avoided talking with me altogether because of this perceived relationship: Were they inhibited or did they hold a grudge toward development agencies?

*An American Woman in an Indian Patriarchal Field*

My relationships with respondents were also shaped by my status as an American woman conducting research within the patriarchal setting of India.[29] My minority, but privileged, status as an American was driven home when I first took a bicycle-pulled rickshaw to reach the UNICEF Office in Lucknow, Uttar Pradesh. On this lengthy ride, as an outsider who looked different—taller, paler, with green eyes—I was the object of most male and female Indians' gaze, as a poor, thin man pulled me through the immensely crowded streets. I felt uncomfortable, but I also felt safe because I was a Westerner, "a rich American" they called me, who would be ascribed high status and power.[30]

Being an American in India sometimes facilitated and sometimes inhibited my interactions with respondents. General curiosity about Americans encouraged some to ask about things such as social norms, daily activities, and meals. Some wanted to know more about women's roles in society while others wanted to practice their English and learn American expressions or slang. These people seemed more willing to accept me as an individual, not necessarily representing my country's norms or political views. Yet others shared disdain for Americans and our political policies, such as our stand on Indian nuclear power, or our social policies, such as women being able to obtain a divorce—too easily some men thought. When these larger concerns entered interactions, relationships were more difficult to nurture and took more time, but respondents' interests in interacting with an American usually enhanced my opportunities to collect data from people in this field site.

My status as a woman—and what that represented in Indian society—also constrained and enabled my work as a researcher. For instance, the society's concern for a woman's safety restricts a woman's movement and, therefore, can be a form of social control and power over her.[31] As a woman researcher I had to balance Indians' need to absorb and control me with my need for independent action. Women and men expressed concern about my solitary travel and told me that I was "brave" for traveling by myself as a woman, especially at night. I was told that this was not a norm for women in India, although I learned that upper-class women would sometimes do so. However, while I was at times anxious, for example, when I was the only woman among many unknown men on an overnight sleeper train car, I refused to be restricted from traveling alone.

Nevertheless, for much of my time in the field, I negotiated arrangements in which my respondents could "protect" me from sexual harassment or other dangers. I stayed with a UNICEF family, traveled with a male TEP trainer, and lived for a while with a teacher, Shail. I was "safer" when I was with the locals, especially my two primary women teacher respondents, Shail and Mamta; they rarely left my side when we were together and they shielded me from any unnecessary objectification.[32] Being with my respondents did control my movements to some extent, yet my goal was to immerse myself in their daily lives. I rarely felt that someone was hindering my independent action or physical empowerment.[33] Occasionally, the women would make well-meaning, alternative suggestions for activities or they would help me to be patient when I became restless with cultural formalities that sometimes seemed to consume most of our time. They would offer their explanations and advice, I would come to better understand the cultural or environmental constraints, and we would often compromise on what to do.

I did at times encounter situations in which patriarchal relations seemed to limit my effectiveness as a researcher. For instance, in one interview, a male administrator asserted his power by steering the conversation in the direction he desired, even though I tried on several occasions to redirect it. In general, however, my status as an American woman—and a "friend of UNICIF"—provided me with more protection, less objectification, and perhaps greater respect.[34]

Moreover, being a woman—and discussing shared experiences with women practitioners—sometimes facilitated my research agenda. As an illustration, during a discussion at her home, Shail told me the story of going to another district to be a trainer for the TEP and being turned away because the male Block leader refused to use a woman trainer. Mamta, a younger teacher with less experience in the program who was also present, explained that she did not perceive any gender bias and that she had not had any such experiences. Yet, she listened as Shail told of several of these bias incidents. Mamta seemed perplexed, unsure of what to think. I suggested to her that she was not wrong and that Shail was not right. "[They are] just two different perspectives. Two different experiences of what you've done so far with the program or with teaching. And that's important for me to understand for my research, to have some different perspectives."

This occasion offered an opportunity for joint reflection on the topics of gender issues and patriarchy. I was made even more aware of how women's socialization often deflects awareness of gender inequities, that women have to consciously learn and be empowered to view their lives and their institutions through a gender lens. Mamta pondered situations beyond her personal experiences and began to gain more gender consciousness about some of the larger, patriarchal institutional structures. Shail felt value in knowing she was helping to make conditions of gender inequity clearer for her junior colleague. Furthermore, the dialogue gave them both a clearer understanding of my research goal to understand and value different perspectives; they learned that I was not looking for an absolute truth. I believe this explanation on my part helped them to trust that I would not judge their opinions as right or wrong. This recognition presumably encouraged them to share a range of insights and experiences with me and offered me the opportunity to have them as collaborators in the research process.[35]

*Discovering Space for Dialogue: Share(d) Advocacies with Other*

In the context of cross-cultural research, at least, researchers and respondents may initially perceive each other as the "other." However, during fieldwork researchers and respondents may discover they share certain advocacies, values, or goals, and this can open a new, shared space that promotes dialogue. Of course, if researchers and respondents discover that they hold conflicting advocacies, it may negatively affect subsequent interaction; "other" perceptions may be reinforced and dialogue will suffer. Moreover, a researcher's interactions with respondents and the relationships thus developed between researchers and particular practitioners or policy makers can affect the quality and tone of relationships with other respondents. Several examples demonstrate these points.

First, as I spent my days with the teachers, Shail and Mamta, I had many opportunities to talk with them individually and sometimes together. The women began to trust me with details of their personal lives, yet with respect to controversial social issues, they were still reluctant to share their ideas. However, my relationship with Shail grew as she heard me talk with others about my views on girls' education and the need for gender equality; she became more trusting and comfortable in expressing her own "feminist" ideas. For example, Shail joined me and listened intently when I spoke with a male administrator about the situation of women in the United States, their rights and opportunities, compared to women in the Indian context; I drew attention to beatings, bride burnings, ostracism, difficult divorces, and silent suffering.[36] Shail told me that evening as we sat in her home that she had agreed with all I had said about women's mistreatment and exploitation. She shared some feelings, told me that she writes about these issues, and later gave me something to read that she had written. Had she not heard my discussion with this male administrator about women's low position in society and problems, she might not have felt safe or trusted me enough to open up and share her views. We had reached a higher level of rapport in which mutual concerns and advocacy of gender equity had moved our own relationship to one characterized by more equality and trust.

Second, shortly after my arrival in Uttar Pradesh, I met Urvashi, the woman trainer in the TEP. However, we had little time to talk individually or do an interview until just before the end of my fieldwork. Thus, I had not built much of a relationship with her when I visited her at her home in Lucknow. That afternoon, when Shail and Mamta, who had accompanied me on this visit, left for their bus trip back to Rae Bareilly—the last time I would see them before I returned to the United States—the three of us shared a difficult, tearful goodbye. Urvashi watched this interaction, perhaps with some surprise but with a growing understanding of the friendships I had developed with these two women teachers. After witnessing that emotional scene, Urvashi seemed to change in her tone, more openly sharing her thoughts and feelings with me during our formal taped interview. In the interview, she discussed physical, ideological, and social obstacles for women trainers and teachers, and we began to understand some similar difficulties of objectification that we both experienced as women involved in training male teachers. This further improved our relationship and dialogue. We have since met at several conferences and remain in touch by email.

She was very hospitable on my recent second trip, and we are working collaboratively on scholarly endeavors on our mutual concerns for gender equity in India and other countries.

The third example illustrates that it was possible to deepen relations with respondents who likely did not share my feminist agenda, but who came to understand that we shared certain views about education. One Sunday afternoon in Rae Bareilly in the company of Shail and Mamta, I attended an "Annual Guardian's Meeting" at the SJS Public School, in which several of their nieces and nephews were enrolled. When the manager of this school heard that I was an American educator visiting schools in the area, several people, including Shail and Mamta, encouraged me to mount the stage and give a ten-minute impromptu talk about my research to the several hundred parents in the audience. I spoke of the progress in girls' education, the poverty of the government schools, and how lucky they were to have their children attend such a well-equipped public (i.e., privately funded) school.[37] I also spoke of the encouraging efforts of the Harchandpur Block teachers who worked with so few resources.

The next day, I discovered that word traveled quickly. Umeshwar, the Block leader in Harchandpur, came to Mamta's school at lunch time, told me he had heard about my good words regarding Harchandpur schools that I had shared with a large audience of parents, and said he was pleased.[38] He stayed throughout the lunch period and beyond. My favorable words about the work teachers in his schools were doing to improve their teaching and access for girls motivated him to talk more with me. Although previously he had not been rude, he had definitely been apprehensive about the notes I was taking and who would receive this information. He may not have totally understood or agreed with my feminist perspective, yet we developed more rapport and trust despite this because I had recognized and shared his views about his Block's efforts to improve girls' education and their schools. My public acknowledgment about my views of his school opened a new space in which we could now share more candidly a discussion about some of the issues to which previously he had supplied only curt answers and given lip service. Upon my return this past summer, he was quite happy that I had remembered his school and chose to visit once again. His trust in me had not faded and he called in several teachers and District Primary Education Programme officers to talk with me that day about controversial issues in the evolution of the TEP and primary education overall.

## Conclusion

My research experiences have taught me that the social construction of knowledge as dialogue is directly affected by the methodology and methods used during the research process. In my study, a qualitative, feminist methodology facilitated the varied relationships I sought to develop, helping me to establish a positive tone, develop understanding of lived realities, and build trust with many respondents, some of whom I now consider my friends. As a participant observer, I realized that I was part of the phenomena I was exploring. Yet my reflection and my reflexivity about my research process and understandings continued to evolve over time, allowing me to arrive at new awareness of the intricacies of the relationships, especially in regard to insider/outsider perspectives and the effects of disclosing subjectivities and advocacies.

Relationships and dialogue with respondents are multilayered and multiphased. Respondents with varied roles and understandings all contribute to a larger dialogue and knowledge construction but often in different sequences of time. As I began my fieldwork, I gained access, and also encountered constraints, through arranged formal connections and structural arrangements: I was the "friend" of UNICEF researcher as well as the American woman "other" with specific research questions and an agenda to try to follow. My discussion about "other" perceptions and my illustrations of field phenomena demonstrate that those with whom I had the least contact and conducted only formal interviews remained "others." Yet, with those whom I experienced some immersion in their lives and with whom I shared some of my values and views, I was able to develop mutual trusting relationships. Trust can lead to building good relationships that create a space in which deeper, more complex, or contested issues can be put on the table and in which more truthful dialogue may emerge.

As relationships developed, they took on new forms. As I spent more time with certain individuals, especially my two main women teacher respondents, stronger, deeper relationships grew. We talked not only as researcher and respondents, but also together as teachers and women, and then as friends. As we laughed together, shared food, rode rickshaws and buses, and sometimes talked into late hours of the night, we became good friends and developed a deep sense of mutual trust and respect. This was partly confirmed when, on our last day together, they signed the consent form waiving their anonymity in the study. I have remained in contact with the two women teachers and the woman trainer between visits and during my subsequent visit stayed primarily with them. The relationships were maintained and we needed almost no time to reach again that level of comfort and trust that we had gained during my first visit. These relationships transformed, moving from the public to the private sphere, from interaction between "others" to a positive insider/outsider balance that enabled intersubjectivity in our dialogue.

Yet sharing trusting, intersubjective dialogue may not result from just understanding their lives, respecting them, or even becoming friends. If you help others to understand your subjectivities and respondents discover you have shared advocacies, can this make you an insider even though your culture, religion, and other viewpoints may be quite different? Can coming from two different cultures (researcher versus practitioner, American versus Indian, female versus male) be eliminated as an obstacle to dialogue when relationships transform through trust and shared viewpoints? Should we recommend that researchers share their subjectivities or make their advocacy clear whenever they attempt naturalistic research? When should they not?

A researcher may not initially intend to advance specific positions or wear her subjectivities on her sleeve. Yet as a relationship develops, she can decide to share her principles, values, and beliefs—in short, her advocacies—about the research topic or other matters. My experience has taught me that sharing these—in a timely manner and with a consistent message regardless of which respondents I am with—will help me experience a more positive research process, establish more meaningful dialogue, and gain more valuable and credible understanding of my research phenomena. To me, this is the essence of being a "participant" observer and the only way that intersubjective dialogue can occur. At least some women teachers and I discovered common subjectivities (a patriarchal society, obstacles for women) and shared advocacies (gender equity, systemic change, and equitable girls' education). The knowledge of our mutual concerns had helped us to build relationships and share more honest dialogue. Their positive perceptions of me as the "other" allowed more rigid researcher-researched relationships to evolve and transform into stronger, private-sphere, friendship relationships with more intersubjective negotiation. When respondents discover that they agree with your advocacies and ideas, cultural and other boundaries may be more easily crossed and dialogue engaged. As noted, this was also possible with male respondents in this setting, although the content of the shared ideas might be different than that which facilitated deepening relationships with women respondents.

As I reflect about how my respondents have affected me and changed my life and research views, I know that I appreciated my role in helping respondents to be reflective and reflexive about their work and their contributions to the larger comprehensive effort of the TEP. I also realize that my presence there provided some benefits for them, especially for my two women friends. For instance, one of the trainers told me that I have brought them attention that has made them feel important. I have also reciprocated with books and other needed professional items and even started a scholarship fund for a girl student in the small primary school Shail has begun. I am their friend in America, and we continue to exchange letters about our teaching and other important personal events in our lives.

The power of human interaction to affect the overall researcher-respondent relationship should not be underestimated. Yet the events, trust building, and dialogue that I have described are not things that can be fully planned ahead of time. Researchers cannot know what the impact of their presence and research will be in the long term or how these may affect people's thoughts and actions. However, they can read studies such as this one and make conscious decisions about choosing a methodology and process that may engender dialogue between researchers, practitioners, and policy makers.

## Notes

1. Sandra L. Stacki, *Partnerships and Processes for Teacher Empowerment: Rays of Hope for Female Teachers in India* (Bloomington, Indiana University: Unpublished Doctoral Dissertation, 1998).
2. I became aware of this teacher empowerment program as I researched issues of teacher empowerment in developing countries at the UNICEF Education Section in New York City.
3. Paulo Freire, *Pedagogy of the Oppressed* (New York: Herder and Herder, 1970); also see Mark Ginsburg and Jorge Gorostiaga, "Relationship between Theorists/Researchers and Policy Makers/Practitioners: Rethinking the Two-Cultures Thesis and the Possibility of Dialogue," *Comparative Education Review* 45 (2) (May 2001): 173–96.
4. See John McNeil, *Curriculum: The Teacher's Initiative*, 2nd ed. (Upper Saddle River, NJ: Merrill/Prentice Hall, 1999); Catherine Fosnot, *Enquiring Teachers Enquiring Learners: A Constructivist Approach for Teaching* (New York: Teachers College Press, 1989).
5. Michael Crossley and Graham Vulliamy (eds.), "Qualitative Research in Developing Countries: Issues and Experience," in *Qualitative Educational Research in Developing Countries* (New York and London: Garland Publishing, 1997), p. 6.
6. Robert Prus, *Symbolic Interaction and Ethnographic Research* (Albany: State University of New York Press, 1996).
7. Donna Haraway, "Situated Knowledges: The Science Question in Feminism and the Privilege of Partial Perspective," *Feminist Studies* 14, (3) (1988): 575–99.
8. See chapters by G. Fiumara, "The Metaphoric Function and the Question of Objectivity," and Patricia Strickland, "Feminism, Postmodernism, and Difference," in *Knowing the Difference: Feminist Perspectives in Epistemology*, ed. Kathleen Lennon and M. Whitford (New York: Routledge, 1994); Nancy Fraser, What's Critical about Critical Theory?" in *Critical Theory: The Essential Readings*, ed. D. Ingram and J. Simon-Ingram (New York: Paragon House, 1991).
9. Steiner Kvale, *InterViews: An Introduction to Qualitative Research Interviewing* (Newbury Park, CA: Sage Publications, 1996).
10. Alan Peshkin, "In Search of Subjectivity—One's Own, "*Educational Researcher* 17 (3) (1988): 17–21.
11. See Eliot Eisner and Alan Peshkin (eds.), "Introduction," in *Qualitative Inquiry in Education: The Continuing Debate* (New York: Teachers College Press, 1990); Maurice Punch, *The Politics and Ethics of Fieldwork* (Beverly Hills, CA: Sage Publications, 1986); Catherine Robb, "Introduction," in *Essays in Feminist Social Ethics* (Boston: Beacon Press, 1985).
12. See Mary Margaret Fonow and Judith Cook (eds), *Beyond Methodology: Feminist Scholarship as Lived Research* (Bloomington, Indiana University Press, 1991); Mary Maynard and June Purvis (eds.), *Researching Women's Lives from a Feminist Perspective* (Briston, PA: Taylor and Francis, 1994); Shulamit Reinharz, *Feminist Methods in Social Research* (Oxford: Oxford University Press, 1992); Margaret Sutton, "Feminist Epistemology and Research Methods," in *Women in the Third World: An Encyclopedia of Contemporary Issues*, ed. Nelly Stromquist and Karen Monkman (New York: Garland, 1998); Judith Stacey, "Can There Be a Feminist Ethnography?" *Women's Studies International Forum* 2 (1) (1988): 21–27.
13. Ibid.
14. Mary Beth Orner, *Teaching Otherwise: Feminism, Pedagogy and the Politics of Difference* (Madison, University of Wisconsin: Unpublished Doctoral Dissertation, 1992), p. 10.
15. Nita Kumar (ed.), "Introduction," in *Women as Subjects: South Asian Histories* (New Delhi, India: Stree Publications, 1994), p. 4.
16. Micaela di Leonardo (ed.), "Gender, Culture and Political Economy: Feminist Anthropology in Historical Perspective," in *Gender at the Crossroads of Knowledge: Feminist Anthropology in the Postmodern Era* (Berkeley: University of California Press, 1991), p. 13.
17. Many documents as well as interviews, observations, and photographs taken during my field immersion informed my interpretations.
18. Internal and external critiques have pointed to the failure to implement proposed reforms: Changes in political party rule, lack of political and ideological support, financial constraints, and centralization perpetuated societal inequalities that contribute to social, cultural, and

gender reproduction. See A. Basu, "Policy and Conflict in India: The Reality and Perception of Education," in *Education and Colonialism,* ed. Gail Kelly and Philip Altbach (New York: Longman, 1978); S. Chitnis, "Gearing a Colonial System of Education to Take Independent India Towards Development," *Higher Education* 26 (1993): 21–41; R. S. Pandey, *National Policy of Education in India* (Allahbad, India: Horizon Publishers, 1992); Department of Education, Ministry of Human Resource Development, India, *Redeeming a Pledge: Status Report, Second Ministerial Conference, Bali* (New Delhi, India: Author, 1995).

19. UNICEF and other donors to universal primary education efforts in developing countries have evolved to enhance national sovereignty and encourage partnerships. "Basic education activities must be considered in their entirety so that the improvements to the system may be made in ways that complement and supplement existing parts of the system." See UNICEF Education Section, *UNICEF and Basic Education* (New York: Author, 1994), p. 7. The government of India also desires partnerships but with discretion over its own affairs and local ownership leading to sustainability—not dependency. "The DPEP [District Primary Education Programme] has broken new paths in international cooperation, in that it belongs to the new genre of the developmental cooperative which emphasizes sustainability, equity, local ownership and execution and is supportive of national policies in the education sector" [National Council for Educational Research and Training, "Evolution of DPEP," *DPEP Calling* 3 (1995): 13].

20. The TEP was initiated in the state of Madhya Pradesh in September 1992. In Uttar Pradesh, to be discussed later, as well as in the other two states, Rajasthan and Maharashtra, the TEP began in 1994.

21. The state-level primary teachers' union, (Uttar Pradeshiya Prathmic Shikshak Sangh, expressed a strong commitment to the project and became involved, although teachers' unions in the other states were not as openly supportive and involved.

22. Teachers, through their union in Uttar Pradesh, Uttar Pradeshiya Prathmic Shikshak Sangh, chose the name Ruchipurna Shikshan, or "Joyful Learning," for their state's program. Uttar Pradesh, India's most populous state with over 140 million in 1996 has recently divided into two states. The smaller northern section has become Utteranchal. Uttar Pradesh has also been noted for high illiteracy rates and gender inequities; approximately 35 percent of rural women can read and write, compared with 66 percent of the men. See AKM Kamaluddin, "A Primary Teachers' Association Initiative for the Universalization of Primary Education," in *Partnerships in Teacher Development for a New Asia* (Bangkok, Thailand: UNESCO, 1996).

23. See Department of Education, Uttar Pradeshiya Prathmik Shikshak Sangh, and UNICEF, *Universalization of Primary Education in Uttar Pradesh: Richipurna Shikshan, a Teachers Initiative—Looking Ahead 1995–1996* (India: Authors, 1995).

24. The women teachers gained more awareness about the patriarchal nature of their society and the structural problems. They became more empowered to participate equally and make decisions along with the men in the program and in their schools. However, evidence of empowerment in the larger societal context was more limited. Even though my key respondents have begun to challenge confining social norms in the public sphere to improve the situation for women and girls, unfortunately a limited number of women teachers have experienced this program. The deep structure of the system still revolves around men's lives. For details, see Sandra L. Stacki, *Partnerships and Processes*; Sandra L. Stacki , "Moving Gender Boundaries: Rays of Hope for Female Teachers in India," *Education and Society* 18 (1) (2000); Sandra L. Stacki, "Wanted—Gender-Sensitive Female Trainers: The Teacher Empowerment Program Responds," *Education as Change* 3 (1) (1999 ); Sandra L. Stacki, "A Decentralized India: New Possibilities for Empowered Teachers," *Democracy & Education* 11 (2) (1997); Sandra L. Stacki and Mary Joy Pigozzi, "Empowering Female Teachers as an Interactive Dialectic Process: Examples from South Asia," *Convergence* 28 (3) (1995): 14–25.

25. UNICEF maintains a strong relationship in India with work in many sectors at the grassroots level. The agency's esteem has allowed it the flexibility to implement innovative programs such as the TEP.

26. A stranger can be threatening by being unknown and different, yet also because she or he cannot be relied upon to behave in familiar ways or trusted to respect the local population's needs and feelings. See J. Davies in ed. Kathleen DeMarais *Inside Stories: Qualitative Research Reflections,* Mahwah, (NJ: Lawrence Erlbaum, 1997).

27. Although some respondents queried the purpose of my research and sometimes looked on apprehensively as I took notes, most understood my doctoral candidate status and no one questioned me publicly or privately about my right to study the program.

28. For example, David Harding, then education chief in India, perhaps even more so than other UNICEF staff, talked about the partnership tensions with the government and a particular miscommunication between UNICEF and the government of India. His frank remarks were made at the end of my fieldwork, after having hosted me at his family home for a few days when I first arrived in India and after having received positive feedback regarding my interactions with many other stakeholders. His candid comments also seemed based on his belief that the New York Education Section of UNICEF would not have helped me get access if they had not thought me worthy of such a research endeavor.

29. Issues of gender and power make research more challenging when a woman, especially a Western woman, conducts research in a cross-cultural and patriarchal field setting. See J. N. Gurney, "Female Researchers in Male-Dominated Settings: Implications for Short-Term Versus Long-Term Research," in *Experiencing Fieldwork: An Inside View of Qualitative Research*, ed. W. B. Shaffir and R. A. Stebbins (Newbury Park, CA: Sage Publications, 1991) pp. 53–61.

30. Peggy Golde, "Women in the Field," in *Anthropology Experiences* (Berkeley: University of California Press, 1986).

31. Ibid.

32. Some men seemed inclined to control women, including me, with their constant gaze; they tried to make women look away or lower our eyes. At the same time, a few men seemed genuinely interested to speak with an American and started a conversation.

33. Many researchers have identified frameworks or models for kinds of women's empowerment, including discussions of physical empowerment that enables individuals to move about freely within their society. See Candida March, Ines Smyth, and Maitrayee Mukhopadhyay, *A Guide to Gender-Analysis Frameworks* (London: Oxfam, 1999); S. Feldman, "Conceptualizing Change and Equality in the 'Third World' Contexts," in *Women in the Third World: An Encyclopedia of Contemporary Issues*, ed. Nelly Stromquist and Karen Monkman (New York: Garland, 1998), pp. 24–36; Nelly Stromquist, "Mapping Gendered Spaces in Third World Educational Interventions," in *Social Cartography: Mapping Ways of Seeing Social and Educational Change*, ed. Roland Paulston (New York and London: Garland, 1996), pp. 223–47; and Caroline Moser, *Gender Planning and Development: Theory, Practice and Training* (New York: Routledge, 1993).

34. This is not the case for the women teachers, who experienced the constraints of patriarchal norms more regularly. For example, Urvashi told me about the problems that she and other women trainers in the TEP faced in discharging their responsibilities, given that traveling alone by a woman was discouraged and there was a lack of sleeping accommodations for women. However, women in India do not always accommodate to these constraints. To illustrate, Shail informed me during my recent trip that she had bought a motorcycle to make her school trips easier and less expensive; this represented an action through which Shail was challenging explicitly some of the gender norms that limit women in her society.

35. With enough understanding that my gender equity goals were similar to hers and trust in me, Shail felt comfortable enough to begin looking over my shoulder and reading my fieldnotes. She read notes when just the two of us talked but also when I was talking with someone else. In this new space that developed, we would sometimes confer about the accuracy of the notes. Thus, practitioners often helped me to interpret data that I had collected.

36. Having reflected on my feminist subjectivities, I was careful during my stay in India not to discuss women's rights publicly, criticize Indian cultural traditions in this regard or any other, or behave or dress in ways that would call any extra attention to me as a Western woman. Yet, when I was asked my views on these issues by someone who was obviously open to an honest dialogue about cultural, social, and gender issues in different cultures, I shared my comparative perspectives about America and India.

37. In India, public schools are private schools managed by guardians; the government schools are publicly funded.

38. The public nature of this event might have helped; the Block leader may have perceived the benefit of how I portrayed his schools to the larger population of public-school, middle-class parents in RaeBareli.

CHAPTER 7

# Reinventing Research for Educational Reform
## Advocacy Research and the Promotion of Participation

CRAIG G. WISHART
JOSEPH DESTEFANO

### Educational (Non)Reform and the Traditional Role of Research

> [I]t must be considered that there is nothing more difficult to carry out, nor more doubtful of success, nor more dangerous to handle, than to initiate a new system. For the initiator has enemies in all those who profit by the old system, and only lukewarm defenders in all those who would profit by the new system, this lukewarmness arising partly from the fear of their adversaries who have the past in their favor; partly from the incredulity of mankind, who do not truly believe in anything new until they have had actual experience of it[1]

The history of educational reform points to the unfortunate truth of Machiavelli's "Law of Innovation." To date, despite international attention to changing education systems across the world, as exemplified by the World Declaration on Education for All,[2] the actual implementation of education reform is very limited and the changes resulting from the reforms are considered insignificant at best.[3] Despite this exasperating and deeply troubling failure to implement broad-scale educational reform, the predominant approach to policy reform remains unchanged, and traditional strategies for linking research to policy and practice continue to be followed.

Reformers frequently assume that insufficient and/or inadequate information or lack of knowledge is the root cause of the failure of educational systems. It is assumed that the lack of technical information, or the inadequate "spread" of that information, is the problem. Accordingly, most educational reform initiatives are, in one sense or another, demonstration projects that are designed to generate concrete, research-based information about good educational practice. And, in fact, these pilot projects often do provide models of what schools and school systems need to do. Indeed, this research shows that models of good educational practice, of state-of-the-art professional development, and of comprehensive school reform can be found almost anywhere. It is assumed that this information alone should be the compelling catalyst for "scaling-up" the reforms to other schools, but it is common to find effective schools just a few miles away from dysfunctional ones.[4]

Although the "technology" of education has been exhaustively researched and the findings from successful innovations thoroughly documented, systemic educational reform and equitable access to quality education for all children have yet to be attained. To assume that we need another new model of good instruction, or more research into how children acquire literacy, or more information on what kind of professional development leads to improved practice, misses the point. That is to say, in reality, the use of the available information is grievously lacking. We know the answers but have not been willing to organize education systems to provide quality learning opportunities for certain children.

The use and misuse of research play critical roles in distanced, unresponsive, and often irrelevant policy making. Because research findings are presumed to be objective, verifiable, and replicable, being articulated by professionals with expert knowledge in the field, the knowledge and experience of other stakeholders are discounted by policy makers. The needs, problems, and solutions are therefore externally defined by the experts, and then justified and implemented according to the prescriptions of the political agenda, which the findings were used to support. Even—or perhaps especially—if the research fully represented the views and interests of the least powerful and seldom acknowledged stakeholders, research findings are subject to rampant misinterpretation and misuse by the policy makers. Evidently, enacting policy reform entails more than generating policy-relevant research and analysis. Both history and common sense have demonstrated that numerous political obstacles serve to block implementation of reform initiatives. In other words, it is not a question of what people *don't know*, but rather a question of what people *won't do* to bring about educational reform.

### Reconceptualizing the Policy Formulation Process

The assumptions on which the research community's activity is based are rooted in misguided conceptions of the process of policy formulation. The "classic" or textbook view of the policy reform process tends to imply that it can be expected to move smoothly through a logical cycle of phases: from agenda setting through problem identification and analysis, to construction of policy options for problem solution, to critical comparison of the policy options in terms of their relative cost-efficiency, and finally to decision making, implementation, evaluation, and back to problem identification.[5] In this scenario, research is a source for hard data and analysis of the facts, serving to inform and shape policy makers' general thinking about the issues and, subsequently, becoming relevant to specific policy decisions. Such technocratic perspectives on the policy process tend to assume, implicitly or explicitly, that there is a consensus on what the problem is, that good analysis will provide the proper solution, and that responsible decision makers and practitioners will ensure that this solution will be implemented to everyone's general benefit.

However, such a linear, logical, and technically rational process to reforming educational policy is seldom, if ever, realized. In actual practice, in developed and developing countries alike, policy formulation and implementation can be and often are a complex result of political pressure, advocacy, coalition building, and the accretion of crisis-management band-aids, as well as—or, in some cases, in place of—technical objective analysis of critical information. We contend that educational policy reform is first and foremost a political process, with reform being shaped by interest groups competing in the political arena to maintain or enhance the benefits they receive within local, national, and global communities.

According to Robert Porter, "the policy process is the product of the way people recognize problems, generate proposals for policy change and engage in political activities such as pressure group lobbying."[6] Throughout this process, Porter contends, advocacy plays a crucial role facilitating and guiding the iterative interactions between three streams of activity: defining a problem for consideration, bringing solutions to the attention of decision makers, and gaining political consensus for action. "Changes occur when these three streams converge, presenting a 'window of opportunity,' [which] can be grasped by the vigilant proponent of reform."[7] This multiple-streams theory of policy reform challenges the prevailing assumption that compelling "objective" information itself is the powerful catalyst of change. Porter argues that "in order to make a difference, not only does information need to be disseminated, but champions—using this information—must make the case for change with those who can actually influence policies and their implementation."[8]

**Redefining the Purpose and Function of Research for Educational Reform**

Against the backdrop of the multiple streams model of policy formulation, it becomes apparent that there needs to be less preoccupation with compiling and validating the "facts" of inequities in education and society and greater focus on giving voice to and mobilizing impassioned advocates of change. Because educational reform is first and foremost a political process, researchers need to recognize and exploit their role in the dynamic interplay of policy activities. Policy reform research must engage innovative, emergent, dynamic, and contextually relevant processes of public engagement to generate this discourse.

Importantly, the processes of engagement should confirm the wholeness of society by embracing the marginalized and silent. It requires processes through which we learn to listen seriously to the voice of the people—"hearing them into speech," as Palmer[9] phrased it, so that they may participate in the discourse. It is a shift in language and activities of communication that compels us to *engage with*, rather than *communicate to*, community stakeholders.[10] It requires unconditional care and deep sensitivity to hear their voice in dialogue, because they have learned that it is much safer to remain silent. Palmer[11] contends that "the silent one is understood as the victim of a system that denies his or her story, that ignores or punishes people who tell tales that threaten the standard version of truth." But through authentic participation in dialogue about their critical social needs, consciousness is raised.[12] This "conscientization is the process by which human beings participate critically in a transforming act. . . . One of the important points of conscientization is to provoke recognition in the world, not as a 'given' world, but as a world dramatically 'in the making.'"[13]

Currently, traditional social science relegates researchers to a passive role in the policy dialogue, in which research findings are being used, misused, and dismissed at will by the policy makers. The prevailing norms of objectivity and value neutrality in modernist social science research effectively place researchers behind a wall of analytical abstractionism that disables them from authentically engaging and learning from their object of study. The credibility and veracity of research are proved by the capacity to eliminate the "observer bias" in assessing the "facts" of social reality unmediated by personal perceptive bias. It is believed that through the application of rational scientific mathematical techniques, the observer is capable of "discovering" the immutable and empirically verifiable laws of social reality. Through the *medium* of language, the researcher gives expression to this objective reality, creating a "picture" of the world.[14] It is assumed that with more information about the world, knowledge advances, and we progressively gain control over ourselves and our social reality.[15]

Yet currently, social scientists are expressing dissatisfaction with the traditional research methodology because of the limited use and relevance of the knowledge generated from their research.[16] For instance, Kenneth Gergen[17] argues that the modernist supposition of objectivity effectively binds the social scientists in an intellectual straightjacket, restraining researchers from fully engaging in the social dialogue and controlling their role in the discourse. Framing "objectivity" as a false consciousness, he argues that because researchers are embedded in human society, social values are *infused* in social science. These values implicitly legitimize particular forms of action and delegitimize others. He articulates an alternative postmodernist position[18] that openly acknowledges the subjective influences and perceptions of the observer on the object of study in social science research. If research is to be socially useful and relevant, then we must openly acknowledge the valuational stance of social science. From this perspective, Gergen posits that the fundamental purpose of research shifts from defining and validating "Truth" to intentionally enhancing the generative capacity of ideas to influence our world. He describes this generative capacity as "the capacity to challenge the guiding assumptions of the culture to raise fundamental questions regarding contemporary social life, to foster reconsideration of that which is 'taken for granted,' and thereby to furnish new alternatives for social action."[19]

Thus, theorists and researchers, while thought to be cloaked in relative obscurity back stage, are in fact found center stage in the "theater" of life.[20] The very act of engaging in an investigation and articulating observations shapes the social reality observed. That is, the words theorists and researchers use to describe our phenomenal-world have created the world we understand and perceive. By implication then, the researcher is not a dispassionate bystander with a trained "objective" eye, but rather an *advocate* of the reality articulated. As Van Maanen[21] observes, the process of research "irrevocably influences the interests and lives of the people represented in them—individually and collectively, for better or for worse."

Given that research may have real consequences for people's lives, it is important to ask about the social relationships in the context of which such research is designed, conducted, disseminated, and interpreted. While there are various arguments for improving communication between researchers and policy makers,[22] attention should also be directed at how researchers relate to practitioners, clients, community members, and other stakeholders. In part this argument is based on a general commitment to the value of participation in democratic societies. We concur with Noam Chomsky and Donald Macedo that:

> It is a waste of time ... to speak truth to ... [those] who exercise power in coercive institutions—for the most part they already know these truths.... One should seek out an audience that matters [and] ... [t]hey should not be seen merely as an audience but as a part of a community of common concern in which one hopes to participate constructively. We should not be speaking *to* but *with*.[23]

When research is informed by and intended to inform a range of stakeholders, it can serve to catalyze the public discourse on reform, which in turn will force the hand of policy makers in compliance with the public will. Research then serves not only as a means of knowledge creation but also a mechanism for engaging public participation in dialogic forms of democratic policy making.

The argument for focusing on researchers' relations with groups beyond policy makers is also based on our recognition of alternative criteria for evaluating social science research. For example, within a "grounded theory" approach one is not primarily concerned with accuracy and correspondence in the sense of empirical verification, but instead highly focused on the utility and applicability of a theory (assessed according to four interrelated properties: fit, understanding, generality, and control).[24] When a premium is placed on emergent conceptualizations that "fit" the situations being studied and are "understandable" to the actors in those situations, research needs to be designed in conversation with and communicated back to the subjects of investigation, thus completing the feedback loop and creating more valid and relevant theory.

We contend that research becomes a mechanism for educational reform when it is appropriately defined as a tool of communication in support of activists.

As a communication tool for advocacy, research can actively promote policy dialogue, intentionally shaping how a problem is perceived and defined, as well as framing the possible solutions. Researchers can contribute to this dialogue in constructive ways by facilitating the creation of the formal and normative environment necessary for broad-based participation to occur, promoting various forms of dialogue, and building the institutional capacity of stakeholders.

Embracing this process approach to research requires a fundamental shift in understanding our roles and knowledge itself. As Majid Rahnema explains, "reality is the unknown which has to be '*dis*-covered' together, free from all presuppositions and influences of the known."[25] Rahnema is pointing to the fundamental characteristics of humility and openness to learning that are critical for researchers and stakeholders to engage in dialogue. The idea of public participation takes on new meaning when the researcher exchanges the hat of *expert* for that of a *collaborator* in the learning process. Advocacy researchers must be prepared to co-generate new solutions to a reality collectively construed and analyzed. Under these conditions, knowledge cannot be envisioned as a static and reified entity that holds truth for everyone, everywhere. As Freire notes, "knowledge involves a constant unity between action and reflection upon reality. Like our presence in the world, our consciousness transforms knowledge, acting on and thinking about what enables us to reach the stage of reflection."[26]

Advocacy research is a dialogic learning process of inviting participants in community to critically unveil their reality and claim their voice. It assumes that "every human being, no matter how 'ignorant' or submerged in the 'culture of silence' he or she may be, is capable of looking critically at the world in a dialogical encounter."[27] Beginning with their existential experience, the researcher joins *with* others in the community to create new understanding of their condition. As participants gradually come to doubt the conventional depiction of reality, they unveil to themselves the truth of their coerced participation in their own oppression, and the potential for changing their condition. Only then will they be capable of giving their own creative self-expressions to the world, and ultimately participate in the process of policy reform and social change. "The more they unveil it, the more their awakening consciousness deepens, thus leading to the 'conscientization' of the situation by the poor class."[28] The praxis of advocacy research is a means of educating for liberation, a means of reigniting hope in the hearts and minds of the oppressed and disenfranchised stakeholders. It cannot be dismissed as mere idealistic banter, for it is the keystone of a life-affirming process that makes us most human.

## Illustrations of Advocacy Research for Educational Reform[29]

Having identified the limitations of modernist forms of research as a catalyst for promoting dialogue (joint reflection and action) about educational research, policy, and practice, and then posited advocacy research as a promising alternative approach, we now turn to examine cases involving efforts to follow an advocacy research model. The cases are situated in Brazil, South Africa, and the United States.

*Brazil: Linking Research and Policy—a Call to Action*

In northeast Brazil, the quality of primary education has been consistently the poorest in the country. Enrollment rates are 22 percent lower than the rest of the country, and completion rates of 10 percent are less than half the national average. In this context, a collaborative effort was launched in 1995 to probe the policy problem with the guiding research question, "Why do schools in the northeast fail to effectively educate children?" Two efforts were undertaken by a broad base of stakeholders, including the educational research community, national as well as state and municipal levels of governments, the federation of teacher trade associations, nongovernmental organizations (NGOs), communities, philanthropic foundations, and international agencies.

First, with the support of the World Bank and the Ford Foundation, a standard beneficiary assessment was launched to learn the needs and interests of the beneficiaries of public education and subsequently inform policy makers. The study probed five major questions:

- What value beneficiaries placed on education
- How they judged the quality of schools
- What they saw as barriers to schooling
- How they saw their role in the educational process
- What suggestions they had for improving education

Unfortunately, although not a surprising result of such traditional research reporting efforts, this effort did not help policy makers (let alone others) to fully understand the results, to make appropriate recommendations for action, to take ownership of the issues, or to mobilize for action.

Meanwhile, a parallel effort (Programma de Pesquisa e Operacionização de Politica Educacional, or PPO) was also initiated. In contrast to the beneficiary assessment, the PPO's goal was more broadly defined: developing strategies for improving the performance of educational systems by operationalizing the results of research. The program design included mechanisms for involving policy makers and other stakeholders throughout the research process, disseminating the findings, using results to make decisions, and mobilizing communities toward reform. The specific objectives of PPO were to:

- Identify the constraints to improving the performance of the educational systems and student outcomes
- Contextualize the results in the northeast setting
- Specify and prioritize solutions for the short-term (actions) and long-term (policies)
- Disseminate and implement these solutions

In order to achieve these objectives, participatory processes were used from the beginning of the study to link the research to policy and practice. Five groups were convened to work in partnership:

- *Coordination Group*—the World Bank, UNICEF, and the Ministry of Education, whose responsibility was to manage the program and assure financing
- *Consultative Group*—composed of leaders whose experience and influence would help to operationalize the study results; including state and municipal secretaries of education from two of the largest northeastern states, presidents of both the municipal secretaries of education and the national association of teachers' unions, as well as a university vice president for graduate research
- *Technical Team*—composed of senior level education policy specialists with experience in advising the government on education policy issues
- *Research Team*—composed of researchers associated with university research centers in the Brazil (northeast, São Paulo, Rio) and the United States
- *Dissemination Group*—composed of stakeholders with expertise in communications and social marketing

The PPO process began with members of the Coordination, Technical, and Research teams meeting to define the problem and plan the study. The Consultative Group provided advice and guidance as the study was conducted and provided recommendations for policy and pilot projects based on the final study results. The Research Team utilized qualitative research (videotaping teaching in the classroom; interviewing students, teachers, principles, community members, and school dropouts) and quantitative research methods (to analyze economic rates-of-return, community factors associated with low achievement, and repetition rates). The Coordination and Technical teams organized the results and proposed recommendations based on the Consultative Team's policy suggestions and the recommendations made by the Research Team. The groups debated over and modified the final set of recommendations, which were compiled into a document, the *Call to Action (Chamada a Açao)*.

With the guidance of the Dissemination Group, the *Call to Action* was formally published and distributed to all education authorities in the northeast as a set of lessons and practices describing the context of the studies, the methodologies employed, and the principal findings and recommendations. Additionally, a video was produced to capture the story of this project and spread the findings and recommendations of the PPO to the teachers, principles, and community members. To further disseminate the work, a campaign was started with a national grocery chain to print on its grocery bags simple messages about the research findings and recommended policies of the PPO. A "how-to" guide for conducting similar studies was developed for practitioners, and a series of eight brochures around the themes found in the PPO was developed for teachers.

While it included an exhaustive research process, PPO was successful because the broad-based ownership of the research findings and policy recommendations created a shared sense of urgency for reform, a comprehensive view of the roles and responsibilities of stakeholders at various levels of the system, and a mobilization of will for change. The process of the PPO engaged everyone in the research, from the children to the policy makers, to uncover and interpret what the problems really were and how they were seen and understood by even the least powerful and privileged stakeholders. Importantly, PPO was not just a research activity, but a decision-making process that emphasized the utility of research for decision making.

As a result of the research process, as well as the innovative communications and social marketing campaigns, "The *Call to Action* is being read all over Brazil. It constitutes more than a research publication. The *Call to Action* is seen as an expression of a consensus perspective and a declaration of the will to act. It has served as the basis for policies at the federal, state, and municipal level, and is leading to broad agreement on specific actions for improving quality [of education]."[30]

*South Africa: APEX–Research as an Opportunity for Dialogic Democratic Policy Making*[31]

On February 2, 1991, President F. W. DeKlerk announced that the apartheid structures of South Africa would be dismantled. Although there was much conflict and strife over this political directive, there was agreement that what lay ahead was an overwhelming and daunting task of transformation. As a result of the long history of racially entrenched inequities of apartheid, the education system in particular was a morass of haves and have-nots. As of 1991, the per capita spending for whites was nearly eleven times higher than it was for blacks. While whites had qualified teachers, the majority of teachers in the disadvantaged, nonwhite education systems were either unqualified or underqualified. The student-teacher ratios in the disadvantaged systems were three to four times higher that those found in the white education system. As a result, the performance of the disadvantaged black educational systems was exceedingly low.

It is against this backdrop of gross educational inequity that the Joint Working Group undertook its charge in late 1991 to put forth and examine viable options for new educational policy in post-apartheid South Africa. Although the Joint Working Group was made up of a number of stakeholder groups, it represented two major voices: that of the democratic opposition and that of the incumbent "white" government. Because of the democratic opposition's lack of trust for the incumbents, who controlled most of the data that informed the existing policy options, there needed to be a means of developing and proposing sound, alternative, information-based education policy options. A collaborative effort was undertaken involving the U.S. Agency for International Development, the Independent Development Trust of South Africa, the Research Triangle Institute based in the United States, and the Education Foundation based in the United States, which became known as the "APEX Team." APEX (Assessing Policies for Education Excellence) was conceived to develop a national-level policy modeling tool for aiding communities and the democratic opposition, the African National Congress (ANC),[32] in designing and assessing new plans for educational resource distribution and administration. The ultimate goal of APEX was to generate policy options that reflected not only concrete data but also the views and opinions of a wide cross section of stakeholders, including the ANC, the Department of National Education (a department of South Africa's apartheid education system), parent-teacher community organizations, and key community leaders. Thus, APEX was designed to be a widely consultative process.

The development of APEX went through several stages, as the APEX team examined its objectives and determined the design and the data requirements for creating a relevant assessment tool. Initially, the APEX team held numerous meetings and workshops, during which they unearthed the difficulties of accessing information not readily available in the public domain and generated a pilot tool that could be used with stakeholders to examine and assess policy options. Groups of stakeholders then convened in Policy Options Workshops in which the APEX modeling tool was used to examine and generate new and existing policy options. Over the following five years, these workshops exposed the APEX tool to a wide cross section of technical and political stakeholders, who challenged the APEX team to explain, reexamine, and reassess the various assumptions, methodological procedures, and other features of the model. As a result, the APEX tool was extensively tested and refined, and additional policy dialogue tools were developed in response to the demands of the participants in a significantly broadened policy arena.

Most importantly, these workshops became the center of an emerging national policy dialogue process, which broadened participation in the policy discussions and expanded influence on decisions. In short, the Policy Options Workshops were rendering the policy formulation process in South Africa more democratic. These workshops became forums for informed dialogue, where stakeholders throughout the system were exposed to the same research data, contributed new information, participated in collaborative discourse, and learned how their particular interests were served or not served by the education system as a whole. Because the workshops were grounded in verifiable research data gathered from such a wide audience of stakeholders, the policy debates were stripped of the harmful rhetoric that feeds on ignorance and falsehoods. Instead, the ensuing policy dialogues were informed by and generated the substantive and information-rich fiscal, political, and systemic issues that characterized the reality of South Africa's education system. Because the process involved the input of the stakeholders, a broad-based sense of ownership of both APEX and the APEX process resulted, which meant that the model became widely accepted as a valid and objective tool for policy decision making.

What emerged from the preliminary workshops was an education policy option, Education Reconstruction Model #1, so named to indicate that it was a dynamic and emergent work in progress. Ultimately, the APEX process produced a number of such models, which served as the democratic opposition's response to the incumbent government's plan for educational resource distribution and administration.

Clearly, APEX was more than a conventional research assessment tool, designed to gauge objective data and yield conclusive results. Using the research data as the common base of knowledge and language, APEX became the catalyst of a nationwide dialogue over the nature and character of post-apartheid education that both facilitated the reconciliation and cooperation among debating stakeholders throughout the education systems and fundamentally altered the policy-making process in the education sector. Throughout this process it was critically important that the APEX team was seen as a public interest group and not aligned to a political organization or side of the debate. Yet, while perceived as politically neutral, the researchers did not mechanically disseminate the research data. The researchers saw themselves as active agents of change and not passive disseminators of information. They used the information to target varied stakeholders and gain widespread participation. Because of the level of participation and acceptance of the APEX, the researchers were able to assemble decision makers at the highest level to engage in the public dialogue. In short, because the APEX team did not confine its research effort to the creation of an abstract analytic tool for policy makers alone, but sought to engage publicly a broad audience of stakeholders in this inquiry, the research process served successfully to generate an innovative democratic policy-making process—a process that to this day is practiced by the ANC-led South African government.

### *United States: DC VOICE: Community-Based Research*

District Community Voices Organized and Informed for Change in Education (DC VOICE) is a broad-based collaborative of parents, teachers, and community representatives committed to strengthening the public voice in public education in Washington, DC. In response to the formal introduction of a standards-based reform initiative in schools throughout the Washington, DC, area in 1998,[33] DC VOICE launched a unique research project in spring 2000 to assess conditions and advocate for improvements of the DC public schools (DCPS). Their report, "Half the Solution,"[34] documented the results of this community-based action research project, capturing the perceptions of parents, teachers, students, and community members regarding the successes and challenges of implementing the *Standards for Teaching and Learning*.

The research effort emerged from the interests of the DC VOICE advisory group, composed of staff, board members, university faculty, teachers, and community representatives, which meets regularly to discuss opportunities to promote the DC VOICE mission. They saw this research project as an opportunity both to collect data on the needs for improvement as well as to educate the community about the *Opportunity to Learn Standards*.[35] The advisory group created a steering committee for this project, composed of advisory group members and other representatives from local community-based organizations. Approximately thirty community-based organizations and local schools, which had first-hand experience of the devastating impacts of insufficient social and economic supports and poor schooling on parents and youth in Columbia Heights and Shaw, DC, were enlisted in this participatory action research to assist in convening public sessions. With $10,000 in local funding and a one-year time frame, DC VOICE created the Research Action Group, which consisted of teams of internal staff, advisory group members, consultants, outreach workers, and local school staff charged with designing and conducting the research.

Using *Opportunities to Learn Standards* as a framework for their inquiry, the Research Action Group generated a series of guiding questions that were posed to the community stakeholders to solicit their interpretation of:

- The types of support needed to improve achievement
- Whether the district's academic standards influence instruction
- Whether current professional development approaches are effective
- The nature of school-community relationships

The teams of researchers conducted seventeen focus group discussions as well as numerous one- on-one interviews throughout the Columbia Heights and Shaw communities. These engaged the participation of more than 150 culturally and racially diverse community members, who were elementary, middle, and high school students; in- and out-of-school youth; youth development program staff; teachers of diverse subjects and grade levels; and native English speakers and language minority parents.

At the conclusion of the year, the Research Action Group compiled and documented the findings from these public discussions with the people most closely associated with the schools—students, parents, teachers, and community members—in a report, concluding that "setting high academic standards is only half the solution to increasing student achievement in DC. The other half is to provide in-school and out-of-school support for students to meet those [standards]."[36] While the report, "Half the Solution," communicated the key findings, which represented and gave voice to the needs, concerns, and conditions of the constituents in these particular communities, it did not propose solutions. To generate these solutions and propose meaningful agendas around which the community could rally, the Research Action Group took the findings back into the community. Five community dialogues were convened, where district administrators, principals, and teachers as well as parents and representatives of community-based organizations discussed the research findings and created specific recommendations to support student learning. With the completion of the fifth community dialogue in the summer of 2001, the Research Action Group is documenting a summation of the community's solutions and recommendations. In collaboration with the organizations and schools involved in the research effort, DC VOICE will be disseminating these research findings and policy recommendations of the two communities throughout DC to further inform, organize, and galvanize the students, parents, and teachers to work together to address the gaps in student support. DC VOICE intends for this final stage of action research to spawn the creation of additional collaboratives of activists and advocacy organizations in the respective communities that will continue:

- Facilitating learning among community stakeholders regarding standards-based reform
- Generating public demand for adequate opportunities to learn in DC schools
- Pursuing specific policy reforms and institutional changes in the school systems

**Conclusion**

We have argued that advocacy research redefines the stakeholders as the appropriate audience for and collaborators in research. As these case studies illustrate, advocacy researchers need to break out their modernist social scientist role as specialists in data collection and analysis. They need to shift their attention from the passive and mechanical application of positivist methods to actively promoting the enabling environment, mechanisms, and capacity for dialogue and exchange with (and among) stakeholders. This is not to say that researchers must abandon the positivist, quantitative methods. Rather, such research methods should be used concurrently with qualitative methods in support of the dialogic forms and processes of stakeholder engagement. In these three cases, the researchers recognized the capacity of their inquiries to intervene in and catalyze the public discourse. Rather than allowing the misuse of the research to foster highly politicized rhetoric, these researchers chose to actively engage the public in the inquiry for understandings and actions.

The PPO in Brazil and DC VOICE in the United States exemplify advocacy research in practice. In these cases, the research process engaged the stakeholders as researchers, who contributed to the design, implementation, analysis, and dissemination of the data to their community. Through their genuine participatory research methods, PPO and DC VOICE engaged the public as a means and end in itself. The researchers' activity was not limited to the collecting of data to test a theory or contribute to academic discourse. Rather, researchers were involved with the stakeholder groups in "a process [that] enables the deprived sections to gain control over their own life situation, resources, knowledge and ideology."[37] They collectively shaped the public dialogue about the issues by promoting processes for policy identification, solution development, and reform implementation. PPO's *A Call to Action* was not a clinical report, typical of traditional research, but it became a living declaration of a community's collective commitment to reclaim their dignity and self-determination.

The APEX process in South Africa further demonstrates the importance of encouraging researchers to consult and deliberate with the various underrepresented constituencies having a stake in policy reform. While the initial design of the pilot APEX tool did not include stakeholders, the ensuing revisions of its design and the policy options generated through the use of this tool were directly influenced by stakeholders participating in the Policy Option Workshops. Because the APEX process engaged such a broad cross section of constituents, the research findings were publicly embraced as the collective voice of a nation and generated the common language for understanding the necessity of dialogic forms of democratic policy making.

In education and other sectors, the sustainability of policy reforms and their implementation is to a large extent due to popular support for the reforms.[38] But as these examples demonstrate, this is not the popular support that is superficially obtained through quick and clever marketing campaigns. The popular support generated by DC VOICE, for example, was based on research practices that directly engaged those affected by the policy in clear communication about the issues, consultation, dialogue, and debate. DC VOICE, like PPO and APEX, is a sustaining initiative because researchers created the conditions for genuine participation in the policy dialogue, in which the public articulated their concerns, identified the problems, set the goals, generated solutions, and participated in championing the policy reform.

For reform initiatives to change schools in a sustainable manner, they need to build internal capacities for change through a deeper intervention into the cultural processes, organizational patterns of meaning, values, and behavior. While obvious to most, but seldom recognized in praxis, all actors who have relevant information and/or a stake in the outcome should participate in the decisions about policy and practice. Advocacy researchers can contribute to the quality of policy reform by grounding their work in the "front-line" knowledge that comes from promoting stakeholder participation in public dialogue about these fundamental questions. For the advocacy researcher, stakeholder participation in defining priorities of investigation and in articulating the issues supplies the "local" information that the bureaucratic channels can rarely access or provide. The most conventional means of accessing information—through conducting surveys, examining reports, and conducting interviews with bureaucratic leadership—are often inversely related to the usefulness of information for policy reform.[39] While the bureaucracies of schools delegate authority, support administrators, and set performance standards, they do not serve to influence creativity and innovation, or fundamentally change the institutional structure and status quo processes they were designed to manage.[40]

In short, advocacy research requires that policy-relevant information emerge from dialogue and deliberation among stakeholders about the issues, in which analyses are debated, different points of view are expressed, and learning takes place. As researchers and other stakeholders collaborate as advocates of reform from the inception of the research projects, the process serves to generate local support and is more likely to result in public consensus and a broad-based sense of ownership of new reform policies.[41] When advocacy research is done well, the parents, students, teachers, administrators, unions, committees, and community—the "roots" of the school systems' culture—come to own the localized reform initiatives that grow from participatory research interventions. With public consensus, constituents are empowered to demand improvements in service and hold the system accountable for results, increasing the likelihood of relevant, meaningful, and sustained change.[42] By advocating for an open "marketplace of ideas," research not only creates knowledge, but also improves policy and practice by engaging the public in dialogic forms of democratic decision making.[43]

## Notes

1. Niccolo Machiavelli, *The Prince* (Cambridge: Cambridge University Press, 1992).
2. UNESCO, *World Declaration on Education for All: Meeting Basic Learning Needs* (Jomtien: 1990).
3. John E. Craig, "Implementing Educational Policies in Sub-Saharan Africa; A Review of the Literature," *Education and Training Series Report EDT79*; The International Bank for Reconstruction and Development (Washington, DC: The World Bank, 1987); R. E. Elmore, "Getting to Scale with Good Educational Practice," *Harvard Educational Review* 66 (1) (1996): 1–25; George Psacharopoulos, "Why Educational Policies Can Fail: An Overview of Selected African Experiences," *World Bank Discussion Papers; 82. Africa Technical Department Series* (Washington, DC: The World Bank, 1990).
4. Henry F. Healey and Joseph DeStefano (1997),*Education Reform Support: A Framework for Scaling Up School Reform* (Washington, DC: USAID project ABEL).
5. *DAE Case Studies* (Washington, DC: USAID/DAE, 1995); Merilee Grindle and John Thomas,*Public Choices and Policy Change. The Political Economy of Reform in Developing Countries* (Baltimore,: The Johns Hopkins University Press, 1991); Wadi D. Haddad and Terri Demsky, *The Dynamics of Education Policymaking: Case studies of Burkina Faso, Jordan, Peru and Thailand* (Washington, DC: The World Bank, 1994); Paul A. Sabatier, "Toward Better Theories of the Policy Process," *Political Science and Politics* (June 1991): 147–56.
6. Robert Porter, *Knowledge Utilization and the Process of Policy Formation: Toward a Famework for Africa* (Washington, DC: USAID Project AFA/SD/HRD/HHRAA/SARA, 1995), p.18.
7. Porter, *Knowledge Utilization*, p. v.
8. Porter, *Knowledge Utilization*, p. v. From Porter's description, policy formulation clearly is not a clean science that follows the logic and laws of cause and effect, proceeding to uncover objective social truth. Consequently and quite understandably, theorists and researchers have desired to separate themselves from the messier stuff in which practitioners and policy makers are immersed in the policy reform game. However, because research influences the outcome of a reform agenda by framing how societal as well as educational problems and goals are identified, studied, and communicated [see Carol H. Weiss, "Perspectives on Knowledge Use in National Policy Making," in *Knowledge Generation, Exchange and Utilization*, ed. George Beal, Wimal Dissanayake, and Sumiye Konoshima (Boulder, CO: Westview Press, 1986)], and

because of the politics of research activity itself, it is difficult to argue for the existence of the supposed borders separating the theorists/researchers from the policy makers/practitioners. Therefore, the "two-culture, thesis" may be perceived as more a self-serving, protective veil of illusion than the reality of the policy reform process [for a critical discussion of the two-cultures thesis, see Mark Ginsburg and Jorge Gorostiaga, "Relationships between Theorists/Researchers and Policy Makers/Practitioners: Rethinking the Two-Cultures Thesis and the Possibility of Dialogue," *Comparative Education Review* 45 (2) (2001): 173–96].

9. Parker Palmer, "Good Teaching," *Change* 22 (1) (1990): 10–16.
10. Susan C. Fisher, *Reasons for Hope, Voices for Change: Annenberg Institute for School Reform* (Providence, RI: Brown University, 1999).
11. Parker Palmer, *The Active Life: Wisdom for Work, Creativity and Caring* (New York: Harper-Collins Publishers, 1990), p. 15.
12. Paulo Freire, *Pedagogy of the Oppressed* (New York: Continuum Publishing Co, 1993).
13. Paulo Freire, *The Politics of Education: Culture, Power, Liberation* (S. Hadley, MA: Bergin & Garvey, 1985), p. 106.
14. Kenneth J. Gergen, *The Saturated Self* (New York: Basic Books, 1991); Jurgen Habermas, *Knowledge and Human Interests* (London: Heinemann, 1972).
15. Robert Cooper and Gibson Burrell, "Modernism, Postmodernism and Organizational Analysis: An Introduction," *Organizational Studies* 9 (1) (1988): 91–112; Kenneth J. Gergen and T. J. Thatchenkery, "Organizational Science as Social Construction: Postmodern Potentials," *Journal of Applied Behavioral Science* 33 (4) (1996): 356–77. Frederick Steier, *Research and Reflexivity* (London: Sage Publications, 1991).
16. William Dunn, "Studying Knowledge Use: A Profile of Procedures and Issues," in *Knowledge Generation, Exchange and Utilization,* ed. George Beal, Wimal Dissanayake, and Sumiye Konoshima (Boulder, CO: Westview Press, 1986).
17. Kenneth J. Gergen, "Toward Generative Theory," *Journal of Personality and Social Psychology* 36 (11) (1978): 1344–360.
18. The postmodern discourse contends that social reality is an emergent and dynamic process of human creation. "Postmodernism . . . decenters the human agent from its self-elevated position of narcissistic 'rationality' and shows it to be essentially an observer-based community which constructs *interpretations* of the world, these interpretations having no absolute or universal status" [Cooper and Gibson, "Modernism, Postmodernism and Organizational Analysis," p. 94]. Accordingly, social science is perceived to be both the creator and the creation of the social reality it seeks to investigate [see Grahm W. Astley, "Administrative Science as Socially Constructed Truth" *Administrative Science Quarterly* 30 (1985): 497–513; P. L. Berger and T. Luckman, *The Social Construction of Reality: A Treatise in the Sociology of Knowledge* (New York: Doubleday & Co, 1966); Kenneth J. Gergen, *Toward Transformation in Social Knowledge* (New York: Springer-Verlag, 1982); Kenneth J. Gergen, "Affect and Organization in Postmodern Society," in *Appreciative Management and Leadership: The Power of Positive Thought and Action in Organizations,* ed. S. Srivastva and D. L. Cooperrider (San Francisco: Jossey Bass, 1990), pp. 153–74; Karl E. Weick, *The Social Psychology of Organizing* (New York: Random House, 1979)].
19. Gergen, "Toward Generative Theory," p. 1346.
20. Erving Goffman, *The Presentation of Self in Everyday Life* (New York: Anchor Books, 1959).
21. Van Maanen, *"Tales of the Field,"* p. 5.
22. Maureen Hillinan, "bridging the Gap between Research and Practice," *Sociology of Education* 69 (1996): 131–34; George Psacharopoulos, "Comparative Education: From Theory to Practice," *Comparative Education Review* 34 (3) (1990): 369–80.
23. Noam Chomsky and Donald P. Macedo, *Chomsky on Miseducation* (New York: Rowman & Littlefield, 2000), p. 21. They qualify their view in stating that "[i]f and when people who exercise power in their institutional roles disassociate themselves from their institutional settings and become human beings, moral agents, then they may join everyone else. But in their roles as people who wield power, they are hardly worth addressing. . . . It is no more worth speaking truth to power than to the worst tyrants and criminals, who are also human beings, however terrible their actions" (p. 21).
24. See B. G. Glaser and A. L. Corbin, *The Discovery of Grounded Theory* (Chicago: Aldine Publishing Company, 1967); Anselm Strauss and Juliet Corbin, *The Basics of Qualitative Research: Grounded Theory Procedures and Techniques* (London: Sage Publications, 1990).

25. Majid Rahnema, "Participation," in *The Development Dictionary: A Guide to Knowledge as Power*, ed. Wolfgang Sachs (Atlantic Highlands, NJ: Zed Books, 1992), p. 122.
26. Freire, *The Politics of Education*, p. 100.
27. Freire, *Pedagogy of the Oppressed*, p. 14.
28. Freire, "The Adult Literacy Process," p. 221.
29. The Brazil and South Africa case studies presented here are extracted from more complete cases that were prepared for use in a World Bank seminar, The Politics of Education Reform, in December 1997. The seminar was put together by Joseph DeStefano and Jennifer Spratt and drew on the Research Triangle Institute's and the Academy for Educational Development's formulation of a comprehensive strategy for working to develop, design, and implement education programs known as Education Reform Support, and of which Joseph DeStefano was one of the principle authors.

    The original Brazil case was put together by Joseph DeStefano and is based on two documents: *A Call to Action: Combating School Failure in Northeast Brazil* (Brazil: Ministry of Education, World Bank, and UNICEF, 1997); *Linking Research and Policy: A Participatory Approach* (Brazil: UNICEF, 1997). The information in those reports was supplemented generously by interviews with Robin Horn of the World Bank and Terri Demsky, who was a consultant to UNICEF on the project.

    The South Africa case study was assembled by Jennifer Spratt of the Research Triangle Institute and is based on the pivotal role this private research organization, based in North Carolina, U.S.A., played in supporting the evaluation of education policy options in South Africa during the transition out of apartheid.

    The DC VOICE case study was put together by Craig Wishart. The Learning Communities Network, under the auspices of the Ford Foundation's Comprehensive Education Reform Initiative, is supporting the efforts of DC VOICE. The case as presented here draws on DC VOICE's report: *Half the Solution: The Supports DC Students Need to Meet High Academic Standards* (Washington, DC, 2001) and on interviews with DC VOICE staff members Erika Landberg and Carmelita Lacey.
30. Joseph DeStefano, Jennifer Spratt, and Terry Demsky, "Cases: Brazil, El Salvador, Haiti, South Africa," in *Stakeholder Participation in Education Policy Reform*, (Washington, DC: Academy for Educational Development, 1997), p. 5.
31. APEX was developed in part under the auspices of the Advancing Basic Education and Literacy (ABEL) project. ABEL was a USAID/R& D/ED project, the prime contractor of which was the Academy for Educational Development (AED).
32. The most powerful member of the democratic opposition, the African National Congress began in January 8, 1912, as an opposition reform organization, became a revolutionary group, and then was formally recognized as an opposition party to the incumbent "white" government of South Africa; since the 1994 elections, it has assumed the role as the governing party of post-apartheid South Africa.
33. The initiative was organized around *Standards for Teaching and Learning*, a guide for academic instruction and assessment.
34. DC VOICE, *Half the Solution*.
35. Wendy Schwartz, *Opportunity to Learn Standards: Their Impact on Urban Students* (New York: ERIC/CUE Digest Number 110, 1995). Based on a set of research findings, seven basic standards are posited to describe the learning conditions required to ensure that students have a fair chance to meet the content and performance standards. In short, they define what it takes to have a good school. DC VOICE adapted these descriptions to seven areas of focus: (1) School Environment, Culture, and Organization; (2) Quality of Instructional Programming; (3) Quality of Teaching; (4) Out-of- School Supports; (5) Parent and Community Partnerships; (6) School Readiness; (7) School Financing.
36. DC VOICE, *Half the Solution*, p. 22.
37. Nalin R. Jena, "An Inquiry Into 'Popular Participation,'" *Participation and Governance* 1 (1): 8–17, p. 12.
38. *DAE Case Studies;* "Practice Pointers in Enabling the Poor to Participate: Intermediary NGOs," in *The World Bank Participation Source Book* (Washington, DC: The World Bank, 1997).
39. Joseph DeStefano, Jennifer Spratt and Michel Welmond, *Stakeholder Participation in Education Policy Reform* (Washington, DC: Academy for Educational Development, 1997).

40. R. E. Elmore, "Building a New Structure of School Leadership," *American Educator* (Winter 1999–2000).
41. DeStefano, Spratt, and Welmond, *Stakeholder Participation*.
42. Luis Crouch et al., *Policy Issues in Education Reform in Africa* (Washington, DC: Project ABE, 1997); Porter, *Knowledge Utilization;* Louise White, "Policy Reforms in Sub-Saharan Africa: Conditions for Establishing Dialogue," *Studies in Comparative International Development* 25 (2) (1990): 24–42.
43. Porter, *Knowledge Utilization;* Weiss, "Perspectives on Knowledge Use."

CHAPTER 8

# Ideology in Educational Research and Policy Making in the United States
## The Possibility and Importance of Transcendence[1]

MICHELE S. MOSES
MARINA GAIR

### Introduction

In March 2001, Republican politicians in the United States House of Representatives put forth an education bill that called for increased student testing in conjunction with punitive measures for schools that consistently post low scores. The sanction for such schools would be a loss of federal funding.[2] Educational researchers and others who oppose high-stakes testing and threat-centered policy ask themselves how this legislation could be proposed in the face of research findings that show its negative impact. One main answer is that in crafting their policy position, the Republican members of Congress in support of the bill decided only to heed research studies that would support their conservative policy initiatives. As Gene Glass points out, the "selection of research to legitimize political views is an activity engaged in by governments at every point on the political compass."[3] In short, political ideology seemed to matter more in policy making than a balanced survey of educational research.

In this chapter, we address the seemingly intractable problem of the influence of political ideology on research questions, results, and use as well as on policy agendas and decisions. The ontological and epistemological premises upon which research is conducted are central to understanding the limited impact of some research on educational policy, the success of particular initiatives, and the modest progress of various other political agendas. The main questions we address are as follows: Can ideological perspectives be transcended within educational policy research? If so, how should we proceed?

As educational researchers, we approach this issue from the perspectives of a philosopher and a sociologist, both concerned with uncovering to what degree educational policy research and outcomes are the result of ideological orientations. Through this discussion, we aim to give attention to the prominence of a researcher's ideological orientation in research designs and products, as well as to challenge policy researchers and practitioners to examine how their ideological assumptions intercede in policy processes. We argue that while ideology is an undeniable factor within educational research and policy making, it can nevertheless be transcended through purposeful attention to critical and deliberative strategies for dealing with disagreement.

To clarify terms, herein we are concerned with all forms of educational policy research, especially those that may have bearing on controversial and intractable educational policy issues, such as vouchers, bilingual education, affirmative action, and standardized testing. Intractable conflicts are characterized as "highly resistant to resolution by appeal to evidence, research, or reasoned argument."[4] By ideology, we mean a politically motivated view of the world: a way of thinking on which one's view of the political, economic, and social system is based.[5]

## The Seemingly Intractable Trio: Educational Research, Political Ideology, and Policy

At heart, the relationship between research, ideology, and policy may be characterized as a complex and interconnected web. The traditional view of this web is that good social and educational policy decisions are generally made based on research evidence and independent of ideological positions. Moreover, the dominant culture of educational community and the society, more generally, in the United States at least, includes a faith in "objective" research findings, especially when presented in the form of statistical data.[6] Research methods stemming from the "scientific" methods of the natural sciences have tended to hold sway over policy makers and the public. Accordingly, there is a common and often unquestioned notion that good, objective research will be effective in helping to resolve policy controversies.[7] Problems surface only when bad or misinterpreted statistics are called upon to justify one particular side of an intractable policy issue. Such data have the potential to distort perceptions of issues, debates, and policies.

However, it is rather more likely that research and political ideology interact throughout the research process, from the choice of research question, to the organization that provides funding for the research, to the way that findings are interpreted. As Donald Schön and Martin Rein insightfully observe, "[p]olicy researchers have tended to be co-opted by one side or another in policy controversies and have done more to fuel such controversies than to resolve them."[8] Too often, policy research and decisions are more the result of ideological orientations than of sound data, experience, and concern for social justice. Ideology frames, distorts, and/or structures findings, the use of final reports, and, eventually, educational opportunities and outcomes. Policy decisions, then, are most often based on a complicated intermingling of research findings, researchers' political ideology, and policy makers' political ideology, among other factors.[9] This is perhaps to be expected when dealing with controversial policy issues of social and educational significance.

Steven Miller and Marcel Fredericks maintain that ideological commitments or preferences often work as "biasing-filters," translating research findings into particular outcomes and acceptable policy decisions.[10] Using the case of the *Bell Curve*[11] debate as an example, they argue: "If one believes, as in the *Bell Curve*, that there are empirical data which clearly support cognitive differences among racial and ethnic groups, that belief system 'intervenes' nicely between the research findings (and approach) and the policy subsequently formulated."[12] Data are often interpreted accordingly to justify ideological stances and belief systems; the values, ideologies, and political motives of the various researchers and policy actors tend to eclipse other factors. As Glass points out, "[s]tudies may be commissioned that support either side of a policy issue."[13] Regardless of what they illustrate, facts alone rarely function to shape policy. Instead policies are grown out of worldviews that are often legitimated in the manipulation, filtering, and massaging of research data.

Drawing on the cases of bilingual education in Arizona and California and of school voucher effects in Florida, we illustrate next how ideology is a key element in policy outcomes.

*Bilingual Education*[14]

The most recent and notable cases of the functioning of ideology with selective research findings in relation to the policy of bilingual education are Proposition 227 in California and Proposition 203 in Arizona. In June 1998, voters in California passed Proposition 227, an initiative called *English Language Education for Children in Public Schools*.[15] The thrust of the proposition was to virtually ban bilingual instruction in public schools, mandating that "all children in California's public schools shall be taught English by being taught in English."[16] Similarly, Proposition 203, Arizona's more restrictive version of Proposition 227, passed in November 2000 with 63 percent of the vote.[17] The Arizona initiative, also known as English for the Children of Arizona, limits instruction to English only and, like Proposition 227, requires English language learners to be placed in English-only immersion classes for a period of one year.[18]

In these campaigns, research findings played a considerable role within the public debate over the issue. Yet both defenders and opponents of bilingual education have interpreted the research in very different ways,[19] selectively using the research to advance particular interests and belief systems.

Proponents of bilingual education generally maintain that public schools have a responsibility to aid English language learners in learning English and to advance their learning in academic subject areas while sustaining their cultural identity. Proponents also maintain that by using English language learners' native languages for instructional purposes, students receive a good start to their overall school career. Drawing on prevailing research, proponents contend that English-only approaches actually limit the learning potential of English language learners and negatively affect their educational achievement and outcomes.[20] Shirley Brice Heath, for one, points out that English language learners are best prepared to learn English in school when they have a solid foundation in their native language.[21] Moreover, monolingual English instruction engenders a form of alienation among English language learners and more often serves to diminish student participation and, hence, their opportunities to learn. Even though a number of research studies[22] have documented the effectiveness of bilingual education programs, bilingual education continues to be a target of criticism and hostility.

Critics of bilingual education draw upon an assimilationist ideology, which frames having a first language other than English as a handicap rather than a benefit.[23] They cite research findings in contending that learning English should be students' central activity, and the students' native language only should be used sparingly as a language of instruction, if at all. Supporters of the "English-Only" movement argue that bilingualism is a threat to American cultural unity;[24] having English as the official language of the nation is necessary in order to preserve the unity of American culture and the full participation of immigrants in mainstream society.[25] There is a notion that immigrants' continued allegiance to their ethnic group is a threat to their being Americans, and thus contributes to polarizing society along language lines.[26] Furthermore, total immersion in the language and culture of mainstream America is beneficial for language minority peoples because it affords them opportunities to pursue education, employment, and success.[27] Such opponents of bilingual education have consistently drawn on research findings to stress the association between the lack of English competency and the existence of social problems, including low academic performance and unemployment.[28]

## School Vouchers in Florida

Jay Greene's published report, *An Evaluation of the Florida A-Plus Accountability and School Choice Program*,[29] is among a number of other illustrations of the practice of selective use of "scientific" findings in order to advance ideological belief systems. The report documents gains in achievement on the Florida Comprehensive Assessment Test in the areas of reading, mathematics, and writing and convincingly establishes a link between the threat of school vouchers for students in low-performing schools and achievement gains in those schools. Greene argues that the threat of vouchers is responsible for the improvement of low-achieving schools: "An accountability system with vouchers as the sanction for repeated failure really motivates schools to improve."[30]

Greene's reading of the "evidence" has the potential to play an important role in policy making at both the federal and local levels across the country. While the statistical model and conclusions of the report have been challenged, policy makers in support of voucher and accountability initiatives may not find the dispute with the mechanisms of the statistical analysis as compelling as the generous conclusions drawn by Greene.[31] Reports such as Greene's are sure to be selectively used by conservative politicians as convincing arguments to defend and facilitate voucher plans. The voucher effect will no doubt be sold to the general public as an effective force in motivating failing schools to improve academic achievement. The argument can be made that the interpretation and use of Greene's research findings may be largely dependent on the particular interests of policy makers. As Miller and Fredericks maintain, "[f]indings are largely irrelevant to policy makers."[32] What is relevant, but overlooked, is how those findings can serve an ideological agenda.[33] The case of Greene's research on the effects of school voucher programs illustrates how ideological commitments often work as "biasing-filters,"[34] translating research findings into particular outcomes and acceptable policy decisions.

### Research, Policy, and Symbolic Politics

Mary Lee Smith, Walter Heinecke, and Audrey Noble argue that (in Arizona, at least) assessment policy change had less to do with research and analysis than with "political spectacle" and issues of power and control over schooling.[35] Policy actions function as political symbolism rather than as rational decision-making endeavors based on facts, evidence, experience, or fair deliberation. They call this "a predicament in the theory of policy,"[36] arguing that the use of persuasive rhetorical devices also functions in distorting social reality and has an influence on effecting educational policy making. Moreover, Smith maintains that educational policies cannot be examined without drawing attention to the symbols that guide them.[37]

We maintain that in addition to the (ab)use of research findings, persuasive rhetorical devices are effective in encouraging policy initiatives. Politicians have consistently employed educational buzzwords, slogans, anecdotes, emotional adjectives, and other figurative language to advance their ideological positions. Because primary sources of research are not readily disseminated or read by the general public, the public's position on educational issues is more often influenced by metaphors than by research findings.[38] In the current wave of reform, for instance, this can be seen in the debate over school performance and declining achievement scores. The public is unlikely to sort through the educational research literature pertaining to test scores and arrive at a balanced understanding of the issue.[39] Instead, metaphors have considerable influence over our understanding and function as powerful tools in organizing public perceptions about an event or a phenomenon. As George Lakoff points out, much of what we read in the newspapers and hear from the political arena is "metaphorical commonsense reasoning" that everyone can understand.[40]

The success of the political right in the United States, for instance, can in part be attributed to a number of shrewd strategies, including language politics.[41] To illustrate more specifically, we take the example of President George W. Bush's phrase "no child left behind," commonplace in recent political discourse.

President Bush maintains:

> The quality of our public schools directly affects us all—as parents, as students, and as citizens. Yet too many children in America are segregated by low expectations, illiteracy, and self-doubt. In a constantly changing world that is demanding increasingly complex skills from its workforce, children are literally being left behind. ... If our country fails in its responsibility to educate every child, we're likely to fail in many other areas. But if we succeed in educating our youth, many other successes will follow throughout our country and in the lives of our citizens.... [No child left behind] will serve as a framework from which we can all work together ... to strengthen our elementary and secondary schools.... These reforms express my deep belief in our public schools and their mission to build the mind and character of every child, from every background, in every part of America.[42]

Because the quality of *our* public schools is conveyed as a "national crisis"[43] that directly affects *us all*, the widespread slogan suggests a natural commitment and responsibility toward children. "No child left behind" echoes a moral idealism. Who would dispute that no child should be left behind? It is an organizing metaphor employed to unite Americans around a larger moral, economic, and cultural agenda. What conservatives have been able to do is successfully use the metaphor to push the educational imperatives it seems to encompass.

## Possibilities for Transcendence

Contending with ideological differences, particularly when they are embodied effectively in metaphors and other symbols, is indeed difficult. Nevertheless, in this section we propose a "critical deliberative strategy" for transcending—not eliminating—the use and influence of political ideology in the context of research-informed policy dialogue. This strategy builds on the notion of critical cultural workers (championed by Paulo Freire) and the concept of deliberative democracy (advocated by Amy Gutmann and Dennis Thompson).

### *Critical Cultural Workers*

Brazilian educator/political activist Paulo Freire argued that while there are exceptional academics and a handful of organizations dedicated to conducting research that serves egalitarian ends, not enough academics are working as critical "cultural workers" who orient themselves toward concrete struggles in the public and political domains in order to extend the equality, liberty, and justice they defend.[44] He maintained that "[t]he movements outside are where more people who dream of social change are gathering," but points out that there exists a degree of reserve on the part of academics, in particular, to penetrate the media, participate in policy debates, or permeate policy-making bodies.[45] He went on to argue that if scholars, researchers, or educators want to transform education to serve democratic ends, they cannot simply limit their struggles to institutional spaces. They must also develop a desire to increase their political activity outside of the schools. To engage as critical cultural workers would require academics to politicize their research by becoming social actors who mobilize, develop political clarity, establish strategic alliances, and work closer to the nexus of power or the "real levers of transformation."[46] In the context of educational research and policy, critical cultural workers would aim to introduce multiperspectival dialogues into dominant political frames of reference, direct less recognized forms of research/findings into policy-making bodies, develop political vocabularies of their own, mobilize the knowledge of those pursuing similar democratic ends, and inform and empower underrepresented groups so that they may develop political efficacy. We argue that such a Freirean-inspired vision is necessary to carve out spaces to advance egalitarian and progressive educational (and other) policies that would benefit all. However, a Freirean strategy requires not a romantic vision, but a collective and concentrated effort.[47]

While critical political leanings such as those espoused by Freire can provide political direction in the struggle for social change, they have been challenged on a number of points. For example, feminists argue that critical theory contains "repressive myths."[48] Feminists argue that the notion of "empowerment" can be imbued with paternalism and perpetuate relations of domination whether it be in the classroom, in academic discourse, or in everyday life.[49] Giving power can also mean the ability to take power.[50] In other words, the efforts to empower people in certain contexts can simultaneously strengthen the privileged position of those dispensing it. In the same sense, a Freirean approach to permeating policy-making contexts may involve a form of imposition by cultural workers, whereby representation, organization, and collective struggle may not necessarily build understanding or political efficacy among groups of people, but merely essentialize or exoticize the other. Similarly, the notion of "dialogue" must also be understood in terms of its potentially reproductive elements and the forms of complicity it can engender. Dialogue is not a neutral or apolitical process, as power, privilege, and persuasion are always present in speech acts. Therefore, as Giroux argues, "cultural workers need to develop a nontotalizing politics that makes them attentive to the partial, specific, contexts of differentiated communities and forms of power" and they should acknowledge "the politics of personal location."[51] Cultural workers cannot assume independence from any ideology, but must pay attention to ideological forces that inform, mediate, and constrain their work. As part of their practice in the context of research-informed policy dialogue, cultural workers must "speak *with* rather than exclusively for others."[52]

### Deliberative Democracy

In examining how to reconcile difficult policy controversies and the role that research findings play within them, researchers have struggled to conceptualize and propose satisfactory strategies. One strand of thought advocates for researchers to join with policy makers in some kind of collaborative research efforts, which would lead to reflective compromises over and solutions for policy conflicts.[53] While this suggestion makes sense, especially because of its emphasis on collaboration and reflection, it neglects an element crucial to the success of any resolution endeavor: deep, mutual understanding. This is where a deliberative democracy can contribute, for example, in clarifying and, perhaps, reconciling conflicting research findings or conflicting values.

Amy Gutmann and Dennis Thompson formulate an alternative conception of democracy—deliberative democracy.[54] Since moral conflict and disagreement are seen as the most difficult challenge facing democracy, Gutmann and Thompson attempt to conceptualize a democracy that places moral discussion in political life at center in order to cope with fundamental conflicts in values and ideology. Their conception of deliberative democracy is characterized by three conditions that regulate and structure the deliberative *process* of politics: (1) reciprocity, by which reason-giving and justification for mutually binding policies are seen as a mutual endeavor; (2) publicity, which stipulates that policy makers, researchers, officials, and members of the public in general should have to justify their decisions and actions in public; and (3) accountability, which requires those who make policy decisions to answer to those who are bound by those policies. In addition to the three conditions, Gutmann and Thompson outline three components that serve to govern the *content* of policy deliberations: (1) basic liberty, which controls what government and society can demand of people and what people can demand of one another; (2) basic opportunity, which concerns the distribution of goods necessary for pursuing a good life (e.g., basic income); and (3) fair opportunity, which has to do with the distribution of goods to people based on their qualifications.[55]

Critics of the deliberative democratic approach have pointed out that its emphasis on argument excludes true communication and participation.[56] For example, Iris Marion Young suggests that to ensure the inclusion of diverse and nonmainstream viewpoints one needs to incorporate the sociocultural practice of storytelling, which compared to processes of argumentation (a) focuses on the lives of individuals, (b) enables people to seek commonalities, and (c) levels the playing field among people participating.[57] Another prominent criticism of the deliberative democratic strategy is that it downplays the role of power and interests within the political and policy process and seems to assume that all participants have equal resources to enable their effective participation.[58] As Pierre Bourdieu theorizes, we live in cultural and social fields of power where various discourses vie for dominance and where the more "competent" and "skillful" actors continuously advance particular ideological stances and belief systems that are difficult to counter, particularly if they have the economic resources and the social contacts to facilitate such efforts.[59] These points are illustrated in Linda Miller-Kahn and Mary Lee Smith's study of parental involvement in the school choice movement in Boulder, Colorado. They describe the ways in which a combination of backstage politics, privilege, and "choice" rhetoric, disguised as an inclusive ideology, more often structured (and controlled) bureaucratic processes in setting educational policy and practice.[60] They point out how the communication skills, knowledge, and social and cultural competencies, more of which were possessed by "local elites,"[61] advantaged them in moving both comfortably and strategically about the school community. Echoing Bourdieu, Miller-Khan and Smith demonstrates how economic, social, and cultural capital coupled with persuasive rhetorical devices function to manipulate the policy-making process, resulting in unequal educational outcomes for students from diverse social class, racial, ethnic, and linguistic backgrounds.

### Transcending Ideology: A Critical Deliberative Strategy

Our key point in crafting a solution to the use of research in ideology-based educational policy conflicts is that neither a critical cultural worker approach nor a deliberative democratic approach can work alone. Instead, combining a Freirean approach and a modified deliberative democratic strategy could help solve intractable ideological policy conflicts because there is an emphasis on dialogue and deliberation with a simultaneous recognition that dialogue and deliberation themselves are not neutral or universal, as power and privilege enter into speech acts. The key is that these strategies are aimed at reaching understanding, and not just at winning.[62] This is no easy philosophy to espouse, especially when winning is such a central cultural element in the United States. Indeed, some scholars on the left have called for a "fight fire with fire" strategy based on beating the conservatives at their own game. For example, David Stoesz calls for liberal policy institutes and think tanks to take up the aggressive ideological policy analysis championed by conservative think tanks, which he says "have developed projects for the purpose of making social policy more consonant with conservative philosophy."[63] However, we are proposing that researchers and other policy actors move beyond a pure ideology-driven endeavor in order to reach a place where discussion, communication, understanding, mutual respect, and critical action are central within controversial research and policy debates.

We should note that some disagreements are not based on deep or even shallow *misunderstandings*, and simply cannot be overcome. Consider the qualitative difference between the debate over phonics and whole language approaches to teaching language arts and the debate over teaching creationism and evolution theory in schools. We can see more possibilities for transcending ideological commitments through critical deliberation and mutual understanding in the so-called reading wars than we can in debates over the origin of humanity. Thus, we are not trying to suggest that the critical deliberative strategy to transcend ideology will work every time, in every type of conflict. We propose only that the critical deliberative strategy has the best chance to influence key actors within research and policy processes. Although in some cases they may never come to agree, the goals of critical dialogue and action, inclusion, communication, and mutual understanding will aid in producing a healthy democratic process in which mutual respect might be reached. Conflict is a necessary part of any such process. Our hope is that the critical deliberative strategy for dealing with difficult conflicts may be used to arrive at even better research and policy processes.

How can researchers and policy makers representing different ideological perspectives proceed to interact regarding a controversial policy issue if they were engaged in a process guided by a critical deliberative approach? To illustrate let us consider the debate over remedial education[64] at the college level, a debate that is characterized by ideological clashes and controversies over research findings. At issue are the primary purposes of colleges and universities in the United States. The question often comes down to whether academic standards or educational opportunity should be the top priority. This largely ideological division has resulted in a national debate in the United States over whether or not remedial education programs have a rightful place at the four-year college level. The different policy actors—in this case college administrators, faculty members, students, educational researchers, and policy makers—have been unable to engage each other in productive dialogue to find satisfactory solutions to the conflict.

Two perspectives dominate the debate.[65] Opponents of remedial education generally come from a more conservative political orientation. They maintain that the students who need remedial courses should be attending community colleges instead of four-year institutions of higher education, and unprepared students are harmed when admitted to institutions at which they cannot compete.[66] Part of the argument is that although remedial programs may be well intentioned, ultimately they are political programs, and not educational ones.[67] Among the number of controversial points that have been raised by opponents, for instance, is that remedial education programs disproportionately benefit students of color.[68] In addition, those opposed to remedial education at four-year colleges question the impact of remedial courses on academic standards, whether or not remedial education policy condones poor academic achievement by students and public schools, and the cost of remedial programs.[69] On the other side, more liberal scholars argue that remedial education centers on creating opportunities, increased retention, and better graduation outcomes for students underprepared for some college-level courses.[70] In the liberal view, remedial education is particularly beneficial for students of color or poor students with decreased educational opportunities or whose K–12 education was historically lacking. For those advancing contemporary liberal ideals in the educational policy arena, remedial education fits into the aims of an education in a democratic society concerned with social justice for disadvantaged students. Abolishing remedial programs, on the other hand, serves to blame and punish some students for circumstances over which they have no control.[71]

We recognize that it may not be possible to transcend completely such a dichotomous view, but believe that if the policy actors were to follow a critical deliberative strategy in addressing this controversial policy issue, a number of factors in the process would change. Although individual institutions would still make the final decisions regarding remedial programs on their campuses, rather than heeding solely or mostly the advice of like-minded faculty members and administrators, college administrators and policy makers would rely much more on the viewpoints of researchers, as they are *somewhat* independent of the thorny issues surrounding educational values. In this sense, researchers fill the role of cultural workers in relation to this political issue. They would be drawn on as essential participants in policy debates, highlighting the points of debate that are clarified by research findings.

To take one example, a prominent objection to remedial courses at the college level offered by opponents of such courses is that they are too expensive.[72] They contend that remedial programs end up costing taxpayers a large amount of money; in effect, tax dollars are spent both for students to learn this material in high school and again for some students to be taught the same material in public colleges and universities. Interestingly, educational research has shown that remedial education programs generally cost slightly less than 1 percent of an institution's yearly budget.[73] In raw numbers, this means that remedial programs cost approximately $1 billion dollars per year of an overall public higher education budget of $115 billion dollars. As such, the programs may cost universities very little to administer and run. These findings make clear the actual financial costs of remedial programs and, as such, aid in the communications of the policy actors.

To take another example, remedial programs also are often criticized because they purportedly serve to lower academic standards and achievement. Researchers Lavin and colleugues found that exposure to remedial courses made no significant negative or positive differences for students in terms of academic achievement, GPA, retention, or graduation.[74] They also found that success in remedial courses did make a difference for students who passed their remedial courses. Such students were more likely to persist and graduate than comparable students who did not take remedial courses. If success at remedial courses correlates with overall college success, and failure at remedial courses correlates with overall college failure, then researchers have contributed an intriguing response to some of the basic criticisms of remedial education. Conservative critics may be satisfied because there is evidence that standards are not substantially lowered by remedial courses. And liberals may be satisfied because students' equality of educational opportunity is expanded by the availability of remedial courses. Furthermore, these findings suggest that there could be a resolution for the conflicting goal priorities within institutions of higher education. Institutions can strive both to contribute to an expansive opportunity structure for all students and to foster high level academic research and scholarship.

In addition, a critical deliberative decision-making process would attend more to the view of those people who have the most to gain or lose depending on the policy decision. Students, those arguably most affected by the outcome of the remedial debate, have had to deal with tangible policy changes at institutions of higher education. While many remedial programs remain in place, others have been reduced or abolished[75]—without student representation in deliberative processes. Certainly, the reasons for students' need for remedial education courses vary, but the acknowledgment or recognition of systemic inequalities that students have experienced would allow actors in this debate to move from monolithic perspectives and perhaps develop a more balanced understanding of the issue. Researchers employing nonmainstream and participatory methods of inquiry, for instance, can introduce a "discourse of difference"[76] into the deliberative process that challenges the mainstream assumptions about remedial education. Embracing research that documents students' lived experiences (e.g., the positive impact of remedial education and various forms of student services on helping disadvantaged students overcome structural inequalities), rather than privileging research that involves pure data gathering, fixed sampling strategies, and generalizable results, can provide a counterargument to the prevailing view within higher education that seems to blame personal or cultural factors such as race, ethnicity, or socioeconomic status for limited academic preparedness. Such efforts toward balanced representation in determining the existence, need, or continuation of remedial education can move the discussion from focusing primarily on individual shortcomings to institutional ones in framing the debate. A critical deliberative approach would take up the voices and lived experiences of those least represented but with the most to gain or lose in the outcomes of the remedial debate. The deliberative process would provide conditions in which those directly affected by policy outcomes are not just invited for emotional appeal, but essential resources and actors in policy negotiations. It would ensure that those most affected would be included in deliberations about what is educationally worthwhile. Furthermore, this calls for educational and other researchers whose inquiries counteract reductionist interpretations, negative stereotypes, and fictionalized representations of remediation, to engage in more of a political struggle. This requires that they function as cultural workers who inform and mediate policy-making contexts, as well as guide the meaning, reception, and use (as well as follow the potential misuse) of their work.[77] These efforts may offset power differentials in the deliberation process by infusing mainstream interpretations of the remediation issue with a multiperspectival discourse and understanding.

As mentioned earlier, inequalities in power relations between those involved in the policy debate are likely to enter into any deliberation and dialogue that may take place. In the case of remedial education, it is often students of color and poor students who come to college from inferior neighborhood public schools that rely on remedial courses to level those public school inequalities. Ernest House points out that "Americans have defined their educational system in such a way as to ensure that African Americans (and often other minorities) are treated in an exclusionary way."[78] Under critical deliberative theory, more powerful policy actors such as high-level college administrators and members of boards of trustees would be obliged to be accountable to the students who need remedial courses in order to pursue selective higher education. Instead of focusing on political outcomes concerning issues like academic standards and achievement, the policy process would endeavor to reach mutual understandings between supporters and opponents of remedial education, by privileging reciprocity and dialogue and building these elements into critical policy debates.

Of course, it is impossible to know what the policy outcome would be if a critical deliberative strategy indeed was pursued in this example, but our hope is that a result mutually acceptable to more interested parties would emerge. While there is no guarantee that political cul-de-sacs can be avoided, our discussion of the case of remedial education shows how research findings may play a central role in a critical deliberative decision-making process. Interactions within the process of critical deliberation would give increased attention to relevant educational research findings rather than allowing ideology alone to drive interpretations of research findings and policy initiatives.

**Conclusion**
Ellen Condliffe Lagemann's historical analysis centers on what she calls the "troubling history" of educational research—an unwillingness to transcend ideological frameworks.[79] Note that we call for transcendence of ideological perspectives, not dismissal or avoidance of such perspectives. It is not objectivity for which we advocate, but a more reasonable, honest approach to educational research and policy. Differences in opinion, ideology, and interpretations of research are legitimate and will continue. Moreover, the contemporary political environment in the United Sates has been described as a "political spectacle"[80] in which contending with ideological differences, particularly when they are embodied in "plain folk Americanisms"[81] and other influential symbols, presents a complex situation, especially for those pursuing more democratic educational outcomes. Recognizing that there is a range of actors, competing discourses, and ongoing processes of change, our central concern in this chapter has been to examine a way, within a democratic society, to discern where politics and ideology are driving research projects, interpretations of research findings, and policy initiatives. We have argued that in examining those cases, a critical deliberative strategy, based on a combination of critical cultural worker orientations and deliberative democratic approaches, would best address intractable conflicts within educational research and policy and transcend the use and influence of political ideology in the context of research-informed policy dialogue. Through

a critical deliberative approach, some leverage can be gained in advancing alternative agendas in the policy arena. By engaging in such practice, we can mitigate unjust educational policies and educational inequalities and, in doing so, build a fuller and richer democracy.

## Notes

1. This chapter was supported in part by a Small Research Grant awarded to Michele S. Moses from the Spencer Foundation.
2. D. J. Schemo, "House Republicans Present a School Bill Mirroring Bush's Plan." *The New York Times* (23 March 2001).
3. G. V. Glass, "What Works: Politics and Research," *Educational Researcher* 15 (1987): 9.
4. D. A. Schön and M. Rein, *Frame Reflection: Toward the Resolution of Intractable Policy Controversies* (New York: Basic Books, 1994), p. xi.
5. M. F. D. Young, "Ideology and Educational Research." in *Poverty, Power, and Authority in Education: Cross-Cultural Perspectives*, ed. E. B. Gumbert (Atlanta: Georgia State University, 1981), pp. 34–43.
6. See J. Best, *Damned Lies and Statistics: Untangling Numbers from the Media, Politicians, and Activists* (Berkeley: University of California Press, 2001).
7. For example, see Young, "Ideology and Educational Research."
8. Schön and Rein, p. xvi.
9. J. W. Kingdon, *Agendas, Alternatives, and Public Policies* (New York: Harper Collins, 1995).
10. S. I. Miller and M. Fredericks, "Social Science Research Findings and Educational Policy Dilemmas: Some Additional Distinctions," *Education Policy Analysis Archives*, January 5; 2000, http://epaa.asu.edu/epaa/v8n3 (September 30, 2001).
11. R. Herrnstein and C. Murray, *The Bell Curve* (New York: Free Press, 1994).
12. Miller and Fredericks.
13. Glass, p. 9.
14. See M. S. Moses, *Embracing Race: Why We Need Race-Conscious Education Policy* (New York: Teachers College Press, in Press), Chapter 3, for a discussion of bilingual education policy.
15. Ron Unz, the primary underwriter and sponsor of the campaign for California's Proposition 227 and a major force behind Colorado's Proposition 203, is a millionaire businessman in California's computer industry with some political aspirations. In 1994, Unz attempted a bid for the Republican nomination for governor, but lost to Pete Wilson.
16. "English Language Education for Children in Public Schools," *NABE News* (February 1, 1998): 12–14.
17. J. Crawford, "Bilingual Education: Strike Two." *Rethinking Schools* 15 (2) (2000): 3, 8.
18. Supporters of bilingual education in other states have reacted against the threat of anti-bilingual ballots. For instance, Colorado successfully staved off having such an initiative on their November 2000 ballot and brought suit against the initiative, which was promoted by a group led by Ron Unz (see note 15), citing the proposed proposition's misleading and deceptive wording. Four months before the election, the Colorado Supreme Court ruled against the initiative on these grounds. In Texas and in Florida, citizens were polled and overwhelmingly reported that they believed that bilingual education was an important program to sustain; see B. Miner, "Bilingual education: New Visions for a New Era," *Rethinking Schools* 13 (4) (1998): 1, 18–20.
19. J. Cummins, *Research, Ethics and Public Discourse: The Debate on Bilingual Education*, paper presented at the National Conference of the American Association of Higher Education (Washington, DC, March 1999).
20. S. B. Heath, "Sociocultural Contexts of Language Development," In *Beyond Language: Social and Cultural Factors in Schooling Language Minority Students*, ed. C. Cortés. (Los Angeles: Evaluation, Dissemination and Assessment Center, California State University, Los Angeles, 1986), pp. 143–86; M. Reyes, "Challenging Venerable Assumptions: Literacy Instruction for Linguistically Different Students," *Harvard Educational Review* 62 (4) (1992): 427–46; L. Wong Fillmore, "When Learning a Second Language Means Losing the First," *Early Childhood Research Quarterly* 6 (1991): 324–46.
21. Heath.

22. See J. Cummins, *The Role of Primary Language Development in Promoting Educational Success for Language Minority Students, Schooling and Language Minority Students: A Theoretical Framework* (Los Angeles: Evaluation, Dissemination and Assessment Center, California State University, Los Angeles, 1981), pp. 3–49; K. Hakuta, *Mirror of language: The debate on bilingualism* (New York: Basic Books, 1986); S. D. Krashen, *Under Attack: The Case Against Bilingual Education.* (Culver City, CA: Language Education Associates, 1996); O. B. Miramontes, A. Nadeau, and N. L. Commins, *Restructuring Schools for Linguistic Diversity: Linking Decision Making to Effective Programs.* (New York: Teachers College Press, 1997); L. Wong Fillmore, "When Learning a Second Language Means Losing the First," *Early Childhood Research Quarterly* 6 (1991): 324–46.
23. Opposition to policies such as bilingual education has been focused primarily on nostalgic notions of Americanization and an ideology of nationalism and cultural maintenance—essentially what critical social theorists have referred to as an ethnocentric fantasy of a common culture; see H. Giroux, *Pedagogy and the Politics of Hope. Theory, Culture, and Schooling* (Boulder, CO: Westview Press, 1997).
24. L. Chavez, *Out of the Barrio: Toward a New Politics of Hispanic Assimilation* (New York: Basic Books, 1991); J. Crawford, *Bilingual Education: History, Politics, Theory, and Practice* (Los Angeles: Bilingual Educational Services, 1991).
25. Chavez.
26. Ibid.
27. Ibid.
28. See, e.g., O. García, "Spanish Language Loss as a Determinant of Income among Latinos in the United States: Implications for Language Policy in Schools," in *Power and Inequality in Language Education*, ed. J. Tollefson (New York: Cambridge University Press, 1995), pp. 142–60; R. Ruiz, "Orientations in Language Planning," *National Association for Bilingual Education Journal* 8 (1984): 15–34; H. Schiffman, *Linguistic Culture and Language Policy* (New York: Routledge, 1996); R. Schmidt, R. "Latinos and Language Policy: The Politics of Culture," in *Pursuing Power: Latinos and the Political System*, ed. C. García (Notre Dame: University of Notre Dame Press, 1997), pp. 343–67.
29. J. Greene, *An Evaluation of the Florida A-Plus Accountability and School Choice Program* (New York: The Manhattan Institute, 2001).
30. Ibid., p. 9.
31. For a discussion on the methodological flaws of the report, see G. Camilli and K. Bulkley, "Critique of 'An Evaluation of the Florida A-Plus Accountability and School Choice program,'" *Education Policy Analysis Archives* (4 March 2001), http://epaa.asu.edu/epaa (20 September 2001); and H. Kupermintz, "The Effects of Vouchers on School Improvement: Another Look at the Florida Data," *Education Policy Analysis Archives* (19 March 2001), http://epaa.asu.edu/epaa/v9n8/ (25 September 2001).
32. Miller and Fredericks.
33. Michael Apple, *Educating the "Right" Way. Markets, Standards, God, and Inequality* (New York: Routledge/Falmer, 2001), pp. 38–41, illuminates the ideological rationale behind voucher initiatives: "Public institutions such as schools are "black holes" into which money is poured—and then seemingly disappears—but which do not provide anywhere near adequate results.... As "black holes," schools ... waste economic resources that should go into private enterprise.... By turning [schools] over to the market through voucher and choice plans, education will be largely self-regulating.... Behind [voucher and choice programs] is a plan to subject schools to the discipline of market competition.... There are now increasingly convincing arguments that while the supposed overt goal of voucher and choice plans is to give poor people the right to exit public schools, among the ultimate long-term effects may be the increase of 'white flight' from public schools into private and religious schools and the creation of the conditions where affluent white parents may refuse to pay taxes to support public schools."
34. Miller and Fredericks.
35. M. L. Smith, W. Heinecke, and A. J. Noble, "Assessment Policy and Political Spectacle," *Teachers College Record* 10 (2) (1999): 157.
36. Ibid., p. 158.
37. M. L. Smith, with L. Miller-Kahn, P. Fey, W. Heinecke, and A. J. Noble, *Political Spectacle and the Fate of American Schools* (New York: Routledge/Falmer Press, forthcoming).

38. Ibid.
39. Ibid.
40. G. Lakoff, *Moral Politics: What Conservatives Know That Liberals Dont* (Chicago: University of Chicago Press, 1993), p. 5.
41. George Lakoff [*Moral Politics*] analyzes some of the reasons for conservative political victories in the United States. He argues that the metaphors prominent in conservative agendas are successful because they are simple, focused, and comprehensive, and as a result, have been able to garner widespread support compared to the "issue by issue" political activity of liberals. The strategic use of metaphor has proven to be an effective practice in policy formation. In addition to commonsense strategies, the language politics employed by conservative politicians are tactically designed to be indisputable. David Gillborn [as cited in Apple, p. 69] maintains that "[t]his is a powerful technique. First, it assumes there are no *genuine* arguments against the chosen position; any opposing views are thereby positioned as false, insincere, and self-serving. Second, this technique presents the speaker as someone... honest.... Hence, the moral high ground is assumed and opponents are further denigrated." See also Noam Chomsky's [*Language and Politics* (Montreal: Black Rose Books, 1988)] argument on linguistic competence.
42. President George W. Bush, http://www.whitehouse.gov/news/reports/no-child-left-behind.html.
43. For example, in 1980s, a number of reports were prominent in criticizing the condition of public education in the United States, arguing that educational institutions were failures as a result of a "rising tide of mediocrity" [National Commission on Excellence in Education, *A Nation at Risk: The Imperative for Educational Reform* (Washington, DC: Government Printing Office, 1983), p. 5]. A drop in academic achievement was attributed to the cultural and political movements of the 1960s believed to have engendered misguided egalitarian reforms. In this view, interdisciplinary and broadly defined programs of study "watered down" the curriculum and in doing so weakened the skills and cognitive capacities believed necessary to maintain the United States' competitive edge within a global economy [Joel Spring, *American Education. An Introduction to Social and Political Aspects* (New York and London: Longman, 1991)]. These reports were embraced by right-wing politicians and generated considerable support during the 1980s. Linking economic productivity to educational performance, conservative politicians structured their argument as a "crisis" in education that required widespread reform efforts. By overstating the severity of the economic and educational crises, these highly critical reports caught the public's attention. The "crisis" in education, albeit somewhat "manufactured," was perpetuated by influential citizens, legislators, journalists, intelligentsia, and financial sponsors of conservative platforms in a manner that created a significant amount of public frustration [see David Berliner and Bruce Biddle, *The Manufactured Crisis: Myths, Fraud, and the Attack of America's Public Schools* (White Plains, NY: Longman, 1995)].
44. P. Freire, *Teachers as Cultural Workers* (Boulder, CO: Westview Press, 1998). This idea also draws on the work of Henry Giroux [*Border Crossings. Cultural Workers and the Politics of Education* (New York: Routledge, 1992)]. According to Giroux, the concept of cultural worker traditionally referred to artists and writers but extends to those in law, medicine, social work, theology, and education. Furthermore, Giroux extends the concept of cultural worker to include the need for multiple solidarities and political vocabularies in extending democratic principles and effecting social change.
45. I. Shor and P. Freire, *A Pedagogy for Liberation: Dialogues on Transforming Education* (South Hadley, MA: Bergin and Garvey, 1987), p. 131.
46. Ibid, p. 131.
47. A useful source of insights is the Freirean-inspired analysis undertaken by Jean Stefancic and Richard Delgado [*No Mercy: How Conservative Think Tanks and Foundations Changed America's Social Agenda* (Philadelphia: Temple University Press, 1996)] of the strategies conservatives have deployed in influencing social policy formulation over the last two decades in the United States. Their analysis of how conservatives have gained control over official English campaigns, IQ and race, Proposition 187, affirmative action, welfare reform, and the culture wars on campuses can inform those with left political ideologies how to penetrate the policy-making process and gain some leverage in advancing alternative agendas in the policy arena.
48. E. Ellsworth, "Why Doesn't This Feel Empowering? Working through the Repressive Myths

of Critical Pedagogy," in *Feminisms and Critical Pedagogy,* ed. C. Luke and J. Gore (New York: Routledge, 1992), p. 91.
49. Ibid.
50. D. Macedo, personal communication, 1999.
51. Giroux, p. 79.
52. Ibid., p. 29.
53. Schön and Rein.
54. A. Gutmann and D. Thompson, *Democracy and Disagreement: Why Moral Conflict Cannot be Avoided in Politics, and What Should Be Done about It* (Cambridge, MA: The Belknap Press, 1996).
55. Ibid.
56. See Smith, Heinecke, and Noble, "Assessment Policy and Political Spectacle;" Iris Marion Young, "Communication and the Other: Beyond Deliberative Democracy," in *Democracy and Difference: Contesting the Boundaries of the Political,* ed. S. Benhabib (Princeton, NJ: Princeton University Press, 1996), pp. 120–35.
57. Young, "Communication and the Other."
58. Gutmann and Thompson, in fact, acknowledge that it may be problematic for their theory to rely on people's ability and, perhaps more importantly, their willingness to reflect and reason beyond their own self-interest and to step into the shoes of another.
59. P. Bourdieu, *The Field of Cultural Production* (New York: Columbia University Press, 1993).
60. L. Miller-Kahn and M. L. Smith, "School Choice Policies in the Political Spectacle," *Education Policy Analysis Archives* (30 November 2001), http://epaa.asu.edu/epaa/v9n50.html (2 December 2001).
61. A. S. Wells and I. Serna, "The Politics of Culture: Understanding Local Political Resistance to Detracking in Racially Mixed Schools," *Harvard Educational Review* 66 (1) (1996): 93–118.
62. Young, "Communication and the Other."
63. D. Stoesz, "Policy Gambit: Conservative Think Tanks Take on the Welfare State," *Journal of Sociology and Social Welfare,* 14 (4) (1987), p. 3. Although we disagree with Stoesz's suggestion to *increase* the presence of political ideology in the policy-making process, we endorse his recommendation that policy-oriented educational researchers combine quantitative, qualitative, and narrative research methods. Such an approach would both challenge the hegemony of quantitative methods, the statistical results from which are easily misinterpreted or manipulated [see Best], and provide a more complete portrait from which to analyze issues and make policy decisions.
64. Loosely, remedial courses are defined as courses dealing with precollege material, which is centered on addressing academic weaknesses [see H. R. Boylan and W. G. White, "Educating the Nation's people: The Historical Roots of Developmental Education, Part I," *Review of Research on Developmental Education,* 4 (4) (1987): 1–4; P. Cross, *Accent on Learning* (San Francisco: Jossey-Bass, 1976); J. E. Roueche and S. D. Roueche, *High Stakes, High Performance: Making Remedial Education Work* (Washington, DC: Community College Press, 1999)]. Although there has been some contention about how to describe the courses that fall under the "remedial" or "developmental" label, most public commentaries outside of academe refer to remedial education, especially when discussing the various criticisms and debates surrounding it. For that reason, remedial education is referred to herein.
65. See M. S. Moses, *Embracing Race: Why We Need Race-Conscious Education Policy* (New York: Teachers College Press, in press), Chapter 6, for a discussion of remedial education policy.
66. B. V. Manno, "Remedial Education: Replacing the Double standard with Real Standards," *Change* 27 (May/June 2000): 47–49; L. Steinberg, "Commentary," in *Remediation in Higher Education: A Symposium,* ed. C. E. Finn (Dayton, OH: Fordham Foundation, 1998), pp. 37–41.
67. L. Cronholm, "The Assault on Remediation: The Triumph of Logic Over Emotion." Baruch College,. http://www.baruch.cuny.edu/president/ remediation.html (17 December 2001); L. Cronholm, "Why One College Jettisoned All Its Remedial Courses," *The Chronicle of Higher Education* (September 24, 1999): B6–B7.
68. L. Guernsey, "Study Finds That 29% of Freshmen Take Remedial Instruction," *The Chronicle of Higher Education* (November 1,1996): A23.
69. See L. Cronholm, "Assault" and "Why One College"; B. V. Manno, "Remedial Education: Replacing the Double Standard with Real Standards," *Change* 27 (May/June 1995): 47–49; L. Steinberg.

70. C. Adelman, "The Kiss of Death? An Alternative View of College Remediation," *Cross Talk* 6 (3) (1998): 11; D. H. Ponitz, "Commentary," in *Remediation in Higher Education: A Symposium*, ed. C. E. Finn (Dayton, OH: Fordham Foundation, 1998), pp. 35–37; J. E. Roueche and S. D. Roueche, *High Stakes, High Performance: Making Remedial Education Work* (Washington, DC: Community College Press, 1999).
71. Critics argue that students in remedial courses are each individually responsible for their underpreparedness. These critics maintain that some students have simply chosen not to take the demanding high school courses that would have better prepared them for the levels of writing, reading, and mathematics expected of college students at four-year institutions. As such, they were unable to score high enough on entrance and placement examinations. The general sentiment is that they are either unintelligent or irresponsible persons who squandered their K–12 educational opportunities. Hence, they do not deserve so-called second chances at the postsecondary level.
72. See Manno; R. Phipps, *College Remediation: What It Is, What It Costs, What's at Stake* (Washington, DC: The Institute for Higher Education Policy, 1998).
73. D. W. Breneman, "The Extent and Cost of Remediation in Higher Education," In *Brookings Papers on Education Policy: 1998*, ed. D. Ravitch (Washington, DC: Brookings Institution Press, 1998).
74. D. E. Lavin, R. D. Alba, and R. A. Silberstein, *Right versus Privilege: The Open-Admissions Experiment at the City University of New York* (New York: The Free Press, 1981).
75. K. Lively, "Cal State U. Revises Plan for Ending Remedial Education," *The Chronicle of Higher Education* (December 15, 1995): A27; P. Schmidt, "A Clash of Values at CUNY Over Remedial Education," *The Chronicle of Higher Education* (March 20, 1998): A33–A34.
76. Espousing the educational philosophy of Freire, Giroux formulates a politics of voice and argues that a "discourse of difference" is necessary to permeate monolithic perspectives and relations of power and privilege (see Giroux , p. 168).
77. Giroux, pp. 246–248.
78. E. R. House, "Race and Policy," *Education Policy Analysis Archives* 7 (16) (1999), http://epaa.asu.edu/epaa/v7n16.html (17 December 2001).
79. E. C. Lagemann, *An Elusive Science: The Troubling History of Education Research* (Chicago: University of Chicago Press, 2000).
80. Murray Edelman, *Constructing the Political Spectacle* (Chicago: University of Chicago Press, 1988), argues that the contemporary political milieu in the United Sates resembles theater, comprised of a range of actors and intricate plots. The curtain conceals the backstage action where irrational and manipulative politics by skilled but immoral actors is really played out.
81. Apple, p. 227.

CHAPTER 9

# Dialogue between "Academic" and "Community" Researchers
## The Possibilities and Challenges of Participatory Research

KEVIN J. GORMLEY

### An Introduction to the Theory of Participatory Research

In the context of community-based research, academic investigators and community practitioners work together to resolve challenges that exist, often in the context of low-income neighborhoods. Participatory research is a specific form of community-based inquiry that affords the equal distinction of "expert" to all involved in the investigation. This privileged label is traditionally reserved only for those with years of formal academic training. Such recognition is possible as scholars within academia confirm that ample knowledge has been discovered by lay researchers, the results of which are not disseminated through academic journals, but through informal networks of communication within innumerable communities and cultures around the world.

As coresearchers, community and academic participants engage in a process of education, research, and action. Research of this kind is educational in nature by equipping all investigators with tools to generate knowledge that can be shared in lay and professional contexts. This form of study is also educational, as all participants learn from each other and are encouraged to become actors in political processes that influence their lives. As a result, this type of investigation not only generates a unique type of researcher but also inspires local practitioners to become grassroots policy makers who influence decisions that impact their community, city, and nation. The processes of research and education lead to stages of action that are intended to be transformative in nature, bringing about dramatic change based on equality, justice, and respect. The products of participatory research are meant to equalize the uneven distribution of social, cultural, and financial capital; empower oppressed groups; and transform social realities that show preference to those who hoard assets and influence.[1]

The fundamental methodological component that differentiates participatory research from other social research is dialogue. In contrast to other types of investigations in which community members serve as informants, advisors, or even collaborators, participatory research emphasizes dialogue as a strategy to overcome structural and cultural barriers to communication between "community" and "academic" researchers through joint reflection and action.[2] By reviewing the writings of Paulo Freire, a number of important components of dialogue are revealed: (a) respect for coequal roles between researchers and practitioners, (b) praxis—action that is based on knowledge generated by the group, (c) voice—affording those who are oppressed to name their world (rather than having it named for them), and (d) lived experience as a critical and valid source of knowledge.[3]

Ginsburg and Gorostiaga state that academic researchers and community practitioners have an opportunity to engage in the most comprehensive form of dialogue through "research as collective praxis," which is exemplified in participatory research.[4] By eliminating the primacy of the researchers' frame of reference, an extensive form of interstructural and intercultural communication occurs. Dialogue invites both researchers and practitioners to critically examine their own knowledge for the purpose of praxis: the development of knowledge for the sake of taking action. Such a process may progress by examining a number of contextual elements:

- Physical conditions of the participant's lives
- Social relations and stratification systems that contribute to creating the contextual conditions
- Subsequent choices available (or unavailable) to the community members through their actions as researchers and citizens
- The possibility of bringing about desired changes

In participatory research dialogue acts as a catalyst for fostering "an understanding based on knowledge of how people and issues are historically and politically situated."[5] The academic and community researchers work together to address social challenges and engage in the dialectic process of conscientization, beginning with learning, then reflection, leading to action, and eventually change in social systems.[6]

Overall, the foundation of participatory research is built upon the theoretical principle that decision making should be guided by the community researchers to the greatest degree possible.[7] According to scholars of community-based research and international development, this type of activity aids in facilitating community ownership of an initiative, and promotes the sustainability of development efforts.[8]

## Bridging the Differences Between Academic and Community Researchers

Conceptual differences exist between academic and community researchers, which are reflected in a number of different forms of expression, including vocabularies, agendas, and worldviews. For academic researchers involved in or concerned with participatory forms of community-based research, the two most evocative concepts are those related to the words "trust" and "power." Volumes have been written and hours of discussion have occurred between academic researchers and theorists intrigued by the prospect of creating dialogue between themselves and their community counterparts. The ethical and moral consequences of community-based work require an intense degree of personal reflexivity as academic scholars seek to counter actions of dominance by esteeming the expertise of their community colleagues and by considering how trust may be earned. Through private reflection and public discourse with practitioners, academic scholars must consider how culture, race and ethnicity, gender, nationality, economic status, and worldviews affect the relationship between academic and community researchers. Such reflections and discussions are imperative if academic researchers expect to effectively engage in activities with community partners.

Among community researchers, the most evocative concepts often center on producing *results* and improvements as well as on enhancing collaborative *networks* and *resources*. They are primarily interested in producing change in the community that is brought about through the use of collaborative networks and the effective application of political, economic, and cultural resources. The motivation is practical more than theoretical.

Comparatively speaking, the motivation for academic researchers is based on the production of ideas and theories, which can help to develop publications, professional integrity, and practical social change. The incentive for community practitioners engaged in community-based study is the production of results that have positive and sustainable impact where they live and work. Therefore, it is observable that the academic researchers and the community investigators are inspired by those issues situated where the stakes are highest and where their lives are affected most. Community and academic researchers share an appreciation for developing trust, equalizing power, producing results, and enhancing networks of collaboration and resources. Yet, these issues are prioritized differently based on their personal and collective needs and the demands of their working/living environments.

Second, academic and community researchers tend to have epistemological differences, evidenced in their appreciation for different types of knowledge connected to the context. That which is esteemed as "knowledge" among academic researchers may not be so among community colleagues. Community researchers may or may not appreciate knowledge that comes from academic circles.[9] They may question not only the veracity of academic "knowledge" but also the scientific paradigm for discovering truth, especially since so much scholarly work has failed to bring about real change and lasting neighborhood revitalization. Community researchers challenge academic knowledge as they grow in their understanding of research and begin probing into the accuracy of studies:

- Who is included/excluded from a study?
- Who devises the research question?
- Is the question/study relevant to the most pressing community needs?
- Are the findings used to bring about progressive change, or just written up and made available to those who might read the research report?

On the other hand, academic researchers may see the informal networks through which information passes in community contexts simply as chains of gossip rather than sophisticated systems through which knowledge is created, evaluated, refined, and handed down to succeeding generations.

Academic researchers are responding to the perception that their work is irrelevant in the real world and autocratic in nature. Barriers are overcome by legitimizing the knowledge of community practitioners as unique and by emphasizing that both can learn from each other. As Freire stated, "through this process of investigation, examination, criticism and reinvestigation, the level of critical thinking is reached among all those involved. Thus, in doing research, I am educating and being educated with the people."[10] This approach not only seeks to make academic researchers' knowledge more relevant but also recognizes the validity of community researchers' knowledge and ways of knowing.

Community researchers are also responding by acknowledging that their systems for creating and transmitting knowledge can be improved with the assistance of academic researchers. Furthermore, through face-to-face interaction, community researchers recognize that their academic colleagues are sincere in their interest to create viable solutions despite continued underdevelopment. Through the process of dialogue with academicians, community researchers can help to accumulate ideas that are more substantive and profound than what they could generate if they attempted to tackle their problems alone. This whole phenomenon is only possible with a participatory foundation that respects all, values ideas and interests of community and academic researchers, and emphasizes working together to create and apply solutions.

## A Case Study of Participatory Research

To illustrate the conceptual issues just summarized, a specific case study of a participatory research project is presented in which I was involved as the academic researcher. The portrayal is built upon stories of the community and academic researchers—specifically about their experiences of working together and appraisals of their efforts to create sustainable change. Documenting the reflection and action of the coresearchers in this case is particularly challenging since rarely did we speak directly about the dialogic process itself. Consequently, a phenomenological approach was used to reveal the essence of the experience and to expose the dialogue that was concealed within the data.[11]

### The Context

The host country for this case study, Brazil, and the low-income community in which the study occurred are important starting points for recounting the stories of this participatory research project. The current federal democratic process in Brazil has been in place since 1988, and appears secure despite nearly five hundred previous years of authoritarian rule. The economic situation of the country as a whole seems optimistic because the staggering levels of international debt and inflation present from previous decades have been brought under control. This has helped Brazil enter into a period of stability and growth. Nevertheless, poverty still grips the heart of this country, which is endowed with abundant natural and financial resources. With the ninth largest economy in the world and a population of 169 million people, Brazil would seem to have the means to overcome its staggeringly high level of poverty.[12] However, as Roett claims, the patrimonial forces of Brazil do not wish to relinquish their hold on power, influence, and wealth—even at the expense of their communities, states, or their nation as a whole.[13]

The educational system in Brazil has experienced marked improvements over the past thirty years with an increase in literacy by 33 percent and a primary school completion rate that has nearly doubled.[14] Yet these findings do not suggest that educational attainment in this country is easily achieved. Figures from 1996 demonstrate that only 19 percent of the population had completed primary education, and only 8 percent had completed high school.[15] With few other options, residents of financially struggling communities seek to overcome the distress of their neighborhoods by striving to find education for themselves and their children, and therein discover a means for self-sufficiency.

The host community for this case study, Jardim Uchôa, is a densely populated neighborhood of five thousand people. This locale is tucked within the urban metropolis of Recife, longitudinally 8 degrees south of the Equator and within the northeastern region of the country, which is renowned as one of the most financially challenged areas in the Western Hemisphere.[16] Settlement of the community began in the 1950s and continued into the 1970s until the majority of the land was claimed.[17] Household incomes in this area overall are modest, but sufficient to modestly support a family with the addition of one or two minor "luxuries" by Brazilian standards (e.g., refrigerator, telephone).

In the 1980s, settlement of the community spread into a swampy area along the Tejipió River.[18] The later settlement can be characterized as a shantytown, or *favela*, bursting with houses that are made of course bricks or wood and are separated by narrow allies and streams of sewage flowing into the nearby river. In 1991, the *favela* of Jardim Uchôa was recognized by the municipal government of Recife and designated as a Special Zone of Social Interest (ZEIS).[19] The ZEIS has a population of approximately fifteen hundred people or five hundred families.[20] These families suffer from extremely low standards of living. For example, according to 1995 statistics, 64 percent of the community residents survived on household incomes of R$60 per month or less.[21]

Statistics on levels of education in the *favela* were equally alarming; only 4 percent of the ZEIS residents had completed eighth grade, and only 2.6 percent had completed high school.[22] At 8 percent, the national average of high school graduates is more than three times this rate.[23] These statistics derive in part from the fact that there are no public elementary or secondary education facilities located in the ZEIS or in Jardim Uchôa, and therefore community residents had to rely on "community schools." These tuition-free and privately operated learning centers offer several types of educational opportunities:[24]

1. Preschool—meals and academic training for children ages three to seven
2. Reinforcement school—support for children ages eight to fifteen who are enrolled in public schools located in nearby communities
3. Vocational education—training for youth ages thirteen to eighteen in areas such as cabinetry, hair cutting, broom making, and cooking
4. Adult literacy programs—typically offered in the evening

Of the four community schools located in or near the ZEIS, three provide preschool, reinforcement, and adult literacy training; the fourth provides all four services. Financially supported through local nongovernmental organizations (NGOs), international NGOs, Brazilian public agencies, and intermittent donations from parents, the schools often scramble to keep their modest facilities in operation.[25] Several fee-charging private schools were also located in the area, but provided minimal service to the families in the ZEIS since few could afford the monthly enrollment fees.

The only public educational center in the community was a municipal crèche, which offered a preschool and recreational curriculum and enrolled sixty children from the ages eighteen months to five years. With approximately twenty-three hundred children under the age of seventeen in Jardim Uchôa, the existing facilities were clearly insufficient to provide for all of the educational needs in the area. The harsh facts of reality stood in stark contrast to federal law, which requires not only that children should be provided with a free public education from the age of seven to fourteen, but also that the schools should be located within close walking distance of their residences.[26] Jardim Uchôa and the ZEIS, like other similar communities in Brazil, appeared to have been bypassed in the implementation of these laws.

*The Research Team*

An initial group of ten community members was introduced to the academic researcher through representatives of the Dom Helder Câmara Center for Studies and Social Action (CENDHEC) and was comprised of five teachers, two school directors, one parent, and two community organizers. Demographically, they were predominantly female (9:1), all residents of the *favela*, and dark skinned (*mulato* or *preto*). The preliminary group issued written and verbal invitations to the remaining adult residents in the ZEIS requesting their participation on the research team. Because of time and resource constraints as well as limited experience with education and community participation, only twenty residents and educators chose to take part in the study as community researchers (including the original group of ten) out of the five hundred families/households in the area.

The research team was composed of ten teachers, three school directors, four parents of students, three community organizers, and myself—the academic researcher.[27] Together, we sought to examine the challenges within the educational infrastructure of the community and to create knowledge that would help direct development projects. The demographics of the community members of the research team remained similar to those of the initial group: nineteen women and one man, all of whom were *mulato* or *preto*, and all but one of whom lived and work in the immediate area. Included among the number of community researchers was a professional social worker from Recife (female and *mulata*) who helped to provide cultural and linguistic interpretation between the community researchers and the academic researcher.

As academic researcher for this study, I sought to break down the barriers that existed between my community colleagues and myself. These walls existed in part because of my appearance and background. I am a Caucasian male from a working-class town in New England, and at the time of this study a doctoral candidate at a large midwestern research university.[28] For the duration of my time in Brazil, I secured a position as a visiting researcher with CENDHEC, which also served as my host institution.[29] I recognized to a greater or lesser degree the privilege I experienced based on race, gender, nationality, education, and professional title. In particular, my nationality proved to be one of the most valuable assets and greatest liabilities. Coming from the United States afforded prestige and opened doors. Yet, as a participatory researcher, I was faced with the challenge of cocreating a team atmosphere in which all were viewed as equal, when in fact there were tremendous differences between the other researchers and me. For example, I would eventually return to my comfortable North American residence upon expiration of my visa, while my Brazilian friends and colleagues would continue to confront the challenges that plagued their neighborhood.

*The Participatory Research Process*
This participatory research project began in September 1997, three months after my arrival to Recife, and progressed through two phases over a nine-month period. In June 1998, the initiative was left entirely in the hands of the community researchers, and through a number of twists and turns was still in operation (at the time of writing this chapter, May 2001) under the name of Project Education for the Future, or *Projeto Como Educar o Futuro* (Project CEF).

During Phase I of the project, the academic and community researchers focused on defining the study in addition to collecting and analyzing data. At the first meeting, the investigators agreed on a research question for Phase I: "How should a community with limited resources define its educational needs?" We proceeded to compile and define a list of forty-five educational needs using a qualitative data collection process. Information was collected using methods that relied on the stories of the researchers themselves and their experiences with schools as teachers, parents, or school directors; narratives from colleagues associated with area schools; and discussions with other residents in the community.

Within the analysis and interpretation process, each community researcher presented to the team the information they had collected; investigators described and defined five to ten educational needs related to the schools serving the ZEIS. Realizing that it would be impossible to address all of the needs compiled, the research team decided to prioritize the list and selected four issues that needed the greatest attention:

1. Getting a municipal school
2. Training teachers
3. Obtaining or developing teaching materials
4. Improving the existing community schools

Building upon what had been conducted in the first phase of the study, the community researchers decided to address two questions during Phase II:

1. How should a community strive to locate resources that would be used to reduce or eliminate the educational needs that they had defined?
2. How should a community seek to sustain an educational development initiative with little or no outside assistance?

This phase of the project proved to be notably more challenging as the community researchers wrestled to balance their time between involvement in the study and other responsibilities. Phase II also proved to be more difficult because the research team was no longer working on describing the problem (Phase I), but was engaging in activities that had unpredictable outcomes—namely, the responses of others to their requests for assistance.

The community researchers and I proceeded by forming four subgroups—one for each prioritized need. The entire team divided into the subgroups with the intent of developing projects to address the related need and to generate political and financial support for their initiatives. The researchers simultaneously addressed the issue of sustainability, the second question for Phase II, by organizing training sessions on how to design a project and how to organize a seminar. The latter became necessary when the research team decided to organize a one-day workshop on the educational needs of Jardim Uchôa.

In the process of trying to develop both the subgroups' initiatives and the one-day workshop, the research team suspended the subgroups' activities until the one-day workshop had been completed. The remaining activities in Phase II included:

1. Completion of the one-day workshop, which produced two valuable products:
    a. Four sets of action plans corresponding to the four necessities
    b. A list of faculty from local universities and other skilled individuals willing to help the research team implement educational development initiatives in Jardim Uchôa

2. Purchase of land in Jardim Uchôa for a municipal school[30]
3. Administration of a final evaluation of Project CEF by the participants
4. Documentation of a final report that detailed the results of the research and outlined action plans for future work[31]

*Decision Making, Participation, and the Role of the Academic Researcher*

In this project, as the academic researcher I repeatedly stated that the community members should make all major and minor decisions in determining the research questions, framing how to address the host of issues that arose while gathering and analyzing the data, and planning the variety of actions and events listed earlier. While I communicated this conception of decision making as empowering, the research team initially struggled with how to function in this manner.

Over time, the research team developed several decision-making methods that embodied the participatory ideal promoted in this type of research. One was a public electoral method in which team members would vote publicly to rank-order a longer list of options and then to select the final choice from among the top three selected options. Another decision-making approach employed a group process in which the ultimate selection would be agreed upon by consensus. The final decision-making procedure relied on anonymous ballots and allowed the participants to elect option(s) without being as subject to influence of other group members. The latter process was rarely used—and only when the group showed symptoms of drifting into "groupthink" (i.e., acquiescing to some form of pressure from a more dominant participant or consenting to an idea that was not actually favored).[32]

Concrete instances may be helpful to provide a sense of how the decision-making methods were implemented and to clarify the roles played by the academic and community researchers. In one example, after a discussion (facilitated by me) the research team agreed on a research question for Phase I of the project. Then with the collaboration of the cultural interpreter I provided initial training in methods of data collection and analysis that were congruent with the community culture. The focus of this training was on basic qualitative research procedures:

- Techniques for interviewing and participant observation
- Triangulation and the need for multiple views of the same information
- The group analysis method[33]

Next the community participants reflected on the conditions of the schools in the area and consulted with their neighbors, adult students, parents of younger students, and professional colleagues to develop a list of forty-five educational needs. From among these, the community researchers (with some facilitation by me) used a voice-vote process to select the four highest priority needs that would become the focus of their later efforts to produce sustainable change.

Throughout this entire process, the community researchers diligently sought clear convincing arguments for why the research process needed to be so laborious. In other words, while the investigation process itself intrigued the academic researcher, the community colleagues were primarily interested in the product. They too wanted reliable and accurate information, but even more they wanted to see tangible results for their labor.

In an example from the beginning of Phase II of the project, the research team discussed some of the strengths and weaknesses of the research they had conducted. They were concerned that the quality of the research suffered because they had not been as active in shaping its direction. In response, the community researchers decided to take more responsibility for what was decided during the biweekly research team meetings. This transition was marked by a change in naming the project from "your" (the academic researcher's) to "our" (all participants') project.

During the final evaluation session of the investigation, the community researchers stressed that they had become essential participants in all that had been achieved. For example, Pia, a community researcher who worked as a neighborhood activist and organizer in Jardim Uchôa, stated,[34] "All of the people [were] involved and participated. Therefore, this stimulated the people to come and present their ideas. Everybody felt at ease. The people thought that they were building something that we really constructed together with the participation of all." Tomas[35] further explained the significance of broad-based participation by the group:

> I have been reflecting here [about the saying], "the sum of the individuals is not equal to that of the collective." The collective always builds something bigger. The individual will make a little step here. Make another there. [Yet], if I arrive in the collective, the thing is easier. I think that the [collective work] is greater because there is a greater [lesson]. There is a greater possibility—a greater participation from people. Therefore, my evaluation is this: that we left the work in the individual to work now in the collective.

According to Pia, broad-based participation was possible because a comfortable atmosphere had been developed in which the ideas of each person were recognized and appreciated. The ambience she spoke of was founded on a sense of trust, which community researchers had for each other and which also existed between the community researchers and the academic researcher. At one point during the "final" evaluation meeting Pia directed part of her public remarks specifically to me:

> Tomas and I were the first people who had contact with you. We knew that you were here to do important work. We trusted you because of those who first brought you here. We already had a determined confidence in

you because of the connection that we have with CENDHEC. We who are here in front of CCEP[36] [i.e., Tomas and I]... [set] our confidence in your work. Therefore, [the community members] understood that your work was serious.[37]

Marcy, a local community schoolteacher and community researcher, wrote an essay written during the "final" evaluation meeting that provided a personal reflection on this theme:

> I remember well the first time you [the academic researcher] arrived. [Your] voice tried to say something, but would [become] confused. The time passed by and at every meeting as you offered your message, little by little, your voice acquired a different tone. You even learned our "Óxente."[38] You were able to bring people together who until recently thought they were separated. It was marvelous. At each meeting, cooperation and unity became present, and these people became a team. Another marvelous person came with you, Ceça, who showed us that we had the will and the unity to attain our objectives.[39] Thus we started off on our battle. Finally, that which I thought would never happen occurred. I came and participated.

These statements represent the sense of trust and camaraderie that developed over time between the community researchers and me. For instance, during one of our many meetings, I jumped up and exclaimed, "I have an idea!" The other research team members simultaneously responded by yelling as if in amazement that I could have come up with an idea, which we all found very amusing. The sense of trust between us was also evidenced in the way the community researchers felt comfortable not only in teaching me their language and in correcting my pronunciation, but also in pointing out cultural differences that became apparent as we worked together.

A case in point: during a research team meeting Ceça commented on a cultural difference between my interest in developing an organized plan, which she and others believed to be very "American," and the more relaxed and less predetermined method, which they believed to be very "Brazilian": "Because it is complicated, isn't it Kevin? Kevin wanted that thing [a specific way] ... the 'now' culture—well organized, step by step.... We have this thing more, 'go here, go there, go here, go there.'" Given this cultural clash, we found ways to meet in the middle between "chaos" and "rigid administration." Much like in any partnership, concessions are made to keep the process functioning. I chose to flow with the regular dose of spontaneity and a bit less systematic planning. The community researchers allowed me to plan (within reason) as long as I maintained a fluid disposition. In the end, we both saw that we benefited from this struggle by learning about the need for both planning and flexibility.

## *Personal Development and Sustaining the Participatory Research Process*

The previous examples not only indicate the nature of the relationships between community and academic researchers but also signal that the research process is one in which personal development occurs among the investigators. Sara, a parent of students at the local community schools and one of the community researcher, explained that her participation in the project had raised her level of critical consciousness: "Before I participated in these meetings, there were things that I didn't know. But afterwards, I began to participate in the meetings, things became clearer in my mind. I understood more—the things here, in the schools." By this, Sara stated that she had learned not only about how the schools functioned but also about the struggles experienced by the teachers and directors because of a severe lack of resources. In addition, she informed the group that she had developed new professional skills. Sara valued particularly the responsibility that she had been given as a receptionist at a seminar the team had organized, as was indicated during a conversation with two other community members of the research team, Ceça and Gina:

CEÇA: She said, "I never have worked that way."
SARA: No, I never had participated [like that].
CEÇA: Never worked as a receptionist.
SARA: A new thing!
CEÇA: Many people could say, "Ah, this is nothing. I don't want to do that. It is nothing." But she said to me, "Wow, I never worked this way. I had never done anything like that."
GINA:[40] It was gratifying?
SARA: Yes! Yes!

Marcy also related how the experience helped her develop not only an expanded sense of personal empowerment but also a feeling that she was part of an effective collective enterprise:

> What I felt at the first meeting, I no longer feel. I now feel a force that rises up from within me, and I know that together we will succeed. Surely, something changed within me because [although] there are always those who try to make us pessimistic, they cannot deter us. It was marvelous and very valuable because I made new friends and I am certain that I can count on them because I feel a deep [sense of closeness].

This optimistic opinion did not universally represent the research team members' views regarding the sustainability of Project CEF. Some community researchers expressed their doubts about the participatory research process being sustained over a longer period. For instance, Gina commented that she believed the enthusiasm would wane:

> Not disrespecting those who are always here [at the meetings], but it is very unclear; many people come hooked [dragged to the meetings]. That person doesn't want to come. On the other side, many come out of consideration for you [the academic researcher]. I hope that this [project] doesn't [end]. But I have little [confidence] in these people.

Indeed, the level of participation among members of the research team rose and then began to decline even during the nine-month period in which I was in the community. I observed that during Phase I of the project, the data collection and analysis stage (i.e., the first three months), attendance at meetings and other activities steadily increased. During Phase II, the research team sought to identify and locate resources (namely outside of the community) and to begin improving the educational infrastructure in the neighborhood. Coordination for this stage proved to be more time-consuming and less expeditious in producing visible results. The community researchers expressed their dissent during this time through their nonattendance. As Tomas explained, attendance declined because "people are accustomed to only participate in some meetings related to something when they see that it has an immediate return." He went on to compare the situation of Project CEF to a meeting with a local social service agency that had received a large pool of public funds for community development. He said that "the auditorium filled so that it couldn't hold any more people because the people were all there with the ambition to receive money." While he was offering a judgment on those who were not participating on a regular basis, he also touched upon the need to quickly respond to the needs of the research team.

*Struggles to Transform Power Relations*

Through my efforts to remain in contact with the community researchers after returning to the United States, I learned that motivation and participation had declined. Nevertheless, many of the community researchers continued to meet, focusing their attention exclusively on securing a municipal school for Jardim Uchôa.[41] This effort continued to move forward. The land had been purchased. The building plans had been finalized. The construction material had been delivered. Then late one evening, the construction crew picked up all of the building materials and relocated them to an empty lot in a nearby community. The community researchers claimed that the neighboring community had profited from better political representation. One of the community organizers from Jardim Uchôa confronted the mayor of Recife, who in return slapped her in the face. Following a number of negative press reports about the incident, the mayor apologized to the community practitioner and committed himself to helping Jardim Uchôa improve its educational infrastructure.

This incident was not the first time the research team and other members of the community had had to confront those in positions of political power. These incidents not only depict the context in which the research team operated but also illustrate how at times the participatory research project enabled them to challenge and perhaps even begin a process of transforming power relations. At the one-day workshop, a representative from the State Secretariat of Education frankly told the investigators and all in attendance that space in public schools existed for all of the children in their community. The research team, citing the data they had collected and analyzed, discredited the official's statement and explained that schools located several miles away were of no use to families with young children, no transportation, and limited finances.

Such public challenges to people in power are significant in that initially, because of their history of oppression, many community researchers exhibited a cultural orientation of repressing ideas and opinions, often called the "culture of silence." Several members of the research team discussed this cultural orientation during one of our biweekly meetings:

SARA: But here the people are accustomed to staying quiet. "Whatever I hear, I will stay quiet. I will not talk."
MARCY: "I will lie."
SARA: It is already in [our] blood. It came like that.
CEÇA: [We live in] a culture of domination. People are not accustomed to complain... nor do they know their rights. How can you complain about activities that you don't know exist [when you don't know they are wrong]?

To overcome this problem, community researchers joined together and encouraged one another to struggle against the forces that prevented them from achieving improvements in their neighborhood:

MARCY: [Sometimes] we don't attain, but we struggle. The importance is not the victory, but the fight.
CEÇA: This here! Look here [at] CCEP... that fell from heaven and came into my hands.
MARCY: It was a struggle. It was a struggle.
CEÇA: So it was. Years of struggle.

## Conclusions

The purpose of this chapter has been to explore the possibilities and limitations of the participatory research approach through a case study of the actions and meanings of a team of community and academic researchers engaged in a participatory research project in northeastern Brazil. Figure 9.1 illustrates the components of the participatory research process in which the *academic* and *community* researchers engage in *dialogue*. The researchers interact within a

```
┌─────────────────────────────────────────────────────────┐
│   Community                      Academic               │
│   Researchers  ←――――――――――→      Researchers            │
│        ↑          ╲    ╱              ↑                 │
│                    ╲  ╱                                 │
│              Participatory                              │
│               Research                                  │
│                    ╱  ╲                                 │
│        ↓          ╱    ╲              ↓                 │
│   The Dialogue                   The Context            │
│   Reflection and Action          Physical Environment & │
│                    ⇐ Effect(s) ⇒  Social/Cultural Relations │
│                      Constraints                        │
│                      Opportunities                      │
└─────────────────────────────────────────────────────────┘
```

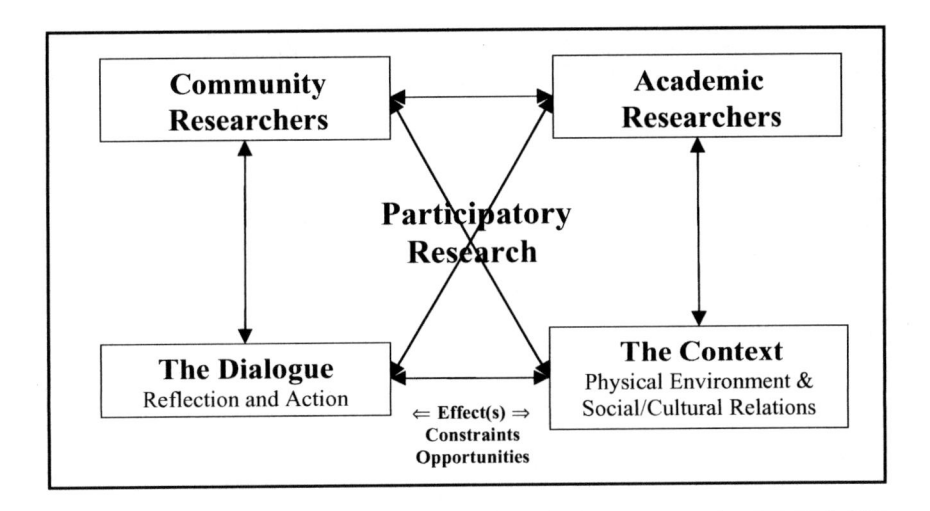

**Figure 9.1.** The components of dialogue in participatory research.

*context* consisting of the physical environment and with social and cultural patterns or relations that are sometimes pliable and sometimes not. The *effect(s)* of the dialogue comprise various forms and degrees of changes in the context, which in turn have implication for the participants and their dialogue. The *effect(s)* is a significant aspect of the model because it refers to the notion that participants, through the process of dialogue (communication as well as joint reflection and action), engage in the context and begin to transform it from the bottom up.

Figure 9.1 also indicates that academic and community researchers in their efforts to achieve dialogue and stimulate change in the context are conditioned by that context. Because of social and cultural realities, academic and community researchers maneuver against constraints and with opportunities that affect dialogue. The social standing of community researchers, being residents of shantytowns, is one typically identified with limited ability to voice their interests and intermittent access to decision-making processes that influence their neighborhood. As demonstrated in the case cited here, participatory research is designed to counter that reality by esteeming the community members as experts about the needs and conditions of their nearby surroundings. As peers in the research process, community and academic researchers interact in an effort to examine the challenges, reflect on these conditions, and develop plans for action and change.

Academic researchers also struggle in their efforts to establish trust among their community peers and a sense of belonging in the context. They are outsiders trying to become insiders. Therefore, a certain amount of time is needed to develop the contextual vocabulary and social skills and to adapt scientific techniques to the unique conditions of the investigation. They also are obligated to their citizenship in academia, which has requirements that are unlike those in the community. They are required to return with information not only that will enhance our knowledge about a certain community but also about how we can contribute to more effective means of low-income community development. What, in fact, was achieved by this particular investigation?

- Did the dialogue facilitate the creation of knowledge?
- Did sustainable change occur?
- Did the investigation facilitate societal transformation?

The reflections of the community researchers were unanimously in agreement that the investigation had produced the creation of knowledge that had been used to direct educational development projects. Regarding the second question, the research team debated as to whether the efforts would be sustainable and whether the group would remain active after the academic researcher departed. A response to the final question concerning social transformation is a bit more complicated than reflecting on the fate of the municipal school and requires a more careful review of the findings.

Observable within this final evaluation meeting was a sense of accomplishment, an appreciation for unity, and an attitude of determination to continue in the struggle for change. Not all group members assessed the results with glowing optimism, as was illustrated previously, nor should they. At what point should they have been satisfied? The construction of a school would not have eliminated poverty in the community nor would it have purged the various forms of racial and financial oppression. Nevertheless, the school would serve as a small piece in the construction of new social norms where opportunities are provided for all individuals regardless of their financial status, ethnicity, race, gender, or heritage.

Concerning evidence of social transformation, Project CEF does not demonstrate large-scale change of global inequities, but local-level improvements in participation and activism as well as some restoration of physical facilities. Because of consistent findings of this nature, participatory research theorists are increasingly softening their tone regarding the potential of the methodology to transform social inequities. Their revisions state that an investigation may serve as part of a network of efforts to overcome systems of disadvantage at a local level, which can informally support similar efforts that occur elsewhere in the world.[42]

Practically speaking, the theory of participatory research does not delineate the complex social and educational process involved in working with community researchers. The theory implies that all research participants are to engage actively in the investigation without any consideration of differing levels of interest and ability. After struggling for a couple of months to promote active participation of all team members, I found it much more constructive to consider our research team as a set of unique individuals who had various levels of capabilities. We had our shining stars and our introverts as well as many optimists and skeptics. This change in perspective enabled me to encourage each community participant to mature to the next level of participation rather than requiring complete dedication by all members initially as I inferred from the theory.

The modifications made during the course of the project demonstrate some of the strengths of participatory research, and also expose some of its frailties. Nevertheless, correcting a theory is not the principal concern when working in the context of a community like Jardim Uchôa. The ethical and moral obligations for an academic investigator in participatory research are not simply fulfilled by meeting the theoretical mandates of a research methodology or by not violating human subjects regulations. In dialogue, community researchers communicate that they want to find a partner who is not like the politicians who are full of empty promises or who take credit for work they have not done. Community researchers gratefully invest their trust and their sense of hope, in exchange for the possibility of creating improvements for their families, neighbors, and community. The ethical responsibilities associated with engaging in community-based research obligate academic investigators to sometimes stretch beyond the boundaries of predetermined theory and conventional research practices to find strategies that are effective. In the case of the Brazilian study, there were examples where the academic researcher—with the help of the community researchers on the team—looked beyond the words of the theory to its essence and found ways to improve the dialogue and facilitate a greater degree of local ownership of the project.

The dialogue between the community and academic researchers also serves as a stage for conducting leadership development. Analogous to Jesus' washing the feet of his disciples, the academic researcher must be willing to be the first one to perform the difficult tasks. Participatory research is a process of servant leadership in which the importance of modeling cannot be underestimated.[43] As a servant, one must be willing to model those tasks that are physically or emotionally difficult to perform. Failure to do so slows the investigation, forfeits an opportunity to develop deeper trust, and risks the sustainability of the project. This point is raised not as an abstraction, but as a lesson learned through trial and error.

Participatory research is a peculiar mix of professional and personal interests. Times together with the community researchers were a mix of struggle and pleasure, and of serious deliberations and spontaneous diversions. Such is the result of using a methodology that expects the academic researcher to become one with the people. The community participants became not only respected professional colleagues, but also personal friends from whom much was learned and with whom much was shared.

The community and academic researchers in Jardim Uchôa engaged in a process of dialogue, and exposed ways in which the theoretical assertions of participatory research were correct and not and ways in which the efforts within this study would be sustainable and not. Potentially more important is that the case study provides a list of some key ingredients that are needed for academic and community researchers to work together. Some of these primary components include formulating the research question(s) as a team, prioritizing the action plans, involving the community researchers in all decisions, and keeping their interest high through tangible results.

Dialogue in participatory research is a partnership—a marriage of sorts—that requires a listening ear and a responsive temperament from both community and academic investigators. Yet, the responsibility weighs heavily on academic researchers, especially those coming from industrialized countries, who must recognize their privilege and the esteem due to community peers. They must initiate the listening spirit in order to demonstrate that they have come to learn from their community partners. Rounding out a balanced approach to participatory research is the need for a healthy dose of flexibility and adaptability. Each party comes into the research with differing interests, abilities, passions, and motivations. This requires a patient spirit from all involved, and a willingness to alter what one may want for the sake of the group. In some cases the variations are more pronounced than in others. In this project the community researchers and their academic colleague were from different countries with different languages, social norms, historical liabilities, and financial circumstances. The research team came to recognize the dissimilarities that existed between them as assets, and grew to appreciate the unique perspectives that could be gained as a result. In participatory research, community investigators gain from attaining a new perspective on creating knowledge and change, and from stimulating a sense of self-respect as lay scientists. Academic researchers also benefit by passing on their passion for discovering truth to a new group of individuals, and by forwarding the knowledge uncovered by the research team into the arena of scholarly advancement.

## Notes

1. For further details on various interpretations of participatory research, refer to the writings of Orlando Fals-Borda, "Some Basic Ingredients," in *Action and Knowledge: Breaking the Monopoly with Participatory Action Research*, ed. O. Fals-Borda & M. A. Rahman (New York: Apex Press, 1991); Paulo Freire, "Creating Alternative Research Methods: Learning to Do It by Doing It," in *Creating Knowledge: A Monopoly? Participatory Research in Development*, ed. B. Hall, A. Gillette, and R. Tandon (New Delhi: Society for Participatory Research in Asia, 1982); Paulo Freire, *Pedagogy of Hope: Reliving Pedagogy of the Oppressed* (New York: Continuum, 1995); John Gaventa, "Citizen Knowledge, Citizen Competence, and Democracy Building," *The Good Society* 5 (3) (1995): 28–35; Budd Hall, "Breaking the Monopoly of Knowledge: Research Methods, Participation and Development," in *Creating Knowledge: A Monopoly? Participatory Research in Development*; Budd Hall, "Participatory Research," in *The International Encyclopedia of Education*, ed. T. Husen and T. N. Postlehwaite (New York: Pergamon Press, 1994); Peter Park, "People, Knowledge, and Change in Participatory Research," *Management Learning* 30 (2) (1999): 141–57; and Rajesh Tandon, "Social Transformation and Participatory Research," *Convergence* 21 (2/3) (1988): 5–15.

2. For the remainder of this chapter, "academic" and "community" researchers shall be referred to without the quotation marks. The author understands that making a distinction between such individuals is problematic since some researchers involved in community-based research may perceive themselves as coming from both contexts. In the case of a participatory research investigation, the academic researcher simply is one who comes from outside of the local context and may not be a subject of the oppression the group seeks to eradicate.
3. See Paulo Freire, *Pedagogy of the Oppressed* (New York: Herder & Herder, 1970), and "Creating Alternative Research Methods," pp. 34–37.
4. Mark B. Ginsburg and Jorge M. Gorostiaga, "Relationships between Theorists/Researchers and Policy Makers/Practitioners: Rethinking the Two-Cultures Thesis and the Possibility of Dialogue," *Comparative Education Review* 45 (2) (2001): 173–96.
5. Song Sil Lee Sohng, "Participatory Research and Community Organizing," *The New Social Movement and Community Organizing Conference,* University of Washington, Seattle, WA (November 1–3, 1995): p. 7.
6. Freire, "Creating Alternative Research Methods," pp. 34–37.
7. Hall, "Breaking the Monopoly of Knowledge," p. 22; Park, p. 143.
8. Michael Bopp, "The Illusive Essential: Evaluating Participation in Non-formal Education and Community Development Processes," *Convergence* 27 (1) (1994): 23–45; Lee L. Williams, "Participatory Research, Knowledge, and Community Based Change: Experience, Epistemology, and Empowerment," in *Research in Community Sociology,* ed. D. Chekki (Stamford, CT: JAI Press, 1999); and Gaventa, p. 35.
9. Scholars of culture and society describe how information that is acknowledged within one environment as being universally true and right is becoming increasingly contested by those from other settings. See Don E. Eberly, *The Essential Civil Society Reader* (Lanham, MD: Rowman & Littlefield, 2000); Alan G. Padgett & Steve Wilkens, *Faith and Reason in the 19th Century* (Downers Grove, IL: InterVarsity Press, 2000).
10. Freire, "Creating Alternative Research Methods," p. 30.
11. Max Van Manen, *Researching Lived Experience: Human Science for an Action Sensitive Pedagogy* (London, Ontario, Canada: State University of New York Press, 1990).
12. The definition of poverty is dependent on the figures that are used to evaluate living conditions. The United Nations' Human Development Index (HDI) is one of the most widely referenced indicators to determine levels of poverty and development in nations around the world. In 1998, Brazil ranked 62nd of 174 countries and was placed among those nations with "high human development" [United Nations Development Programme, *Human Development Report: Consumption for Human Development* (New York: Oxford University Press, 1998)]. Among the most noted figures from the HDI for Brazil were those of average life expectancy (66.6 years), adult literacy (83.3 percent), and adjusted gross domestic product per capita (US$5928 annually). What is not reflected in these figures is that 50 percent of the annual income was earned by 1 percent of the population [Statistics from 1993 in R. Andrew Chesnut, *Born Again in Brazil: The Pentecostal Boom and the Pathogens of Poverty* (New Brunswick, NJ: Rutgers University Press, 1997)]. Depending on the levels of income considered to be the demarcation of poverty, some scholars agree that approximately 50 percent of the Brazilian population live in poverty [see Helio Jaguaribe, Wanderley G. dos Santos, Marcelo de P. Abreu, Winston Fritsch, and Fenando B. d'Ávila, *Brasil, 2000; Para um Pacto Social [Brazil, 2000; For a Social Pact]* (Rio de Janeiro: Paz e Terra, 1986); and Cecilia L. Mariz, *Coping with Poverty: Pentecostals and Christian Base Communities in Brazil* (Philadelphia: Temple University Press, 1994)]. In 1999 Brazil's HDI rank was lowered to 79th, repositioning the country as one with "medium human development." The 1999 HDI also concluded that 28.7 percent of the population in Brazil lived on US$1 per day or less [United Nations Development Programme, *Human Development Report: Globalization with a Human Face* (New York: Oxford University Press, 1999)].
13. Riordan Roett, *Brazil: Politics in a Patrimonial Society,* 5th ed. (Westport, CT: Praeger, 1999).
14. Instituto Nacional de Estudos e Pesquisas (INEP), *Estatísticas da Educação Básica no Brasil [Educational Statistics for Brazil]* (Rio de Janeiro: Instituto Nacional de Estudos e Pesquisas, 1996).
15. Ibid., p. 3.
16. Instituto Brasileiro de Geografia e Estatística (IBGE), *Anuário Estatístico do Brasil, 1995 [Statistical Yearbook of Brazil, 1995]* (Rio de Janeiro: IBGE, 1996).

17. Valária Nepomuceno and Luciana de F. P. Santos, *Escola e Criança: Feito Um paro o Outro—A Situação Educacional na Comunidade de Jardim Uchôa [School and Child: One Made for the Other—The Educational Situation in the Community of Jardim Uchôa]* (Recife, Pernambuco, Brazil: Centro Dom Helder Câmara de Estudos e Ação Social, 1997).
18. Assies documented that many *favelas* are located in swampy areas that had previously been deemed inhabitable. The homes of those in the shantytowns are often filled with squalid water from the nearby rivers during the rainy season. Nevertheless, for decades desperate individuals and families have flooded into Recife and "invaded" public and private lands that were not in use, especially the muddy flats of riverbanks. See Willem Assies, *To Get Out of the Mud: Neighborhood Associativism in Recife 1964–1988* (Amsterdam: CEDLA Latin American Studies, 1992).
19. Cécar Caloni, Laura Rosa, Evania F. Galindo, and Luciana de F. P. Santos, *Diagnóstico Rápido Participativo: Comunidade de Jardim Uchôa—Recife [Rapid Participatory Diagnostic: Community of Jardim Uchôa—Recife]* (Recife, Pernambuco, Brazil: World Vision, 1998). The municipal government's designation of the *favela* in Jardim Uchôa as a ZEIS was significant because it officially denoted that the city recognized the area as legitimate. Before being acknowledged by the city, the area simply did not exist within the scope of city planning and services. Trash removal, road construction, utilities, and other publicly funded infrastructures are not afforded to an area until the city recognized it as an established community. The designation of "ZEIS" is granted to a newly settled area once it has reached a certain level of order and has matured to the point of advocating for itself. In such communities, one will typically find the presence of two types of organizations that serve as hubs for self-advocacy: an educational center (e.g., a community school or crèche) and a homeowners' association. See Kevin J. Gormley, "Education for the Future: Participatory Research as a Link between Non-formal Adult Education and Community Development in Brazil," *Dissertation Abstracts International 60* (5): 1709 (Digital Dissertations No. ATT 997 2965).
20. Mécia A. de Silva and Patrícia B. de Luz, *A Organização para a Participação Popular nos Espaços do PREZEIS: A Experiência na Comunidade de Jardim Uchôa [The Organization for Popular Participation in the Spaces of PREZEIS: An Experience in the Community of Jardim Uchôa]* (Pernambuco, Brazil: Universidade Federal de Pernambuco, Recife, 1995).
21. R$60 was half of the minimum salary per month [Secretaria do Governo de Pernambuco, *Sistema integrado de informações sobre áreas de pobreza urbana na região metropolitana do Recife: Volume II, Relatório por núcleo João Paulo II* [Integrated System of Information about Areas of Urban Poverty in the Metropolitan Region of Recife: Volume II, Key Report, João Paulo II] (Secretaria do Governo de Pernambuco, 1995)]. The Brazilian Institute for Geography and Statistics (IBGE) evaluates the threshold of poverty per household at two minimum salaries per month, or R$240 (See IBGE in Roett, p. 228).
22. Secretaria do Governo de Pernambuco, p. 9.
23. See INEP, p. 3.
24. Nepomuceno and Santos, pp. 3-17.
25. The primary sources of income for the community schools in and near the ZEIS came from World Vision (an international, faith-based NGO) and a host of small public and NGO assistance initiatives. The schools functioned as a cooperative, sharing resources with each other to ensure sustainability of their educational mission.
26. While Brazil's constitution guarantees a publicly funded primary education, universal secondary education is still an unrealized objective. Public educational facilities in Brazil do not provide student transportation. Therefore, access to education should be evaluated foremost by the proximity of students' residence to schools, especially to primary school students, as noted in Centro Dom Helder Câmara de Estudos e Ação Social (CENDHEC), *Educação para Todos [Education for All]* (Recife, Brazil: CENDHEC, 1993), p. 15.
27. I chose to conduct this research project in Jardim Uchôa because it possessed a significant need for improvements to the local education infrastructure, while at the same time maintained a modest level of security and organization such that I could enter without an escort. Yet it was not until an initial group of community researchers agreed to participate with me that the investigation actually began.
28. This study was conducted as part of a dissertation study in the area of international development education.
29. Funding for this research was provided through a U.S. Federal David L. Borin Fellowship.

30. The purchase of land for a municipal school was the result of efforts initiated by CENDHEC before the commencement of Project CEF, but was aided through the activities of the research team.
31. While the report was developed by the research team for its own use, CENDHEC also received a copy and stated that it planned to use the document as a model demonstration of community participation in educational development for the metropolitan region.
32. Irving L. Janis, "Groupthink," in *The Effective Manager: Perspectives and Illustrations,* ed. J. Billsberry (London: Sage, 1996).
33. See Matthew B. Miles and A. Michael Huberman, *Qualitative Data Analysis,* 2nd ed. (Thousand Oaks, CA: Sage, 1994).
34. The names of the community researchers have been changed in accordance with human subjects research protocol.
35. Since Tomas was the only man on the research team, I purposely have refrained from disclosing any details about him since doing so would compromise his anonymity.
36. CCEP is a community school in Jardim Uchôa and participating entity in this study.
37. My relationship with the community contrasted with their perception of some local officials. According to Ia, a community researcher and community schoolteacher: "The councilman here only lies to you. [He] promises, asks for your vote. The person comes and goes. We see lots of proposals put on Jardim Uchôa, everything. But after the election, whether he wins or not, he never shows up. He only shows up here four years later [to ask for our votes again]."
38. "Óxente" is a distinctive way of saying "My goodness!" in northeast Brazil.
39. Ceça was the cultural interpreter for the PR project.
40. Gina was a community researcher involved in this study, community schoolteacher, and resident of the area.
41. In addition, every so often, news arrives from the community of small improvements, for example, the building of a new crèche and improvements to area community schools.
42. See Park, p. 143; and Williams, p. 17.
43. Richard K. Greenleaf, *Servant Leadership* (New York: Paulist Press, 1977).

CHAPTER 10

# Enhancing Dialogue among Researchers, Policy Makers, and Community Members in Uganda
*Complexities, Possibilities, and Persistent Questions*[1]

JOSEPH CARASCO[2]
NANCY CLAIR
LAWRENCE KANYIKE

## Introduction

From Ugandan independence in 1962 until the early 1970s, Uganda's education system was considered one of the best in Africa. For about a decade after independence, access for nonelites improved and quality was maintained. However, from the early 1970s to the mid 1980s education, like other sectors, suffered considerably from dictatorship and political instability. During the middle 1980s the political situation began to stabilize. It was then possible for the Ugandan government to initiate a comprehensive reform program to improve the quality of primary education. The objectives of this reform include rehabilitating and strengthening the teaching profession, enhancing community participation in improving education quality and equity, allocating resources for materials, revamping the examination process, revitalizing educational publishing, and rehabilitating schools and teachers' colleges.

This study relates directly to one of the reform objectives: enhancing community participation in education quality and equity. Its purpose is twofold: to illuminate the complexities and possibilities of participation as a method to improve education quality and to understand how dialogue among researchers, policy makers, and community members (teachers, parents, and pupils) may contribute to better schools.

### Dialogue Among Researchers, Policymakers, and Practitioners

According to Freire,[3] dialogue includes reflection and action. It is multidirectional between and among education stakeholders and its ultimate purpose is transformation. In the Freireian view, dialogue among education stakeholders would allow for multiple voices that have mutual influence upon each other. By viewing each other as potential creators and users of knowledge, researchers, policy makers, and practitioners may penetrate traditional barriers to communication. This presents a more participatory view in which everyone in the system has much to learn about reaching ambitious goals for student learning, and challenges the traditional linear notion of knowledge transfer from theorists/researchers to practitioners/policy makers.[4]

The problems of nondialogue among researchers, policy makers, and practitioners are well documented.[5] Cultural difference theory[6] offers an explanation to this problem, suggesting that researchers/theorists and policy makers/practitioners represent different cultures. The two cultural groups view their roles, responsibilities, and commitments to collaboration differently. In addition, differing conceptions of how knowledge is created and used[7] offer insights into the divide between researchers/theorists and policy makers/practitioners. The traditional linear models suggest that knowledge is created by researchers and disseminated to policy makers and practitioners. This view diminishes the necessity for dialogue: researchers create knowledge and policy makers/practitioners consume it. Moreover, the politics of knowledge is a formidable force.[8] Those with the power and status "to know" frequently set the research agenda and interpret the results,[9] and those with limited power generally remain silent. Finally, language frequently keeps researchers, policy makers, and practitioners from engaging in dialogue. In multilingual countries, the language of research and policy are held frequently in the dominant language. Those who do not speak the language of power are left out of important discussions.

Despite the problems, most education stakeholders agree that research findings should be utilized more effectively in improving schools.[10] For instance, while some scholars are concerned that more dialogue would compromise their "objectivity,"[11] many argue that research will be more relevant and better understood if researchers, policy makers, and practitioners collaborate.

## Improving Education Quality (IEQ) Project

The Improving Education Quality (IEQ) project,[12] funded by the United States Agency for International Development (USAID), responds to policy needs for research-based information for improving education quality in developing countries. Partnerships are fundamental to IEQ: All projects are collaborations among a number of host country institutions, educators, and researchers. U.S. team members supply supplemental technical knowledge and skill as they work together with their host country counterparts.

IEQ Uganda began in 1995 with a meeting of national education stakeholders to discuss the information needs for primary education reform. The meeting resulted in a research agenda: Two large-scale baseline studies were commissioned and completed by the IEQ researchers between 1995 and 1997. Both studies employed quantitative and qualitative research methods to understand the overall conditions of Ugandan primary schools. Among the many findings, IEQ researchers observed that the culture of the school and the teachers' role were central to overall pupil performance.[13]

The publication of the first two IEQ studies resulted in a policy dialogue about the general education conditions and contributed to policy decisions regarding textbook guidelines and incentive grants for girls' education.[14] However, IEQ researchers from Uganda and the United States remained unsatisfied. The same faces as always were around the policy table and there was some question as to whether the findings would impact on the quality of schooling at the local level. Given the dismal conditions and climate of many schools in Uganda[15] and the implementation of Universal Primary Education (UPE),[16] IEQ researchers sought a methodology that would combine investigation with action, be democratic in nature, and include local community members in the policy dialogue about education. Participatory action research (PAR)[17] is one such method within the family of participatory approaches.[18]

**Participatory Action Research**

PAR is an iterative process that combines dialogue, investigation, and action. Participants assess their situation, analyze data that they themselves have collected, act on the findings, and begin the process again. It is based on several assumptions. PAR assumes dialogue with practitioners and other local people will produce rich insight. They have the ability and the position to assess their situation, analyze information, and create an action plan for improvement. A second assumption is that in-depth participatory work in a few communities/schools can provide insights that are relevant to other communities/schools and policy makers. Finally, PAR assumes that human behavior is contextual and dynamic—that humans function in changing and adaptive ways.

PAR differs from traditional, extractive research. First, PAR results in action at the local level as well as information for policy makers and other stakeholders. With practice, this kind of research can become a normal aspect of continuing staff development or community mobilization. Second, PAR seeks to involve people, who under other approaches have been passive "subjects," as active participants in the research process—problem identification, data collection, and analysis.[19] Third, participatory action researchers approach the work as interactive partners with community members.[20] They serve both as researchers and facilitators: encouraging participation, prompting dialogue, building relationships, collecting data, and so on. Finally, PAR findings are immediately given consideration at the local level because community members have been actively involved in the research process. In short, PAR is a potentially positive, proactive resource for change.

The power of PAR comes from dialogue among local stakeholders and researchers, but the power of this approach must be kept in perspective. PAR represents a radical change from traditional research, cultural norms, and the way that many educators and community members function. Radical change in belief and behavior does not happen overnight, and for some it does not happen at all. Despite the fact that researchers and community members engage in the PAR process together, the status of researchers and community members frequently remains static. In other words, traditional barriers to communication may remain. PAR may "romanticize the goodness and democratic tendencies"[21] of local people and researchers and ignore the ways in which those with (or without) power may be reluctant to change. Moreover, the intensity of the effort cannot be underestimated: PAR is labor intensive, and initial results such as attitude change among some participants are not universally visible.[22] Finally, PAR takes time: It represents a tremendous amount of learning and reflection for all. Nevertheless, participatory approaches to improving education have resulted in positive change especially among communities where there are disadvantaged groups (poor, rural, female) and where demand for education exists but the government has failed to provide adequate resources.[23]

## Method

To illuminate the complexities and possibilities of participation as a method to improve education and to understand how dialogue among researchers, policy makers, and community members may contribute to better schools, we (the authors of this chapter who were members of the IEQ core research team in Uganda)[24] used interpretive theory[25] and qualitative data collection and analysis methods.[26] Interpretive theory focuses on the specifics of meaning and action in day-to-day life and considers the context within which these actions occur as influential on human behavior. It considers the multiple realities that exist in any community.[27] We conducted this interpretive, qualitative analysis of the process in which we and other members of the IEQ core research team took the role of participant observers as community members, teachers, and pupils sought to improve education through participatory action research.

In addition to participating in PAR activities, IEQ core research team members collected data on the PAR process to understand how dialogue among researchers, policy makers, and community members may contribute to better schooling. Primary data include IEQ core research team fieldnotes, analytic memos, and IEQ participants' formal meeting records or minutes. Other data include meeting artifacts, such as flip charts, pupils' work, lesson plans, community maps, notes from home visits, photographs, and descriptive informal conversations between the IEQ core research team members and members of the school. IEQ core research team field notes captured the content of the PAR meetings, interactions among participants, body language, and laughter and silence. Analytic memos captured interpretive reflections regarding any aspect of the work. Raw fieldnotes and analytic memos were written by hand and taken to Kampala where they were entered into a word processor. All data produced directly by the participants (lesson plans, maps, flip charts, etc.) were kept at the schools and reviewed in the field. They were the property of the participant groups that produced them.

Data were analyzed through interpretive data analysis methods.[28] Analysis occurred in and out of the field. In the field it was ongoing and participatory: It included IEQ core research team members and participants conferring regularly about their emerging understandings during community meetings and individual interactions. Out of the field, IEQ core research team members (Carasco, Clair, and Kanyike) conducted a formal data analysis that consisted of displaying and verifying the data. First, the data were examined and codes were developed and revised. For example, "decision making" was an initial code that was eventually subsumed under "dependence." Data were imported into Folio Views (data management software) and sorted for patterns and discrepant cases. Throughout the analysis, IEQ core research team members conferred regularly in order to explain and verify findings.

Throughout the eighteen-month study considerable attention was given to developing the capacity of IEQ core research team members and community members to collect, analyze, and interpret data in depth and with rigor. For instance, in November 1998, IEQ core research team members participated in a qualitative research workshop to prepare for formal data analysis.[29] IEQ core research team members reviewed formal qualitative data analysis steps,[30] critiqued fieldnotes, discussed differences between fieldnotes and analytic memos, developed preliminary data codes, and began the coding process. Nevertheless, the limitations of this study are because of the team's experience with interpretive methodology. This was the first experience with interpretive research for some of the IEQ core research team. Some IEQ core research team members did not systematically take fieldnotes or keep analytic memos during the site selection process;[31] therefore, we can only recollect the conversations among the IEQ core research team and the education authorities in Kampala. Second, some of the fieldnotes lack the perspectives of our school partners. There are more accounts of the PAR process and fewer reactions and direct participant quotes.

## Findings

As stated previously, the purpose of this study is to illuminate the complexities and possibilities of participation as a method to improve education and to understand how dialogue among researchers, policy makers, and community members may contribute to better schooling. In this section we describe three aspects of the PAR process (site selection, group formation and action, and Quality Learning Exhibitions) and discuss three broad interrelated themes (power, dependence, and distribution of resources) that represent some of the complexities and possibilities.

### Site Selection

The site selection process in itself was participatory. We took into account the relevant Ugandan educational administrative structures, that is, the national

Ministry of Education and Sports (MOES), district education authorities (DEOs), and the Teacher Development and Management System (TDMS).[32] A major site selection objective was for the education authorities to identify with the research so that they would support it. Pursuing this objective was risky since previous IEQ research had shed less than positive light on the education system. The task was to explain the purpose of PAR in a climate in which there was fear of research findings and evaluations.

We proposed to work at three school sites within one administrative cluster to minimize the effects of cultural, language, and socioeconomic factors. This proved challenging as Ministry of Education (MOE) people had difficulty understanding the reasons for studying only three sites. We reviewed the MOE's criteria for assessing coordinating center performance, while simultaneously discussing the selection criteria with senior MOES and TDMS officials and DEOs. Site selection discussions were important as they provided opportunities to learn about sites and listen to education authorities' concerns. Moreover, these discussions provided opportunities to explain PAR and get early acceptance for the research.

We used purposeful sampling strategies to select the school communities. Five criteria guided selection: (1) a community's willingness to participate and interest in the research; (2) the school/community's readiness for positive change (e.g., evidence of community and parent involvement in a Parent Teacher Association, cooperation among the members of the school and its supporters, collaboration between the DEO and Coordinating Center Tutor, a functioning TDMS structure, and teacher and pupil commitment to the work); (3) the stability of teacher staff; (4) physical accessibility and availability of accommodations in the community; and (5) recommendations by the relevant education authorities (MOEs, TDMS, and DEOs).

Two of the authors (Carasco and Kanyike) visited nearly all of the thirty schools recommended by education authorities, and after further discussion with various stakeholders, in March 1998 three rural schools in a rural county in a southwestern district were selected because they best met the criteria.

The district is approximately 240 kilometers from Kampala in the southwestern part of Uganda. There are two major towns in the district. Much of the population resides in rural areas outside of the towns. This area has drawn an increasing number of new settlers from other parts of the country. Ranching and dairy farming are the main economic activities. Historically the people were pastoralists and nomads, but recently they have settled and started some agricultural activity such as cultivation of beans and maize. The main language is Runyankore. Two of the three schools are located in a small trading center (population two thousand). The third school is twenty kilometers from town off a dirt road that connects small trading centers. School A has sixteen teachers and nine hundred pupils. School B has ten teachers and six hundred pupils. School C has nine teachers and five hundred pupils.

*Group Formation and Action*

In April 1998, a one-week community-based workshop was organized to introduce teachers and community members to PAR. The workshop sessions were conducted in English and the local language; translators were available and participants could use either language.[33] Workshop objectives and activities included exploring quality learning, practicing Participatory Learning and Action (PLA) tools,[34] and developing an action plan for the work in the three schools. Participants in this introductory workshop included head teachers, teacher representatives, PTA representatives and School Management Committee (SMC) representatives from the three schools, and IEQ core research team members.

Immediately after the April 1998 workshop, IEQ core research team members met with the head teacher from each school to arrange a schedule for initial meetings of a teacher group, a community group, and a pupil group. From April 1998 to September 1999 these nine groups (three at each school) met to explore how they themselves could improve the quality of education in their community.

Initially, all groups engaged in several activities aimed at building relationships and confidence, exploring quality learning, and collaboratively setting an agenda for the work. The IEQ core research team spent significant time in the field visiting homes, participating in meetings, and talking informally with locals. At the outset, the IEQ core research team member in each school took the lead in organizing the meetings and chairing them. After two or three meetings each of the teacher and community groups elected a chair and a secretary to record the proceedings and decided when and for how long they would meet. The IEQ core research team continued to facilitate the pupils' meetings during times when the pupils would not miss any formal classes.

Over time and as groups gained confidence, PAR activities focused on identifying problems associated with schools and potential solutions. Following are a few examples of PAR activities by group:[35]

- PAR activities with the teacher groups began with discussions on the conditions that support quality learning. All teacher groups discussed and revised their lesson plans based on the conditions that they had named. Two teacher groups developed and practiced a peer assistance system in order to improve their classroom practice. Through data collected from the peer assistance instrument, teachers discovered that although they had studied teaching methods, they had not understood them sufficiently to apply them in class. One teacher group developed a pupil evaluation instrument and learned that many of their pupils could not see the blackboard.
- Two of the three community groups identified pupil absenteeism as a barrier to their children's education. They collected data on pupil absenteeism by making community maps and visiting homes. They

also studied their children's daily schedule to see how it influenced attendance. After data analysis and dialogue some parents reduced their children's workload of domestic chores so they could attend school more often. One of the community groups decided to visit their children's classrooms to get a better idea about the school conditions. They noticed the classroom had no benches, desks, lockable doors, or window shutters. They decided to contribute the money and labor for new benches and developed and initiated plans for building new classrooms.
- Through PAR activities, the three pupil groups discussed characteristics of good teachers and pupils. From these characteristics, pupils chose areas for action. In one group, pupils took action to solve pupil tardiness. They drew community maps indicating the homes of all of the pupils in the PAR group. For each pupil, they indicated the distance between the home and school. Then they identified classmates who lived near each other, pupils who were frequently tardy, and those who were not. The outcome of their analysis was a system whereby pupils would help each other get to school on time.

*Quality Learning Exhibitions*

In October 1998 and September 1999, the schools and the IEQ core research team hosted the Annual Quality Learning Exhibitions. During exhibitions, pupils, teachers, and community members met with local, district, and national leaders to discuss their PAR experiences in studying and improving education in their communities.

During the afternoon, dialogue groups were facilitated so all participants could discuss education issues further. Questions were raised and solutions offered regarding pupil discipline, language of instruction, coeducation, and handicapped pupils' rights (to name a few). The discussions were held in English and Runyankore, and translators provided simultaneous translation during large group discussions.

The Quality Learning Exhibitions were significant. This was the first time that many of the community members, teachers, and pupils had the opportunity to discuss education issues with district and national education authorities. The confidence with which they presented their perspectives on education was noteworthy. Both exhibitions ended with a sense that local communities have the power to engage in dialogue with researchers and policy makers and improve their situation.

*Power*

Power differences among individuals and groups are a fact of human society. The question then becomes how power is managed so that it does not inhibit dialogue among groups. We have evidence of how power impacts participation throughout the education system: examples of policy makers' and the funding agency's influence on the IEQ research design, implementation, and dissemination and evidence of power differentials among and between people—researchers to head teachers, head teacher to teacher, teacher to parent, adults to pupils, to name a few. However, we focus mainly on the head teachers' power and the IEQ core research team's role for a number of reasons. First, tremendous authority is vested in head teachers by the rules and regulations governing schools. In practice all stakeholder groups, including outside researchers, both above and below the head teachers in the education hierarchy, regard head teachers as the school authority on a day-to-day basis. At the school level the teachers, community members, and pupils are accustomed to head teachers dominating decisions and dispensing favors. Community participation, a goal of education reform, conflicts with this "natural order" in the schools as it invites all to become involved.

Evidence of the head teachers' great power emerged during the site selection process at the school level. Constrained by time and a desire to respect the hierarchy, we initially discussed possible participation in the research with head teachers. On all occasions, the head teachers instantly agreed that "their" school was willing to participate. There was no expression by the head teachers of consulting anybody else before deciding to involve the school in the research. The head teachers mentioned that they would inform their teachers and the community, but those head teachers were confident that those stakeholder groups would not refuse to participate.

The second encounter with the head teachers' power occurred during the identification of teachers to represent their colleagues at the April 1998 workshop. We realized that if we left the process of identification to the head teachers, the possibility of a head teacher hand-picking "his people" as the teachers' representatives was very high. Therefore, we requested to be present when the elections for teacher representatives took place. In one school, the head teacher was present during the elections. He assumed the role of chair and openly suggested to the teachers whom they should elect. There were only two female teachers present and they decided between themselves who would attend the workshop. With respect to the male teachers, there was voting by raising hands, and the head teacher's favored candidate got elected. The candidate who lost appeared bitter about the result.

During the first few teacher meetings, teachers rarely talked. Even when discussing a simple matter such as fixing a date for the next meeting, teachers were reticent. During an early teacher meeting, one teacher asked in the presence of the head teacher whether he could contradict the head teacher (MO *fn* April 30).[36] That only one teacher had the confidence to ask such a question underscores the risk involved. Contradicting a head teacher carries risks, since head teachers have the capacity to engineer the transfer of "troublesome" teachers and even interfere with the teachers' inclusion on the payroll.

Head teachers dominated the conversation at the initial teachers' meetings. We discussed this observation initially at IEQ core research team meetings and decided to exclude head teachers from teachers' meetings. At two of the schools, the decision was made after the first teachers' meetings when we realized head teachers created an environment that made it difficult for the teachers to express themselves freely. We approached the head teachers and advised them that it might be more productive if the teachers met on their own to discuss matters that concerned them. The head teacher of one school responded that he had no problem with this arrangement. He had heard from a fellow head teacher that the IEQ core research team had already conducted meetings with the community members and teachers of School C without the presence of the head teacher (MO, *fn* June 2). In the third school, we observed the situation before taking action with the head teacher. But at the third teachers' meeting, matters came to a head when deliberations completely stalled within half an hour of the meeting.

> An IEQ core research team member spontaneously arranged for some group discussions and then advised the head teacher discreetly that his presence may be a major problem. The head teacher seemed to agree because he left the meeting a short while later. (JC, *fn* June 5)

On another occasion in the same school, the head teacher made a decision about an IEQ teacher meeting on behalf of all the teachers, without consulting them. An IEQ core research team member writes and reflects.

> Thursday 11th was a working day and she (CCT) went for the meeting. The head teacher told her that the teachers had not agreed on the meeting, so they were not ready for the meeting. The CCT further explained that later some teachers came to her and said that they were actually ready for the meeting but when their boss (head teacher) spoke the way he did, they had nothing to do but keep quiet. The impression I got was that the head teacher did not want the meeting on that day to take place. So he used his position to speak on behalf of the rest of the teachers. Aware of the dictatorship in primary schools, it is not surprising to me that the teachers could not speak out their minds openly and make other suggestions. (MO *fn* June 15)

A few teachers appeared to support the dictatorial practices of head teachers. When these teachers were asked why some of their colleagues were not attending IEQ meetings, they responded: "Some teachers are not attending because you (members of the IEQ core research team) had said that participation in this research was voluntary. I think these teachers who do not attend should be reported to the head teacher" (MO *fn* June 16).

Other teachers, however, indicated a less positive appraisal of the head teachers' power. For example, during a teachers' meeting, they were discussing their situation before IEQ. They mentioned some of the things they had learned from

PAR and then made comparisons to previous staff meetings that had always been chaired by the head teacher:

> Charles (a teacher) caused laughter when he reported that "I used to attend meetings with no notice by the head teacher or heads of departments." An IEQ core research team member wanted to know more so she asked a question, "Did you feel free to participate in the meetings that you did not plan for?" Hamida (another teacher) testified, "We could participate but not fully." Charles pointed out a weakness of such meetings, "[W]e do not know where the agenda comes from and the teacher is not encouraged to talk about the problem he/she is facing in teaching." Peter interjected, "[E]ven up to now the situation of those meetings ha[s] not changed." (DN *fn* Aug 29)

In addition to illuminating the head teachers' power, these data suggest the power that we held as members of the IEQ core research team. For example, by initiating PAR we exercised a certain amount of power over the community. We were the ones with the knowledge of the PAR approach. Moreover, we grappled with how central power was to our actions and decisions. Sometimes our actions replicated the status quo. For example, in order to get the cooperation of the head teacher, a vital prerequisite to beginning PAR, we began dialogue about PAR with the head teachers. To some extent, this action may have reinforced the head teachers' authority.

On the other hand, we used our power strategically to intervene when the head teachers' actions might influence an election or inhibit participation in meetings. For example, after observing the influence of head teachers over teachers in meetings, we discussed these observations with the head teachers. By engaging in dialogue together we were able to persuade the head teachers to let the teachers meet on their own. This space was critical for teachers to gain their voice.

We also reflected frequently on power issues and disagreed with each other about working within the existing school structure. An IEQ core research team member reflects:

> We want the community to be able to express itself. However, that is but one of the objectives. We also need to create an environment in which a category of stakeholders can express itself without fear in the presence of other categories of stakeholders. We need to bridge the gaps. LK fears that constantly citing power relations as a reason to keep groups apart may have the negative effect of fossilizing both our fears and the traditional power relations themselves. The proposal that inter-category (teachers, pupils, and community) be channeled via the school research committees is good, but it is also limited. The committees will essentially be a bureaucratic structure, another "appropriate" channel for

communication.... "Appropriate" channels of communication are many times tools for domination and control. (JC *am* June 14)

Enhanced community and teacher participation as an education reform goal conflicts with the authority that characterizes the head teachers' role. The evidence suggests that outside stakeholders—in this case IEQ researchers—can have impact on the head teachers' dominance by engaging in dialogue with them. It also suggests that without reflection, a key component of PAR, outsiders can replicate the existing authority structures.

*Dependence*

Dependence is another theme that emerged from the data. Dependency manifested itself in two ways: dependence on others and dependence on outside knowledge. The evidence suggests that both individuals and groups were dependent. Like power, dependence has historical roots and can severely limit individuals' and groups' ability to engage in dialogue. Nevertheless, the evidence suggests that through extended dialogue and with time, individuals and groups became more independent.

*Dependence on others.* In the first few weeks of convening meetings, the teachers and community members had difficulty taking organizational responsibility for the meetings. Making the necessary administrative arrangements for seating, chairing, recording, and facilitating the meetings was problematic. In addition, planning meetings was difficult. Initially, we (IEQ core research team members) carried out these tasks. However, we began to deliberately raise issues of organizational responsibility at the meetings. An IEQ core research team member's field notes illustrate what happened after teachers evaluated their meeting:

> After the evaluation, a core team member reminded participants on the need to further discuss the following issues (i.e., replacing teachers' recorder/secretary, safeguarding of IEQ materials like flip-chart paper, attendance, and time management) with a view of looking for strategies to ensure efficiency and effectiveness. (DN *fn* June 22)

It took about three months for teachers to take over the organizational aspects of the meetings. It was not easy for the IEQ core research team to hand over some tasks. After two months of teachers' meetings in one school, a problem of chairing arose:

> The chairperson did not turn up for the meeting. So I asked for someone to volunteer to chair the meeting. I encouraged them by referring to one of the principles of PLA (our work), "Be ready for the unexpected." It took us quite a while and no one volunteered to chair the meeting. I suspected that since most people who turned up for the meeting had not been with us for the last two to three months, they felt that they

would not guide the meeting appropriately. To proceed, I decided to chair the sessions. (MO *fn* July 23)

It is interesting to note that when the teachers came to evaluate this incident later, one teacher said, "It is like asking a visitor to participate in serving food." In Ugandan society, visitors or outsiders are served by hosts. The teachers were expressing that this is their community and they are the hosts: They should have taken responsibility and chaired the meeting. The teachers were not proud of the part they played in that incident (MO *fn* July 28).

Community members also exhibited dependence on others, especially local authorities. They looked initially or solely to the Local Committees (local administrative authorities) and religious organizations to solve problems, especially to mobilize people to attend meetings. When things did not go well in mobilization exercises organized by community members, the responsibility was placed squarely on the local authorities:

> One participant hailing from a village cell complained that the people turned up on the specified day but there was no facilitator who showed up. Mrs. Mugenyi (facilitator) was absent and Mugabe admitted that because of a busy schedule he was unable to attend. Both facilitators from another cell (village) were absent too. Only one IEQ community member was present. The LC I chair did not show up either. Kategaya (an IEQ community member) blamed the failure to hold the meeting on LC I chairman. "They did not mobilise the community" he said with concern (DN *fn* July 25).

*Dependence on outside knowledge.* We (the IEQ core research team members) began the work by stressing to community members, teachers, and pupils that we are all researchers (*abacoondozi*). The idea that every person has knowledge to contribute was a foreign concept to community members, teachers, and pupils. The most telling evidence of this is the way that the community named and described the IEQ core research team. They called us teachers (*abasomesa*). The significance of this label, "teachers," in the local context is that teachers are perceived as the sources of knowledge. Community members see themselves as learners dependent on teachers for knowledge. The learner's actions must be sanctioned and guided by the teacher, in this case an IEQ core research team member. There is no room for the learner to create knowledge. Much as the IEQ core research team tried to discourage it, the community's attitude was rooted in fact. Two of the IEQ core research team members were senior academic staff at some of Uganda's premier educational institutions of higher learning.

One example of the participants' hesitancy to adopt the role of "teacher" or knowledge creator occurred at a community meeting. An IEQ core research team member asked if they had any recommendations for improvement of IEQ work. One person responded, "The ball is in your court, tell us what to do and we will follow because we are interested in improving education for our children" (DN *fn* May 25). A community member at another school was perplexed about the role that the IEQ core research team had given him. He asked at the very first meeting: "How come you, the professors, are asking us, the unlearned, to do the research ourselves?"(MO *fn* June 6).

Dependence on others to build knowledge among the community changed in subtle ways over time. On the one hand, there is evidence that community members began to trust their knowledge; on the other, they still looked to us to validate their responses. During a village mobilization meeting, one senior community member appeared to vent her frustration about the IEQ project in this manner:

> [W]e had expectations for material benefit and when this did not happen, people were discouraged. We are the people with answers to solve the problems of poor education. However, some people are finding difficulties with this research when they ask, "[W]hat do we learn when all the answers we give are presumed to be correct?" (DN *fn* June 8)

Like the community groups, the teachers also demonstrated a similar dependence on outside knowledge. For example, the teachers had spent a considerable amount of time discussing which conditions are necessary for quality learning from their own experiences and understanding. Then they went on to discuss how they could create these conditions with the use of various teaching methods that they had listed themselves. But the teachers seemed unsure about the knowledge that they had created, especially when an IEQ core research team member pointed out that what had been recorded was what worked for them on the ground and had not been taken from a textbook. Then one teacher asked, "But are these conditions that we have listed correct?"(DN, *fn* July 1). And they did not seem to highlight knowledge they had generated, for example, by connecting these conditions to the design of the self-evaluation.

> An IEQ core research team member asked, what are the sources of information/data for self-evaluation and how does one go about carrying out self-evaluation? Charles outlined the following sources: lesson plan based on different steps, i.e., setting of objective, introduction phase, content, sharing of experiences, evaluation of pupils and finally you evaluate yourself as a teacher. Another core research team member reminded the teacher of the conditions they had generated for quality learning. Charles quickly admitted the omission, "[O]hh, I had forgotten, those conditions should be considered first." (DN *fn* July 31)

*Distribution of Resources*

Distribution of resources is the final theme that emerged from the analysis of the data. We anticipated some of the community expectations that we knew we could not satisfy. For example, we were constrained by the IEQ project itself. IEQ was not funded to directly add material benefits to the schools, such as iron sheets for roofing or teaching materials for classroom use, although a result of PAR may be the acquisition of material resources through networking and community mobilization. Moreover, participatory work is voluntary: There would be no payment for participating in IEQ. In conditions of scarcity like those in the three rural schools, this pressure for material help and the impact it had on everyone's ability to engage in dialogue cannot be underestimated. The issue of payment for participation or materials for schools persisted throughout our work. Teachers and community members raised the issue directly and indirectly many times.

All the head teachers we interviewed responded affirmatively when asked whether they wanted their school to be involved in the IEQ project. In Uganda, the word "project" is often associated with substantial sums of money. Even though we informed the head teachers at the start that there would be no funds for individuals involved or for the school, head teachers nevertheless appeared to be eager to participate in the IEQ work, hoping that in the future some material rewards would come.

At one school, the material problem persisted in different guises. For instance, the teachers at this school did not turn up on time for any of the IEQ meetings. After about six weeks, we asked them why they continually came late. One teacher responded, "We have no watches, so we cannot tell whether it is time or not. Let the donor give us watches" (MO *fn* June 16). Another example occurred two months later during a teacher meeting. The teachers at this same school were discussing their participation in the upcoming Quality Learning Exhibitions, and three male teachers stated that they did not want to participate unless they were "facilitated." The "facilitation" referred to here was not just tea and lunch, but cash given to the teachers. The IEQ core research team member explained that no payments to participants were possible (MO *fn* Aug 20). Eventually the teachers at this school decided to participate even though they were not "facilitated."[37]

It was not only the teachers who expressed concerns for material benefit. The community members did the same. In the initial community meetings, we distributed one ballpoint pen and one twenty-four-page notebook to each member who attended the meeting. It was made clear then that the offer was *entandikwa* (seed support) and a one-time contribution to enable the research to get off the ground. Within a few weeks at one school, a community member asked, "Last time you gave the participants exercise books and pens, will you do this again?" (DN *fn* May 23).

In another example, we were visiting homes in order to mobilize the community. One IEQ core research team member asked a community leader if there were any problems with the IEQ work so far. He responded, "[P]eople's needs are insatiable.... They have not been used to such meetings but they like the books and pens which you gave them" (DN *fn* May 24). Two weeks later in discussing how to get more people to participate, the head teacher of that community suggested "that as a way of encouraging people to come for the research, something, say a cup of tea, could be organized in the middle or at the end of the meeting" (DN *fn* June 7).

Finally, participants persistently expressed the demand for improvement of the schools' physical infrastructure, the building of water tanks and valley dams. We reiterated the limits of our mandate: that IEQ was funded to do research on improving education and this did not include the improvement of physical infrastructure or any income-generating activity. Some community members appeared dissatisfied with this response. After three months of IEQ meetings, the community expectations, at least those held by some members, still seemed to be at variance with those of the IEQ core research team. During a discussion based on their community map drawing, Mr. Mugabe (elder) told fellow participants not to add any more resources to the map. He argued that if the map looked complete, IEQ would not contribute resources (DN *fn* July 23).

These examples illuminate the kinds of requests for material resources. Given the conditions of the three school communities, these requests are understandable. For the most part, we (the IEQ core research team) held firm because we were working within project parameters and undergoing periodic scrutiny by project funders and Ugandan education authorities. Moreover, the examples illustrate the inequities in the research process. Some IEQ core research team members were being paid for their work; community members were not. Such inequity can influence the possibility for dialogue between groups.

**Persistent Questions and Discussion**

As was stated earlier, the purpose of this study is to illuminate the complexities and possibilities of participation as a method to improve education quality and to understand how dialogue among researchers, policy makers, and community members (teachers, parents, and pupils) may contribute to better schools. The themes that emerged in this research represent the enormous dilemmas in moving toward more participatory ways of ultimately improving education within the context of Ugandan society. They suggest the tremendous effort, time, and learning required of all committed to participatory approaches. We are not naïve about the cultural, political, and historical context of Uganda and the global social order in which countries compete for resources. Participation is rarely practiced in Ugandan education institutions, school governance,[38] and classroom practice; thus we have been exploring ways of being and doing that challenge the political and social order.

In addition to these dilemmas, the findings also give evidence of participants beginning to speak out, trust their knowledge, and act independently regarding improving education in their community. One has only to look at the videotapes[39] of some community members, teachers, and pupils presenting their perspectives at the Quality Learning Exhibitions. Our findings are similar to those of other participatory efforts in schools and communities in other countries.[40] Power relations, dependence on others and outside knowledge, and distribution of resources are issues in other stories of PAR.

PAR as a method to improve education is situated in broader issues that are critical to understanding how increased dialogue may be possible. Each issue raises persistent questions that emerged directly from our fieldwork, asking how power, dependence, and distribution of resources influence dialogue among researchers, policy makers, and community members. Our responses to these questions are partial, ambiguous, and dynamic as they represent an interpretation of events at a given point in time.[41] More dialogue is needed within the education community, and we invite readers to consider these questions and become part of the conversation.

*How Can Power Be Understood in a Way That Promotes Dialogue among Researchers, Policy Makers, and Community Members?*

Power challenges dialogue throughout the education system: head teachers to teachers, researchers to community members, adults to pupils, to name a few. Dialogue promotes participation in decision making and action among all stakeholders, especially those at the grass roots. Can power and dialogue be reconciled?

A closer look at the head teacher-to-teacher relationship and the ways that we (the IEQ core research team) exercised power in order to facilitate dialogue adds insight. In Uganda, the role of the head teacher in participatory approaches is problematic. On the one hand, head teachers are used to manage the day-to-day activities of a school. Generally unchecked by higher-ups in the education hierarchy, these head teachers have an enormous amount of power over teachers, community members, and pupils. Initially, we decided that it was important for teacher, community, and pupil groups to work independently to learn autonomy in practice. Through our intervention, all groups have been meeting without the head teacher.

There is evidence that the teachers, community members, and pupils have learned that they are able to make positive contributions to improving education without the presence of the head teacher. But participation means inclusion. We know that when the head teachers were present in the teacher and parent groups there was the potential for "engineered consent," the illusion of participation.[42] To date the solution has been for head teachers to meet among themselves. However, the ultimate goal is for all stakeholders groups to be able to meet together to name and solve problems that impact education in their community.

Without ongoing reflection and dialogue it is likely that those in power will continue to replicate the status quo. For example, when we began PAR we intended to work as diligently with the pupils as with the community members and teachers. Despite our intentions, we experienced some difficulties because of adults' conceptions of how to work with the pupils. There was a natural replication of the power structure. Just as the head teacher held power over the teachers, the adults held power over the pupils. For example, at an IEQ core research team meeting we discussed pupil participation. Responses among some of the IEQ core research team members regarding how to work with the pupils ranged from dictating activities for the pupils to leaving them out altogether. Dictating pupil activities is in direct conflict with PAR, and leaving them out not only violates one of the principles of participatory work but also loses valuable pupil insights into improving education. The IEQ core research team spent considerable time discussing this issue. Discussions resulted in convening the pupils using the same PAR process as that of the teachers and community members. The outcome was positive: Pupils participated in the policy dialogue on improving education and they solved some of the problems that they themselves had named.

Finally, the concepts of power and dialogue are housed in the larger social, political, and global world order. Although the IEQ core research team was committed to dialogue and the principles of participatory practice, we were frequently constrained by those who held power over us. For example, Ugandan policy makers wanted us to work in more communities and produce faster results. The funding agency wanted more "concrete" evidence: how participatory approaches contribute to higher test scores. Our meetings with Ugandan policy makers and funding agents were spent trying to "convince" them of the study's value as opposed to engaging in dialogue about the actual circumstances of the local communities. For the IEQ core research team, these meetings were frequently lost opportunities for dialogue.

Power is a formidable force in potentially inhibiting dialogue and participation. However, the evidence suggests that researchers and community members can reconcile power differentials by naming and discussing the issue and by strategically intervening. Although national policy makers and funding agents participated in the Exhibitions for Quality Learning, we have less evidence that we can engage in truly multidirectional dialogue that puts improving education at the center of the discussion with national policy makers and funding agents.

*How Can the Teachers, Pupils, and Community Members Become More Independent? What Is the Role of Outsiders in Promoting Independence?*

In the beginning we initiated most of the participatory activities—starting with organizing meetings, conducting meetings, and defining key questions to improve education. We understood the contradictory nature of our work. We were the ones who initiated PAR in the three schools; thus, a dependent relationship between the school communities and the IEQ core research team was inherent in the process.

Gradually, we shifted responsibility to teachers, pupils, and community members: They organized and facilitated the meetings. However, we experienced an interesting cultural dilemma. We were regarded as "visitors," and culture dictates that one does not ask visitors to leave one's home. Even making suggestions by word or action may be considered rude. Therefore, teachers, pupils, and community members continued to indicate to us not only that they are dependent on us but also that they want to continue the dependence! We explained that the ultimate responsibility for improving education in their schools is on them. There will be a time that we will not be needed, and there was pressure for us to expand PAR to other schools. We continued discussing this issue with them.

The outsiders' role is one of balance. On the one hand, we had the power, skills, and resources to initiate the participatory process. On the other hand, it was up to us to model inclusiveness and power sharing.

*How Can Research/ers, Policy Makers, and Community Members Learn to Construct Knowledge and Work Collectively in Ways That Are Consistent with the Culture?*

The IEQ core research team sought to encourage all participants to construct knowledge and contribute ideas, although this notion contradicted how most Ugandans have been socialized. In Ugandan society it is the teacher or expert who holds the knowledge. As the result of such encouragement and the experiences in the PAR process, teachers, community members, and pupils slowly began to realize that they could construct their own knowledge and that their experiences are as valid as those of others "more learned than themselves," as they put it.

Moreover, we were all learning how to participate and work collectively. We believed that opportunities to learn together are necessary for our work. There was an initial tendency for some community and IEQ core research team members to put their individual benefits above the collective benefit, especially in sharing of information. While common sense would dictate that the stronger one's team members, the stronger the team, IEQ core research team members were initially hesitant about openly discussing each other's perceived weaknesses in relation to the project's objectives. However, we learned to provide information and opportunities to all community and IEQ core research team members, rather than a selected few. Moreover, we were dealing with the power and knowledge differences within the IEQ core research team itself. Participatory approaches meant refraining from issuing commands to others even when one had the power to do so.

*Is PAR Sustainable If the Material Needs of the Participants Are Not Being Met at the Workplace or If School and Community Resources Are Less Than Adequate?*

The current economic situation in Uganda is harsh and has been so for a long time. By the mid-1980s schools had gone through almost two decades of very difficult times because of political and social instability. Schools then were dependent largely on parental contributions and a primary teacher's salary was less than $10 a month, way below a living wage. However, for more than a decade now, there has been increased political and social stability in most parts of the country. The state has gradually reorganized the education system and there is increasing demand for accountability. Despite improvement, the salaries, now about $75 per month, are still considered by teachers to be below a living wage. Therefore, school staff supplement their incomes by engaging in activities unrelated to their official jobs, for example, small-scale farming, petty trade, and so on.

The IEQ project has brought the extra workload that PAR demands in a school. We think teachers and the community are crucial to improving education quality, and we have been persuading them that it is in their professional and community interest to engage in PAR. Some teachers appear to be convinced, but in order for the work to be sustainable, it may require more than a few. PAR has long-term benefits for a community, but results such as changing attitudes are not initially visible.[43] We wonder whether PAR results will be sufficient to sustain the participatory activities with other material priorities. Can PAR compete with other activities necessary to make a living wage?

There is evidence that some teachers and community members would rather that the IEQ project merely give material resources. Some community members and teachers have directly said that a new school roof, more textbooks, or a new road will greatly improve education. We understand this request, given the lack of material resources, and we have responded in numerous ways to requests for material resources. We were aware of the imbalance of material benefits that this project has brought to some Ugandans. For example, some IEQ core research team members were paid, yet the community members were not. In addition, we were aware of our power limits. Despite dialogue with national stakeholders and funding agents about the research process, there was an unspoken agreement that financial decisions would be made elsewhere. This nondialogue among researchers, policy makers, and community members about distribution of material resources must be reversed.

## Conclusion

Given Uganda's history, participation and dialogue as approaches to improving education challenge systems to which researchers, policy makers, and communities are accustomed. PAR raises interesting dilemmas and questions that defy existing political, social, and cultural structures. These dilemmas and questions warrant discussion within the education community if we continue to claim that PAR is a viable alternative to ultimately improving education at the local level.

We have attempted to illuminate some of the complexities and possibilities of participation as a method to improve education and to understand how dialogue among researchers, policymakers, and community members may contribute to better schools. The problems associated with dialogue among researchers, policy makers, and community members are perpetual: They existed before our work and will continue to exist. This study adds power, dependence, and distribution of material resources as major themes that represent challenges for increasing dialogue.

Amidst the challenges, change has been initiated and the dialogue continues. We understand the difficulties ahead: sustaining PAR with less support as the project has not been refunded[44] and continuing the dialogue among researchers, policy makers, and community members on how to improve education. Nevertheless, we believe that this study has relevance beyond education. Dialogue and participation, while extremely challenging in certain contexts,[45] have the potential to transform communities. While the backdrop of this study is improving education, it allows researchers, policy makers, and community members to practice processes of inclusion, participation, and democracy. These processes are fundamental to individual and community well-being. It is possible that the praxis of the community with this research will encourage them to examine their role in improving other aspects of their lives.

## Notes

1. This chapter was originally published in the special issue of the *Comparative Education Review* [45 (2) (May 2001): 257–79] focused on "The Relationship between Theorists/Researchers and Policy Makers/Practitioners." We are grateful to all those at the selected schools for their participation and contribution in this pioneer project. In addition, we thank USAID (contract number HNE-I-00-97-00029-00) for its funding and support. Finally, we appreciate the Acting Secretary and our colleagues at the Ugandan National Examinations Board (UNEB) for their support.
2. Dr. Joseph Carasco was on Kenya Airways Flight 431 that crashed on January 30, 2000. He did not survive, but his work lives on. It is with great humility that we revised this article for publication. Mrs. Modesta Agita Omono, another IEQ core research team member, was on that flight as well. We honor the lives and work of our colleagues and friends. We dedicate this article to them.
3. Paulo Freire, *Pedagogy of the Oppressed* (New York: Seaburt Press, 1970), pp. 76–77.
4. Brenda Turnbull, *Technical Assistance and the Creation of Education Knowledge* (Washington, DC: Policy Studies Associates, 1996).
5. Mark B.Ginsburg and Jorge Gorostiaga, "Relationships between Theorists/Reseachers and Policymakers/Practitioners: Rethinking the Two Cultures Thesis and the Possibility of Dialogue," *Comparative Education Review* 45 (May 2001): 173–96.
6. Henry Levin, "Why Isn't Education Research More Useful?" in *Knowledge for Policy: Improving Education Through Research*, ed. Don Anderson and Bruce Biddle (London: Falmer, 1991), pp. 72 and 77.
7. Bruce Biddle and Don Anderson, "Social Research and Educational Change," in *Knowledge for Policy: Improving Education through Research*, ed. Don Anderson and Bruce Biddle (London: Falmer, 1991), p. 6.
8. Michel Foucault, *Power/Knowledge* (New York: Pantheon, 1980).
9. D. Pan, "Ivory Tower and Red Tape," *Telos* 86 (1990): 109–17.
10. Fernando Reimers and Noel McGinn, *Informed Dialogue: Using Research to Shape Educational Policy around the World* (Westport, CT: Praeger, 1997), p. 5.
11. J. Bradley Cousins and Kenneth Leithwood, "Current Empirical Research on Evaluation Utilization," *Review of Evaluation Research* 56 (3) (1986): 331–64.
12. The Improving Education Quality Project (IEQ) is USAID-funded and undertaken by the American Institutes for Research (AIR) in collaboration with the Academy for Educational Development (AED); Education Development Center (EDC), Inc.; Juarez and Associates, Inc.; and the University of Pittsburgh's Institute for International Studies in Education (IISE).

13. Joseph Carasco, John C. Munene, Deborah H. Kasente, and Mathew Odada, *Factors Influencing Effectiveness in Primary Schools: A Baseline Study* (Kampala, Uganda: Ugandan National Examinations Board and Improving Education Quality Project, 1996); John C. Munene, Mathew Odada, Deborah Kasente, Joseph Carasco, W. Epeju, W. Obwoya Kinyera Sam, O. K. Modesta Omona, and George A. Kinyera, *Teachers' Work Experience and Pupils' Schooling Experience as Determinants of Achievement in Primary Schools* (Kampala, Uganda: Ugandan National Examinations Board and Improving Education Quality Project, 1997).
14. Joseph Carasco, Lawrence Kanyike, and Nancy Clair, "From Baseline to Insight: A Look at the Process of Change through Uganda's Improving Educational Quality Project," paper presented at the 10th World Conference of Comparative Education, Capetown, South Africa, 1998.
15. See Carasco et al., 1996; Munene et al., 1997.
16. UPE is Universal Primary Education. This reform has caused considerable controversy in Uganda as many schools do not have the infrastructure to provide education for all students.
17. Peter Reason, "Three Approaches to Participative Inquiry," in *Strategies of Qualitative Inquiry*, ed. Norman K. Denzin and Yvonne S. Lincoln (Thousand Oaks, CA: Sage, 1998).
18. Robert Chambers, "Origins and Practice of Participatory Rural Appraisal," *World Development* 22 (7) 1994; and Eileen Kane, *Seeing for Yourself: Research Handbook for Girls Education in Africa* (Washington, DC: World Bank, 1995).
19. Ernest T. Stringer, *Action Research: A Handbook for Practitioners* (Thousand Oaks, CA: Sage, 1996).
20. Despite that researchers approach the work as partners with community members there is still differential status and division of labor between researchers and community members.
21. Reason, 1998, p. 84.
22. Nancy Clair, "Teacher Study Groups: Persistent Questions in a Promising Approach," *TESOL Quarterly* 32 (3) (1998): 465–92.
23. Andrea Rugh and Heather Bossert, *Involving Communities. Participation in the Delivery of Education Programs* (Washington, DC: United States Agency for International Development, 1998).
24. The IEQ core research team consisted of Joseph Carasco, Principal Researcher, Makerere University; Lawrence Kanyike, Research Leader, Ugandan National Examinations Board (UNEB); Modesta Omona, Lecturer, Institutes of Teacher Education, Kyambogo (ITEK); Vincent Birungi, Tutor, Bushenyi Core PTC; Denis Nuwagaba, Action for Development (NGO); Imelda Kemeza, CCT Kazo Coordinating Center; Nekemiah Mwesigna, County Inspector of Schools, Kazo County; Patience Namanya, recent graduate, Makere University; Nancy Clair, Senior Research Advisor, Education Development Center, Inc. (EDC). At the beginning of 1999 N. Mwesigwa was transferred and replaced by Michael Tindikira. All team members are Ugandan except Clair, who is North American.
25. Frederick Erickson, "Qualitative Methods in Research on Teaching," in *Handbook of Research on Teaching*, 3rd ed., Merlin C. Wittrock, (New York: Macmillan, 1986), pp. 119–61.
26. Mathews Miles and Michael Huberman, *Qualitative Data Analysis,* 2nd ed. (Thousand Oaks, CA: Sage, 1994).
27. Norman K. Denzin and Yvonna S. Lincoln, "Entering the Field of Qualitative Research," in *The Landscape of Qualitative Inquiry,* ed. Norman K Denzin and Yvonne S. Lincoln (Thousand Oaks, CA: Sage, 1998), p. 27.
28. Miles and Huberman, 1994; Amanda Coffey and Paul Atkinson, *Making Sense of Qualitative Data* (Thousand Oaks, CA:Sage Publications, 1996).
29. A PAR workshop had already been held with IEQ researchers and community members.
30. Miles and Huberman, 1994.
31. Carasco and Clair had numerous ongoing discussions about data representation in oral cultures. Carasco questioned the necessity of written fieldnotes in oral cultures.
32. At the time of this research TDMS was the organization responsible for implementing most of the primary education reforms. TDMS is comprised of a small core technical staff at headquarters and a network of core primary teachers' colleges (Core PTCs) responsible for zones in the country. There are eighteen core PTCs. The schools within the jurisdiction of each Core PTC are grouped in clusters called coordinating centers, each supervised by a coordinating center tutor (CCT).
33. During meetings, community members, teachers, and pupils used the language with which they were most comfortable. Teacher meetings were conducted in both languages; community

meetings were in Runyankore; pupil meetings were in both languages. Translators were used in meetings when all stakeholders were present.

34. Kane, 1995.
35. For further details on teachers, pupils, and community members' perspectives on improving education see IEQ Core Research Team, *Perspectives of Quality Learning: From Research to Action* (Kampala: Ugandan National Examinations Board and Improving Education Quality Project, 1999).
36. Initials refer to IEQ core research team members; *fn* refers to field notes and *am* to analytic memo.
37. In Ugandan English, "facilitation" is slang for payment to induce somebody to accomplish a task. It originally acknowledged inadequate salary scales.
38. Ugandan school governance is representative. PTA and SMC members represent the community regarding education. The potential for participation is there if a representative structure in place. The challenge is to widen opportunities for those who are not represented and to apply principles of participation.
39. Nancy Clair, Lawrence Kanyike, and David Smith, producers, "Joining Hands in Education" (Washington, DC: Improving Education Quality Project, in poroduction).
40. Clair, 1998; Rugh and Bossert, 1998; Sheldon Shaeffer, ed., *Collaborating for Educational Change: The Role of Teachers, Parents and the Community in School Improvement* (Paris: International Institute for Educational Planning, 1992).
41. Clair, 1998.
42. Graebner cited in Michael W. Apple and James A. Beane (eds.), *Democratic Schools* (Alexandria, VA: Association for Supervision and Curriculum Development, 1995).
43. Clair, 1998.
44. IEQ core team members have continued the work without funding from USAID. They are disseminating project publications (the Principles and Case Study) throughout the country. Imelda Kemeza (letter to Clair, May 2000) writes that a head teacher's house is currently under construction in one local community.
45. Joe Kincheloe, "Meet Me behind the Curtain: The Struggle for Critical Postmodern Action Research," in *Critical Theory and Educational Research*, ed. Peter McLaren (Albany: State University of New York Press, 1995).

CHAPTER 11

# Policy Making, Critical Analysis, or Both—What Role for Educational Research?
## *The Example of "Lifelong Learning"*

HOLGER DAUN

### Introduction

The functions of research in relation to politics/policy making and to the economy (both service and commodity production) have been changing.[1] First, the generation of knowledge is increasingly taking place outside the traditional locus of scientific research—the universities. Secondly, terms and concepts invented in the policy realm or appropriated by policy makers from other realms are placed in the service of global capitalist competition and transferred to researchers for operationalization and measurement.

The purpose of this chapter is to highlight some aspects of these recent developments, focusing specifically on the relationship between policy and research in the field of lifelong learning.[2] "Lifelong learning" is a term that previously was conceived as equivalent to the broad term "socialization," but in recent years lifelong learning has become more narrowly focused on the formation of the economic and modular man.[3] The realm of research in lifelong learning has been drawn into a corporate capitalist constellation, which is not very likely to generate or even tolerate a detached and critically reflective role of research. The new discourse is impregnating international and comparative education; its terms are being uncritically adopted and taken for granted by researchers. Learning is seen primarily as participation in the educational arrangements resulting in skills and knowledge that are measurable and related to work roles. This implies that researchers are increasingly involved in monitoring and assessing individual "learners" and thus entering into individuals' private lives.[4]

This chapter explores the evolution in policy and research arenas of the concept of lifelong learning. It traces the transformation of adult education policy discourse from a focus on lifelong education (conceptualized initially in relation to socialization or human development) to a focus on lifelong learning (viewed primarily as human resource development to improve economic productivity). Next the context in which this occurred is described. Finally, the role that researchers have played—and should play—in dealing with the transformation in the policy discourse in adult education is critically discussed.[5]

## Lifelong Learning as Socialization for Life

Since the first human beings appeared, everybody has been learning throughout life. "Learning is as integral an aspect of living as breathing. People are lifelong learners whether they wish it or not."[6] Learning throughout life has been a research theme from two different perspectives: socialization and development psychology.[7] Here the focus is on socialization, which has been defined as "the genesis and change of human personality over the entire lifespan from birth to death and for all socio-cultural conditions"[8] and as "a continuing, lifelong process" that takes place in the context of the family, school, peer group, occupational setting, and radical resocialization settings.[9] When the interaction between the socializer and the socialized is deliberately formalized and institutionalized for explicit teaching, it may be seen as education. Socialization theory and research have been grounded in different disciplines (psychology, social psychology, social or cultural anthropology, sociology, and so on), reflected different perspectives,[10] and focused on different periods in individuals' lives.[11]

## Adult Education: From Humanistic Awakening to Vocational Training

In recent years, however, this broader focus on socialization has been neglected in discourses on lifelong learning and adult education, being replaced by a narrower concern with workforce preparation.[12] Initially adult education emerged from the grassroots level—social, religious, and cultural movements—and was organized for humanistic and sometimes altruistic reasons. In the Nordic countries such learning took place in study circles, *Folk High Schools,* and so on. This socialization was principally nonformal and informal[13] and was an alternative or complement to the formally organized education system. Apprenticeship had existed in the private companies since the Middle Ages but did not make up part of the movements just mentioned. Later, vocational and in-service training were introduced in the companies. All these phenomena came to be included in "adult education."[14] With increasing influence from economic interests, the demands for improved efficiency of vocational and professional training, and the growth of the international organizations, adult education more and more came to be seen as training for competence in the economic affairs. From the 1970s the frontiers between vocational and professional training, on the one hand, and adult education for critical understanding, on the other hand, "have been blurred."[15]

The label *lifelong education* was used as early as the 1920s; it was an English term for Nordic adult education, *folkupplysning* or *folkbildning* (people enlightenment).[16] When it was placed on the international agenda by the Organization for Economic Cooperation and Development (OECD) in 1973, lifelong education was defined as "a comprehensive educational strategy for all post-compulsory or post-basic education, the essential characteristic of which is the distribution of education over the total life-span of the individual in a recurring way, i.e. in alternation with other activities, principally work, but also with leisure and retirement."[17] And UNESCO's discussion of lifelong education gives emphasis to "equality and equal opportunity, opening up of the educational system, education as preparation for life and the need for adult education, participation and solidarity, learning throughout life."[18]

However, in the mid-1990s, there was a definite shift in the discourse. Lifelong *education*—as well as permanent and recurrent *education*—was firmly replaced in the lexicon by "lifelong *learning*."[19] The term *lifelong learning* had been previously used by OECD and UNESCO, but principally as an argument for reorganization of adult education rather than as an operative concept, and until the 1990s it did not attain a strategic position in the discourse.[20] In 1996, OECD appointed a task force whose aim was "to analyse the shifting meanings of ... lifelong education and lifelong learning."[21] UNESCO subsequently adopted the latter term and saw a "need to clarify the meanings of literacy, lifelong learning, continuous learning, and adult education."[22] At a 1996 meeting the education ministers of the OECD countries identified "lifelong learning" as the point of departure for adult education policies and research. The document from the meeting highlights labor force preparation[23] and argues that lifelong learning is required because of economic competition and rapid technological and societal change.[24]

**Lifelong Learning: A Functionalist and Totalizing Framework**

A closer look at the new discourse on lifelong learning reveals that the overall point of departure is a functionalist and consensus-oriented paradigm, emphasizing an organic notion of society as a living organism with its own goals and purposes.[25] Moreover, society is represented as atomized; it is an agglomeration of freely choosing individuals that have the same opportunities. When individuals choose properly, it is advantageous not only to them but also to society as a whole.[26] For example, UNESCO's major focus on the structural problem of inequalities becomes expressed in the language and spirit of a 1996 document as a consensus and utopian view of the individual as a free agent in the "global village."[27] In the 1999 documents, UNESCO seems to adapt to globalization and market forces.[28]

The concept of "lifelong learning," as it now is used, may be seen not only as a purposive measure to improve competitiveness and welfare of the population and as a way to respond to the demands emerging from reflexive individuals, but also as a means to persuade the reluctant and resisting sections of the population to enter commodified relationships and to become competitive. It is also a way of making people in the South believe that their poverty is the result of a "low level of human resource development" and that lifelong learning will release them from poverty.

While tensions may exist, there are no fundamental conflicts of interests, for example, between individuals and companies,[29] and there are no relevant contradictions between gender or ethnic groups. Nor is anything said about the mechanisms that create inequalities (educational and other forms). It is taken for granted that lifelong learning gives everybody similar chances. "Educational provisions" are seen as neutral in relation to different groups of individuals, and individuals are seen as having identical access and opportunity in education and society. To the extent that there are inequalities in society (and the world), they are because of differences in knowledge and not inequalities built into social and economic structures. And education or learning are perceived to remedy such inequalities by helping to distribute knowledge.

Furthermore, the lifelong learning approach is "totalistic" in at least two ways: (1) All aspects of life (public and private) are to be included, and (2) the individual is to be monitored and assessed in all domains throughout life. In policy development related to lifelong learning the total situation of the individual is implied. Lifelong learning focuses on activity "not only [in] the setting of formal education but also [in] the less formal settings of the home, the workplace, and the community";[30] those concerned with lifelong learning should "pay less regard to the role of formal institutions and more to non-formal and informal learning in a variety of settings—at home, at work and in the community."[31] Thus, informal, nonformal, and formal learning in all situations and periods of an individual's life are included in the concept of lifelong learning.[32] Moreover, lifelong learning encompasses people's social relations and networks, which to a large extent are a private matter. While social networks have come to be seen as an important component of social capital,[33] they are now to be framed for purposes of policy as an auxiliary to the formation of human capital[34] and not as something having a value for its own sake or for solidarity and altruism.[35]

In policy discourse related to lifelong learning the individual is to be monitored in different life situations, throughout life and with more and more sophisticated methods. It is not enough to know the amount of human capital (i.e., work-related knowledge and skill) that individuals possess. Measurements will be refined (e.g., through biographical research) so that private processes can be publicly recognized.[36] Just to register and analyze the total scope of individuals' lives is not enough; whole life worlds are to be rationalized and penetrated through monitoring and evaluation.[37] Thus, it is argued that "opportunities to learn outside the formal system are to be placed on an equal footing with those occurring within. An important condition for this is that such learning is properly evaluated."[38] All aspects of the results of individuals' socialization are now to be measured and monitored for purposes of their potential for economic productivity.[39]

Within the discourse of lifelong learning one can detect an unproblematized conception of learning. A large number of phenomena are now termed "learning." Individuals are termed "learners" and institutions and various arrangements are said to provide learning. It should not be possible to state a priori that learning is taking place and that people are learners, but this is very common also in researchers' terminology. Moreover, learning is not defined and why and how learning occurs is not mentioned in any of the works consulted for this chapter. The reason is that the learning itself is not important; what is of interest are the results of learning. What will be measured counts as results of learning and researchers are expected to trace the individuals and find out where they have learnt what.

To better understand how and why lifelong education (as socialization for critical participation in adult life) has been transformed into lifelong learning (as narrowly conceived, workforce training, but with a totalizing reach), one needs to examine the economic and political dynamics within national and global contexts during the past thirty years. In particular, I will highlight economic globalization and the restructuring of the state.

**Globalization and the Restructuring of the State**

With economic liberalization and rapid technological development, globalization processes started to accelerate in the 1970s. Local and national economic activities and economic policies have since had to adapt to the global conditions.[40] Globalization has resulted in increasing gaps between the North and the South. Wealth is accumulating in the North, while large areas of the South have become marginalized, being "bypassed by the intensified circuits of trade, capital and investments."[41] Globalization creates contradictions along a "three-part hierarchy in social structure": a top layer of people who are directly integrated into the global economy exists in most countries but principally in the North, a category of people serving those directly involved in global affairs, and those who are excluded from the global economic flows.[42] The responses to economic and technological globalization differ somewhat among countries because of their economic and political structures, which have also been changing.

Such changes can be captured by two trends affecting the functioning and authority of nation-states. First, the role of the state has been reorganized through processes of deregulation and privatization. This trend has been influenced ideologically from the right (i.e., neoliberal arguments about the inefficiency of nonmarket-based, government bureaucracies) and from the left (i.e., deinstitutionalization critiques, which began in the late 1960s, that large scale arrangements create anonymity and alienation and limit direct and participatory democracy).[43] At the same time, paradoxically, deregulation and privatization have in certain ways made the state more interventionist[44]—in the domain of retrospective monitoring of outcomes and goal attainments among different bodies.

Second, in the context of globalization international bodies increasingly substitute for national states in their policy formulating tasks and take over policy making and research. Globalization makes the principal functions of the state

**Table 11.1** Relationships Between the Realm of Research and the Realms of Policy Making and Commodity and Service production

| REALM OF RESEARCH | GREY ZONE | REALMS OF POLICY MAKING AND COMMODITY AND SERVICE PRODUCTION |
|---|---|---|
| Basic research (for the sake of discovery and curiosity) | Commissioned research (in the service of society but on its own conditions) | Evaluation (in the service of policy makers and on their conditions) |
| Critical analysis | | Commissioned investigation |
| Applied research (in the service of society) | | Concepts and research questions formulated by politicians and/or administrators for policy purposes |

more complex than before and it makes states struggle not only for people's entrance into the exchange in commodified relations but also for people's will to become competitive.[45] Thus, international agencies engage in their own production of knowledge, and it is from such activity that the world models derive. These models, consisting of "tacit understandings," explicit recommendations, and so on, prescribe the role of the national state, education, research, and so on.[46]

## Educational Research and Knowledge Production

During the "national" period in industrial societies, some empirical research was conducted in the service of the national state. Yet the boundaries between and the functions of the policy realm and the research realm were relatively clear. Most of the research took place at universities, and basic research, for instance, had a distinct role. There was a role for critical research, especially in adult education. Formulating policy, implementing policy, and conducting research on policy constituted different "spheres" of activity.[47] On the other hand, educational researchers have for a long time complained that research findings have not been used to a large extent in policy making.[48] However, the ideal picture presented in Table 11.1 has never existed in most of the countries in the South, since much of the research on and in them has been initiated from and conducted by researchers from the North.

The position of research is now being altered in two principal ways: (1) relations between the research realm and the surrounding society are changing, and (2) the generation and production of knowledge increasingly takes place outside the universities.[49] According to Etzkowitz and Leydesdorff: "The university and the firm are each assuming tasks that were once largely the province of the other. The boundaries between public and private, science and technology, university and industry are in flux."[50] The "New Knowledge Production," as it is designated by Gibbons and colleagues, has several interrelated characteristics, a few of which can be mentioned. The relevance and validity of scientific knowledge are now determined not only by scientific criteria but also by criteria linked to utility, marketability, and reflexivity. Knowledge production becomes part of a larger process in which discovery, application, and use are closely integrated. As a consequence, the "tradition of university-based research is threatened by the encroachment of industry and profit-making mentality and values."[51] This applies in particular to technology, natural science, and economics, but similar processes are taking place in humanities and social (including educational) science.[52] In the same way, the major international agencies (e.g., OECD, UNESCO, and the World Bank) and many NGOs have established their own research bodies or hire researchers to work according to terms of reference and on items defined by the policy makers.

### The Role of Researchers in Lifelong Learning: Uncritical Acceptance or Critical Analysis

Lifelong learning has become a buzzword coined in policy-making bodies in the North. This may be interpreted as an effort to respond to three different challenges that national states as well as international agencies have been encountering: (1) global competition in the economy; (2) demands for participation, deinstitutionalization, and deschooling raised by critical and reflexive individuals; and (3) resistance to commodification and rationalization of lifeworlds and revival of cultural particularism, sometimes resulting in demands for multicultural legitimacy. The language of the "lifelong learning" discourse seems to be formulated so as to respond to all these challenges by using vocabulary constituting a mix of neoliberal and "civilian" or "communitarian" terms, while privileging workforce preparation.

The discourse is agent- and consensus-oriented; everybody should be involved and have options. The individual is free to choose. The picture of education that emerges in the writings is very complex, probably because the appeal is addressed to all interests and all layers in society. On the one hand, education and educational change are seen as a "dependent variable." That is, economic and social factors (globalization and global competition) drive education. On the other hand, in the national context, the opposite holds: Education (or lifelong learning) is seen as the motor of development; nations will be competitive and cohesive as a result of such efforts.

Lifelong learning is a policy metaphor, which some educational researchers have accepted uncritically. Although its meaning is yet to be clarified, lifelong learning has become a term commonly used in the realm of research and has become taken for granted in many researchers' vocabulary and thinking. These researchers not only have accepted the renaming of lifelong education and socialization as lifelong learning, but they also have appropriated lifelong learning as an object of research; it is not an object for discourse analysis but for operationalization and measurement in the way suggested by abstract empiricism.[53]

They now assist in (1) finding phenomena that are seen to correspond to the new term, (2) measuring this economically driven socialization now called lifelong learning, and (3) improving the techniques of monitoring and assessment of the individual from "the cradle to the grave" and in all aspects of life.[54]

What, then, should be the role for educational research? Policy-making bodies have an interest in empirical findings that are easily translated into knowledge/information on which policy decisions can be made.[55] However, traditionally there are researchers who have the ambition to theorize, make deeper analyses, and reflect on broader social implications as well. Such humanistically and critically oriented research is time consuming, but it is needed for at least two reasons.

First, objects of research should be placed in a holistic context, which ultimately means, in the context of the international division of labor, involving both production and consumption. For instance, it is necessary to ask why certain countries are unable to finance their education systems. Research should focus on the economic forces that make the international division more unequal today than it was thirty years ago and how this fact affects education in the South. As it is now, there is a risk that "lifelong learning" becomes part of a whole package of cultural imperialism items produced in the richest countries. The relationships between global capitalist processes and poverty, inequality, and oppression are not at all considered in the lifelong learning discourse. Therefore, the initiative of naming and defining phenomena, especially education and learning, should be taken back by the realm of educational research and placed in a holistic context including culture and the conditions for socialization as well.[56]

Second, the drive for global competitiveness results in restructuring of economic branches, widening gaps between people within and between countries; increasing uncertainty regarding job and income prospects for large sections of the world's population; putting pressure on people to become more competitive; and thus heightening stress, marginalization, and exclusion. It should be the role of educational researchers to place all the mentioned things on the research agenda.[57]

Governments and international bodies increasingly have been supporting cognitively, economically, and technically oriented educational research, a fact that led researchers to an "one-dimensional" (i.e., economic) view of human beings. In medium and long terms, humanity cannot afford this. Instead, substantial moral and financial support should be given to critical and alternative research focusing on the concept of and policy issues involved in "lifelong learning."

## Notes

1. H. Etzkowitz and L. Leydesdorff, "The Endless Transition: A 'Triple Helix' of University-Industry-Government Relations." *Minerva, A Review of Science, Learning and Policy* 36 (1998).

2. Other examples are "empowerment," "social capital," and "human resource development."
3. The term "modular man" has been borrowed from E. Gellner [*Conditions of Liberty. Civil Society and Its Rivals* (London: Harnish Hamilton, 1994)], but has been given a somewhat different connotation here. Modular man is here defined as a rational and utility-maximizing individual, multiskilled and geographically, culturally and professionally mobile.
4. P. Jarvis, "A strategic research agenda for lifelong learning in learning societies," in *Lifelong Learning Policy and Research*, ed. A. Tuijnman and T. Schuller (London: Portland Press, 1999).
5. Some delimitations have been made. The analysis focuses only on OECD and UNESCO, and only some of their documents have been analyzed. It is possible that other views have been expressed in other organizations' documents and within other OECD and UNESCO documents.
6. I. Baptiste, "Beyond Lifelong Learning: A Call to Civically Responsible Change," *International Journal of Lifelong Education* 18 (2) (1999): 95.
7. Development psychology for a long time studied only childhood and adolescence, which to a large extent correspond to primary and secondary socialization, but since the 1960s the adult phase of the individual's life has received more attention. See D. H. Hargreaves, *Interpersonal Relations and Education* (London: Routledge & Kegan Paul, 1972); J. J. Goodnow, "The Socialization of Cognition," in *Cultural Psychology. Essays in Comparative Human Development*, ed. J. W. Stigler, R. A. Shweder, and G. Herdt (Cambridge: Cambridge University Press, 1990); M. Grossen and M. Nicolet, "Origine sociale et performances cognitives: contribution psychosociologique à une redéfinition de la problematique," in Nicolet ed. A.-N. Perret-Clermont and M. Nicolet *Interagir et connaître* (Cousset: Editions Delval, 1988); J. Haldane, "Psychoanalysis, Cognitive Psychology and Self-Conscious-ness," in *Mind, Psychoanalysis and Science*, ed. P. Clark and C. W. Crispin, (New York: Basil Blucmen, 1988); C.-G. Janson ed. *Seven Swedish Longitudinal Studies in the Behavioral sciences*, Report 2000:8 (Stockholm: Forskningsrådsnämnden, 2000); A.-L. Lange, *From Child to Adult* (Stockholm: Stockholm Institute of Education, 2000); D. M. Rakfy, "Phenomenology and Socialization: Some Comments on Underlying Socialization Theory," in *Childhood and Socialization*, ed. H. Dreizel (London: Collier McMiallan Publishers, 1973).
8. B. Brezinha, *Socialization and Education. Essays in Conceptual Criticism*, trans. James Stuart Brice (Westport, CT: Greenwood Press, 1994), p. 4.
9. A. Sturman, "Socialization," in *International Encyclopedia of Education*, ed. T. Husén and N. Postlethwaite (Oxford: Pergamon Press, 1994), p. 5588.
10. Socialization research has during the past two decades shifted from role theory to more agent-oriented theories. In classical studies, socialization was seen as a "one-sided" process: transmission from the socializer to the socialized. Humanist- and interactionist-oriented theories view socialization as a mutual, interactive process in which (micro) realities are constructed. Individuals themselves are coproducers of realities, including roles. Learning takes place practically everywhere and learning by being and doing are important principles. Some approaches have made attempts to integrate different perspectives and different analytical levels. See, for instance, P. L. Berger and T. Luckmann, *The Social Construction of Reality* (Harmondsworth: Penguin, 1967).
11. See, for example, G. A. Almond and S. Verba, *The Civic Culture* (Boston: Little, Brown & Company, 1965); A. E. Mazawi, "Contested Regimes, Civic Dissent, and the Political Socialization of Children and Adolescents," in *Citizenship and Citizenship Education in a Changing World*, ed. O. Ichilov (London: The Woburn Press, 1998); P. Woods, *Sociology and the School: An Interactionist Viewpoint* (London: Routledge & Kegan Paul, 1983).
12. Similarly, before the 1980s, politicians and researchers tended not to perceive children in the "preschool age" to be amenable for institutionalized education of the structured type given in primary education and, generally, there was no perceived need to monitor their level of knowledge and skills; see J. K. Bishop, "Play. Its meaning and being," *Early Childhood Development and Care* 26 (1986): pp. 65–78; U. P. Green, "Teachers and the Play Curriculum: Issues and Trends," *Early Childhood Development and Care* 17 (1984): 13–22; D. Elkind, *The Hurried Child: Growing Up Too Fast Too Soon* Botan: Addison-Wesley, 1981).
13. A. M. Thomas, "Adult Education: An Overview," in *The International Encyclopedia of Education*, ed. T. Husén and N. Postlethwaite (London: Pergamon Press, 1994).
14. Consequently, very different schools of philosophy have been behind this education; K. Rubenson, "Livslångt lärande: Mellan utopi och ekonomi" ("*Lifelong Learning:*

*Between Utopia and Economy"*), in *Livslångt lärande (Lifelong Learning)*, ed. P.-E. Ellström, B. Gustavsson, and S. Larsson (Lund: Studenlitteratur, 1996); L. Srinivasan,*Perspectives on Nonformal Adult Learning* (New York: World Education, 1977).
15. A. M. Thomas, p. 144.
16. O. E. Johansen, *Adult Education and Training in the New Millenium. Changing Parameters in New Paradigms?* (M.A. thesis, Stockholm: Institute of International Education, 1997), p. 36.
17. OECD, *Recurrent Education: A Strategy for Lifelong Learning* (Paris: OECD, 1973b), p. 16.
18. E. Faure et al., *Learning to Be* (Paris: UNESCO, 1972).
19. The term *permanent education* was suggested by the Council of Europe and used by UNESCO. Like lifelong education, permanent education had a broader and more holistic view, while recurrent education was more narrowly linked to work life than the two other concepts [Faure et al.; OECD, 1973b)]. *Recurrent education* includes postcompulsory education, on-the-job training and in-service-training, and more liberal adult education. The latter was initially critical and utopian but later became more and more instrumentalist [P. Freire, *Pedagogy of the Oppressed* (Harmondsworth: Penguin, 1992); Rubenson.)].
20. OECD, 1973b, p. 18) had argued for the perspective of "lifelong learning" from the beginning of the 1970s: "The concept of lifelong learning assumes a more precise sense in that it accentuates the need for adaptability through a constant registering and processing of information, formation of concepts, and development of attitudes and skills.... Education... cannot... be a permanent or continuous process.... It leaves vague the question of how lifelong education opportunities will be provided, and how they interact with lifelong learning."
21. A. Tuijnman, "Research Agenda for Lifelong Learning: A Report by the Task Force of the International Academy of Education", in *Lifelong Learning Policy and Research,* ed. A. Tuijnman and T. Schuller (London: Portland Press, 1999).
22. UNESCO (1999a), *Symposium on Basic Education and Lifelong Learning. Final Report. Beijing and Bangkok, 8–12 September,* 1998. The OECD and UNESCO perspectives differ somewhat, in that UNESCO views lifelong learning not only in an economic context but also in terms of human rights, tolerance and understanding, democracy, responsibility, universality, cultural identity, peace, environmental preservation, knowledge sharing, poverty alleviation, population control, and health [UNESCO,*Learning: The Treasure Within.* Report to UNESCO of the International Commission on Education for the Twenty-first Century (Paris: UNESCO, 1996)]. However, UNESCO also stresses training for economic activity in its conception of lifelong learning, stating: "[Learners] must also be prepared for a radically new labour market in which traditional wage-employment may be the experience of only the minority and self-employment in various forms may offer a high potential for economic independence in a new era of entrepreneurship" [UNESCO, *Lifelong Learning and Training: A Bridge to the Future. Second International Congress on Technical and Vocational Education* (Seoul, 26–30 April, 1999b), p. 5].
23. Although the language of the OECD writings is predominantly "economistic," it carries elements of the emancipation discourse, when it is stated that "modernity has reached a stage of reflexivity as a result of rapid change into society... [and] individuals have become freer of social structures than ever before." [Jarvis, p. 123]. Furthermore, while it is sometimes stated that all dimensions of individuals' lives are to be covered in lifelong learning, it should be noted, for instance, that the cultural dimension is mentioned only as a factor affecting the individual's motivation to learn and a country's definition of and priority to lifelong learning [see T. Schuller, "A Research Agenda for Lifelong Learning: Rapporteur's Report", in *Lifelong Learning Policy and Research,* ed. A. Tuijnman and T. Schuller (London: Portland Press, 1999), p. 25].
24. OECD (1996), *Lifelong Learning for All. Meeting of the Education Committee at Ministerial Level,* 16–17 January 1996 (Paris: OECD), p. 21: "We are all convinced of the crucial importance of learning throughout life for enriching personal lives, fostering economic growth and maintaining social cohesion, and we have agreed on strategies to implement it... supporting the growth of other formal and non-formal learning arrangements..., [fostering] coherent links between learning and work..., [and] rethink[ing] the roles and responsibilities of all partners—including governments—who provide opportunities for learning."
25. R. Brown, *Explanation in Social Science* (London: Routledge & Kegan Paul, 1963); E. Nagel, *The Structure of Science* (London: Routledge & Kegan Paul, 1961). Terms such as "learning society," "learning organization," and so on, are either metaphors or functionalist views. In

26. M. Rygg, *Lifelong Learning. A Study of Conceptual Development* (M.A. thesis, Stockholm: Institute of International Eduation, 1997).
27. UNESCO, 1996.
28. UNESCO, 1999a, 1999b. That a*market-oriented view of needs* dominates in discourses on lifelong learning can be seen in that simplistic assumptions of classical economic theory are taken for granted: (a) Individuals demand education of the type provided; (b) individuals' needs are seen as identical to the needs of the state or capital; (c) individuals' demands are based on preferences and not deeper values and economic conditions; and (d) needs are effectively articulated and manifested as formal demands in educational markets. However, all these assumptions are highly questionable [see B. Crowley, *The Self, the Individual and the Community. Liberalism in the Political Thought of F. A. Hayek and Sidney and Beatrice Webb* (Oxford: Clanderon Press, 1987); L. Doyal and I. Gough, *A Theory of Human Need* (London: MacMillam, 1991)].
29. A. Hasan, "Lifelong Learning: Implications for Education Policy," in *Lifelong Learning Policy and Research*, ed. A. Tuijnman and T. Schuller (London: Portland Press, 1999), p. 54.
30. OECD. 1998, p. 5.
31. Tuijnman, p. 6.
32. UNESCO, 1999b, p. 41.
33. J. Coleman, "Social Capital in the Creation of Human Capital," *American Journal of Sociology* 94 (1988) (supplement): 95–120; R. Schuller and J. Field, "A Social Capital, Human Capital and the Learning Society." *International Journal of Lifelong Education* 17(4)(1998).
34. Schuller, p. 28.
35. A. Etzioni, *The Spirit of Community. Rights, Responsibilities and the Communitarian Agenda* (London: Fontana Press, 1995); J.-M. Hoerner, *Le tiers-monde. Entre la survie et l' informel* (Paris: Harmattan, 1995).
36. Jarvis, pp. 121–122, raises doubts in relation to this point: "As a private process, learning needs public recognition in a market-oriented learning society. [But h]ow can private processes be publicly recognized and should they even always be?"
37. Interestingly, this focus on monitoring is stressed in the context of supposedly promoting learner centeredness. It is stated that lifelong learning should be organized "from the learner's point of view" [Hasan, p. 56] and be centered around the "*learner and learner needs*" [OECD, 1998, pp. 7–8] and "the needs and potential of the individual in the society" (UNESCO, 1999b, p. 2]. However, this is not learner centeredness in the Maslowian sense that people learn for their own curiosity or self-actualization [A. Maslow, *The Further Reaches of Human Nature* (New York: Viking Press, 1971)]. Instead, the learner is responsible for choosing, demanding, and participating in educational programs that increase knowledge and/or skills that show up on tests, which are increasingly used to measure the capacities of adult individuals to function in the workplace [Jarvis, pp. 121–22].
38. Tuijmman, p. 18.
39. Hasan; UNESCO, 1999b.
40. P. Brown, A. H. Halsey, H. Lauder, and A. Stuart Wells, "The Transformation of Education and Society: An Introduction," in *Education. Culture, Economy, Society*, ed. A. H. Halsey, H. Lauder, P. Brown, and A. Stuart Wells (Oxford: Oxford University Press, 1997); M. Castells, "The Informational Economy and the New International Division of Labor," in M. Carnoy, M. Castells, S. S. Cohen and F. H. Cardoso, *The New Global Economy in the Information Age*. (University Park: The Pennsylvania State University, 1993); R. Cox, "A Perspective on Globalization," in *Globalization: Critical Reflections*, ed. J. H. Mittleman (Boulne CO: Lynne Rienner Publishers, 1996); S. Gill, "Globalization, Democratization and the Politics of Indifference," in *Globalization: Critical Reflections*, ed. J. H. Mittleman (Boulder, CO: Lynne Rienner Publishers, 1996).
41. D. Ghai, *Economic Globalization, Institutional Change, and Human Security* (Geneva: United Nations Research Institute for Social Development, 1997), p. 3.
42. Cox; Gill; J. H. Mittleman, "The Dynamics of Globalization," in *Globalization: Critical Reflections*, ed. J. H. Mittleman (Boulder, CO: Lynne Rienner Publishers, 1996).
43. Etzioni; R. Flacks, "Think Globally, Act Politically: Some Notes toward New Movement Strategy," in *Cultural Politics and Social Movements*, ed. M. Darnovsky, B. Epstein, and R.

Flack (Philadelphia: Temple University Press, 1995); R. Mayer and R. Roth, "New Social Movements and the Transformation to Post-Fordist Society," in *Cultural Politics and Social Movements,* ed. M. Darnovsky, B. Epstein, and R. Flacks (Philadelphia: Temple University Press, 1995); A. Giddens, "Brave New World: The New Context of Politics," in *Reinventing the Left,* ed. D. Miliband (Cambridge: Polity Press, 1994); I. D. Illich, *Deschooling Society* (Harmondsworth: Penguin Books, 1971).

44. States tend to intervene in society to promote their legitimacy and to motivate their citizens via three modes: (1) regulation, (2) economic measures, and (3) scienticization, information, and persuasion [see R. Dale, "The State and the Governance of Education: An Analysis of the Restructuring of the State-Education Relationship," in *Education. Culture, Economy, Society,* ed. A. H. Halsey, H. Lauder, P. Brown, and A. Stuart Wells (Oxford: Oxford University Press, 1997); M. Neocleous, *Administering Civil Society. Towards a Theory of State Power.* (London: Macmillam, 1996)].

45. Neocleous; C. Offe, *Modernity and the State. East, West* (Cambridge, MA: The MIT Press, 1996); M. Waters, *Globalization* (London: Routledge, 1995).

46. J. W. Meyer, J. Boli, G. M. Thomas, and F. O. Ramirez, "World Society and Nation-State," *American Journal of Sociology,* 103(1)(1997).

47. Arvidson.

48. T. Husén, "Educational Research at the Crossroads. An Exercise in Self-Criticism," *Prospects* (XIX)(3)(1989); T. Husén and M. Kogan (eds.), *Educational Research and Policy. How Do They Relate?* (Oxford: Pergamon Press, 1984).

49. M. Gibbons, C. Limoges, H. Nowotny, S. Schwatzman, P. Scott, and M. Trow, *The New Production of Knowledge* (London: Sage Publications, 1994).

50. Etzkowitz and Leydesdorff, p. 203.

51. Gibbons et al., p. 76.

52. Gibbons et al.

53. "Abstracted empiricism" is the term used by C. W. Mills, *Power, Politics & People,* ed. Irving Louis Horowitz) (London: Oxford University Press, 1967).

54. See, for instance, C. Bramford and T. Schuller, "Measuring Lifelong Learning," *The SCPE Newletter, Findings, Ideas, Projects across Scotland* 66(Spring 2000): F. Orivel, "From Adult Education to Lifelong Learning," *CESE Newsletter* 42 (March 2000).

55. See, for instance, N. Stromquist and J. Samoff, "Knowledge Management Systems: On the Promise and Actual Forms of Information Technologies,"*Compare,* 30(3)(2000), 323–32.

56. See, for instance, M. A. Apple, "Between Neoliberalism and Neoconservatism: Education and Conservatism in a Global Context," in *Globalization and Education. Critical Perspectives,* ed. N. C. Burbules and C. A. Torres (New York: Routledge, 2000); A. Hickling-Hudson, "Beyond Schooling: Adult Education in Postcolonial Societies," in *Comparative Education. The Dialectic of the Global and the Local,* ed. R. F. Arnove and C. A. Torres (Lanham, MD: Rowman & Littlefield Publishers, 1999).

57. For an example of such research, see D. A. Wagner, *Literacy, Culture and Development. Becoming Literate in Morocco* (Cambridge: Cambridge University Press, 1992).

CHAPTER 12

# "Designed" Dialogues
## The RealPolitics of Evidence-Based Practice and Education Policy Research in England

SUSAN L. ROBERTSON
ROGER DALE

## Introduction

While it is widely acknowledged that the ideological and structural conditions under which researcher–practitioner–policy maker relationships take place—their form, content, site, and scope—shape the nature of the agency of the researcher–practitioner–policy maker, it is rarely possible to discover exactly how the various elements of those conditions combine and with what outcome. Our aim in this chapter is to focus on an instance where the nature of these relationships is more visible—because it is deliberately "designed" by a particular subgroup of policy makers. The notion of the possibility of this relationship being the result of explicit intention[1] rather than wholly contingent (albeit within a relatively narrow range of possibilities) does, however, require us to examine—at a theoretical level—how these contingencies are narrowed and "design" made possible.

This chapter, then, is a case study of a novel and distinct formulation of the researcher–practitioner–policy maker relationship: a study of the politics of a "designed dialogue" by the state within the education sector in England.[2] We take this as a case through the analysis of which it may be possible to derive a clearer understanding of the relationship among these three groups. There are two strands to the argument that we derive from this case. Formally, we posit the need to conceive of the nature of the researcher–practitioner–policy maker relationship at a more "distant"—meso rather than micro[3]—level of focus, and a higher—conceptual rather than associational—level of abstraction. Substantively we suggest that the particular content of this relationship demonstrates, paradoxically, by its near-denial of partnership, the critical need for partnership. To do this we need to make problematic the status and the presence, in particular arenas, of the groups of actors we call policy makers, researchers, practitioners, state agencies, and state agents. There is, in the literature on the topic which is critically discussed elsewhere in this volume, the sense that these categories of actors *always already* exist in particular forms and that the issue for the analyst is how the sets of conditions that frame their relationships combine, and with what effect, in different circumstances. There is also a sense that the relationships within and between the groups are more or less equal, collegial, and voluntary. The notion that these relationships can be designed—and, more importantly, not by objective analysis or on the basis of objective research, but by one of the parties to the relationship—challenges these assumptions. Note that we are not suggesting here that the various groups have always enjoyed equal power or that one or more of these groups have always dominated within the relationship. The case we discuss goes beyond that; it concerns not just the fact of domination within the relationship and how that might require the dominated to adjust, but the designation and control of the role and activity of the dominant and dominated in the relationship. To guide our examination we sought to address the following questions:

- How and why did this version of the "truth" about the "problem" of educational research, and what counts as a solution to it, come to dominate official thinking in England?
- To what extent was this "truth" a rationalization by key political actors and state-agency officials, who have at their heart the need to create the conditions enabling a new rationality to emerge?[4]
- Did the proposed solution to the problem of educational research— of partnership, capacity building and evidence-based practice—carry within it the possibility of an authentic dialogue between theorists/ researchers and policy makers/practitioners and with it the possibility of a transformation in the researcher–policy maker–practitioner relationship as alluded to by Hargreaves, Hillage and colleagues, and Tooley and Darby?[5]
- Or, is it the case—as some analysts[6] have also suggested—that by tactically managing *"what counts as knowledge"* and *"what knowledge counts"* the state's new rationality for governance is strategically re/oriented toward controlling the conditions for and investment risks involved in knowledge production (theorists/researchers) and knowledge consumption/transformation (practitioners/students)?

## The "Problem" with Educational Research(ers) in England

The case study starts from the familiar position of mutual misunderstanding, or neglect, between the three parties. The position is stated in the form of a press statement from the United Kingdom Department for Education and Employment (DfEE) that accompanied the release of the Hillage Report, *Excellence in Research in School*:[7] "Too much research neither helps teachers by showing them what works best in the classroom nor provides policy makers with rigorous research on which to build their ideas."[8] At another time and place, such observations might have gone the way of predictable complaints about ivory tower academics, theoryless practitioners, and pragmatic policy makers—each side located in an oppositional and virtuous space—then ignored. However, the Hillage Report did not go unnoticed.

We want to suggest two significant reasons for this. One was the New Labour government's determination to "shake up" education. It had insisted on "Education, Education, Education" as the central feature of its overall policy in the 1997 election campaign that bought it to power. However, it was soon clear that this did not mean more of the same that earlier Labour governments had offered, or even attempted. In fact, the seeds for what became a bipartisan critique of the education system—if not of its direction and role—had been laid by the last Labour Prime Minister, James Callaghan, in his famous Ruskin College speech in 1976. The essence of that speech was that the providers of education—the education profession, broadly conceived—had "captured" the educational apparatus to such an extent that they were able to control its direction and its modes of operation. Redressing this capture became a central plank of Margaret Thatcher's and subsequent Conservative governments, and it has continued to inform New Labour's approach.

The second reason was the incorporation into the state's project of the organic intellectuals of both Thatcherite/Conservative and New Labour/Third Way projects in the forms of Professors David Hargreaves and James Tooley, respectively. With their involvement, the "anti-provider capture" thrust, which comprised key dimensions of the overall education policy—seeking to alter the capacity and the governance, as well as the mandate, of the education system—also provided the basis for the attempted imposition of a "new rationality" on the redesigned researcher–practitioner–policy maker relationship.

The significance of the Hillage Report lies in the weight it lends to an earlier diagnosis about the problems in the relationship between educational researchers and practitioners made by Cambridge Professor David Hargreaves.[9] In his Annual Teacher Training Agency Lecture in 1996,[10] Hargreaves argued that not only did educational research lack an adequate evidence base, but that much of the research—unlike that in the field of medicine—was second-rate. Hargreaves claimed that the effectiveness of schoolteachers could be improved substantially if teaching was a research-based profession, and he blamed educational researchers in the academy for the fact that it was not.

The government's searchlight fixed on the educational research community. This time the Office for Standards in Education took the initiative by commissioning the controversial academic James Tooley—well known for his pro-privatization stance[11]—to report on the state of educational research in England. Hardly surprisingly, Tooley and Darby's 1998 report, *Educational Research: A Critique*,[12] fanned the flames in claiming that educational research was shaped by a left-wing ideological agenda. Their report was regarded by some within the educational research community[13] as a thinly disguised attack on those who had sought to oppose the government's neoliberal agenda for the restructuring of the education system.

The Hillage Report, then, was no isolated bit of reportage that could be and would be ignored by an academy already weary from the continuous changes that had begun with Thatcher and pursued with equal zeal, if in different directions, by the new Labour government elected in 1997.[14] Hillage and colleagues reasserted the reasons for change and, in so doing, signaled the seriousness of the state's determination to act. The Hillage Report was commissioned by the DfEE with the specific objective of improving the relevance and value of educational research to teachers and policy makers. The review thus sought to provide the DfEE with an overview and assessment of research relating to schools in England. In Hillage and colleagues' view, educational research—by this they mean academic[15] research focused on various aspects of education—was neither sufficiently oriented to practice to be helpful to teachers nor sufficiently rigorous to be of value to policy makers.[16] In short, they concluded that the failure of the academy to inform effectively educational policy and practice required a new way of thinking about how the activities of researchers should—by design—be related to policy and practice arenas.

In this chapter we explore the relationship between researchers, practitioners, and policy makers[17] through a systematic analysis of the emergence of a particular type of "designed dialogue," evidence-based practice, a form of interaction between researchers and practitioners designed by national government policy makers. In particular, we look closely at the official diagnosis of the "problem" of educational research (its quality, relevance, ideology, and communication) and the "solution" (the production and use of "evidence" as a basis for policy and practice).

## The Official Problem—Rationalizing as Strategy

On a broader political canvas, the annual lecture of the Teacher Training Agency (TTA) might be viewed as an agenda-setting occasion, an agenda that simultaneously mirrors, creates, and legitimizes the strategic intentions of the state as they relate to the teaching profession. The TTA emerged from the Council for Accreditation of Teacher Education (CATE)[18] in 1994, extending and adding to its already powerful hold on the training of teachers through new processes of audit and inspection of training providers. Both CATE and the TTA were crucial instruments in the Conservative government's project to radically transform the teaching profession. In essence, the state's argument was that teacher training courses diminished the effectiveness of teachers and that in their training programs teachers were exposed to useless theory that limited thinking and did not enable them to develop as individuals. A complex grid of policies (in the form of government circulars) resulted in the creation of new institutions and practices to shape teachers' work. According to Furlong,[19] these initiatives had two interrelated purposes:

> First they aimed to re-establish a national system of accountability in initial teacher education, challenging the right of those in higher education to define the nature of teacher professionalism underpinning initial teacher education. In addition, they aimed progressively to introduce a more practically focused professionalism, by opening up training courses to the realities of the "market."[20]

It might be argued then that the driving intent in the state's strategy was the radical reconstruction of the governance of teacher training through controlling teacher knowledge and the conditions under which that knowledge was acquired and developed. One clear outcome of this strategy was the demise of the *teacher as expert* and the construction of the *teacher as the competent practitioner*.[21] The TTA played an increasingly significant—although not exclusive—part in this strategy. That the TTA had such penetrating reach into the education system in general was because of its formal legislative requirement that it develop a strategy that linked funding of programs to quality of programs. The reach of the TTA, however, was extended and amplified because of the breadth of its initial remit from the Secretary of State. This enabled the expansion of boundaries and, along with other state-funded institutions such as Office for Standards in Education (Ofsted), legitimated its spread through the assertion of a moral duty to guard over the public interest in what Dahl[22] has called the Guardian State.

It is within this context that we locate the moment of rationalizing—of naming "the problem" and in so doing generating the conditions for its logical solution—the intractability of the educational research community, and the problematic nature of educational research. According to Hargreaves, educational research had failed to make a contribution to fundamental knowledge because it was not cumulative, and it had failed to affect practice because it was not relevant to the practical concerns of teachers. Not only was it a matter of quality but the public did not get value for money: "Something has indeed gone badly wrong. Research is having little impact on the improvement of practice and teachers I talk to do not think they get value for money from the £50–60 millions we spend annually on education research."[23] To support his argument about the poverty of educational research in informing practice, Hargreaves contrasted the role of research in education with the contribution of research to the practice of medicine. Hargreaves drew upon the recent development of evidence-based medicine as a model of partnership between researchers and practitioners. In evidence-based medicine, clinical decision is founded upon, and justified in terms of, research findings about the relative effectiveness of different medical treatments.

Martyn Hammersley,[24] a well-known academic from the Open University who writes on educational research, in his response to David Hargreaves's TTA lecture published in the *British Educational Research Journal*, sought to assess Hargreaves's criticisms of educational research outlined earlier and the remedies that he proposed. Hammersley stated that he could sympathize with some aspects of Hargreaves's claims. Much educational research *was* small-scale, one-off, not cumulative, and not replicated. However, this assumed that the only approach to research was based upon a scientific model that—in Hammersley's view—had long since been discredited within education for its failure to deal with complexity and contingency. Further, as Hammersley[25] points out, it is not always clear what criteria Hargreaves is using in stating that there has been *no* knowledge development in education. Nor is it necessary to see knowledge built up in the way in which it might be within the tradition of the physical sciences. Rather, Hammersley argues, knowledge about, for example, the dynamics of classroom life,[26] or, we would add, the relationship between social class and processes of social stratification,[27] are all bodies of research that enable us to say something important about education.[28] However, what is clearly on Hargreaves's agenda is that educational research should be "evidence based". But again, as Hammersley points out, only a particular kind of way of knowing the world (positivism) passes the test of acceptable official knowledge here. We thus have to ask ourselves: "What is and is not being accepted as evidence here, and what counts as basing claims on evidence?"[29]

Hargreaves's claims in his TTA lecture produced two further lines of inquiry pursued by the state, each consolidating the state's rationalizing over the poverty of educational research within the academy. The first was by the state's agency concerned with monitoring and inspecting standards in education—the Office for Standards in Education (Ofsted). Ofsted commissioned Tooley and Darby to review and provide a critique of the state and status of educational research. Tooley and Darby took the key elements of Hargreaves's 1996 lecture and devised criteria with which to make an assessment on a selected sample of journal publications.[30] The criteria were (1) a serious contribution to fundamental theory of knowledge, (2) relevance to practice, and (3) coordination with preceding/follow-up research.[31] One of the main conclusions by Tooley and Darby was that there was what they called evidence of partisanship (a proxy for left-wing ideology) in the conduct, presentation, and argument of a significant number of the research publications reviewed.[32] Other areas of concern raised by Tooley and Darby related to the methodologies used by academics within education, to matters of "quality" in publishing in education journals and of nonempirical research, and to the nature of the refereeing process for research and publication.

It seems to us that Tooley and Darby's review, and their location as organic intellectuals aligned with neoliberal agendas, shaped in significant ways the nature of the criteria that generated their concerns and conclusions. Their questions about "quality" and the adequacy of research theory, its practices, methods, and findings, including its value and relevance, were profoundly shaped by their own theory about the way the world does and should work and, within that, what constitutes valuable and relevant research. As we see here, the word "quality" acts as a neutral language, yet it is a term that profoundly reflects particular interests, in that there is still considerable disagreement among social scientists about approaches to research within the social sciences (for example, the newer qualitative tradition is often regarded as not rigorous research). The use of the word "quality" was particularly directed at research that might be called policy critique raising questions about, for instance, whether policy critique in education has any relevance to teachers' practice. The answer must surely be "yes," but not necessarily found in the more obvious and direct way that seems to be what Tooley and Darby have in mind. What they do appear to have in mind is to show that this sort of research produced by the education community is potentially dangerous in that it is shaped by an assumed left-wing ideological agenda that "will influence the ethos of schooling for generations to come."[33]

It is instructive to examine the sort of research that caught the eye of Tooley and Darby as "poor" research; the example was research on the parental choice of schools conducted by the so-called Kings' Group.[34] The purpose of the Kings' Group research was to explore the ways in which the relationship between social class and school choice operated. The case against this research advanced by Tooley and Darby was that the study was flawed on methodological grounds, although as Ozga[35] observes, "these are a proxy for his disagreement with their view of the market". This is partly revealed in Tooley and Darby's observation about the authenticity of the markets that the Kings' Group study observed. In Tooley and Darby's judgment, the markets, which exist in England and which produced increased social class inequalities, are not real or authentic and, if they were real markets, according to Tooley and Darby, a different outcome would have been observed.

The second line of inquiry was one pursued by the Department for Education and Employment when they commissioned the Hillage Report.[36] The main aim of the Hillage study was to report on the direction, organization, funding, quality, and impact of educational research primarily related to schools.[37] However, as Ozga[38] observes, Hillage and colleagues—with the guidance of the DfEE project managers and project steering committee (which included David Hargreaves)—concentrated their attention on a narrower range of objectives—the quality and utility of educational research and how it might be "improved"—ignoring the broader tasks of an overview of educational research and its relationship to policy. In their report they concluded that educational researchers involved in the production of knowledge must aim toward research that is forward looking, policy relevant, and practical[39] by:

- Creating more strategic coherence and partnership
- Improving the capacity of research to provide support to policy makers and educational practitioners, through improving quality

- Enhancing the capacity of policy makers and practitioners to receive such support, through improving their involvement in the research process and the development of mediation processes
- Establishing a commitment to evidence-based policy development and approaches to delivery of education[40]

The Hillage solution was a template potent with politics, carrying within it the implied ills of the research fraternity. Further, for a report concerned with *Excellence in Research in Schools,* the consultation and data gathering from teachers (twenty three interviews with teachers and head teachers[41] as well as seventeen others[42]) could hardly be said to demonstrate an adequate basis for researching and reporting on teachers' and head teachers' views.[43] That aside, the Hillage Report particularly sought teachers' views on definitions of best practice and the role of research in assisting them to select "teaching options." Here educational research is reduced to that knowledge immediately useful to solve problems of practice or to inform policy decisions. That is, educational researchers must produce a series of "options" from which practitioners and policy makers might select.

## Strategy, Tactics, and State Power

So far we have been exploring the strategy and tactics used by the state and which enabled the state to challenge and thus redesign the basis of communication especially between researchers and practitioners. Evidence-based practice, a concept that national government policy makers appropriated from the work of theorists/researchers (Hargreaves; Tooley and Darby), not only addressed all of the complaints that were laid against researchers and teachers as knowledge producers and consumers, but evidence-based practice requires and indeed depends upon authoritative definitions of what counts as evidence and for what. Our argument here is that what is also at issue is *who has control over official knowledge* and *how that official knowledge is produced, distributed, and consumed.* In discrediting academically produced knowledge as irrelevant, impractical, theoretical, ineffective, ideological, and so on, the state was reformulating what knowledge was produced and by whom and what counted as useful knowledge. In the Hillage Report,[44] for instance, the problems of relevance and accessibility of research are seen to arise because the research effort "is predominantly supply (i.e., researcher) driven." In offering a view from the DfEE, Judy Sebba[45] also observes that one of the main conclusions to be drawn from the "quality of educational research debate" was that "the research agenda was too supplier-driven and that this was exacerbated by the process of research funding. Pressure on researchers to produce empirical findings in published journals of international repute reflected different priorities to those which 'users' in the system need to inform policy and practice."

In the struggle over who controls knowledge production and its distribution in education, the power of the state can be seen as rested in its capacity—through its agents—to mobilize partial truths and offer them as complete accounts of the problems of educational research and who was to blame. The partial truth mobilized here is the disjunction between the academic research community and the interests and needs of practitioners and policy makers. However, as Ginsburg and Gorostiaga[46] note, this disjunction is presented as two distinctive cultures, despite the fact that it can be demonstrated that there is considerable movement between these two, making their apparent distinctiveness less certain.

We concur with Ginsburg and Gorostiaga[47] on this, but want to stress a point that we feel they make too lightly. We argue for a stronger and more contested version of "cultures;"—as made, remade, and managed as a result of struggles between social actors over status, power, and resources within existing institutional and ideological conditions. The problematic relationship between educational researchers (for instance, academics) and educational practitioners (for instance, teachers) has, in the United States and United Kingdom at least, historically been shaped by these struggles. It would have been more than surprising, then, had teacher practitioners rushed to the defense of the academic research community as the academics found themselves under attack from the state. The structural locations of academics in universities versus practitioners in schools and their differential resources and assets (cultural, economic, organizational, and social[48]) create different work, market, and status situations.[49] Although not impossible, dialogue and partnership are nonetheless more difficult under these circumstances.[50] In this particular case, not only have the various interest groups different statuses and authority, but they are also potentially unwilling actors on the stage designed for them and managed by the state (viz., national policy makers).

### The "Evident" Solution—Constructing a New Rationality

It is our view that the new rationality imposed by the state to be negotiated through a new "designed dialogue" has, at its heart, the object of controlling the production, distribution, and use of knowledge by researchers, policy makers, and teachers. As we have argued earlier in this chapter, throughout the 1980s and 1990s, the key state agencies focused their attention on teachers, their work and professional training. At issue were the considerable discretion teachers had over their work, what they labored on (curriculum), how they labored (pedagogy), and how well they labored (assessment). By the mid-1990s, attention turned to the academy and the nature of the knowledge that was being produced in and about "education." By strategically targeting the educational research community and tactically managing to create an official version of the "truth" about the "problem" and its "solution," in part by promoting the analyses of theorists/researchers associated with both major political parties, the state now had a pincerlike grip on the knowledge producers and consumers—researchers and practitioners. This was a case of strategic navigation—the moral duty of a Guardian State. This involved the state in more closely managing the conditions for the efficient production of learners for the knowledge economy. It involved the creation of a differently designed relationship between educational researchers, policy makers, and practitioners that was strategically coherent, developed through partnerships to generate practical understandings and questions about teaching and learning, and drew upon evidence about what worked.

In shaping the new rationality, a central idea advanced by the state agencies and agents was that for research to be more valuable, especially for practitioners, it must be "useful" and "practical". The discursive force of the mobilization of valuable knowledge as "useful" and "practical" is made sensible through its implied opposite—of valueless and therefore useless research being "impractical theory". For Hillage and colleagues, Hargreaves, and Tooley and Darby, the "useful/practical" and "useless/theoretical" binary secures a strategic separation between academic researchers and policy makers/practitioners—between those who live in an esoteric and imagined world apart from and looking backward[51] and those who inhabit the "real" world that requires action and decisions for the future.

The second idea advanced as part of the new rationality is that research should be coherent and strategic, and forward looking. Educational research should prompt policy and practice, not follow it. It is useful at this point to ask ourselves what type of activity Hillage and colleagues are talking about here when they are critique educational research as "backward" rather than "forward" looking. Surely all educational research is, at least in some way, backward looking as it gathers data on events that have passed, but perhaps this critique should not be interpreted in such a literal manner. Indeed, we believe a more plausible account of this criticism is that what is being dismissed is a certain type of research—critique, which offers an alternative way of knowing the world aside from the "official".

Researchers are also encouraged to package the results of their research for easy consumption by practitioners. In a paper presented to the British Educational Research Association 2000 Conference, Philippa Cordingley from the TTA outlined the findings of the National Teacher Research Panel[52] funded by the TTA and the DfEE. Cordingley[53] reported that the panel identified four aspects that would enable teachers to make use of research. These included gaining teachers' interest, credibility for research in the eyes of teachers, enabling access, and supporting teachers in interpreting the implications of research for their own context.

According to the Teacher Research Panel, interest is secured through relevance.[54] While relevance certainly is likely to create the conditions for engagement, the more interesting features to us in Cordingley's paper are her explanations of the challenges teachers are facing and her suggestions for how relevant research might overcome these challenges. For instance, she observes:

> The enormous pressure on teachers' time means that they are attracted to research that helps them do *more effectively and/or more efficiently* what

they have to do anyway. This might include national priorities such as literacy, numeracy and ICT;[55] all, *unsurprisingly* current priorities for teachers regarding research. But they also look for research that helps them address specific teaching and learning problems they see as persistent features of classroom life. Overcoming disaffection, improving *motivation* and improving *questioning* skills are common examples of additional issues highlighted by large numbers of teachers in TTA surveys as priorities.[56]

What should be noted here is, on the one hand, the conception of the problems that teachers face and the solutions identified (motivate students, use better questioning techniques) and, on the other hand, the view of the teacher and the role research might play in teachers' work (make them more efficient and effective vehicles of the official knowledge and the production of efficient learners). The emphasis in the text on the "basics" of literacy, numeracy, and ICT gives some clue to the nature of the "official" knowledge with which teachers should be concerned. There is little sense here that teachers might be able to use research to better understand the reasons for learning problems as they relate to the complexity of cultural, social, economic, and political factors that shape the lives of students, their interests, and their capacities. Rather, here the learner is pathologized (as lacking motivation or unable to ask questions) while the teacher is the vehicle for efficiently and effectively passing on knowledge specified in the curriculum. In this partnership with teachers, the role of the academic researchers is to produce knowledge in a form that enables teachers to be more efficient and effective in adding value and increasing student attainment. This point is reiterated in the TTA's paper posted on its website concerning evidence-based practice: "classrooms are complex work settings. Effective teachers must internalize knowledge and skills so that they can deploy them quickly and efficiently."[57]

Academic researchers are viewed as assemblers and packagers of particular forms of knowledge for quick and easy digestion by teachers, who are regarded passively and instrumentally, both as consumers of pedagogically "relevant," research-based knowledge and as deliverers of state-prescribed curriculum. And as the practitioners' decision-making role is circumscribed, the locus of the discretion for academic researchers is, as the following passage reveals, narrowed down to decisions about the nature of evidence and its convincing link to performance.

> *Convincing evidence* that research has engaged rigorously with impact upon learning is, in itself, capable of stimulating initial teacher interest, though broader qualitative and/or quantitative evidence will also be needed to sustain that interest through the complexities of interpreting *the implications of findings for teachers' own particular contexts*. The Panel felt that teachers are not looking for over simplified cause and effect

propositions but for evidence that research is focused on improving teaching and learning and that *recommended strategies* have been shown to at least be *linked to such improvements*.[58]

We can see here that evidence-based teaching is associated with a particular form of research: "scientific" research evidence that offers itself as *convincing*. According to Hargreaves,[59] convincing research is research that can "demonstrate conclusively that if teachers change their practice from x to y there will be a significant and enduring improvement in teaching and learning."

As we noted at the beginning of this chapter, this evidential base rests upon a particular type of knowledge gathered in a particular way: positivism. Positivism is a way of mapping and knowing the world that can be quantified, accumulated, and replicated.[60]

It is instructive to examine the sort of questions teachers *might* be engaged with and pose for themselves as practitioners in classrooms and how it would engage teachers in thinking about the nature of the evidence available to resolve the problem. We draw here upon two examples from teachers involved in *The Evidence Based Teaching in Primary Science Project* at Nottingham Trent University, United Kingdom.[61] One teacher (Eleanor) asks: *How can I encourage children to take ownership of their science lesson in contexts of planning and assessment which appear to constrain this?* A second teacher, Paul, asks: *How can I help children to build their imaginative, lively curiosity so as to propose and follow through investigations more scientifically?* In the first case, Eleanor will have to seek out research that appears to demonstrate how ownership can be attained. However, what does ownership mean in this case? Does it mean submitting homework? Or, will it be measured in terms of "time on task"? Will these be adequate measures of ownership? What part might the social context for learning play in ownership? In the case of Paul, his question raises issues again of what the evidential base might be here. How is curiosity conceptualized here? What might be the evidence that would demonstrate curiosity? And so on.

**Knowledge and Its Management: When Knowledge + Control = Designed Dialogue = Monologue**

These two cases and the discussion throughout this case study highlight the issues that are involved in the state imposing conditions on the nature and form of the relationship, particularly, between academic researchers and practitioners.[62] Insisting on evidence-based practice as the means through which this conversation between researchers and teachers is to be constructed and carried out results in a number of important problems for developing a dialogic partnership and a transformative relationship,[63] with the result being that a monologue is more likely to ensue.

First, evidence-based practice fails to take account of the complexities of education that arise from the multiple goals of education[64] and the diverse settings and subjects where education takes place. In relation to multiple goals, these will include goals directed at the learner, such as affective (e.g., attitudes), behavioral (e.g., skills and actions) and cognitive (e.g., achievements, beliefs), as well as wider social, political, economic, and cultural goals that different stakeholders and political and economic actors might have. These multiple goals translate into a complex array of potentially contradictory goals. If we apply this to the two evidence-based projects referred to earlier, ideas like "ownership" and "imaginative and lively curiosity" could mean very different things depending upon the sometimes varied goals of the teacher, parents, students, administrators, community, and so on. In other words, what might count as evidence of outcomes will vary, and sometimes vary considerably. Complexity is also a result of the very diverse settings and diverse nature of students (as a result of individual capacities and cultural identities—for instance, ethnicity, gender, social class). Whose evidence will count for whom and under what circumstances? We can very rapidly appreciate the problems teachers and researchers face when the complexity of context confronts the one-size-fits-all tendency of evidence-based practice.

Second, it is not easy, even if desirable, to produce the sort of scientific evidence for all learning tasks and educational settings that Hargreaves and others are seeking, not only because of the many and complex variables that are at play in classroom life, but because—if it were feasible—that sort of "scientific" research sought by Hargreaves is ethically problematic. In other words, experimental and quasi-experimental approaches—where interventions are made in one setting and not another, with all other variables held constant—are ethically difficult as education is both a universal entitlement and a high-stakes commodity.[65] Again, the foundation on which the partnership is to be built—evidence-based practice—is flawed because of its own contradictory assumptions about the teaching-learning setting.

Third, teaching or pedagogy—by definition—involves a level of discretion that cannot be taken away if teaching is to be performed.[66] This irreducible minimum might well be constrained in various ways, as, for instance, by the ways in which teachers must work with the national curriculum and new forms of assessment and auditing. However, the different social contexts and different needs and abilities of students will always require a set of conditions that hold open some space for determination by teachers. Once again, the notion of evidence-based teaching misunderstands the very nature of teaching itself and the conditions that might best produce learning in students.

Fourth, it is naïve to assume that partnerships can be constructed with little recognition of the different stakes in existing arrangements held by the various social actors. As we see in this case study, the state not only recognized the nature of the vested interests of various groups but also sought to impose its own definition of the problem and its solution on the social actors involved (primarily university-based researchers and school-based practitioners). However, it ought to be anticipated that social actors will seek to retain and maintain these existing arrangements as they involve power, status, and other resources. The state—in part through the words and deeds of a subgroup of policy makers—may well seek to impose a form of communication in the form of "designed dialogue" between researchers and practitioners/policy makers. However, we argue that not only does the form and content of the partnership matter, but equally as important is how the previously dominated/dominant "partners" see their roles. Changing this "assigning" of interests means that both academics and teachers need to view these "roles" as social and political constructions that need to be deconstructed if new forms of partnership are to emerge.[67]

Finally, this sort of "designed dialogue" that is viewed as an imposed partnership by the social actors involved may well be jettisoned because of the state's own problems of securing legitimacy for its project. In the case of this "designed dialogue," the state's apparent interest in controlling both the nature of knowledge production and how it is used has been the object of critique by both teachers and academic researchers. Rationalities become commonsense and hegemonic only when they are widely, albeit unevenly, accepted. There is little evidence so far that this is the case in England.

## Designing Dialogue: The Conditions for Reflexive Dialogue and Critical Practice

In this analysis of a case study of a "designed dialogue" between researchers and practitioners/policy makers in education in England, we show how an existing set of relationships and its overriding rationale is challenged and replaced by one very different in its form and substance. Theoretically, the analysis has drawn on Claus Offe's[68] insight about the political nature of the attribution of interest group status. This led us not to take the nature of the relationship between and among researchers, practitioners, and policy makers at any given time at face value, as having been arrived at somehow voluntarily, spontaneously, and collegially in the circumstances. Rather, we view the nature of such relationships as the outcome of conflicts of interest between the groups that may have been submerged or stabilized for long periods but which are vulnerable to changes in macro-political juncture. This involves conceptual inquiry into what creates the particular form of the relationships we observe and a consequent shift in the institutional level of focus—from micro to meso—required for our analysis. That has enabled us to make visible the conditions that enabled the design in a particular setting and in the presence of groups of actors.

The shift from a micro to a meso level of focus also enables us to identify the potential and conditions for them to be changed and improved. One suggested way in which they might be changed, and which arises from the sort of analysis we have attempted here, is to work with the notion of an "evidence-informed" rather than an "evidence-based" practice. Within a framework of "evidence-informed practice," researchers, practitioners, policy makers, and others would be able to assess the variety of sources and types of evidence and ask: *What works for whom? When? Why? What are the conditions (political, economic, social) that might contribute to this? Under what circumstances might these be reproduced? How might I use this evidence to inform my practice?* This then leads to a *critical practice*, a practice that is centered not upon an unreflexive notion of what works—for we have argued here that this fails to grasp the complexities of education both in terms of its goals and its practice—but a reflexive notion of what matters and works for whom, why, and with what outcome. This raises the possibility of multiple evidences, multiple practices, and multiple conceptions of attainment, which, surely in a knowledge society, is what must matter.

## Notes

1. Note that this does not mean that the intention will be successfully implemented, or that there will not be side effects, although these are not our central concern here.
2. The use of England as a case is because—unlike elsewhere where there is a more implicit understanding of the nature of the policy maker/practitioner relationship—here there is an explicit attempt by the state to shape the nature of the relationship between academics, policy makers, and practitioners.
3. What we mean by "meso" rather than "micro" level of focus and level of abstraction is that on the one hand we argue that we are better able to understand the complexity of everyday concrete events by seeking to distill and abstract from these events underlying causal patterns. We argue that that although an event is always located within a complex set of events, understanding an event means locating that event within a wider set of social relations and processes. In this chapter we are suggesting that a meso level analysis will enable us not only to take some distance but also to work toward an analysis that sees the relationship between structure and agency as dialectic.
4. We use the idea of "rationality" here following Bent Flyvberg, *Rationality and Power: Democracy in Practice* (Chicago: University of Chicago Press, 1998). He suggests the idea of rationality not in the Enlightenment sense of a concept that is well-defined and independent, but one where power is linked to rationality and is also context dependent.
5. See David Hargreaves, *Teaching as a Research-Based Profession: Possibilities and Prospects*, Teacher Training Agency Annual Lecture, 1996; Jim Hillage, Richard Pearson, Alan Anderson, and Penny Tamkin Hillage, *Excellence in Research in School. Research Report No. 74* (HMSO: Norwich, 1998); J. Tooley and D. Darby,*Education Research: A Critique* (London: HMSO, 1998).
6. See, for example, J. Ozga, *Policy Research in Educational Settings: Contested Terrain*, (Buckinghamshire: Open University Press, 2000); W. Humes and T. Bryce, *Scholarship, Research and the Evidential Basis of Policy Development in Education*. Paper presented to the ECER (23 September 2000).
7. The Hillage Report [Hillage et al.] was conducted by a team from the Institute for Employment Studies, which presents itself as "an independent, apolitical international center for research and consultancy on human resource issues. . . . in employment and training."
8. Press statement, Department for Education and Employment (1998, p. 6).
9. The choice of Professor David Hargreaves was viewed as a sign that the state sought to begin the process in a more confrontational way. Hargreaves has been well known over his career as an academic for taking on the educational establishment. In the 1990s, he argued for a radical restructuring of the schooling system, claiming that the system was not adequate to meet the needs of the twenty-first Century.
10. See Hargreaves.
11. James Tooley has publicly aligned himself with the pro-privatization stance of the neoliberals. He is employed as a consultant by the Business Roundtable on education matters.
12. Tooley and Darby. The appointment by the state of Professor Tooley (Newcastle University), like that of Hargreaves, was seen to be provocative.
13. See Ozga.

14. Some of this continuity was the result of key individuals being kept on from the Conservative to the Labour administration. A notable example here was the Chief Review Officer Chris Woodhead.
15. There is an implicit notion here that it is only academics that are engaged in research in the area of education. However, following the outsourcing of its research activity, a considerable amount of "research" for the DfEE is conducted by a range of consultants and private organizations (such as Price Waterhouse). These research studies are conducted for government agencies as policy advice and therefore not made available to those engaged in teaching. It should be noted that DfEE-funded research does not exhaust the educational research funding and output. The Education and Social Sciences Research Council (ESRC) also funds a considerable amount of research in the area of education. However, there is a great deal more latitude for researchers who work on ESRC-funded projects.
16. The separation of practical research and rigorous research is an interesting one; the implication here is that practitioners are not concerned with the basis of the evidence, but its formulation as a solution, while policy makers are concerned only with the evidence and not the implied solution. We would argue that this is a false opposition, that practice and policy must be committed to the same principles of rigor.
17. While the reports refer to academic researchers, policy makers, and practitioners, in the various texts policy makers are often left out of the equation. This seems to suggest that the argument is really about the academics and their relationship to practitioners.
18. CATE was one of the early births in the radical changes that began with Callahan's "questioning" of the postwar educational settlement in his speech at Ruskin College in 1976. CATE was charged with the responsibility for overseeing initial teacher education in England and Wales on behalf of the Secretary for State.
19. See J. Furlong, "Reforming Teacher Education. Re-forming Teachers: Accountability, Professionalism and Competence," in *Education, Reform and the State: Twenty-Five Years of Politics, Policy and Practice*, ed. R. Phillips and J. Furlong (London: RoutledgeFalmer, 2001), p. 125.
20. What they mean by this is the introduction of market-based modes of coordinating various forms of education provision, competition, contracts, and auditing.
21. See Furlong.
22. See R. Dahl, *Democracy and Its Critics* (New Haven, CT: Yale University Press, 1989).
23. Hargreaves, p. 143.
24. See M. Hammersley, "Educational Research and Teaching: A Response to David Hargreaves' TTA Lecture," *British Educational Research Journal* 23 (2) (1997): 141–61.
25. Hammersley, p. 44.
26. See P. Woods, "Ethnography as the Crossroads: A Reply to Hammerlsey," *British Educational Research Journal*, 13 (1987): 297–307; P. Woods, "Ethnography and Theory Construction in Educational Research," in *Field Methods in the Study of Education*, ed. R. Burgess (Lewes, England: Falmer Press, 1985).
27. B. Bernstein, *Pedagogy, Symbolic Control and Identity: Theory, Research, Critique* (London: Taylor and Francis, 1996).
28. Indeed, it could be argued that Hargreaves's own scholarly contributions [for example, D. Hargreaves, *Social Relations in Secondary Schools* (London: Routledge and Kegan Paul, 1967); D. Hargreaves, S. Hester, and F. Mellor, *Deviance in the Classroom* (London: Routledge and Kegan Paul, 1975)] are rooted in the very tradition of which he is critical.
29. Hammersley, p. 44.
30. They reviewed 264 articles in leading academic journals and undertook a more detailed examination of 41 articles.
31. Tooley and Darby, p. i.
32. Interestingly, they do not view their own position as partisan and ideological.
33. Tooley and Darby, p. 35.
34. The Kings' Group refers to a group of researchers—Stephen Ball, Richard Bowe, and Sharon Gewirtz—working on school markets at Kings College, London. See S. Gewirtz, S. Ball, and R. Bowe, *Markets, Choice and Equity in Education* (Buckingham: Open University Press, 1995).
35. Ozga, p. 65.
36. See Hillage et al.
37. Ibid., p. ix.

38. Ozga, p. 30.
39. Hillage et al., p. xi.
40. Hillage et al., p xii.
41. There are, in England, around five hundred thousand teachers in schools (see National Union of Teachers statistics).
42. The others are made up of various types of agency officials, including Ofsted Inspectors, Teacher Training Agency officials, and Department of Education officials.
43. It should be noted, however, that the National Teacher Research Panel, which is funded by the TTA and the DfEE to provide teacher perspectives on the promotion of research and evidence-based practice, does go some way to redress this.
44. Hillage et al., p. xi.
45. S. Sebba, "The Department for Education and Employment (Schools Research)," in *What Works? Evidence-Based Policy and Practice,* ed. H. Davies, S. Nutley, and P. Smith (Bristol: The Policy Press, 2000), p. 240.
46. M. Ginsburg and J. Gorostiaga, "Relationships between Theorists/Researchers and Policy-makers/Practitioners: Rethinking the Two Cultures Thesis and the Possibility of Dialogue," *Comparative Education Review* 45 (2) (May 2001): 173–96.
47. Ginsburg and Gorostiaga.
48. See S. Robertson, *A Class Act: Changing Teachers' Work, Globalisation and the State* (New York: Falmer/Garland, 2000).
49. See D. Lockwood, *The Blackcoated Worker* (London: Unwin University Books, 1958).
50. The possibility of dialogue is central to intellectual projects such as critical pedagogy or action research.
51. Hillage et al., p. xi.
52. The purpose of the panel was to provide expert teacher perspectives on the promotion of research and evidence-based practice.
53. See P. Cordingley, "Teacher Perspectives on the Accessibility and Usability of Research Outputs," paper presented to the British Educational Research Association Conference, Cardiff, September 2000.
54. Teacher Research Panel, Teacher Training Agency (2001), *Improving Standards: Research and Evidence-Based Practice,* http://www.canteach.gov.uk/info/library/tta00_03.pdf (p. 2).
55. ICT refers to Information and Communication Technologies, such as computers.
56. See Cordingley, p. 3; our emphasis.
57. Teacher Research Panel, Teacher Training Agency, p. 2.
58. Cordingley, p. 2; our emphasis.
59. Hargreaves, p. 2.
60. For an extended discussion of positivism as a research approach, in contrast to other approaches, see T. Popkewitz, "Paradigms in Educational Science: Different Meanings and Purposes to Theory," in *Paradigm and Ideology in Educational Research: The Social Functions of the Intellectual* (New York: Falmer Press, 1984).
61. See *The Evidence Based Teaching in Primary Science Project,* http://education.ntu.ac.uk/research/ebt/who.html.
62. Since the focus in much of the state's discussion is on the academic researcher–practitioner nexus, referring primarily to evidence-based practice rather than evidence-based policy, our discussion here is focused on the researcher-practitioner relationship.
63. By "transformative relationship" we mean the conditions that might enable critical reflection, critical understanding (including the theory frames we use to understand the world), and critical theorizing of events. This is dialectic, it moves from the simple to the complex, from the concrete to the abstract.
64. See C. Fitz-Gibbon, "Education: Realizing the Potential," in *What Works? Evidence-Based Policy and Practice,* ed. H. Davies, S. Nutley, and P. Smith (Bristol, England: The Policy Press, 2000).
65. See, for example, Hammersley; P. Mortimore, "Does Educational Research Matter?" *British Educational Research Journal* 26 (1) (2000): 5–24.
66. See R. Dale, "The McDonaldisation of Schooling and the Street-Level Bureaucrat" (Review Essay), *Curriculum Studies* 2 (2) (1993): 249–62.
67. Some of this work is currently going on in ESRC projects recently funded under the Teaching and Learning program. Projects that were funded were required to take place in partnership

with teachers in educational settings and where teachers participated in the research process. Our experience as researchers in one of these ESRC projects suggests to us that it is only possible to transform existing practices when the taken-for-granted statuses are problematized and reconceptualized around new ways of thinking and using language to describe the various roles.

68. See C. Offe, "The Attribution of Interest-Group Status," in *Organizing Interests in Western Europe*, ed. S. Berger (Cambridge: Cambridge University Press, 1981).

# Index

Asian Development Bank 65, 69, 74–76

Bilingual education 6, 145–146
Brazil 5, 20, 131–133, 164–178

CHEPS (University of Twente) 3, 37, 44–45
Collaborative action research 18
Collective research and praxis 19, 33, 161
Communication among researchers, policy makers and practitioners
  approaches toward enhancing 1, 14–21, 91, 96, 225–226
  one- and two-way 15, 37
Community members as researchers 11, 14, 135–137, 162–164, 166–167, 189–190
Community participation 11, 14, 127–139, 161–178, 189–198
Comparative (and international) education 9, 83–92
Critical analysis 213–214

Decision-oriented research 17
Democracy
  public and privatized notions 11, 32
  "deliberative" 22, 150
Dialogue
  approaches to promoting 14–21, 118–121, 155–156, 164, 199–200, 232–233
  as joint reflection and action 15, 22, 109, 174–178, 183–184
  critical deliberative strategy for 22, 148–155
  cultural/ideological constraints to 24–25, 104–6, 119–120, 175–76, 199–200, 227
  "designed" 3, 6, 18, 219, 227, 232
  methodology for 110–112
  structural/political economic constraints to 24–25, 104–6, 154–5, 175, 199–200, 227

Education
  planning in 66–69
  reform of 125–126
  sector assessment in 65, 69–72
England 219–233

Ford Foundation 131

Gender issues 101–102, 106–107, 114–118
Globalization 211–212

Ideology and research 143–5, 151–55, 221
Improving Educational Quality project 184–85
India 109–120

Knowledge utilization 1–2, 86, 227–230
  conceptual model of 2
  instrumental model of 2
  strategic model of 2
Knowledge
  non-positivistic 87–88
  positivistic 85–87, 230
  production of 85–86, 89–90, 212–213, 226

Lao People's Democratic Republic 5, 63–78
Lifelong learning 24, 208–211
  as socialization 208
  as workforce preparation 208–209
  for human development/awakening 208–209
Literacy programs 97–104

Mali 23, 97–107

Netherlands 47–54

OECD 208–209, 213

Participatory research 10, 19, 161–162, 174–178
Participatory action research 10, 185–190, 193–194, 199–203
Partnership 75, 219–220, 225, 230–232
Policy
  definitions of 88
  process 2–3, 37–38, 54–56, 126–127
  types of 62–63, 68
Policy makers
  culture of 4–5, 7, 8–9, 96

Power relations 8, 23, 42, 154, 173–174, 190–194, 232
Practice
  critical 232
  "evidence-based" 3, 230–232
  "evidence-informed" 3, 232
Practitioners
  culture of 4–5, 7, 8–9, 96
  peripheralization of 84–91
Praxis 10, 19
Professionalism as ideology 11, 14

Research
  advocacy 6, 10, 20, 21, 130–137
  collaborative action 18
  collective (and praxis) 19, 33, 162
  contract 45–46
  cross-cultural 116
  decision-oriented 17
  participatory 10, 19, 161–178
  participatory action 10, 185–190, 193–194, 199–203
  policy 3, 17, 39–40
  practitioner 17
  uses of 39–40, 61–62, 72, 147, 220, 223
Researchers
  academic (or university-based) 162–167, 220–222, 229
  community members as 11, 14, 135–137, 162–164, 166–167, 189–190
  culture of 3–4, 5–6, 7–8, 96, 162–164
  students as 189–190
  teachers as 10, 88–89, 95–103, 109–120, 189–190

School principals (head teachers) 191–193
  as researchers 189–190
Sector assessment 65, 69–72

Social change/transformation 128–130, 161–162, 176, 203
South Africa 21, 133–135
State 211–212, 227–228
Students
  as researchers 189–190

Teachers
  as consumers/users of research 86, 223, 227–232
  as participants in policy making 88–89
  as researchers 10, 88–89, 95–103, 109–120, 189–190
  education of 91, 112–113, 223
  empowerment of 109, 112–113
  voices of 91, 193
Theorists
  culture of 3–4, 5–6, 7–8
Theory
  versus policy/practice 83
Two cultures thesis 37, 83, 104, 184, 227
  description of 3–5
  limitations of 5–11, 95, 105–107, 227

Uganda 183–203
UNESCO 209, 213
UNICEF 6, 109, 113–114, 132
United States
  Arizona 145–146
  California 145–146
  Florida 146–147
  Washington, DC 21, 135–137
USAID 24, 184

Western and non-Western countries/cultures 23, 96, 106
World Bank 74, 131, 213